PERSONAL ENCOUNTERS

A Reader in Cultural Anthropology

PERSONAL ENCOUNTERS
A Reader in Cultural Anthropology

Linda S. Walbridge, Ph.D.
Indiana University

April K. Sievert, Ph.D.
Indiana University

Boston   Burr Ridge, IL   Dubuque, IA   Madison, WI   New York   San Francisco   St. Louis
Bangkok   Bogotá   Caracas   Kuala Lumpur   Lisbon   London   Madrid   Mexico City
Milan   Montreal   New Delhi   Santiago   Seoul   Singapore   Sydney   Taipei   Toronto

McGraw-Hill Higher Education ⨂
*A Division of The **McGraw-Hill** Companies*

PERSONAL ENCOUNTERS: A READER IN CULTURAL ANTHROPOLOGY
Published by McGraw-Hill, a business unit of The McGraw-Hill Companies, Inc.,
1221 Avenue of the Americas, New York, NY, 10020. Copyright © 2003 by The
McGraw-Hill Companies, Inc. All rights reserved. No part of this publication may
be reproduced or distributed in any form or by any means, or stored in a database
or retrieval system, without the prior written consent of The McGraw-Hill
Companies, Inc., including, but not limited to, in any network or other electronic
storage or transmission, or broadcast for distance learning. Some ancillaries,
including electronic and print components, may not be available to customers
outside the United States.

This book is printed on acid-free paper.

1 2 3 4 5 6 7 8 9 0 QPD/QPD 0 9 8 7 6 5 4 3 2

ISBN 0-7674-2603-7

Publisher: *Phillip A. Butcher*
Sponsoring editor: *Kevin Witt*
Senior marketing manager: *Daniel M. Loch*
Media producer: *Shannon Gattens*
Senior project manager: *Rebecca Nordbrock*
Production supervisor: *Susanne Riedell*
Designer: *Jean Mailander*
Supplement producer: *Nathan Perry*
Photo research coordinator: *Brian Pecko*
Art director: *Robin Mouat*
Cover design: *Linda Robertson*
Cover image: *© Cory Langley*
Interior design: *John Edeen*
Typeface: *10/12 Palatino*
Compositor: *G & S Typesetters*
Printer: *Quebecor World Dubuque Inc.*

Library of Congress Cataloging-in-Publication Data

Personal encounters : a reader in cultural anthropology / [edited by]
Linda S. Walbridge, April K. Sievert.
      p. cm.
   Includes bibliographical references and index.
   ISBN 0-7674-2603-7 (softcover : alk. paper)
   1. Ethnology—Field work.   2. Ethnology—Philosophy.   3. Ethnologists—
Anecdotes.   4. Ethnographic informants—Anecdotes.   5. Participant
observation—Anecdotes.   I. Walbridge, Linda S.   II. Sievert, April Kay, 1953–
GN346 .P47 2003
305.8'007'23—dc21   2002029371

www.mhhe.com

The editors dedicate this book to each other.

Contents

Preface

We designed *Personal Encounters: A Reader in Cultural Anthropology* for undergraduates in introductory cultural anthropology courses. We have each taught many introductory courses and neither of us has been wholly satisfied with the materials available. The idea for this collection came out of a discussion about a story that Linda had written about her driver in Pakistan, Riaz. Linda found Riaz to be a thoroughly enjoyable person, intriguing in his perspectives on the world, and indispensable in many ways. April pointed out that such stories are what students like and remember best. We mused how Riaz's story could be used to introduce the complexities of social status in a caste system. We decided to put together a reader filled with original short stories about individuals like Riaz, and use these stories to reveal the abstract concepts in anthropology. These stories also show how anthropologists interact with individual people in other cultural settings.

While talking our idea over with colleagues, we found that they too had stories they wished to tell. We found numerous anthropologists who wanted to participate, to share their personal encounters and fieldwork experiences in a way that would engage students while teaching about the complexities of culture. The reader consists of 31 new articles specially produced for this volume. They are written with an eye toward capturing students' interest and offering glimpses of real life in a variety of cultural settings. The memorable stories point to major topics of concern to anthropologists working in the modern world: globalization, social status and inequality, rapidly changing political situations, the spread of HIV/AIDS, medicine, and the ways in which people cope with death and dying. The geographic breadth of the articles, from Mongolia to Mexico, and the contexts, from Islam to popular music, help to show students the diversity found in the world even as globalization brings us into closer contact. These essays show how traditional anthropological concerns such as marriage remain useful in understanding broad processes like culture change, while giving students a view of the current directions in cultural anthropology. The authors also address issues of ethics in anthropological work. We hope this is an introductory text that both instructors and students will truly enjoy using and that it will encourage lively discussion.

ACKNOWLEDGMENTS

The editors wish to thank Andrew Corey, Jeanne Humble, Winifred L. Mitchell, and four anonymous reviewers for their comments and suggestions. We are indebted to Sheree Sievert for her assistance with editing and formatting the articles and to Kristina Faber, who read and edited section introductions. We would like to thank Jan Beatty, then editor of anthropology at Mayfield Publishing, for her encouragement and support. We thank the staff at McGraw-Hill, all of whom have been a delight to work with. We also thank John Walbridge, whose expertise he was always happy to share.

Julianna Acheson: I wish to acknowledge the Fulbright Foundation, International Research and Exchanges Board, Western Washington University for a summer research grant, and Narodopisny Ustav (Ethnology Institute) in Bratislava, Slovakia.

Carolyn Behrman: I wish to acknowledge the single mothers interviewed in this research. Pilot research was conducted with Rebecca Huss-Ashmore with the support of a grant from the University of Pennsylvania Research Foundation. Research assistance was provided by Jessaca Leinaweaver and other students from Whitman College.

Anne Bennett: Appreciation goes to the Syrian families who took me in and showered me with warmth and hospitality. Funding for this project came from the Fulbright Foundation and practical assistance came from the Institut Francais d'Etudes Arabes in Damascus, Syria, where I was a research associate in the second year of fieldwork.

Sherylyn Briller: I would like to acknowledge the Wenner Gren Foundation and the International Research and Exchanges Board for funding the research. Thanks also to dissertation committee members, Drs. Goldstein, Beall, Binstock, and Ikels; my Mongolian colleagues, especially Barsbold Batbold and her family; and the people of Moost.

Holly Buchanan-Aruwafu: I wish to thank Rose Maebiru, Francis Aruwafu, Ken Konare, Prof. Lenore

Manderson, and Dr. Dennie Iniakwala. I wish to acknowledge SSHRC (Social Science and Humanities Research Council of Canada) and the University of Melbourne.

Elizabeth Cartwright: My research was supported by the Inter-American Foundation and a Spicer Research Award from the University of Arizona.

Lisa Cliggett: I thank Richard Wilk, Elizabeth Colson, and Thayer Scudder for their encouragement and support, and the people of Sinafala and Mazulu for sharing their lives and experiences. Fulbright IIE, the National Science Foundation, and the Oversees Development Agency provided funding for this research.

Courtney Coffey: I wish to thank Kurt Thomson, Jiang Danian, Tuoya Gegen, Wang Zhusheng, Fang Hui, and Yunnan University for their much-appreciated support of my research in China.

Paul Derby: I wish to thank the American Institute of Indian Studies for the language study grant to get me to India; also Dr. Susan S. Wadley, my advisor and inspiration from Syracuse University; the shopkeepers and workers of Banaras, especially Thomas, who befriended me and gave me a home away from home; and, of course, my wife Lorraine.

Carolyn Epple: I thank Diné cultural teachers, National Science Foundation, Sigma Xi, the volume editors and reviewers, and Ossy and June Werner.

M. Ligaya Hattari: My gratitude to Dr. Lisa Faithorn and Dr. Margaret Mackenzie of the California Institute of Integral Studies for teaching me the joy of engaged mindfulness, Dr. Linda Walbridge for her cheerful enthusiasm throughout this project, and my partner Manson Marpaung and my son Jaguar for their love and understanding.

Mary Hegland: For research funding and support, I am grateful to the Social Science Research Council and the American Council of Learned Societies as well as to Santa Clara University.

Vaughn Koops: Thanks to the Cook Islands Public Health Department, to Sarah Bailey for her support, and to all of our friends and neighbours in Rarotonga.

Larry Kuznar: I wish to thank Mark and Karen Aldenderfer and the Southern Peru Copper Company for support during my association with Manuel. Most of all, I thank the Aymara herders for giving me a glimpse of their lives.

Sarah Lamb: Research in West Bengal was generously funded by Fulbright-Hays American Institute of Indian Studies and Wenner Gren fellowships. I am grateful to Kayera Bou and the people of Mangaldihi, who shared their stories and lives with me.

Barry Lyons: I wish to thank John Schechter, Guillermo Delgado, Bruce Mannheim, and Richard O'Connor; the Social Science Research Council, University of the South; and Wayne State University for research support.

Pamela A. Maack: Thanks to Susan Hunter of USAID; Fred Kaijage, Patrick Massawe, and Andrew Kiondo of the University of Dar es Salaam; Gregory Maddox and Kate Maddox, my fieldwork companions; and my husband, Jay Hendrickson. Also thanks to Philates Simon Njuyuwi of the Ngome Street Children's Project for caring for our children, Eliasa included.

Robin O'Brian: Thanks to Sigma Xi, the UCLA Latin American Center, and UCLA Department of Anthropology for funding. I also thank Christine Eber and Allen W. Johnson for their comments.

Susan Peake: My paper owes its existence to the insights of Blue Boy, who knows who he is. I thank him sincerely for sharing the most personal details of his life with me and others. Thanks also to Sporting Wheelies of Australia for their fine work and for putting me in contact with this extraordinary human being.

Jason Pribilisky: Thanks for this article belong, of course, to Arturo himself. Additionally, I wish to thank Susan Wadley and students in Introductory Cultural Anthropology classes at Syracuse University and Ithaca College who read and commented on the draft.

E. Moore Quinn: To Liam O'Cuinneagáin, upon whom this story is based, ná lige Dia lamh. The same greetings extend to Bríd Bean Uasal Chuinneagáin; Soasamh Watson; the entire staff at Oideas Gael in Gleann Cholmcille, County Donegal, Ireland; and all of those who read earlier drafts of this manuscript. Finally to my friend and colleague, Séamus Pender, for the continuing love and support. Bhain mé sult as ag obair libhese go léir.

Alan Sandstrom and Pamela Effrein Sandstrom: We thank the American Council of Learned Societies, Foundation for the Advancement of Mesoamerican Studies, Inc., and Indiana University–Purdue University Fort Wayne for providing financial support for our research and Michael A. Sandstrom for his drawings of the paper figures.

April K. Sievert: As author of "Smoking Sage," I wish to thank Doug Harris, Dakota pipe-maker, my former students in Human Origins at Indiana University–Purdue University at Indianapolis, and Carolyn Epple, who provided comments and suggestions.

Jeanne Simonelli: I wish to thank the people of Tecolotes for their infinite patience and faith. Partial support for this work comes from the Archie Fund, the Pro Humanitate Fund, and the Mellon Foundation, facilitated by Wake Forest University.

Debra Spitulnik: I am indebted to the National Science Foundation, the U.S. Department of Education, University of Zambia, ZNBC, Peggy Barlett, Peter Brown, Don Donham, Hudita Mustafa, Keith Nalumango, and Michael Spitulnik.

Sarah Strauss: Research was facilitated by the financial support of a Fulbright-Hays Doctoral Dissertation fellowship (1992); writing up of this work was aided by visiting scholar support from the Swiss Federal Institute of Technology (EAWAG) in 1993–94 and the University of California at Davis (CCRHSC) in 1994–95.

Frances Trix: I would like to acknowledge the people of Alma el-Chaab, Lebanon, and Prof. Raji Rammuny, emeritus, University of Michigan, my first Arabic teacher.

Linda S. Walbridge: I wish to thank Seyed Moustafa for all he has taught me. As for Riaz, I cannot imagine Pakistan without him. I also wish to thank Dr. Talib Aziz for his help, and, as always, my husband John.

Kathleen G. Williamson: Thanks to Jane Hill, Richard Henderson, and Lawrence Taylor for reading my article and offering suggestions. Also thanks to friends and family in Ireland.

Significant Others: Introduction to Personal Encounters in Cultural Anthropology

April K. Sievert
Indiana University

ANTHROPOLOGY AND CULTURE

How did an eight-year-old boy come to spend two years living on a bus? Why did a family leave their grandmother alone on a mountainside? Why would a woman educated in America seek medical help from shamans in Indonesia? Questions such as these can be addressed using methods of **cultural anthropology**—the field of study devoted to understanding variation in human **culture**—a set of beliefs, attitudes, and behaviors shared by a group of people that distinguish them in some way from other people. Cultural anthropologists seek to understand different facets of human societies and explore how such institutions as religion, politics, and economics relate and influence each other and combine to create culture. Explanations of culture therefore do not come easily, because there are always many angles to consider. Many anthropologists view culture as **holistic**, as a complex system combining interrelated learned behaviors, within the limits set by the biological species, *Homo sapiens.*

Nosy people, anthropologists are always observing and always asking questions. Anthropologists conduct interviews and write **ethnographies**—books or articles that describe and explain the cultures or cultural contexts they are trying to understand. Once students of anthropology start to see cultural behaviors as links within complex networks of ideas and traditions, these cultures can come alive, and be seen in all their dynamic, ever-changing richness. It may make perfect sense that some people eat guinea pigs, marry their cousins, keep their hair hidden from view if they are women, or perform any number of traditional customs, once a student has an idea of how these different facets interrelate. Anthropologists pay specific attention to these interrelations. For example, an anthropologist might find that a specific group of people who herd large animals in a desert environment also practice elaborate hospitality, restrict women's movements outside the home, have strong kinship ties, and place a high premium on family honor. Anthropologists, through intensive studies, often uncover cases where seemingly unrelated practices both form and reflect a cultural group's worldview.

ANTHROPOLOGY AND THE INDIVIDUAL

Early anthropologists viewed culture as a definable entity, something they could simply document. They merely had to look for certain traits, make lists, and then compare those lists. But anthropologists now recognize that there are problems with this idea of culture as a set of easily definable traits, especially since within each group there are variations in how people speak their languages, how they behave, how they view the world, and what they believe. Any group is composed of individuals. No two individuals will learn, perceive, and interpret their cultures in exactly the same way—there is always variation. There is variation within cultural contexts because differences in age, sex, gender roles, status, ethnicity, nationality, "race," or religion create different cultural worlds for different people, even within the same group. Therefore, a single individual cannot be representative of an entire cultural group. Neither can an entire "culture," if distilled to a set of traits, take into account the range of individual variation. However, as each individual develops and adopts cultural behaviors, they do become the **agents** of culture, carrying culture with them, wherever they go and whatever they do. All people learn, react to what they learn, and have some latitude in selecting attitudes and ideas that suit them. Individuals abide within cultural contexts that affect their lives, actions, and attitudes. Culture certainly molds individuals, while individuals in turn influence cultural changes. Parents teach their children; children teach their own children. Generation upon generation learns cultural ways, yet children never become exact cultural copies of their parents.

With this dynamic view of culture in mind, what can individuals teach us about the cultures in which they live? Individuals show us the variation. Thus, anthropologists always try to collect different perspectives from different members of a society. By speaking to many individuals, anthropologists can begin to see where similarities and differences lie, and they can formulate general ideas about prevailing attitudes and beliefs. Yet anthropology starts with one person talking to another person, either in a chance meeting or in a more formal **interview.**

As anthropologists, we often cross paths with specific people who leave indelible impressions on our memories and on our lives. Whether sought out as **cultural teachers** during **fieldwork,** or encountered by happenstance during the course of research or teaching, individual people teach anthropologists. Often we sit and chat with colleagues at conferences, only to hear the words, "I met the most remarkable person . . ." What better way to introduce students to anthropology than to tell the stories of just such remarkable people? Thus, we believe that sharing the stories of such remarkable people is one way—and an excellent way—to introduce students to the field of anthropology.

For this introductory reader, we collected tales of personal encounters between anthropologists and the people they meet. Personal stories help us to engage with members of another society or culture—to join them as they deal with an array of contemporary issues. As we get to know the people whose lives are presented here, we gain some insight into how specific individuals reflect their broader cultural environments. The people introduced here are very real people, with very real emotions, reactions, and concerns. In getting to know these individuals—Riaz the driver, Paddy the Irishman, Liu Hui, the business-woman—you get to know something about the cultural contexts in which they live, about the conditions they deal with every day, about the opportunities they find or create, about their responses to a changing world, about their families and their lives. Many of the concepts covered in an introductory course in anthropology are abstract, but culture itself is not simply a mass of abstractions.

Although the articles are all about real people, in nearly every case, their names have been fictionalized. Anthropologists' **ethics** give us the responsibility for protecting people's privacy, and therefore their identities. We assure our cultural teachers (sometimes called **informants**) that their identities will be kept confidential. In some cases, there might even be danger for people, if their names, locations, and actions are divulged. For similar reasons, the names of smaller villages and places mentioned here are usually pseudonyms, again to protect our cultural teachers.

In some of the cases presented in this reader, the anthropologists have cultivated long-term relationships and friendships with these individuals in the context of doing fieldwork, as Kuznar did with his friend Manuel, an apprentice shaman. Others are cases of accidental anthropology, in which an anthropologist meets a person outside of the classic context of fieldwork yet learns from him or her. I certainly did not expect to find a Dakota pipemaker among the students in an introductory physical anthropology class. His presence made for a serendipitous journey into the world of Native American stone pipes, their use, and their special meaning.

TOPICS FOR *PERSONAL ENCOUNTERS*

Anthropology is only a bit more than a century old. As early anthropologists such as Franz Boas, Bronislaw Malinowski, Ruth Benedict, and Margaret Mead set out to collect information, they concentrated on topics such as **language, kinship, subsistence,** and **marriage.** Since these ethnographic pioneers started working, the cultural world has become more interconnected in response to global communication and interaction. Now, at the beginning of the twenty-first century, no unknown peoples are hidden away in remote rainforests. No societies depend solely on mobile **foraging** (hunting and gathering) lifestyles. Foraging, where it still occurs, does so within a broader system that always includes access to the products of agriculture.

The world is carved into nations, and all societies, whether small or large in scale, are under the political control of nation-states. The demise of cultural isolation has accelerated **acculturation**—the blending of cultural characteristics into wider and usually more dominant cultural contexts. Economic goods such as clothes, medicines, and electronics are transported freely around the globe. An information revolution in the form of the Internet has made contact with other cultures virtually instantaneous. These changes are part of a phenomenon known as **globalization.** Migration continues to move people along with their languages, religions, and national identities across wide distances—a situation sometimes referred to as **transnationalism.** This process can be seen in the article "Tears for the Saint, Tears for Ourselves," where we follow Seyed Moustafa on a journey that has his family fleeing his native Iraq to eventually settle in the United States. In migrating, Seyed Moustafa and his family join the ever-increasing populations of immigrants, immigrants who bring language, religion, customs, and some excellent cuisine with them as they form new communities in new places.

Because of these rapid cultural changes, the topics or themes presented here reflect the current directions taken by anthropologists. As we solicited the papers, we discovered that the most popular topics researched now by anthropologists concern economic and political change, gender roles, medical issues, belief systems, and death.

In this volume, you will find sections on fieldwork, economics and work, changing political realities, gender, social status, health and healing, religion and belief, death and dying, material culture and art, and globalization. In each section, we present articles that illustrate the theme and in most cases underscore how rapidly the cultural universe is changing. These articles show that the pace of change is not the same everywhere, nor does it equally affect every aspect of a society. In some contexts we see resistance to change, and the reasons for this resistance may be as intriguing as the reasons for its occurrence.

The articles in this reader focus on the challenges of the modern world; however, the more traditional concerns of anthropologists are deeply embedded in the articles. For example, **kinship,** a fundamental concern to anthropologists, is not the focal point of any single article, nor does it get its own section heading. However, kinship provides a context for behavior in many cultures and can be examined within many of the articles. You will see how kinship affects social and economic relations in, for example, the way that family members cope with the death of their brother in "Death of an Irishman" and in the way that a weaving cooperative is set up in "Rosa, Weaving Women into Life." As you read these articles, consider how marriages, families, and kin relations affect the lives of people whose stories are told here. We offer readers the opportunity to see the many facets of culture interacting within the context of each article.

When we solicited these articles, we told the authors that we wanted them to write in a style that students would enjoy. They weren't to use theory and jargon. They were to tell a story, usually about a single individual, and through that story reveal a snapshot of the culture within which this individual lives. We hope that you, as students, will agree that they have been successful in making peoples of other societies come alive.

USING *PERSONAL ENCOUNTERS:* A GUIDE FOR FACULTY

Each section of articles has an introduction explaining that topic. These introductions offer the student more background on topics, introduce specific terminology,

and point out the importance of understanding how these topics contribute broadly to culture. Each individual chapter has a short introduction explaining the context for the article and giving relevant background material regarding the story's setting. We highlight the cultural themes through discussion questions that precede each article. These questions guide students toward the important issues presented in the articles.

We organized the topics in the reader in such a way to complement the structure usually found in introductory cultural anthropology textbooks—fieldwork discussed first and globalization, a topic that can relate to any facet of culture from economics to religion, last. However, the holistic nature of the discipline ensures that any one article could fit under more than one of the section headings. For example, although Strauss's article on yoga is placed under the theme of globalization, it also provides an example of attitudes about health and healing. Likewise, although Briller primarily discusses social status, the subsistence strategies of pastoralists are also referred to in her story. To make selecting articles for assignments more flexible, we include Table 1 as a guide for faculty.

Articles focus on societies from around the world, yet several countries, such as India, Mexico, Ireland, and Zambia, are represented by more than one story. These can provide information on several aspects of a single country or area so students can begin to see variation present within a single world region, thus gaining a broader view. For example, in the two articles set in Zambia, one occurs in a remote rural village, the other in the largest city of Lusaka. In a few cases, such as Pribilsky's article about a man who lives in two worlds, his village in Ecuador and New York City, the articles are relevant to more than one region or country. The breakdown of articles by region is shown in Table 2. We hope these two tables can serve as guides for faculty who may consider using articles in this book for anthropology courses that target specific topics or specific regions.

Articles were chosen for this reader on the basis of the topic covered and the readability of the work. We want these articles to be accessible to introductory students. Each article has both narrative and sufficient anthropological context and analysis to allow the student to understand what they are reading. However, there is variation in the complexity of the articles, and some may prove more challenging than others. We hope that this variability will match the diversity in student abilities and provide something for everyone.

TABLE 1   Anthropological Topics and Relevant Articles

Topic	Authors
Fieldwork	Derby, Koops, Kuznar, Maack, Pyburn, Sandstrom and Sandstrom
Subsistence	Briller, Cliggett, Kuznar
Economics and Work	Acheson, Behrman, Coffey, Derby, Maack, O'Brian, Pribilsky, Walbridge (*Driving*)
Politics and Political Change	Acheson, Hegland, Quinn , Simonelli, Walbridge (*Tears*), Trix
Migration and Refugees	Maack, Pribilsky, Walbridge (*Tears*)
Language and Communication	Lyons, Quinn, Spitulnik
Health and Healing	Buchanan-Aruwafu, Cartwright, Hattari, Koops, Maack, Strauss, Williamson
Gender	Behrman, Buchanan-Aruwafu, Cliggett, Coffey, Epple, Hegland, Lamb, Kuznar, Peake, Pyburn
Kinship, Marriage, and Family	Epple, Hattari, Hegland, Koops, Lamb, O'Brian, Pribilsky, Simonelli, Williamson
Social Status	Walbridge (*Driving*), Briller, Lamb, Cliggett, Coffey, Hegland
Religion and Belief	Bennett, Hattari, Kuznar, Sandstrom and Sandstrom, Sievert, Walbridge (*Tears*), Williamson
Death and Dying	Bennett, Hattari, Trix, Williamson
Material Culture	O'Brian, Sievert, Sandstrom and Sandstrom
Art and Popular Culture	Lyons, Sandstrom and Sandstrom, Spitulnik
Culture Change	Acheson, Behrman, Coffey, Derby, Hegland, Kuznar, Maack, Pribilsky, Sandstrom and Sandstrom, Simonelli, Strauss, Walbridge (*Tears*)
Applied Anthropology	Cartwright, Maack, O'Brian, Pyburn, Simonelli
Globalization and Transnationalism	Coffey, Derby, Hattari, O'Brian, Pribilsky, Spitulnik, Strauss, Walbridge (*Tears*)

TABLE 2   Regions Covered and Relevant Authors

Region	Authors
Africa	Cliggett (Zambia), Maack (Tanzania), Spitulnik (Zambia)
Australia and the Pacific	Buchanan-Aruwafu (Solomon Islands), Koops (Cook Islands), Peake
Middle East	Bennett (Syria), Hegland (Iran), Pyburn (Yemen), Trix (Lebanon), Walbridge (*Tears*) (Iraq)
Europe	Acheson (Slovakia), Quinn (Ireland), Williamson (Ireland)
South and Southeast Asia	Derby (India), Hattari (Indonesia), Lamb (India), Strauss (India), Walbridge (*Driving*) (Pakistan)
East Asia	Briller (Mongolia), Coffey (China)
Latin America—Mexico	Cartwright, O'Brian, Sandstrom and Sandstrom, Simonelli
Latin America—South America	Lyons (Ecuador), Kuznar (Peru), Pribilsky (Ecuador)
Native North America	Epple, Sievert
North America/United States	Behrman, Epple, Pribilsky, Sievert, Walbridge (*Tears*)

PART I

Anthropology and Fieldwork

Photo by John Walbridge.

Before a person can be enlisted into the ranks of "real" sociocultural anthropologists, he or she must go through a sort of rite of passage called "fieldwork." This is a lengthy process involving research in another culture, generally involving the learning of another language. It may or may not involve formal questionnaires and statistical analysis, but it definitely does involve "participant observation." The researcher lives with the people under study and participates in their everyday activities. In this way the anthropologist begins to see the culture through the eyes of the people he or she is studying, while learning to view his or her own background, and, indeed, all of humanity, in a new light.

This is a more difficult task than it may seem on the surface. Many researchers experience what is called **culture shock** when they initially enter a different setting and experience drastically new customs. Anthropological research cannot be conducted by the same rules used in physics or biology because the sociocultural anthropologist, often called an ethnographer, has the task of capturing the uniqueness of a culture that has resulted from its own creative use of symbols. Tools such as mapping an area, census taking, and administering questionnaires may also be used, but nothing takes the place of immersing oneself in the way of life of a group of people. Through participant observation, analysis, and self-reflection, anthropologists hope to rid themselves of **ethnocentrism,** that is, viewing other peoples' beliefs and customs in terms of their own standards. The field of anthropology has usually subscribed to a belief in the concept of **cultural relativism,** which states that each way of life should be evaluated according to its own standards of right and wrong. However, there is also a realization that to carry this concept too far can lead to condoning universally unacceptable behaviors such as racism or even genocide. Anthropologists realize that they have to attempt to see things through the eyes of others while still maintaining standards about important matters having to do with fundamental human rights. Certainly one contribution anthropologists can make through their understanding of human behavior is to help reduce the degree of **stereotyping** found in societies, especially that which involves inaccurate and demeaning ways to describe others so as to support the privileged status of one group over another.

Anthropologists have paid considerable attention to their methodology and how they write about a society. Ideas about how research should be conducted have changed over the decades. During the early years of the field of anthropology, researchers believed that they could remain in the comfort of their own home or university and simply rely on reports sent home from various parts of the globe. But anthropologists such as Bronislaw Malinowski in Europe and Franz Boas in the United States broke with this "armchair" model of studying cultures. Through their own fieldwork they shifted the focus of anthropology from hearsay to observation. Secondhand reports were considered insufficient; the ethnographer had to be there to see and experience the culture, to learn a new language and speak to people in their own tongue.

In the nineteenth century and the first half of the twentieth century, much of the world was under European colonial rule. Peoples in Asia and Africa were excluded from government and many other areas of life. Hence, to a large extent, they were not permitted to develop politically and economically. Anthropologists often saw these societies as being locked in the past and wrote about them accordingly. With the end of colonial domination, societies around the world have undergone tremendous change as they grapple with defining themselves as nations and developing governmental systems and economic bases that fit their situations. While the challenges for these countries are enormous, anthropologists also face challenges: they must find ways to understand and write about rapidly changing societies where old categories and ideas are often discarded. Also, because of the legacy of colonial rule and the lessons learned from it, anthropologists have become more reflective about the possible influences that they might have on the people they contact. Increasingly, they are realizing that what they say and write can have an impact on the people they are studying—for better or for worse.

One of the challenges for anthropologists is that of studying societies fraught with the traumas brought about by modernity, and by marginalization on the postcolonial world stage. These traumas can take the form of civil wars in which various ethnic groups struggle for power in recently created states. Or they can be the ravages of diseases brought about by mass migrations resulting from warfare or economic turmoil. The ethnographer can find him- or herself no longer simply studying a people, but also struggling to find ways to alleviate their suffering.

Increasingly, anthropologists are called upon to use their skills as fieldworkers to address a variety of problems facing a society. While many anthropologists devote their working years to the study of one region or country, at other times they are forced by circumstances to turn an "anthropological eye" on cultures with which they have little familiarity. In other words, it is their skill as researchers that is in demand rather than their specific knowledge of a place. Increasingly, the field of **applied anthropology**—in which anthropological methodology, findings, and concepts are put to use to attain social goals—is gaining in importance in fields such as medicine, business, and law.

While fieldwork may be the hallmark of sociocultural anthropology, it is now being used by scholars in fields such as history, sociology, political science, and criminal justice. Indeed, the fieldwork techniques used by anthropologists—surveys, interviews, observations, and participation in social and cultural practices—can be applied to a wide range of research problems in a number of fields.

Whether an anthropologist studies a remote small herding village in Asia or a bustling city in the United States, fieldwork is the common denominator that links anthropologists' perspectives the world over.

Paul Derby arrives in the bustling, crowded pilgrimage city of Banaras, India, where he is overwhelmed by new sights and sounds and by hawkers of goods. Happily he finds a cultural teacher in the form of Thomas, a money changer, seller of silks, and shop owner who appreciates the potentially dire effects of the "evil eye."

When K. Anne Pyburn endeavors to conduct a study of women's agricultural potential in Yemen without knowing a word of Arabic, she is taken in hand by Raja, a hospitable woman who reveals that Yemeni women may have some freedoms that Pyburn had never considered.

Pamela Maack finds Eliasa, a Tanzanian child orphaned by the HIV/AIDS epidemic in Tanzania. Through Eliasa, we glimpse how crushingly devastating AIDS is for families, and through Maack, we glimpse the emotional challenges that anthropology often presents.

Other articles with relevance to fieldwork:

A Virgin to the Vaka by Vaughn Koops

Manuel, Apprentice Yatiri by Lawrence Kuznar

The Shaman's Art by Alan Sandstrom and Pamela Effrein Sandstrom

1

The Evil Eye Is Bad for Business

Paul Derby

Castleton State College

Hugging the banks of the holy Ganges River, Banaras may be the oldest and most important religious site in India. Every year, millions of Hindus make pilgrimages to the city to bathe in the dirty but spiritually purifying waters of the Ganges to cleanse away their sins. Along with these religious pilgrims come thousands of foreign tourists and religious scholars seeking a glimpse of the great religious tradition of the East. But the spirit alone cannot support a great city, however holy, and the pilgrims are the industry that feeds Banaras. This article introduces Thomas, whose business is one small cog in this complex and ancient industry. This article also tells of Paul Derby's immersion into the culture of Banaras; not the culture of the pilgrims, tourists, and scholars that has so often been written about, but of the people who live and work in this bustling, old, decrepit city. This is another Banaras where about one million permanent residents are jammed into a five-mile stretch along the Ganges with hundreds of thousands of pilgrims, temples too many to count, and *sadhus* (holymen), sacred cows and monkeys, oxen carts and bicycle rickshaws, beggars and lepers.

As you read, consider the following questions:

1. What can you learn about doing fieldwork from this account? Have you ever been in a situation that was so radically different than what you are used to? How might you react to such an experience?
2. How might you feel if suddenly people could not understand what you were trying to say, or if you did not understand the language being spoken to you? How do you think you would feel if strangers were making fun of the way you talked or looked or acted? How would you feel if you did not like the people you met, and how would you deal with that situation?
3. What can be said about the relationship of belief in the evil eye and the adoption of a capitalist economy in India?
4. Can you compare the evil eye to anything from your culture? Is this just superstition and magic?
5. What does this article tell you about relationships and power in Indian culture? Why are the right connections important in business? Why was Mohun forced to leave his family just because he married a woman from a different caste? Why did Thomas allow Rama to bother him?

THE *MALIK* AND THE *DALAL*

"Ye kya hai?" (What is this?) I pointed up at the three chilies, one lemon, and three more chilies hanging on a string from a nail above the doorway on the outside of a little shop in the city of Banaras, India.

"Ye ajib chiz ke bad mujhe batao?" (Tell me after this strange thing?) I was trying out my very best Hindi, which brought peals of laughter from the shopkeeper.

"Mujhe is ajib chiz ke bare me batao." (Tell me about this strange thing). So I was corrected by my friend Thomas, a businessman and owner of this small cloth and souvenir shop just around the corner and up the street from my apartment at the southern end of Banaras.

Banaras was not a pleasant place for me to live. It is crowded, dirty, and hot. There were many times in the first two months of my nine months of fieldwork that I just wanted to go home: home to a bed that didn't require mosquito netting around it to protect me from malaria and home to people who spoke the same language as me and didn't make fun of me when I made a mistake. But I stayed and I'm glad that I did, because in time I got to know the real people behind the façade. The people, my friends, who made this whole thing work. Thomas was probably the most important of these friends.

Thomas specializes in foreigners. Outside of his shop are *dalals,* or commission men, so named because, if they are successful in enticing the visitor to Thomas's

4

shop, they are rewarded with a 10 percent commission on the sales. In fact, that is how I came to meet Thomas. I had been in Banaras for only three days. I had come to the city to do fieldwork on spirit possession. On a previous trip to India I witnessed a young girl possessed by the ghost of her recently dead uncle. I was fascinated by her as she whirled around and cried out to a Muslim saint, asking the saint to "burn the ghost out of her." My research plan was to visit a similar Muslim shrine in Banaras that was known to have some possessed children. I planned to interview the children and their families and write about the causes of possession among children in North India. But as is common in fieldwork, my research changed drastically. The change began as I was meandering around what was to be my new neighborhood for the next nine months. Then a short, scrawny man approached me and changed my life. He smiled at me, and I could see his teeth were stained red from the betel nut he was chewing, and he had a thick streak of white paint from the Brahman priest of the Hindu temple in the middle of his forehead.

"You want see good cloth?" he asked.

"No," I said and kept walking.

"Silik, famous Baransi silik?"

"No," I repeated, trying to sound firm and resistant to sales pressure. I was afraid if I tried my Hindi on this man, he would somehow see my weakness and I would succumb to his pressure.

"Change money?"

"No thank you." I walked faster. Exchanging currency, especially American dollars for Indian rupees, is a significant portion of the profits for tourist-based businesses. They exchange for dollars and hold them until the rate of exchange is favorable.

"You have cash? Very good rate."

I was uncomfortable now. Basically, I never got used to these strong-arm sales tactics. So, when I heard expressions such as, "Come in, come in! Just looking. Don't buy anything. Just looking," I felt like running.

Then, if I am lured into a shop, I have to bargain, something for which I received no training in my hometown. But I must admit, there is an art to bargaining. Once I was persuaded into buying a pair of *faux* Ray Ban sunglasses, the asking price of which was about $50 U.S. Trying to appear sophisticated, I scoffed. The shopkeeper eyed me narrowly, "How much you give?" After 25 minutes and much exasperation on my part, but none it seemed on his, I bought the glasses for $3 U.S. We so-called capitalists in the United States have a lot to learn from these people. Of course, they've been at it for a long time. Haggling over goods and services is a part of everyday life in a society where people are born into occupational castes and

have to negotiate with people of other castes for goods and services.

Back on the street my commission man remained undaunted. "You want nice kurta?"

Ah . . . , actually, I did need a new kurta pajama outfit. The kurta is a large, long shirt made of light cotton or silk. They look kind of like a nightshirt my dad wears to bed, and they are comfortable. And I had to have something cooler than the shirts and pants we in the West wear. An hour on the streets of Banaras in September and I am dripping with sweat. I couldn't wear shorts. They are not respectable. And I don't want to be mistaken as a tourist; after all I am an anthropologist. That was it. I caved.

"Okay," I said, "where to?" The commission man smiled broadly, and walked me from the crossroads up the dirt street to a tiny 8' by 10' showroom. The sign above the door read, with the typical misspelled English words:

THOMAS'
LA SOIE THE SILK DIE SEIDE
Manufacturer's Exporter
&
Authurised Restricted Money Changers

And right there below that sign was the strange chilies-and-lemon combination.

Inside the shop, a single bulb hung from a wire suspended from the ceiling. It burned meekly, emphasizing the dingy decor. The walls of the shop were plaster on concrete and painted a faint blue all around. The air was thick and smelled of a mixture of smoke from burning incense and bidis (the Indian cigarettes that nearly all men of Banaras smoke constantly) and BO. Some finished kurtas and a few "Western-styled" shirts hung on a hook screwed into one concrete wall. Two bhatik wall hangings were pinned onto a strung wire on the opposite wall. One hanging depicted the Lord Shiva in his majestic and ascetic cross-legged yogic pose. The other revealed the awesome goddess Kali: her red, blood-covered tongue lolling from between fangs; a necklace of human skulls barely covering her dark, naked breasts and red nipples. At her feet was the same Lord Shiva, but here he was not so mighty. Kali wildly danced or stomped him defiantly! Or was the Lord Shiva, the master of Banaras, allowing her this moment?

"Hello. Come in. Sit down." Thomas's English was much better than his commission man's. His hand directed me toward the floor. Sitting meant sitting cross-legged on the large, lumpy mats or mattresses on the floor. I removed my shoes at the doorway, as is proper etiquette upon entering one's home or shop in India, and plopped down across from Thomas. I looked around the shop and back at the entrance to the street.

The man who brought me here pulled shut a curtain at the entranceway. The street was gone; I was trapped. Here I was sitting alone among strangers, people I knew nothing about. I was already skeptical and defensive about the hard-sell, and I remember thinking, "How am I going to get out of here?" I was frightened, but I also found myself wondering about these people: Who were they? What are their names? What are they like? What are they thinking about me? This was going to be an experience.

Thomas was tall for an Indian, close to six feet with a large frame, and very dark skinned.

"Mohun, *chai lena!* (Bring tea)," Thomas ordered Mohun, the hawker who brought me here.

Mohun yelled from the doorway. "Chai . . . three glasses."

Thomas was the *malik*, the owner, and he was clearly in charge. Thomas comes from the very south of India, from the state of Kerala, which has been Christian almost as long as Christianity has existed. The people of Kerala believe that St. Thomas the Apostle traveled to India and brought about the conversion of the people. Thomas describes himself as a "good" Christian and does "not believe in all of those Hindu gods and rituals. They have many strange ideas." He often made it a point to inform his customers he was a Christian, not a Hindu, believing that foreigners from the Christian West would rather deal with a Christian than a Hindu.

The state of Kerala boasts the highest literacy rate in India, and many speak and write English, but Kerala also has high unemployment rates. As a result, educated persons often migrate from Kerala to find work in other parts of India, especially government positions that require a good knowledge of English. Thomas would have no part of the government. Instead, in 1985 he left Kerala with his wife and son and came "to do business in the Hindu holy city of Banaras." As Thomas explained it to me, "I came to Banaras to make money. I could speak English and heard this was important in the tourist trade. I heard Banaras was the place tourists come, and I wanted to meet them." His mastery of English is certainly an advantage, and his manner with tourists is patient and honest, yet persuasive. Through trial, error, savvy, and *bakshish* (bribes) he managed to carve out a modest spot within the fiercely competitive marketplace of Banaras.

But Thomas's modest success came slowly and not without tribulations. When he first came to the city, he rented a shop in Banaras's primary market of Godaulia. In Godaulia Market, up from the main ghat (steps that descend into the holy Ganges) of Dasashvemed, there are literally hundreds of shops, dozens of which depend solely upon tourism to survive. Within the entangled and seemingly endless, winding back alleys, one can buy anything that can be had in Banaras: from the famous Banaras silk saris and brocades, to jewelry, coffee, toys, statues of Hindu deities and Buddhas, flowers, incense, candy, audio tapes, movie videos in English and Hindi, books, sitars, and tables (Indian drums played with the fingers). Even Indian beer can be purchased somewhere in that cacophony of shops and markets. Thomas set up a small store and made arrangements with Muslim weavers to buy silk brocades and fabrics. He found the competition fierce. That first shop failed, but he does not blame himself. Instead, he blames this early failure on others, saying that he could not rely on his sources for good silk. They would cheat him by giving inferior pieces or by charging him more than they would the other, established sellers. Also, Thomas complained that his commission men would play him against other shop owners for greater commissions. I understood this problem. On several occasions I was lured by commission men trying to make sweeter deals behind the backs of their bosses. Mostly, though, Thomas blamed the other shop owners. He believes they conspired and colluded to drive him out of business. In such a hyper-competitive small business industry in India this is hardly surprising. And Thomas was an outsider without all the benefit of good local connections. Still, Thomas persevered.

Three or four years back Thomas moved to the southern end of the city. Here tourists are fewer, but there are also fewer shops. This proved to be a good move. With two small hotels in the immediate area and a few tourists getting off here from a one-way ride up the holy Ganga River, there is a slow but steady stream of potential customers. Also, many foreign scholars gravitate to the southern end of the city because it is the area close to Banaras Hindu University, and the all-important American Institute library. But more importantly Thomas had significantly cut down on competition. Nevertheless, outside the shop or at the nearby crossing, commission men from other shops tried to sway people away by offering free bicycle rickshaw rides, better rates, or superior products, or by denigrating Thomas's business. However, Thomas found a good commission man of his own. His name was Mohun.

Mohun was from Bengal. He claims with great pride, "I am a Bengali brahman." His father and brothers all worked on the railroad, and so did Mohun when he was a young man. Then one day, according to Mohun, an accident occurred killing a fellow worker at the rail yard. I never fully understood the story of who was killed or how, but Mohun feared the railroad's retribution and the often "punish first, ask questions later" brutality of the police. He never returned to work at the rail yard. Nor could he live at home. Not because of the "accident," but because of his marriage to a low-caste, non-brahman woman. Of this I think Mohun was most proud. He spoke often and with a gleam in his eye of what he in English called his "love marriage." The result of his misfortune at the railroad and his happy, if ill-advised, marriage was poverty and abandonment by his family. Mohun and his wife were destitute and needed to move to Banaras to live with relatives of her family. There Mohun could find work only as a commission man. He dreams of opening his own shop, once actually approaching me for financial backing. I could not help him. After all, I was just a poor graduate student here on a grant, but even so, I wouldn't help him, because I doubted he could succeed in this cutthroat business. Both he and Thomas knew that the dream would probably never be realized. Mohun does not have the English skills or the capital necessary to start his own shop. More so, he does not have the network of connections to make a go of it. Banaras is a city of who knows whom. One's power resides in one's important connections. To enter the market, one has to be quick-witted, cunning, diplomatic, and ruthless. Mohun is a gentle man and a dear friend but no *malik*, no entrepreneur.

Being a commission man produces little steady income, but Mohun has survived by it. Like Thomas, Mohun used to work in the Godaulia Market. His previous boss, he claims, treated him poorly, and sometimes cheated him out of earned commissions. He met Thomas through a mutual friend, a Muslim fabric weaver, and decided he would be better off working for Thomas. Past favors were called in and Thomas went to Mohun's boss and paid a fee to get him. Mohun is now under exclusive contract with Thomas. It was Mohun who had lured me into Thomas's shop.

The first day that I met Thomas and Mohun, the three of us talked and drank tea. I ended up ordering two kurta pajama outfits, to be made by Thomas's subcontracted tailor. I did not realize it then, but these two men were to become my closest friends in India. We spent nearly every day in that showroom. I had not intended it, but their world became the focus of my fieldwork. I did not take notes that first day, but when I returned to my neighborhood apartment, I wrote frantically about what I had seen and heard. I knew something good had happened. After that I always carried my journal and often a mini-tape recorder. I also kept a journal in which I would summarize the day's events. My research became exciting to me. I had found a place where the culture of Banaras resides. I had met people who live and breathe this city. I had to know them. Over the next nine months, I bought plenty from them, and brought in many other *videshi grahuk* (foreign customers). In exchange for my role as "a commission man," Thomas and Mohun vowed to teach me Hindi and teach me their trade. Most days, however, I

just walked in, sat down, drank tea, chatted, and observed Thomas and Mohun's everyday lives. It was through this daily contact that I came to understand the evil eye.

HIS EVIL EYE; YOUR BLACK FACE

It was three weeks after that first encounter and 10 degrees cooler when I asked about the three chilies, one lemon, and three more chilies suspended from the string and affixed by a nail over the threshold of Thomas's shop. By then, I had learned that they were a common fixture in other shops as well.

"Ye ajib chiz ke bad mujhe batao?" (Tell me after this strange thing?) I erred.

After the laughter from my Hindi faux pas died down, Mohun became serious. He pulled at the corner of his right bottom eyelid with his index finger and whispered, *"bura ank."*

"The bad eye?" I understood this basic Hindi, but looked to Thomas for verification of its English translation.

Thomas nodded, then commented emphatically, "Oh yes, the bad eye brings bad luck. An onlooker from outside may peer into the shop, and if they have a bad eye, it is dangerous."

"You mean someone with a deformed eye is harmful?" I asked.

"No," Thomas went on, "if the person with the deformed eye is a customer, it is okay."

Now I was confused. "How can this be?"

"Anyone," Thomas explained, "can possess the evil eye. It is not a physical deformity. It happens when someone wants something bad to happen to you."

Thomas paused and then recited an obviously common rhyme, *"Bura nazar wala; Teri muhn kala."* (His evil eye; Your black face.) Perhaps a more literal translation is "The one possessing the evil eye will turn (or make) your face black." Being "black-faced" is a common insult in India. It implies that a person is of low caste, stupid, unsophisticated, unwanted, and unfortunate. It also can mean that a person has been the victim of the evil eye.

People in various parts of the world, including South Asia, believe that the person who has the evil eye is envious or jealous of another's material things or personal qualities. For example, a boy who is jealous of his friend's new toy may be said to possess the evil eye. Or a woman who looks at another woman's baby too lovingly may be suspected of envy and thus be dangerous. Casting the evil eye may be intentional or not. The person who intentionally casts the evil eye is supposedly malicious; the person who does so unintentionally simply has a weak moral character. In either case the evil eye brings harm and misfortune to others. It is blamed for the destruction of property, and for illness and death, particularly the deaths of young children. Potential victims must use caution. For example, they should not flaunt their material wealth, because this will cause others to envy them. In addition, people use amulets or charms to protect themselves and their property. And because children are especially vulnerable to the evil eye, the first gift given to the newborn is often a special bracelet that acts to ward off the harmful effects. Other amulets used to ward off the evil eye include stones placed at the entrances to villages and fetishes made of chili pepper placed around the necks of oxen and cows. Likewise, trucks, buses, and rickshaws commonly have shoes hanging from their bumpers or drawings of shoes painted on their vehicles. These objects ward off the malevolent glances of others, glances that are the cause of many traffic accidents.

Thomas went on. "The evil passerby can cast the bad glance." By evil passersby, Thomas principally meant the busybody competitors and people outside the shop who wished him ill will. Principally, these are the commission men from other shops trying to steal his customers. There were others who might also want to ruin his business or reputation, such as his landlord or that crazy *chai-wala* (tea maker) across the street.

The *chai-wala*, Rama, was indeed a problem. Large and loud, he constantly barged into the shop demanding cigarettes or food from Thomas and his workers. He also routinely threatened me by saying something bad would happen to me if I didn't give gifts to my friends, which of course included him. Gift giving is expected, but subtlety is required in asking for them. Rama's open and outrageous demands even made Thomas and his workers uncomfortable. "He is crazy," Mohun used to say behind Rama's back. Rama does have large, wild eyes, and it was very clear no one trusted his presence. Personally, I was afraid of him. If I saw him hanging around the shop, I would try to sneak by and come back later when he wasn't there. At first I felt guilty about this, but then I realized that it was a romantic notion to think I could become friends with everyone. People are not always pleasant or nice. I guess that is a universal. And Thomas did not like him around much either, but there was little he could do because Rama was having a flagrant affair with Thomas's widowed landlady. The landlady made much trouble for Thomas. She constantly threatened to raise his rent or kick him out. Thomas worked hard to appease her, and this, unfortunately, included suffering Rama's uncouth behavior.

Still, when a customer entered the shop, Thomas demanded that Rama leave. Usually Thomas did this in a way to conceal his real intention, generally by asking Rama to go prepare and bring tea, something that the Indian merchant offers both as a sign of hospitality and as a way to make the customer feel obligated to buy something. I noticed that he also closed the curtain to his doorway whenever he was involved in a sale.

I was beginning to understand. Thomas wanted to keep the outside outside. He did not want others, potentially dangerous competitors or the nosy neighbors or the landlady's informant, to know or meddle in his livelihood. These outsiders could cast the evil eye, and the evil eye is bad for business. Thomas blamed his previous failure on the malicious and envious intent from others. In a real or symbolic sense, their evil eye or bad intentions caused his misfortune.

And what of the three chilies, one lemon, and three more chilies hanging at the threshold of Thomas's shop? It is an amulet to protect or ward off the negative effects from the evil eye—in this case, the evil eyes of other shop owners and commission men. "This thing wards off an evil glance. It keeps out the bad luck. You have to be careful when doing business. That is why we keep the curtain shut, and that is why we have that," Thomas said as he pointed up at the three chilies, one lemon, and three more chilies protectively hanging at the threshold of Thomas's shop in the holy city of Banaras, India.

Thomas's shop was not my intended fieldwork study in Banaras, but it proved to be my greatest glimpse into the culture of that complex city-industry. This is where I could learn about the people and the culture. These people are the lifeblood of that city. But they are people like you and me. People who work, go home, have families, have problems, and feel joy and suffering. Serendipity led me to Thomas and Mohun. I was fortunate to be let inside their lives and their culture. *Namaste.*

SUGGESTED READINGS

Eck, Diana L. (1982). *Banaras: City of Lights.* New York: Alfred A. Knopf.

Pocock, David F. (1981). "The Evil Eye: Envy and Greed Among the Patidar of Central Gujurat," in *The Evil Eye: A Folklore Casebook,* ed. Alan Dundes. New York: Garland Publishing.

2

Worthless Women

K. Anne Pyburn
Indiana University

Anthropologists are often hired to apply their skills and knowledge in solving social problems, or providing information to policy makers. Sometimes, an anthropologist may be called upon to work in unfamiliar settings, with unfamiliar people. This article illustrates the uncertainty, loneliness, and ethnocentrism that accompany anthropologists into new or strange settings. In this case, anthropologist Pyburn is hired to work on issues of women's gardens in Yemen, an area quite foreign to her.

Yemen is an arid and mountainous country spread along the southern coast of the Arabian peninsula. Bordering the Red Sea and Gulf of Aden, Yemen has as its capital the city of Sana'a. Yemen's 10 million people follow Islamic traditions in which women are expected to fill strictly defined gender roles, though there is variation in the manner of observance.

Pyburn finds that her preconceptions of Arab women are challenged as she witnesses a communion of women at an afternoon party. She comes to understand, through the hospitality of Raja, an office worker, that women in Yemen respond to patriarchal society in creative ways. When women and their ideas are discounted, it is sometimes possible to use this negligible status to accomplish things, because there is a certain amount of freedom in being ignored.

As you read, consider the following questions:

1. How did the anthropologist's lack of preparation actually help her to do her job in this case? In what ways was she actually well prepared for the project she undertook? What kind of preparation would you want before taking on a challenge of this type?
2. Identify instances of ethnocentrism, culture shock, and cultural relativism in the story.
3. What does this article show about Western conceptions of female beauty?
4. Explain how anonymity and "worthlessness" can be used to advantage by people with little overt power.
5. How might the experience of entering an unknown culture differ when the traveler is a tourist or a businessperson?

I was a ridiculous choice for the job I was hired to do in Yemen. I was supposed to evaluate a U.S.-funded education program intended to improve the productivity of women's gardens. I spoke no Arabic and had no scholarly background or experience with Islamic cultures. I knew nothing about gardening; I am not even able to grow houseplants; I had no interest in gender studies. At the time, I was an archaeology graduate student who had been excavating at a Maya site in Belize, Central America—about as far from Yemen as a person can get.

The U.S. government employee who hired me told me he was impressed with my ability to deal with tough field conditions despite being a woman. My excavations in Belize required me to live in the jungle for months; cope with insects, reptiles, and other threatening fauna; eat unfamiliar food; and run a project staffed by men unaccustomed to a female boss.

So uppermost in the mind of my employer (or so I thought) was my ability to handle a tough field situation that required a woman. Yemen, he said, was very hot, and inhospitable to American women, with no provision for foreign tastes. I would have to wear long sleeves and long skirts, cover my hair with scarves, and cope with being unwelcome. Uppermost in my mind was a chance to travel, do something useful, and earn an unbelievable amount of money for a graduate student. It never occurred to me that I was chosen precisely for what I did not know.

The United States had built an agricultural college and funded scholarships to teach Yemeni agricultural extension agents how to grow more and better food

9

from small domestic animals and kitchen gardens. These agents would then take their training home to their villages and teach their friends and relatives how to better feed their families. Unfortunately, men who graduated from the school were heading into cities for the white-collar jobs they could claim with the extra education. Women were not attending at all, so I was supposed to find what would attract them.

I did my best to prepare myself to do the job properly. I read everything I could find about Yemen, which I discovered to be near the top of Amnesty International's list of human rights violators. I read state department bulletins, literature produced by government studies, and what ethnographies of Arab women I could find. I purchased a cool but modest wardrobe and steeled myself to be hot and tormented. I got on a plane for Egypt, where I spent five days before going on to Yemen. I had justified the interruption of my dissertation by believing that any archaeologist ought to see Egypt, and this was my chance.

THE LESSONS OF EGYPT

I got off the extremely long flight to Cairo and onto a sort of assembly line, where tourists are processed according to nationality and wealth. I attempted to control my destiny by trying to get a taxi to the hotel where I had reservations, but the customs agent only smiled at me kindly and gave my bags to a relative who took me to the taxi of another relative who took me to the hotel of another relative. Here I attempted a second time to take control of my situation by demanding a room with a lock on the door. The hotel staff very graciously moved me to a room with a broken lock. I managed to wedge an enormous overstuffed chair between the door and the bed, making the door absolutely unopenable. Then I slept, but woke up hourly worrying about being burned alive should the hotel catch fire.

The next day I went to Luxor. I insisted on a private car for the overnight train trip even though the ticket seller tried to dissuade me, which meant that I paid for a private car and was given a roommate who also had paid for a private car. I had more adventures in Egypt, but I had already been given two lessons I would need in Yemen. First, my money and background meant less than my gender. Being a woman meant I was in charge of nothing, not even my own life, regardless of how much I was willing to pay. Second, a woman traveling alone has some freedom other tourists do not, because women are inconsequential targets to the men who run the industry. The normal ruts of tourist travel are designed to manipulate men.

THE TAJ SHEBA

Thus insufficiently acclimated to life in Islamic society, I landed in the Yemeni capital city of Sana'a expecting to be treated as I had been in Cairo. I was ignored. The customs official looked at me as though I was something stuck to his shoe, and no one saw any problem with me struggling with my own luggage out of the terminal. Outside, where people were gathered awaiting arrivals, a broadly smiling and handsome Ali Amadi grabbed my suitcases and told me in beautiful English that he would be my driver and full-time assistant and he ushered me into a beautiful new Land Cruiser with a freezer-like air-conditioning system. I wondered when the hardship would appear.

After a brief visit to the American diplomatic compound where I was given a series of warnings about getting out of the car or going out alone, Amadi took me to the fanciest hotel in town. I argued mildly, thinking there might be some mistake, since I was a researcher (expecting hardship) and not a diplomat, but he insisted my reservations were for the Sheba, where all U.S. government people stayed. I acquiesced, assuming the arrangement was temporary, and spent the weekend in a gilded room with a television showing Western channels, a wet bar, and a pool (all forbidden to Yemeni citizens). But I had no contact with any people from Yemen. From the inside of the hotel, I could have been anywhere; even the hotel staff was European. I would have to find somewhere else to stay.

Monday morning Amadi took me to my first appointment in a city office where I was introduced to a female bureaucrat whom I will call Raja. She wore a calf-length polyester trench coat over her street clothes and a scarf over her head that tied under her chin. I kept expecting her to take her coat off, until I realized that the few other women in evidence were also wearing them. By 8:30 it was well over 100 degrees and the building was not air-conditioned, but Raja mysteriously did not sweat. I was wearing opaque cotton gauze clothing for modesty and coolness, and I had become a dripping mess during the walk from the air-conditioned car to the building. My hostess was cordial, but clearly had no idea what to do with me. I suspected she knew as much about kitchen gardens as I did, but I was afraid I might insult her if I assumed she didn't know (since it might be her job to know) or assumed that she did (since she might not wish to be seen as anything but a sophisticated urbanite). We mostly smiled uncomfortably at each other while Raja tried to unobtrusively get some work done and I pretended to be happy to sit and sweat. She was busy and people constantly came and went from her office. It was apparent that her position was considered high "for a woman." However, most offices were run by men and were busier and better furnished. Raja once rolled her eyes at her female colleagues after the departure of a man with particularly officious body language. When she caught me smiling she grinned back at me. It was the first hint of understanding between us.

A TEA PARTY

At about 3 P.M. Raja signaled it was time to go. I thought she was taking off early for my benefit, but I later found out she had started work at 6 and was leaving at the normal time. This schedule is a sensible adaptation to the heat of midday, but also an accommodation to a certain Yemeni custom that I was about to experience. Amadi told me Raja was inviting me to a party, and I replied that I didn't want to intrude on her private life. I could tell there was something off about this attitude; either the concept of intrusion was not socially relevant, or else it was her job to entertain me. I was hot and jet-lagged enough to feel slightly panicked at the idea of trying to be gracious in a completely alien social context where no one could talk to me. My hostess was charming but not exactly warm and friendly.

Nevertheless, I felt that I ought to do this, and I was very ready to get out of the hotel, so I agreed to go. Amadi drove us to a house in a suburb of Sana'a that looked exactly like a middle-class subdivision in America. We went in a side door where a servant ushered us through a bare kitchen into a living room with only a large stereo at one end and some cushions on the floor. I was invited to sit; Raja smiled widely and surprised me by taking off her scarf and disappearing into the back of the house.

I felt slightly uncomfortable in this empty house, and wondered how there could be a party without furniture. Almost immediately three more women came in the side door and took off, not only their scarves, but also their trench coats. This kept me very busy for the next few minutes trying not to gape, since I was floored by what they had on—and did not have on—underneath.

They greeted me casually, apparently getting some explanation of my presence from the servant who took their coats. Nobody spoke English or seemed to expect me to speak Arabic. I think I was introduced, but I could not pick a name out of the musical, laughing splatter of words. The three women were different ages: one a teenager and the other two middle aged. Removal of their coats left them wearing transparent fabric draped artistically over brightly colored underwear.

The fabric had nonrepresentational designs (graphic depictions are forbidden) in loud turquoise and red and royal blue splashed over the transparent fabric making some small patches opaque, but matching the turquoise or red or blue brassiere underneath. The fabric designs were accented with silver or gold and topped with huge quantities of gold jewelry at neck and wrists—ankles were decorated as the coats came off. My first reaction was that the women were comical looking with their pointy colorful underwear and gaudy gilded dresses. I guessed the sheer fabric was a concession to the heat.

They settled in, spreading a cloth and the pillows (with which I was beginning to feel some kinship as another inert silent presence in the room) on the floor in front of me. Three more women veiled in black from head to toe arrived. Some conservative Yemeni women wear veils that they look through, so not even their eyes are visible. These they unceremoniously shucked off in a back room I could glimpse down a corridor, revealing similar party clothes, but even more jewelry. Raja emerged with them wearing orange and gold over an orange brassiere. By this time the teenager had approached the stereo and put on Arabic rock-and-roll music, with a heavy beat and guitars whamming out a sort of—well—almost a belly dance tune, I thought hilariously. I guessed that it was my ignorance making me think all Arabic music sounded like belly dance music and I prepared to try to learn the difference. I wondered if I should get up to greet arrivals. No one else was sitting, but I liked feeling unobtrusive.

The teenager started to move her hips to the music almost immediately. It was a startlingly sensuous movement, something few American teenagers would do in front of older female relatives. I was embarrassed and fascinated at the same time. She was very fat by American standards, where she would likely be doomed to ridicule, but something about this young woman exuded not only confidence but a sort of happy sexuality. The undulations, interrupted by several musical changes as she appeared to be seeking something she liked, escalated to full-scale dancing in about five minutes. Much to my amazement she was belly dancing vigorously about four feet from where I sat, as other women came in, chatted, and took off their outer garments. No one but me seemed particularly aware of her amazing display.

She combined jerks and wiggles with undulations and small twirls in a lovely way. I had never seen anything like it. Within minutes my aversion to her figure completely reversed. Her movements did not attempt to compensate for her size or to deny her bulk; they displayed the fat, and to great advantage. She caused her large breasts to jiggle and her belly to move unexpectedly and independently; her hips and thighs seemed to blossom erotically from impossibly small feet. I was enchanted. It was as though a door on a completely different and completely female type of beauty had been opened to me. I felt goosebumps creep up my arms despite the rising heat of the rapidly filling room.

When Raja and another older woman stood up beside the dancing teenager and began to give her lessons, my mouth fell open. They were actually fatter than she was and even a bit saggy here and there. They both had breasts bigger than my head and rolls of fat visible through their sheer garments. And they were absolutely superb. I suddenly realized that the body fat American women are so ashamed of can give women a sexuality and power I had never imagined. The dancers were proud of their bodies, and their movements proclaimed their luscious vitality. And these women were not out of shape, not by a long shot. They were doing things with powerful muscles where I had no muscles at all.

Suddenly I began to remember things I had read about Yemen and realized this was not something staged for my benefit; I was just a woman at a party for women. My fear of being singled out switched to a sense of camaraderie; I felt hugely complimented to be included as a woman rather than excluded by special treatment designed for a foreigner. These parties actually happen almost daily. Women party only with each other, and belly dancing (perhaps invented as an exercise to prepare for childbirth) is an activity women do together for their own pleasure. If you have seen a belly dancer for an audience in a restaurant or a strip club, forget it—this was nothing like a public performance. The women in this room were confident elite women celebrating their bodies and sexuality in a way that Americans simply do not experience. Belly dancing for men is traditionally done by male prostitutes. These dancing women were certainly not lesbians, nothing that simple, but if there had been a man in the room it would have spoiled everything. But *I* was included; *I* was seeing something no male anthropologist would ever see. The contrast between the lonely culturally sanitized hotel and this rich assault on my preconceived ideas delighted me. I was ashamed of my ignorance and humbled by Raja's generosity. I felt a twinge of pity for the men who had hired me. There was something here they never expected me to discover because they had no inkling of its existence, something much more important than the dancing—the pleasure of simply being a woman.

At this point I felt slightly unhappy. I love to dance. The anemic ersatz rock and roll had been replaced by something raucous and wild and so loud I could feel it vibrating under my skin. Women were taking turns dancing, since the room was too small for everyone to dance at once and I really *really* wanted to join them. I wasn't sure how they would feel about it, but I almost certainly would have tried it if I had had anything to dance with. For the first time in my life I felt sorry for myself for being thin. My personal belief that I needed to lose another five pounds to make my thighs absolutely smooth dissolved into a realization that in this context, I was the ugly one, homely and pitiful with an androgynous shape and nothing interesting to wiggle or sway.

And I also felt like I was the one from the oppressive culture. I was the one whose whole existence was controlled by strict conceptions of what I should look like and how I ought to be sexual even alone with other women. No one watching these women could think women should look otherwise. The anorexic look of Western fashion models suddenly seemed sickly, pathetic, and repressed; by comparison what I was seeing in this room was powerful and threatening. I suddenly wished every man I knew could see what I was seeing—a sexuality simultaneously compelling and probably terrifying to some men. But I also knew that no man would ever see it without spying. This was absolutely exclusively female, and I was probably the only woman in the room who was thinking about men at all. Absolute patriarchy had made men absolutely absent here. No admittance, no knowledge, no control, no power.

The cloth was spread with cakes and candies and warm Cokes and hot tea. All the sweet things were provided to cut the bitter taste of Qat (*Catha edulis*), a leafy plant Yemeni people love to spend the afternoon chewing. It has the effect that drinking 10 cups of coffee would have if you could do that without getting jittery. It makes you feel bright and happy and very wide awake. I tried it without feeling it at the dance party, though later I did not know why I couldn't sleep. The next day I moved out of the Sheba Hotel for good. I wanted to be as close to Yemen as I could get.

IN TRANSLATION

I asked permission to live in the Fulbright residence where I could live with people who spoke Arabic and could teach me about Yemeni culture. Through them I met people from different countries who were in Yemen to provide economic and technical assistance and who taught me a lot in a short time. Although I got differing perspectives on Yemen from the variety of people I interviewed, two points were made in one way or another by everyone I met. First, the idea I had from my reading and talking to American officials about the situation of women in Yemen was vastly oversimplified. Yemen is not a single culture with a conservative religious base, but an amalgam of many cultures with a tremendous variety in the manner in which religion

FIGURE 1   Yemeni market scene. *Photo by K. Anne Pyburn.*

and gender propriety are observed and expressed. No one set of rules or restrictions could ever apply to all Yemeni women.

The second thing I learned was that American government employees were infamous for knowing nothing about Yemen. The fact that I spoke no Arabic and had no background in Yemeni or Arabic studies surprised no one. On the other hand, everyone was surprised that I was trying to learn. At a party of British medical workers one evening I casually mentioned an ethnography I had read. My hostess responded by treating me as a sort of curiosity, actually taking me around the room and introducing me to her colleagues as "an American who has *read* something."

In hindsight, I believe that the men who hired me to go to Yemen wanted to stop trying to train female extension agents, but their decision to scrap the plan was being blocked by an objection from somewhere in the bureaucratic hierarchy of Washington. They needed a woman to verify their contention that it was impossible to train women extension agents in Yemen. The last thing they wanted was an Arabic-speaking woman specialist who might advocate for women's programs. At USAID where I was warned about getting out of my chauffeured car, there seemed little interest in Yemenis as people; cultural values were treated as something that interfered with American assistance.

These gentlemen had not gotten the lessons I learned in Egypt. They believed American money and know-how should be enough to overcome the cultural values that interfered with their plans. If they ever had any intention of helping women at all, they must surely have realized that women would be disinclined to violate the strictures of their religion and the opinions of their families to live among men to take classes. And women who did this would not be allowed to teach the innocent daughters of their neighbors after showing their contempt for family values, any more than men trained to grow kitchen gardens would be able to teach women with whom they were not allowed to speak.

But by picking the most useless woman they could find, me, the Americans made a mistake. I was so far outside their corporate culture, I didn't even comprehend what underlay their warnings or superior attitudes. Raja and her friends charmed and engaged me immediately. I wanted to respond to their generosity by doing my job well. I wanted to do something to help Yemeni women feed themselves and their families. I set out to find a way to make the agricultural extension program work. It was years before I figured out why the solution I designed made people so angry. I found that some women in some communities could take training and come home to teach other women. Each village would have to be approached differently and respectfully, but it could be done and it could be successful.

ON WORTHLESSNESS

People who have no options can find power and a degree of freedom in anonymity and "worthlessness." Worthlessness made me invisible enough to survive five days alone in Egypt; it makes dancing parties possible for Raja and other elite Yemeni women; and it would make it possible for confined women to get new information about growing kitchen gardens through their personal networks of worthless relatives. Although outside Muslim countries women are ostensibly free to wear what they please and go where they wish, the truth is that if women do not conform to particular norms of dress, weight, behavior, and location, they risk being harassed and even harmed. We don't see the boundaries on women in our own culture, because we have grown up with them. That's just the way things are. The same is true in Yemen; most women are not particularly aware that staying inside and wearing a veil are repressive; that's just the way things are and to try to change things is expensive, dangerous, and impossible. Better to find ways within the boundaries to achieve a measure of freedom and contentment.

What shocked me most was the realization that wearing more revealing clothing lays Western women open to criticism of their body types by a male-dominated culture, whereas Yemeni women's shapes are not available for discussion. Of course, Yemeni men see their wives, but are not in much of a position to make unflattering comparisons. How different it must be, and how liberating, to only ever have your figure evaluated by other women.

My employers refused to accept my recommendations, accused me of fabrication, and at one point demanded that I name the women I had interviewed who offered to get help to isolated women. Realizing that refusal to give the names would doom my suggestions to oblivion, I also realized that divulging names would put women in jeopardy, possibly for their lives, since disobedient women are treated mercilessly. I refused to give the names; the grumbling died down. Much later I heard that the director of USAID had said indeed it was probably time to do something for women. In a way, by keeping the veil over my consultants, I maintained their power; if I had named them not only would I have put them in danger, I would have placed their strategy under attack.

I support people who are trying to improve the situation of women in Muslim countries. But only ignorance would suppose that Christian-based Western attitudes toward women are dramatically better. The difference, I now believe, is one of degree rather than of kind. The subtlety and power of the coping mechanisms developed by women all over the world to one of the most self-consciously repressive systems on Earth are impressive. They have my deepest respect, and when I remember Raja dancing, they have my envy.

SUGGESTED READINGS

Hansen, Eric. (1992). *Motoring with Mohammed: Journeys to Yemen and the Red Sea.* Portland, Oreg: Boston: Houghton Mifflin.

Fernea, Elizabeth Warnock. (1965). *Guests of the Sheik: An Ethnography of an Iraqi Village.* New York: Doubleday.

3

Eliasa and the Kwacha Video Coach

Pamela A. Maack
San Jacinto Community College

Usually, an anthropologist's first fieldwork experiences occur during graduate school when they are collecting data for their doctoral dissertations. These experiences may constitute their first time in a culture radically different from their own and may prove to be intellectually and emotionally challenging. Often, return fieldwork trips can involve the anthropologist in applied research projects. Specifically, those anthropologists working in developing nations may find themselves called upon to participate in a development project aimed at improving the lives of the people they have come to know. Seeking to affect change also can prove intellectually and emotionally challenging.

Pamela Maack, who had done previous work in Tanzania, a country in East Africa, worked on a large project to study the effects of death from one of Africa's major killers, the disease HIV/AIDS. Tanzania is a country of extremes, from the high volcanoes of Kilimanjaro to the bustling spice-growing island of Zanzibar. Maack traveled to many locations in Tanzania in doing her study, and she interviewed people all along the way. She brings us the story of one boy, who himself had migrated across the nation. We see how she had to look at different kinds of information—history, economics, anthropology—in order to make sense of how a devastating disease is spread. We also see how anthropological fieldwork rarely leaves the anthropologist unchanged.

As you read her story of Eliasa, keep in mind the following questions for discussion:

1. How does the article depict the holistic nature of anthropological fieldwork?
2. How did the author's fieldwork experiences seem to affect her? How did events in her life change her perspective?
3. Anthropologists try to let informants convey the important issues in their life. What did Eliasa know about the world? What was important to him?
4. What factors affect the transmission of HIV/AIDS in Tanzania?

In the east African country of Tanzania, they say that passengers prefer small boys to call the buses. "Calling the buses" is a rough translation of a Swahili phrase that refers to the way the destination of coaches are announced to the milling crowds at the noisy, disorganized bus depots in east Africa. That they prefer small boys is good because Eliasa is small. Very small. Not much bigger than my own 4-year-old daughter, Kate, who squirms next to me radiating that almost obscene Pepsodent-white, corn-fed-beef healthy American glow. But Eliasa is 10 years old. He is sitting across the table from me at the Ngome Street Children's Project in Kihesa, Iringa, Tanzania. He has been brought to tell me about his life because he is an orphan and I am looking for orphans.

It was 1994 and I had the unenviable task of conducting a "rapid assessment survey" of the state of families coping with the AIDS crisis in Tanzania. This survey was to be very different from the carefully planned, overthought research of my dissertation some seven years earlier. This survey was applied anthropology with an impact.

It began innocently enough as an informal study group organized by the AIDS sector analyst for the U.S. Agency for International Development (USAID). The group was struggling to devise a research protocol when I was asked to join. AIDS is killing millions of parents in Africa. What was happening to their children? To answer this question, we had to find the children. Where were these orphans? With virtually no birth control available in a country of some 35 million people and no condoms produced or distributed in the country, every sexual encounter could result in a pregnancy or a death from AIDS. The fumbling attempts of teenagers to express their newfound sexuality and love for another human being; a young mother's desperate

15

attempt to earn food for her child through petty pros- titution; a young male's celebration of his masculin- ity upon the receipt of his pay packet—all these events can end in birth and in death. To be an anthropologist means accepting what it means to be human. It means accepting that all humans are fallible, that they operate with imperfect information and uncertain goals—that they make mistakes.

It also requires that we understand how culture shapes the consequences of those mistakes. What did I know about the cultural context of Tanzania in 1994 that would help determine how to lighten the burden of families struggling with AIDS? The International Red Cross and the U.S. government set an agenda: how can we help? It was a new question for me with a radi- cally different perspective. In retrospect my disserta- tion work seems both detached and self-absorbed at the same time. I struggled with my goals: how do I eat; how do I bathe; how do I get this woman to open up to me; how can I get this man to sit down and talk with me. How do I get what I want? Now I was being asked to do something much different: "We want to help— how can we help?"

And, boy, did I want to help. I had never made peace with the poverty of Tanzania. I had cried over it, become enraged at it, grown weary of it and tried to run away from it but I had never found any acceptance of it. The cost of being an anthropologist, of accepting that all people are fully and completely human, is the knowledge that all humans are not fully and com- pletely equal. Tanzania is one of the 10 poorest coun- tries in the world with a per capita annual purchasing power of $550—poverty is evident in any direction you look. You are surrounded by squalor, filth, chronic malnutrition, disease, and pain and I could find no way to turn from it, no way to blame the victim so I could feel better, no way to make them more bizarre and therefore less human. Each and every day, they seemed just like people to me. And then there were the children.

During my dissertation research I was young and had the arrogance of the childless. Children were loud, noisy distractions. Then my daughter was born to me and the world shifted. With her, my heart was ripped out of my body and given legs. After her birth, I could never look into the eyes of a child and not see my daughter. How can we help was a loaded question for me.

DEFINING THE PROBLEM

The first step in devising a solution to a problem is to define the scope of the problem. We had precious little information to go on. While the group comprised educated and dedicated scientists, none of them were Tanzanian. In fact, few of them had any experience in Tanzania. That was my strength—I had lived "in the villages." I knew Tanzanians. Perhaps more than that, I knew the history of Tanzania and had a feel for the complex nature of its development.

From my understanding of the history of a third- world, postcolonial nation-state, I was a little surprised at the study group's assumptions. The group had as- sumed family members would be taking in orphaned children. Sadly, I was more cynical. In a country where people are poor and getting poorer—where the spaces between meals can be measured in days not hours— what would another mouth mean?

But it was more than my cynicism; I didn't under- stand their monolithic view of culture. They were op- erating on the assumption that you could simply list the cultural mores of a particular group of people and then you would know where the children were. If the people were matrilineal, the children would be with the mother's family; if patrilineal, with the father's. What were the rules of fosterage? What did the cultural traditions say? It wasn't a form of anthropology I rec- ognized. Hadn't we left the static assumptions in the 1960s? For me culture is complex and dynamic. Tanza- nians don't have set fosterage rules any more than the majority of Americans who are raising children within nuclear families.

There is a popular saying that it takes a village to raise a child. Whenever you hear this repeated, it sup- posedly is an African proverb. Whatever the origin of the phrase, it is a good illustration of the erroneous assumption that Africans live in peaceful, unchanging farming villages, adhering to age-old tribal customs. To proceed upon this assumption would be to com- pletely ignore the reality of life in Africa both today and over the past several hundred years. Nearly all third-world nations have been colonies of a European nation. To be a colony means that the nation existed to serve the needs of others. Those needs were to sup- ply the colonizer with money and goods. When earn- ing money becomes the goal for the nation as a whole, static subsistence-based villages can no longer exist (if they ever did).

Any attempt to help the families and children cop- ing with AIDS in Tanzania needed to begin with an understanding that the disease is not spread evenly across the landscape but is instead concentrated in cer- tain regions and, perhaps more importantly, in areas within regions. We needed to understand the economic conditions that governed the movement and concen- tration of people because this affects both the acquisi- tion of AIDS and the structure of families within Tan- zania. AIDS is a disease of disruption. It thrives in those areas where people are least likely to achieve successful, stable sexual relationships. It is not a disease of placidity, rootedness, or monogamy—it is a disease of trucks, markets, roads, and money. The story of areas where AIDS is thriving is the story of population mobility, single mothers, broken families, shallow kin networks, underemployment, and poverty.

Because the Tanzanian government was lacking the money to pay for the blood test kits to even diagnose HIV, we could not pinpoint those areas from any reported HIV/AIDS rates. But I believed we could easily find those areas hardest hit by AIDS by examining human behavior. Which areas within Tanzania had the greatest numbers of people with the least stability in their lives? We had to go well back in history to find the beginnings of poverty and instability.

Tanzanian history was marked by stories of coercion. From the East African slave trade to the postcolonial and independent Tanzanian nation, common people have sought to control their destiny often with little room for economic and social success. The land that would eventually become known as Tanzania became introduced to a global economy dramatically as part of an ancient slave trade connecting the interior of Africa with the Indian Ocean slaving frontier. Most Tanzanians know well the stories of a time when a human life was worth a quantity of salt. Just as we are constantly seduced by the next electronic gadget that will transform our lives, those early Africans sought to make sense of a world of seductive perversion. The cloth, salt, and manufactured goods offered in exchange for a human life were often a temptation too great to resist. The consequences were disruption of family life, rearrangement of local political power, and economic underdevelopment.

Wage labor was introduced to the territory when it was incorporated as German East Africa. In their brief tenure, the Germans sought to make the territory productive through plantation agriculture. Specifically, they began a number of rubber plantations. My informants from my dissertation research in the Morogoro region of Tanzania remember this as a period of conscripted labor when young men were forced, under threat of whippings, to leave their homes and work as virtual slave labor on these plantations. World War I was fought through Morogoro; and to the burdens of forced labor was added the burden of forced provisions for the German troops. When the territory became a British protectorate after the war, the British forced the Germans to pay reparations to the people of Morogoro for the supplied provisions. Wherever I traveled in the Morogoro area, the people remembered the amazing experience of being paid for these crops.

Under British colonial rule, the road to success for most young men would not be as mere farmers nor through the minimal education system supplied by the British but, instead, through the route of wage labor and petty trade. In an effort to escape the poverty and stagnation of rural villages, young males increasingly sought jobs in the cities, leaving family at home. Women and elders struggled to take up the slack for absent sons and husbands. Maintaining any family life became increasingly difficult for Tanzanians.

At the time of Tanzanian independence in 1961, the country was economically subdivided. These areas included plantation agriculture (for example, sugarcane, coffee, and tea); vast labor reserves (areas known for producing the young males who would migrate to the plantations looking for jobs); growing cities and towns, attracting those seeking full and partial employment; and in-between scattered areas that still struggled with subsistence-based farming and cash-crop production. The meaning of "family" could be very different in each of those areas. The potential for stable husband-and-wife relations also could be very different, as could the potential for HIV infection. Throughout the postindependence period these subdivisions grew and shifted, but the basic patterns remained the same.

FINDING AIDS/HIV INFECTION

Like people in America or others in developed countries, most Tanzanians would like to have a good job and a stable family life. In the United States, young people are taught to go to school, get a good job, and have a family. Because of its poverty, few Tanzanian young men and women are given the opportunity to go to high school, let alone college. Gainful employment, as we know it, is also rarely available. These rather simple economic realities mean that stable family lives are difficult to achieve in Tanzania.

We found AIDS in the cities, towns, and centers of cash-crop production known for "doing business"— the east African expression for taking products from one area of the country and selling them in others. In Tanzania, large numbers of people continue to live and farm in rural areas. However, great numbers of people also flock to areas with favorable crop production or employment opportunities. This activity takes place in business centers that arise in areas of cash-crop production and in cities and towns. These activities are often divided by gender. The transport and reselling of various crops, commodities, and consumer goods is mostly done by men. Women are most often relegated to the less prosperous service sector: brewing and selling local beer and preparing food. It is these geographic areas of population aggregation that are hardest hit by AIDS.

For women in these areas, engaging in various forms of prostitution is not a choice but a necessity.

Denied any opportunities for employment, many brew local beer and cook food to sell in order to survive and support their children. Their earnings are alarmingly low. Men will not come to drink your beer or buy your food if they are not also able to obtain sexual favors. With so many women competing at these occupations, few women can hope to say no. In addition, many women tend to migrate to these regions looking for money to improve their standard of living or support children born out of wedlock. Women also may choose to migrate to areas known for hiring large numbers of migrant labor. Examples include the huge, sprawling shantytowns outside of sugar estates and tea plantations. At most of these estates, young men seeking seasonal labor arrive by the thousands. For a period of time they make relatively good money, often spending it on the beer, food, and sexual services women provide.

Under such economic circumstances, it becomes apparent why families in Africa seldom follow a nuclear family pattern. In fact, very few couples get married in many parts of Tanzania today. Women may have several children by different fathers. Children may never have even met their fathers. Many women in Tanzania are part of cultures that deny or limit their ability to own houses, land, and animals. Their access to these essential resources is mediated through men. Men are highly mobile as they seek to "do business" or work seasonal jobs. Women rarely receive support from one established husband. They must enter into multiple or serial relations with men in the hope of obtaining support. Although for most women in Tanzania having children is not a matter of choice, women can hope to create more permanent ties with men by having their children. Unfortunately, many women end up supporting these children on their own. AIDS/HIV infection is most likely to hit these areas and unfortunately these are the areas least likely to provide a social safety net for children whose parents have died. Children with no family to take them in would most likely show up in towns and business centers.

FINDING ELIASA

I found Eliasa at the Ngome Street Children's Project in the town of Iringa. In Iringa you can buy onions, potatoes, and tomatoes—lots of tomatoes. You can pull in, fill up your truck, and move on, taking with you lots of juicy, red fruits and the death sentence of HIV/AIDS. Eliasa was living in the home with 19 other boys between 5 and 17 years of age. Of the 20 boys in the home, 15 had no parents.

All the boys had come to live in this home because their counselor, Mwalimu Philates Simon Njuyuwi, of-

fered them a home and an education. (*Mwalimu* is a term of respect in Swahili; it translates to the English equivalent of teacher but it carries more authority.) Njuyuwi found all 20 boys living on the streets of Iringa. Eight of the boys lived in the market area. They would offer to help you carry your baskets for a few coins. The other 12 boys lived around the bus depot where they offered to carry luggage for tips. Even very small boys can carry things.

Mwalimu Njuyuwi went every day to the areas of town where food might be thrown out as trash. Here, around the college and the secondary school, he found the boys collecting food—pretending it was for their dogs back at the homes they did not have. He learned their names and gained their confidence. Meanwhile, he prepared a home for them. He could get support from neither the Tanzanian bureaucracy nor from UNICEF, but he did receive financial help from the Catholic church and the people of Italy. He hoped to open his home in June 1994, but he was forced to open a month ahead of schedule. In May, the local police swept the bus depot and picked up 15 children and charged them with loitering. Nine of these 15 were found to have no parents to look after them. Mwalimu Njuyuwi started his home with these nine children. The other 11 joined soon after. Some of these children were originally from Iringa, but others came from different areas within Tanzania: Singida, Shinyanga, Dodoma, Dar es Salaam, Morogoro, and Bukoba. Of these 20 children, six had lost their parents because of AIDS. Eliasa was one of these children—and he had quite a story to tell.

As he told me this story, I struggled to come to terms with his perspective. From my grounded American existence, I found in his tale a strange mixture of detailed knowledge and complete oblivion. As he spoke, he displayed little emotion. At one point, moved by his story, I reached across the table and stroked his cheek—his expression remained unchanged.

ELIASA ARRIVES IN IRINGA

Eliasa began his journey when he was approximately eight years of age in Bukoba, Tanzania, the region around Lake Victoria in northwest Tanzania. He awoke one morning to find his only surviving relative, his older brother, packing up lake fish to take to Dar es Salaam, the large port city on the other side of the country. His brother was trying to "do business." Eliasa followed him—first on the boat to Mwanza, on the other side of the lake, then on the train. He hid under the seats, curling around the legs of passengers. He was a very small boy. During their days of travel, he shadowed his brother. Several times his brother looked back at him, but no words were ever exchanged. When they reached the bustling train station in the over-crowded city of Dar es Salaam, his brother hurried to lose him in the crowd. Eliasa saw the crowds close in around him and his brother vanished. He never saw him again. Somehow, Eliasa made it to the bus depot and he sneaked onto a bus of unknown destination, once again compressing his small frame into the spaces under people's feet. That bus brought him to Iringa.

ELIASA'S LIFE IN IRINGA

Eliasa traveled to Iringa on the "Songola Luxury Coach." He remembers the name of the bus. He re-members a lot about buses—until a month ago he lived on one, the "Kwacha Video Coach." The Kwacha Video Coach offers travelers to the Mbeya region, south of Iringa, a ride, complete with videos playing from a small television set suspended at the front of the bus. For the past two years Eliasa made his home in the stairwell of the Kwacha Video Coach, traveling with the bus as it left Iringa at 10:00 A.M., arriving in Mbeya and leaving again at 4:00 P.M. bound for Kiera, arriv-ing there at 8:00 P.M., and leaving to return to Iringa at 4:00 A.M. the next morning. Eliasa had no education. He cannot read or write, but he knows well this sched-ule and the cost of a ticket (600 shillings). Eliasa is al-lowed to sleep, when he can, on the floor of the bus and eat from the trash cans in the depots at the various stops. Most importantly, he is allowed to earn tips by helping the passengers on the Kwacha Video Coach. For this he has to be small, and funny, and entertain-ing. The smaller the boy, the better the chance of a tip. Most of the boys are small. When Mwalimu Njuyuwi brought the boys to the Ngome Street Children's Proj-ect, they were suffering from stomach amoebas, hook-worm, roundworm, and malnutrition.

ELIASA BECOMES AN ORPHAN

Eliasa was born in Bukoba, the region of Tanzania ad-joining Lake Victoria and bordering Uganda. Its bor-der with Uganda, the African nation with the high-est incidence of AIDS, can explain why Bukoba has the greatest incidence of HIV/AIDS in Tanzania. Why Uganda? There have been many theories advanced: in-fected monkeys from the heartlands of Africa; truck drivers and boat captains on their way to the interior regions; civil unrest. Few people outside Tanzania have the information to answer that question the way that the people of Tanzania do—the way that Eliasa does. In 1978 the troops of Field Marshall Idi Amin Dada of Uganda invaded Tanzania by crossing the border into Bukoba, birthplace of Eliasa. They brought with them the ultimate destruction: tanks, bullets, and AIDS.

Eliasa's parents both died of AIDS. Actually, there is no way of determining precisely what killed Eliasa's parents. Test kits for AIDS are not being used for diag-nostic purposes in Tanzania. They cost too much. AIDS is a diagnosis of rumor. People in Tanzania die from many treatable conditions: malaria, tuberculosis, diar-rhea, viruses, and bacterial infection. All are exacer-bated by chronic malnutrition and grinding poverty. Death is common in the country and AIDS is just one more possibility. In an area experienced with HIV/AIDS, if one-half of a recognized couple dies and then the other partner succumbs, then the couple are as-sumed to have died of AIDS. But Eliasa had more proof.

That June day in 1994 Eliasa sat across the table from me and quietly told me how his parents became sick and died. Their death left Eliasa and his older brother alone. They ran from their father's house be-cause they had to escape the *ukimwi* in the house. (*Ukimwi* is a Swahili term that translates roughly as devils or evil spirits.) The *ukimwi* were there—his brother saw them. The *ukimwi* made his parents sick and killed them. "They were brought by Idi Amin," is what Eliasa quietly told me—Idi Amin—a man who ruled and rampaged long before Eliasa crouched hun-gry and tired at the feet of the passengers of the Kwacha Video Coach. Eliasa was very astute for such a very small boy.

Over the years, Eliasa has stayed in my mind. I met many other children whose stories were in many ways worse than his, but his has always haunted me. Per-haps because Eliasa did originally come from a stable home, his story seems more tragic. Perhaps it is his ex-pressionless face that stays with me; if he had only given me a smile, I could pretend he was okay. Perhaps it was all the questions that I still had about his life. What was it like for him in Bukoba before he lost his parents? Does he ever think about his brother? Did he think his brother was mean or cruel to shake him off? Somehow the enormity of his story quelled many ques-tions for me. How could I ask him these things? How could I probe at his pain?

In the end, I think what I will never shake is how right he was. In 1978, Field Marshall General Idi Amin Dada, then-ruler of Uganda and a man of apparent in-sanity, invaded the small, peaceful country of Tanza-nia. In retrospect we realize that his 100,000 soldiers brought with them the yet-to-be-identified disease of AIDS. They raped and pillaged Eliasa's home area of Bukoba long before he was born. The evil spirits con-tinued down the transport lines of Tanzania, traveling along with the agricultural products that fuel the na-tion. Years later, Eliasa's brother would follow its route as he took his load of lake fish across the country. Eliasa himself spent his young life following the paths and routes it took on the buses. Today the evil spirit is still killing. I wish Eliasa did not have to understand that.

SUGGESTED READINGS

Devita, Philip R., ed. (2000). *Stumbling toward Truth: Anthropologists at Work.* Prospect Heights, Ill.: Waveland Press.

Dettwyler, Katherine. (1993). *Dancing Skeletons: Life and Death in West Africa.* Prospect Heights, Ill.: Waveland Press.

PART II

Economics and Work

Photo by Linda S. Walbridge.

When we consider the economic conditions of today's world, the strongest images we have are of high-tech millionaires and starving masses in war-torn areas. A tiny minority in this world actually control great fortunes. A significantly larger proportion live in poverty and fight hunger on a daily basis. But much of the world's population falls somewhere in between these two extremes, trying to cope with both economic insecurities and limitations on the one hand, and opportunities on the other.

While at one time, economic anthropologists concerned themselves with understanding how various societies acquired adequate subsistence, today the issues are somewhat more expansive. Production of goods and services is now often vested in corporations, and these entities have heavily altered the way that people do business. Although there are numerous societies that focus on herding

21

and horticulture to meet daily subsistence needs, nearly everyone has access to goods produced through large-scale, intensive agriculture and industrialized manufacturing. This means that markets and stores are critical to meeting people's needs and nearly everybody in the world shops. Markets also provide outlets where surplus goods from small-scale production, cash crops, and nonindustrialized manufactured goods can be sold.

In addition, many people now make economic ends meet by performing services, and wage work has increased dramatically over the last 50 years. Factories in Asia and elsewhere now employ millions of people that have migrated from rural areas to find work in burgeoning cities. Mechanized transport makes both personal travel and the transfer of food and durable goods faster, and economic networks now often extend beyond village and kin groups. Likewise, as agricultural production becomes more industrialized and corporate, entire families travel from natal areas to find work at large farms and plantations, or in cities.

Nations do not always completely control their own economic activities. For example, economic sanctions levied by one nation over another for political reasons may limit the opportunities for people living within those nations. Large overriding organizations such as the International Monetary Fund (IMF), World Bank, and World Trade Organization (WTO) often control the ways in which countries become industrialized, affecting the trade relations between countries and regions, and thereby impacting the people within them. New trade alliances such as the European Economic Union (EEU) and the North American Free Trade Agreement (NAFTA) are changing economic and business opportunities across the globe.

However, the presence or actions of large-scale business entities does not completely override local economic networks that may have as their foundations kin-based relations. Families are still the basic units of production and consumption. Even though minted money may be the primary medium of exchange in most areas of the world, barter and reciprocity still function within complex market economies. What appears on the economic landscape is a mosaic of activities—large and small scale, corporate and cooperative, national and family-oriented. Arching over these are major economic operating systems such as capitalism,

with its emphasis on individual endeavor, and socialism, with its emphasis on collective provision. And within these systems are economic operating systems like capitalism, with its emphasis on individual endeavor, and socialism, with its emphasis on collective provision. And with these systems are people, lots of people trying to feed themselves or their families, meet their commitments, and build decent lives. As these systems change, with capitalism rapidly becoming the model for much economic activity, people's strategies must also change.

The ways in which people work are highly variable. As we see in the following articles, there are many solutions to meeting basic needs, to forging and maintaining economic networks, and to meeting periods of paucity or plenty in a rapidly changing world.

Traditional skills, such as Rosa's weaving, may be valued by people outside her community in Chiapas, Mexico, but how can she market her craft so that she and her family can make ends meet? Robin O'Brian learns to understand the resourcefulness that rural people need in order to cope with changing economic needs and expanding economic markets.

Elicia, a single mother who lives in a trailer in the state of Washington, shows Carolyn Behrman that in order to make ends meet, some people must wring every productive minute out of a day. Poverty and economic insecurity may plague the poor in the United States, but in Elicia's case they are met with diligence, cleverness, and hope.

Sunday dinner at Hanka's house in a small village in the Spis region of Slovakia is always a special occasion, but it is made even more memorable when there is a guest. In this case, Julianna Acheson, a relative of Hanka's family, points out the effects that changing the national economic system from communism to capitalism has had on peoples' subsistence strategies.

Other articles with relevance to economic activity:

The Evil Eye Is Bad for Business by Paul Derby

Eliasa and the Kwacha Video Coach by Pamela A. Maack

Driving the Memsahib by Linda S. Walbridge

The Model Worker Talks Back by Courtney Coffey

Living the Chulla Vida by Jason Pribilsky

4

Rosa, Weaving Women into Life

Robin O'Brian

Elmira College

Mexico is a complex and diverse country, with a wide range of ecologies and cultures. A nation of more than 97 million inhabitants, nearly 4 million live in the southern state of Chiapas. The population is made up of indigenous or native peoples who are the descendents of the ancient Maya, who speak Mayan languages and prefer their work as farmers and weavers; and Ladinos, or the people who are members of the dominant Mexican culture. Ladinos can be rural or urban, poor or well-to-do, but Ladinos dominate Chiapas. Ladinos speak Spanish, control government and economics, and generally dominate indigenous people economically and politically.

Rural indigenous agricultural communities like San Pedro Chenalhó cluster around the highland city of San Cristóbal de las Casas. San Cristóbal draws indigenous people for a variety of economic and social reasons: some move to urban settlements like La Hormiga to escape religious persecution. Others, like Rosa and her sister, visit family, attend meetings, and go to the co-op store there. Both before and after the Zapatista uprising of 1994, Rosa and other indigenous women and men worked as farmers and weavers in their rural agricultural communities, but retained strong ties through kinship, *compadrazgo* (god-

parenthood), and friendship to people in the city. But as farming became less productive, they found themselves increasingly dependent upon the city economically. Here women sold crafts or worked as maids; here men became manual laborers. Indigenous women and men remain tied to both their rural communities and the city, though now they see their relationships to both through the lens of political change.

As you read, consider the following questions:

1. What option do the Maya weavers have for earning money from their weavings? What do nonweavers do to earn money?
2. How does Rosa integrate weaving into domestic life?
3. What kinds of communities do indigenous people live in? Do their economic strategies differ? How?
4. How do women in Rosa's community work together to improve conditions in their village? Do women in La Hormiga do similar things? What might these be?
5. What Maya traditions are important to Rosa? How does she emphasize these in her economic and political work?

Sebastiana and her sister Rosa were banging on the metal gates of the house where a friend and I had rented rooms. It was a dreary night, rainy and dark, typical weather for this mountain city in the Mexican state of Chiapas. The two sisters, each with her baby daughter, were in town to drop off weavings at the co-op store and pick up the cash from any sales they had made. They would spend the night with their brother Pedro, a teacher who lived not far from me in San Cristóbal, and return to their own town of Chenalhó in the morning.

My friend Laura and I invited them into her room, out of the rain. "You can stay here for a while and see if the rain stops," I said.

"Would you like some hot tea? Would you like sweet rolls?" asked Laura.

"Oh, it's not far," said Rosa, pulling her *mochibal* (shawl) up over her head. "We won't get so wet. We have skin, don't we?"

Reluctantly, I led Rosa and Sebastiana back outside to the patio. It began at that moment to rain with renewed vigor: sheets of water drummed on the roof, poured over the eaves, splashed on Sebastiana's bare feet.

"Well . . ." Rosa surveyed the rain, running in rivulets on the patio. "Maybe we will stay a few minutes."

In addition to visiting the co-op store, Rosa told us she was thinking of taking some of the weavings she hadn't sold to one of the *artesanía*, or crafts, stores in the center of town. She'd never done it before and was reluctant to do so, saying, "The stores don't pay enough. They pay very little and then charge much more. It's exploitation. They exploit us because we are poor."

I'd met Rosa several months earlier, when another friend who knew her well brought her, her little daughter, and her husband Juan to meet me. I was hoping to talk to her about her work as a weaver and a cooperative leader, but my meeting also gave me a chance to play a role in the co-op: Rosa asked all of us to be judges in a weaving competition, to judge the weavings she had and decide who should win the small cash prizes for skill and creativity. Juan dumped a bag of bright cloth on the foot of my bed, and we carefully inspected the weavings. During the judging, Juan and Rosa sat on the straight wooden chairs by my writing table. After the judging I volunteered to make tea and when I returned, Rosa was writing a letter at my desk while Juan sat talking to my other friends. Everyone was ignoring a large puddle on the cement floor of my room, though when I noticed it, both Juan and Rosa giggled. It turned out that the baby left it.

Rosa and Sebastiana were fairly traditional women who spent most of their time in Chenalhó. There they wove and cared for their families and farms. They came to San Cristóbal sometimes but never sold their high-quality weaving to tourists in the streets or plaza there, and they had never marketed to *artesanía* stores. Rosa's experiences with the *artesanía* stores were not pleasant. She told me later that the store she visited offered only 5,000 pesos apiece for the *sirvilletas* (dinner napkins) she had—about $1.75, not enough to cover the cost of the thread. The stores' practices mirrored much of Maya relations with Mexicans, called *Ladinos* in this part of Mexico. *Ladinos* dominated the culture, the economy, and the political life of San Cristóbal, and while Maya people were everywhere, they were distinctly second class.

When I met her, Rosa was working as the leader of a weaving cooperative, a position she had held for nearly 10 years. She took this obligation seriously, as a service to her people and her community, even though it added to her considerable workload as a farmer's wife and the mother of five small children. Rosa's position in the cooperative also revealed her skill as a weaver and her literacy in Spanish; her visit to my house on that rainy night was part of her obligation to serve her cooperative members.

Women have belonged to weaving cooperatives since the 1970s. Cooperatives allow women to work in their rural towns and to speak their own languages rather than Spanish. The cooperative structure also duplicates the collective way of working that Maya communities follow, valuing mutual support and responsibility. Rosa, her sisters, and mother have been active in cooperatives since the early 1980s, when they joined first a government cooperative and later a new independent cooperative, San Jolobil ("The House of the Weaver"), that sold weavings in San Cristóbal.

Rosa and her sister were close, but their lives were different. While Rosa lived with her husband and children in a small thatched home, weaving, cooking, and doing the other things that Maya women did, Sebastiana, her husband, and their two young children lived with her elderly parents in a different hamlet. The youngest of her parents' children, Sebastiana and her mother wove and cooked together while her husband did the farming. This was a help because Sebastiana's father was now too ill to do much work in the fields.

Sebastiana and her mother were weaving when I once went to visit. After traveling with others who knew the way, we arrived after two hours of steady walking, mostly uphill. When they saw us they put down their weaving and went into the adobe kitchen house, inviting us to follow. Sebastiana's mother set out small chairs for us to sit on, and Sebastiana put wood on the fire. While her mother examined the beans and put water on for sweet, weak coffee, Sebastiana heated

FIGURE 2   Young Maya woman weaves *sirvilletas* for later sales to tourists. *Photo by Robin O'Brian.*

an old iron frying pan over the fire, adding cooking oil and a number of eggs. We went outside to wash our hands and when we returned, a small table had been placed in front of our chairs.

Meanwhile, Sebastiana's husband Felipe had returned from the fields and was wiping his face off with the old T-shirt he had been wearing. Sebastiana placed a small table in front of him and handed him a large basket of tortillas and a small bowl of water. Her mother dished up beans and eggs and handed them to us, following with cups of warm coffee. Sebastiana handed a bowl of eggs and beans to Felipe and took her small daughter on her lap, feeding her bits of tortilla and food from her own bowl. Sebastiana's little boy Mateo periodically dipped into his father's bowl.

Although Sebastiana seemed relaxed and cheerful chatting to Felipe, she watched constantly, and when Felipe was finished eating, she cleared the table and dishes away. Then she added a bit of corn flour to another bowl of water, mixing it thoroughly with her fingers. He drained it in a single draught and returned it to her.

After the meal Sebastiana returned to her weaving. She unrolled her loom and settled back into it, resuming her weaving of a wide length of brightly striped cloth. Her small daughter played around her, and she occasionally spoke to the child as she played nearby. Because Sebastiana and her husband still live with her parents, her mother and father are a presence in their children's lives. Her son, who is older, is going to school, learning Spanish, and beginning to behave like an older child, sometimes caring for his little sister as well. In the household where she lives, Sebastiana is able to devote much of her time to her weaving. Both Rosa and Sebastiana speak Spanish well, but Sebastiana prefers Tzotzil, the Maya language spoken in this region. She is a quieter, sturdier presence than Rosa, whose quick wit and easy laugh often ease tensions.

Rosa and Sebastiana continued to weave because it allowed them to earn a little money in a traditional way, doing the kind of work that Maya women value. For Maya women, clothing woven at home remains an important symbol of belonging, both to ethnic group and community. It also demonstrates the woman's important role in her family because women prefer to clothe their families in handwoven materials. Maya women incorporate important religious and spiritual meanings into appropriate clothing. They prefer their own traditional clothing to commercially made Western clothing out of a sense of obligation to community members and gods. They also suggest that wearing Western clothes would deceive Ladinos or other non-Maya people who might want to talk to them. Many Maya women here still speak little or no Spanish and would not understand. Such difficulties would create misunderstanding and imbalance. The signal of clothing eliminates this. Weaving is also strongly linked to a woman's social status and wearing appropriate clothing makes her a "true woman," a member of her community in ways that are very different from those generally found in the United States.

But the need to earn money affects everyone, and not everyone belongs to a cooperative. Many women who work as crafts sellers and maids come from the small squatter settlements that encircle San Cristóbal. Such communities resemble, as much as they are able, small Indian communities, with thatched homes, sheep and chickens, and tiny cornfields, as if to suggest that though the residents live in San Cristóbal, they remain rural Maya farmers, attached to their fields and animals. As a practical matter, though, there is no land for farming, and the residents usually work in San Cristóbal. Some women sell crafts to tourists while others work as maids for Ladino families, cleaning, doing laundry, and preparing meals.

Everyone works and even little girls sell to tourists in town. For example, María, a young girl from La Hormiga, a poor neighborhood on a hill near San Cristóbal, showed me her small handful of braided bracelets called pulseras. "I need to sell these," she said. "Do you want to buy them?" She sat down on the bench next to me, pulling her bare feet up under her brown wool skirt.

María was extremely disheveled: wisps of hair were escaping from her loose braids; her stained and patched blue blouse was pulling out of her skirt.

"Where do you live?" I asked.

"I live in La Hormiga," she said.

"I know La Hormiga," I told her. "What are you selling here?"

"I'm selling pulseras. Won't you buy my pulseras? I need the money to buy my shoes."

"I don't have any money." I showed her my empty purse.

"I must go then; I must sell my pulseras."

"Good-bye, then," I said, watching her walk purposefully across the plaza.

María also earned a little money for her family. She, her mother, and her brothers and sisters, all sold something to tourists: the woven bracelets, gum, candy. By continuing this they could just manage to keep their family going. But she didn't know the work of weaving, and it showed. Weaving is a skill learned over years, from a mother or grandmother. Rosa learned weaving from her own mother, but María's mother is working on the plaza, too, and doesn't have the time to teach her. The skill is lost, and girls like María sell things that don't take much skill to make and don't make much money for the maker.

But Rosa did not need street sales and stores in San Cristóbal. Her beautiful weavings could be sold for far more than a braided bracelet. Working with other women, her skills and ability to lead benefited more than just her own family, and the weavings themselves sometimes demonstrate a little about Maya life to outsiders. Rosa and the other women in the weaving cooperative know that weaving is a kind of language, a kind of message. Once, after noticing that the symbol of a man appears as a common weaving design, someone asked about symbols of women in weaving. Rosa's elderly aunt, who also wove for the cooperative, recalled that women appeared as symbols on ceremonial weavings used during fiestas. Rosa and the other cooperative members began weaving the symbol once more, and now Maya women as well as Maya men are woven into Maya cloth. In fact, one of the ironies of weaving for money is that the symbols of women are very popular with the buyers.

I last saw Rosa on another impromptu visit. This time it was a sunny Saturday morning, and she was traveling with Juan. They were visiting San Cristóbal to run a number of errands, chasing down a local curer, visiting her brother and other friends in town, buying a few items in the San Cristóbal market. We invited them in for breakfast, cooking eggs in a skillet while Rosa warmed tortillas on the stove, her hands flipping the blue tortillas off the fire before they burned. As we ate, Rosa speculated about the craft stores once again.

"It's exploitation. Do you notice how much more they charge for things after they pay us? We do the work but they make the money."

Although I saw Rosa last nearly 10 years ago, I have heard about her from others who return more often to Chiapas. I send occasional gifts and letters, and I hear about her life. She has had another daughter, born during a time of great struggle, the political uprising that began early in 1994. The uprising, begun by a group called the EZLN, or the Zapatista National Liberation Army, overtook the city of San Cristóbal and other towns in Chiapas to draw attention to numerous economic inequalities. Because so many Maya were farmers, the EZLN worried about the new NAFTA treaty that would allow American and Canadian corn to be sold locally. The Zapatistas also wanted Maya land rights protected from cattle ranchers. And the factors that prompted Rosa to join a weaving cooperative and sent girls like María into the plaza—limited land, economic exploitation, lack of health care—all these and more led both Mayas and other Mexicans to begin the uprising, which continues today. Rosa still weaves, but she is inspired by the message of the uprising, and much of her energy is directed into the new political movement and its promise of change and equality for Maya men and women. The skills she learned representing the weaving co-op serve her well as a political activist. She has begun a second cooperative, one that bakes bread for the community. She says, "I like working with women."

Her political work keeps her even busier and she has stepped down from her position as weaving cooperative leader. But her mother and her sister Sebastiana have assumed this role jointly, so that the weaving cooperative can continue. And Sebastiana also is a member of "Las Abejas" (The Bees), another group that supports political change through nonviolent action. Rosa still weaves in addition to her other work. In spite of the changes in her life, the need to weave for money continues. And Rosa's new work can be more dangerous. Working to support political change has killed people in Rosa's community; right before Christmas three years ago, men killed nearly 50 people during a mass in a distant part of Chenalhó. Most of the dead were women and children, and many were members of Las Abejas. Although Rosa really can't spare the time, she is working with the women from this part of her town, and she suggests that these women's needs are greater, their poverty and suffering deeper.

Of course, most women suffer when their children are hungry and they do what they can to help themselves and their families, often doing the work they also do at home: weaving, embroidering, cooking, cleaning, child care, keeping themselves and their families precariously afloat. Urban women in places like La Hormiga may have fewer options if, like María, they cannot weave, but they work hard at selling crafts or housekeeping. Rural women can weave high-quality items that provide an income; if they are cooperative members they also can remain in their communities and work among relatives and friends performing traditionally respected work.

Rosa has always valued her people's traditions. She dresses in the clothing she and her sisters weave. She places her faith in saints and in curers, speaks Tzotzil and Spanish. But the uprising has deepened her commitment to her people and her way of life. She asks why it is that exploitation and poverty fall so heavily on her people, and why it is that changing this is so threatening, for example, to those who killed people in church. It's this continuing commitment to her people, her family, her children, that keeps her participating, now even at some risk to her own personal safety. But Rosa is still a woman who weaves women into the daily texture of Maya life.

SUGGESTED READINGS

Eber, Christine. (2000). *Women and Alcohol in a Highland Maya Town: Water of Hope, Water of Sorrow.* Austin: University of Texas Press.

Cancian, Frank. (1992). *Decline of Community in Zinacantan: Economy, Public Life, and Social Stratification, 1960–1987.* Stanford, Calif.: Stanford University Press.

5

A Mother's Work

Carolyn Behrman
University of Akron

Approximately 15 million Americans, nearly one in 16, live in trailers. As our population and our cities grow, the number of trailers in use as full-time residences also grows. With the increasing gap between rich and poor in this country and the large number of people living at very low income levels, the relative affordability of trailers makes them very attractive. A survey done in eastern Washington showed that a disproportionate number of trailer households were headed by single parents, usually women. These households had lower incomes than those with more than one adult but had just as many children. This matches the trend overall in the United States where an increased number of female-headed households and children live in poverty.

Many people who live in trailers are also under-employed. Often, the readily available jobs in the United States are not full-time positions. Rather, they are low-paying, part-time jobs with no benefits and little hope of promotion. This trend can be linked to both local and national economic factors. Legislation such as the North American Free Trade Agreement (NAFTA) makes agricultural businesses like those based in eastern Oregon and Washington compete with businesses in Mexico and elsewhere that make use of far cheaper labor pools. Increasing the use of part-time, lower-wage workers is one way for companies to keep costs down and remain competitive. When employers use this strategy in today's modern *market* economy, workers find it necessary to develop creative but often exhausting strategies to maintain an adequate level of subsistence. They often piece together tightly packed work schedules involving multiple jobs along with relying heavily on informal networks of support and reciprocity with neighbors, co-workers, family, and friends. The effects of these strategies and counterstrategies on one worker's life are demonstrated in this workday tale of a single mother living in a trailer park in Walla Walla, Washington.

As you read, consider the following questions:

1. What is Elicia's subsistence strategy? What would you say were her short- and long-term goals? What effect do you think her subsistence strategies will have on her ability to achieve those goals?
2. What pressures did Elicia's employers face and how did they cope with them? What does the article reveal about recent changes in the American economic system?
3. How do Elicia's living conditions differ from or resemble conditions for single mothers in other cultures you are familiar with? Why do you think Elicia lives alone with her son? What alternatives in terms of residence and subsistence can you suggest for her?
4. Flexibility is highly valued in the American labor market today. Workers value flexible schedules and employers value flexible workers. But the idea of flexibility suggests that something or someone will "give" or adjust readily to change. Which aspects of Elicia's daily life are flexible? Who or what "gives" when circumstances demand it?
5. Identify examples of reciprocity operating throughout Elicia's story. How does redistribution in the United States affect Elicia or her family? How does the larger market economy in the United States affect them?

I had been waiting for Elicia* for nearly an hour. Sitting in my car on the shoulder of the semicircular driveway leading into the trailer park, I contemplated the row of

*The names of individuals and of the trailer park have been changed to protect the privacy of the participants in the study.

battered mailboxes atop the low rail fence, the large, old sign that read *Mobile Manor* in ornate lettering, and the bleak December sky. It was a cold afternoon and there is not much in flat, eastern Washington to block the wind that periodically nudged the car and seeped through the door, slowly turning my fingers white.

Finally, Elicia pulled past me on the driveway and fitted her car into the patch of concrete at the end of her trailer. I helped her carry a box of food, a huge package of diapers, a plastic laundry basket of clothes, and a grocery bag into her trailer while she collected Peter from his car seat. Elicia struggled to unbuckle and lift the large, sleeping two-year-old. Peter looked even larger than usual in the arms of his small mother because he was wearing a full snowsuit and wrapped in a heavy blanket. "Heater in the car went out," she said by way of explanation for the child's wrappings as she removed her own coat, hat, and gloves.

The single-wide trailer was furnished sparely. The table on which I had placed the groceries was dotted with crumbs and sticky patches of old juice. Elicia talked as she put things away. Last night had been a bad night for sleep, and this had been a more complicated day than usual because Peter had an ear infection. She had had to get him to the clinic between jobs—leaving one early and getting to the next late. Everyone had been irritated with her.

Elicia slipped the bundle of diapers under the sink. The box I brought in contained nonsaleable items and leftovers from her first job of the day at a local bakery. These items, in a combination of white bags, plastic, and foil, were left in the box on the table. The groceries in the bag were from a chain discount store that sells factory seconds and nearly-out-of-date items from retail stores. The dented box of cereal, canned soup, frozen pizza, and cheese sticks went into the cupboard and refrigerator. Finally she tipped the laundry basket out onto her bed and pushed the basket into a corner. She had done the laundry at her second job—chambermaid for a small motel. Elicia hoped she would not get into trouble for using the washing machine at work. Her mother, who usually does her wash while taking care of Peter, did not get to it because Peter had been miserable with his earache. They really needed clean laundry.

Elicia opened one of the packages from the box—slices of coffeecake with cream cheese filling already on a paper plate. She set it beside the box for us and put a kettle on the stove. I sat at the table while Elicia moved around the trailer getting nightclothes out for Peter, using the bathroom, changing into her uniform. There is not much privacy in older trailers; what you cannot see, you can hear. We chatted about Peter, Elicia's mother, my children, and the weather. The water boiled but Elicia had no time left for a cup of tea so I made only one. She pointed out the emergency numbers on the refrigerator and handed me a ripped pharmacy bag containing Peter's antibiotics and a plastic measuring spoon. "He gets another dose around nine," she told me. Then she thanked me and headed out for her third job of the day, helping to cook, serve, and clean up after the evening meal at a nursing home. It was after four and she was in danger of being late for this job too. She had left the trailer to drop Peter off and get to her first job at 5:30 this morning and she would not be home again until after 9:00 tonight.

I am an anthropologist, not a professional childcare provider. Normally Peter spent the afternoons and evenings at a neighbor's when Elicia was working. This service cost Elicia $10 out of the $26 she made each shift at the nursing home. Elicia had told me that she regretted how little time Peter got to spend in his own home. I was babysitting Peter at home as a way to show my appreciation for Elicia's participation in my research.

I am interested in urbanization and the changing U.S. economy as they affect poor and, specifically, single mothers. After completing a survey on work, subsistence strategies, and family health in the trailer parks of cities in eastern Washington and Oregon, I embarked on a more intensive study of single parents and work. Elicia was one of the people I asked for further interviews. I asked her if I could shadow her for two nonconsecutive days to observe the way she planned and carried out her workdays. Elicia is very practical and, although she agreed, she made it clear that fitting an anthropologist into her schedule would be neither comfortable nor easy.

FLEXIBILITY FOR A WORKING MOM

Elicia was a single parent working multiple part-time jobs and relying on a perilously small network of family and friends for assistance and support. Like many single parents, she obtained health insurance for her child through a state program but had no health coverage herself because her employment was not full-time. Elicia was 23 and held a high school diploma. She had worked several jobs since high school including two years full-time at a local factory that canned the vegetables and fruits grown in this rich agricultural region of eastern Washington. That job had benefits and the opportunity for promotion. But Elicia's mother, who had worked at the canning factory for many years, had been denied retirement benefits on what Elicia saw as a contrived technicality. She quit and has remained wary of working for large organizations. Instead Elicia opted for a series of overlapping part-time jobs. She said that having several gave her flexibility. She could quit one job without losing all of her income. I asked her what circumstances might arise that would cause her to quit a job. She said that she left one part-time job because it was demeaning and she had been sexually harassed. She left another because she was pregnant and needed to spend fewer hours a day on her feet. And she left a third because "my mother heard about the opening [at the nursing home]. It pays much better, fits my hours and it's in the kitchen. Kitchen is good for me and I like that it's not the same everyday; it's good work."

Elicia's workday was tightly structured but flexible. On days when she worked all three locations—the bakery, motel, and nursing home—she and Peter left the house at 5:30 and drove to her mother's house. From there she drove to the bakery, arriving at or just before 6:00 A.M. when her shift started. She sliced and bagged bread and filled trays until 6:30 when the doors opened. From then until the 10:00 A.M. lull she worked the counter. She did not take a break available to her at 10:30 because she wanted to garner "credit" with her co-workers in case she needed to arrive late or leave early (like on the day I babysat when Peter had the ear infection). Normally, she would leave the bakery at 11:00, drop some baked goods off at her mother's, see Peter briefly, and hurry to the motel.

She changed there, cleaned rooms and bathrooms, and made beds until 3:30. There were days when she had few rooms and was done early, but there were others when she was not finished by 3:30. On days with time to spare, she would pick up Peter and they might go briefly to the park, get an afternoon snack, or run errands. Then they returned home. Elicia would change and then take Peter to the neighbor's before setting off for her last job. On long days at the motel, her mother, who needed to get to her own job as a waitress, took Peter to the neighbor and Elicia went straight to the nursing home.

Work there started at 4:30. She began by assisting with food preparation and setting up the dining area. She served the meal to residents and some of the staff, transported residents' meals along with other staff meals around the home, and then returned to quickly eat her own dinner before beginning the cleanup. The kitchen generally settled down by 7:30 or 8:00 in the evening and then she assisted the staff in helping residents to bed. Her shift ended at 9:00. Peter, who took long naps at his grandmother's in the morning and afternoon, was often awake when she retrieved him. Her favorite time was putting him to bed on nights when he had stayed awake for her. Elicia ended her day with household chores done in the company of the television.

Elicia admitted her schedule was tiring and that she was barely making ends meet even with three jobs. However, Peter was not with strangers and she could see him between jobs on most days. She also had time to explore other job possibilities or take care of personal business. Elicia valued her self-reliance and her relative independence. She was proud of the fact that with this schedule, she was, in effect, her own boss.

Elicia's preference for flexibility and a sense that she had some control over her work had its negative consequences. By choosing multiple part-time positions she carried the burden of a complicated daily schedule with potentially conflicting demands. She placed herself in the most "easily fired" category at each place of employment and denied herself access to the benefits that accompany the rigid structure of a full-time job.

WAGE WORK IN CONTEXT

What is the larger context within which Elicia was working? Unemployment in the area was relatively low, but underemployment was common. Many of the people surveyed had some work but not the number of hours they felt they really needed. The vast majority of jobs advertised that winter were for low-wage work totaling fewer than 35 hours per week. The canning factory where Elicia had worked was reorganizing shifts from eight- to six-hour blocks. The new 3:00 P.M. to 9:00 P.M. shift would be staffed largely by high school students and other young adults. This shift would be undesirable for workers with school-age children, particularly single parents. And working only the six-hour day shift would not constitute full-time employment. Workers would have to compete for one or two additional shifts each week to make a full 40 hours and qualify for benefits. Elicia saw advantage in her frantic but flexible schedule for personal reasons. Employers clearly also saw advantage in building in flexibility by offering shorter shifts for low-wage jobs to high-turnover employees like high school students and migrant workers in the winter.

Elicia's current employers also faced pressures and found ways to keep costs down by reorganizing work schedules and relying on part-time workers. Local bakeries were once staples in established communities. Economic pressure on a small bakery comes in part from ways that industrialization has changed the way we make and buy bread. With mass production of bread and other baked products containing preservatives, and "in-store" bakeries in large chain supermarkets, local bakeries have become specialty shops. The bakery where Elicia worked depended on a healthy national economy so shoppers would feel comfortable spending a little more for luxury items like freshly baked bread. It was not a particularly profitable small business. To remain open the bakery employed only two full-time people (the bakers) and approximately 18 other part-time workers who clocked in for half-day shifts with no real benefits beyond goods they could take home from the store. It was rare for anyone to work a full 40-hour week, and no one ever worked overtime.

Local conditions rather than national factors influenced work at the motel where Elicia was a chambermaid. The small city where she lived was not on a major interstate highway, and few tourists make their way to the southeastern corner of Washington. Motel guests tended to be in the city in connection with one of its major employers: the state penitentiary, the Veterans' Administration hospital, or one of three colleges. Because there were several chain motels in town, the independently owned motel where Elicia worked was seldom full. Elicia received an hourly wage, and her hours varied depending on the number of rooms to be cleaned. Few rooms meant she could either leave early and take the lower pay or fill out her hours doing odd jobs for the motel owner. Unlike at the bakery, Elicia had no contract at the motel. Her continued employment depended on her good relationship with the owner-manager, and she knew that she might be replaced without notice. Because of the large number of students and low-income wage workers in the city, there was a shortage of affordable housing. Elicia worried that in response to this need for more low-income housing, the motel owner might transform the motel into a rental property, letting rooms out on leases and eliminating the need for a chambermaid altogether.

The nursing home industry in Washington State as elsewhere has been under a great deal of financial pressure. A Seattle newspaper reported recently that nearly one out of every five nursing homes in the state was likely to file for bankruptcy or close in any given year. Insurance providers pressure nursing homes to reduce costs, and everyone from clients, to state inspectors, to health-care workers pressures them to maintain or improve their standards of care. It is an industry that must respond to regulation and pressure from many sides, and it must use trained, licensed workers for much of its staff. Nursing homes like Elicia's spent as little as possible and demanded as much as possible (in terms of work hours and activities) from unskilled workers. Hiring part-time workers for all unskilled positions and using those workers to fill in gaps as needed kept costs down overall.

Although Elicia preferred the flexibility of self-scheduling, it is important to recognize the other force at work here. Employers build flexibility into the workplace to improve the efficiency or success of the business, not to accommodate workers' needs.

MOTHERHOOD IN A TRAILER PARK

Earning a wage was only a part of Elicia's work life. She took her responsibilities as a parent very seriously. Being the mother, the one who is depended upon, is "my happiness and my hardship," she told me. In arranging for Peter's care, she relied chiefly on her own mother but also on friends and the neighbor whom she paid. Elicia saw her choice of the trailer park as a temporary one based largely on her role as a mother. For the most part, she was happy that she had purchased the trailer, but she hoped to be out of it before Peter was too far along in school.

Elicia had never lived in a trailer before moving to Mobile Manor shortly after Peter's birth. She had been surprised by the sense of community in the trailer park. It was "more like a neighborhood" than she expected. People greeted each other, lent each other a hand, and had the mutual dislike of the park manager to unite them. But it was not a setting oriented toward children. Although some urban trailer parks have small play areas, Mobile Manor did not. Most urban trailer parks that are not restricted to retirees have

FIGURE 3 A yard with children's toys in an urban trailer park. *Photo by Carolyn Behrman.*

diverse household configurations, and Elicia's was no exception. In a single row in Mobile Manor there were two single-parent families; two families with two parents; a single older man; a single middle-aged woman; an elderly couple; a household of two adult brothers; a household of two college students; and a mother and adult daughter. Despite her assertion that the trailer park felt like a neighborhood, Elicia observed that there were "generally no people out and about to speak of. There's no place for the children to play because, like, I've got the biggest yard here and there's no grass. Sometimes you go outside and see all those dark trailers and pulled blinds, no sound of people you just know are there and it feels sort of spooky, lonely out there."

Elicia also was concerned about the significance of coming from a trailer park for a child going to school. The stereotyped image of trailer park kids as "white trash" worried her; she did not want that stigma to hurt Peter. Moreover, she had observed family life in the park and noted many unsupervised kids. There were rumors that a local gang was based there. "I guess trailers can get a bit small for growing kids and there just seem to be fewer grown-ups around than in regular neighborhoods—you know, working on their yards and stuff. I need to be sure that someone would notice and tell me if I was at work and Peter skipped school or something."

Formal schooling for Peter was something that Elicia saw as a pivotal point in their future because she then could commit to a more rigid work schedule. The guilt connected with relying on her mother and the financial drain of child care would be lifted. Peter would become more self-reliant as well. But all this reinforced her conviction that their trailer park residence needed to be temporary. The survey showed that, other than retirees, most trailer park residents assumed that their stays would be short-term. Elicia may not follow the trend, but the majority stayed significantly longer than they had hoped.

SELF-RELIANCE

Elicia bought the trailer with money she saved while working at the canning factory when living at home with her mother, a $2,000 "gift" from Peter's father who had been uninvolved in their lives since then, and a loan from her mother. With this money down, Elicia entered into a rent-to-own arrangement with the real estate company that owned the trailer and managed the park. Although her monthly payments were relatively low, she was responsible for maintenance, and she believed she would lose her entire investment if she failed to pay off the debt before she moved next.

She did not think she could sublet or sell her debt to a third party. This meant that she had placed her savings in a property that could only depreciate. Because she did not yet own the trailer, she couldn't use it to secure any sort of loan, and her income barely covered her monthly expenses. Consequently, Elicia's free time was dedicated to what, as an anthropologist, I would call "urban food foraging." Her wages produced no significant surplus, so she relied on leftover resources from jobs (like the baked goods) and offerings at the discount food store, church give-aways, Goodwill, and yard sales to feed and clothe herself and Peter. She chose not to apply for public assistance, and she was uncomfortable using the soup kitchen and food pantry that gave food to the needy. She felt those resources were for people who were truly destitute.

ISOLATION

The night I babysat, Elicia came home after 9:30. Peter had been a little fussy, but ibuprofen helped him go to sleep again after dinner. I called my own children at home with my husband to say "Good night." I had cleaned up a little and folded the laundry, which I hoped would not embarrass Elicia. When she came in, I had expected her to want me to leave right away, since she would have to be up and on the go again early the next morning. But she asked me to stay for another cup of tea. She told me some funny stories about the other workers and the nursing home residents. There were a lot of Hispanic workers. (Some were from Mexican migrant labor families who chose to settle or winter-over in the area before the next agricultural season's work began.) Elicia said an elderly woman had become greatly upset because she thought that an attendant had called her a "bitch." It turned out that the attendant had been commenting on a photograph by her bed of her grandchild at the "beach."

I mused that it must be nice to finish the day with a group of fellow workers. But Elicia said she was not close to the others. She had the most in common with the Hispanic women, many of whom also cobbled together part-time jobs and dealt with small children. But the culture barrier was difficult for her, and her unusual shift (from 4:30 to 9:00 first in the kitchen, then delivering dinners, and finally assisting with bedtime wherever she was needed) meant that she was not with any particular staff member for long. She felt a lack of connection to other adults in her life right now.

"I feel alone a lot. It is funny because it's only at the motel that I'm ever really alone. One of the hardest parts of this is that there is really no time for friends. Sometimes I think about how my mother used to take us to the park and talk with the other moms. She takes

Peter to the park and she sometimes finds those moms (but now they're grandmothers there with their grandkids). I don't know if that is a change for sure. I mean I don't know if there are more people like me who need their parents' help to make it. But this is hard on me, the working-too-much and the too-little-sleep and the not-getting-to-be-with-him [Peter]. But when you're barely making it to get by, it's just that I don't get to talk with the other moms either. You might be the closest thing I have to a friend right now since at least you keep coming around here to see what I'm up to and how I'm doing. I miss friends."

ELICIA IN THE BIG PICTURE

It is possible to critique Elicia for taking on too much responsibility and avoiding reliance on the system of full-time employment and its attendant benefits to support herself and her young son. But as Elicia pointed out through the example of her mother, an important impact of economic change in this country for some workers has been the development of a distrust of employers and the system of full-time employment. In some sectors of the economy, job stability and the reliability of long-term benefits have been undermined.

Economic and social systems are bound together in every culture. Changes in economic strategies will influence the ways that people think about and rely on social supports. At the societal level, we might respond to these changes in economic circumstances through efforts to promote workers' unions, fight for living-wage legislation, improve affordable day-care options, and/or broaden the reach of social services and charity. As an individual, Elicia chose not to make use of social service support beyond Peter's health care. Her strategy for survival in the market economy involved multiple part-time positions and a heavy reliance on her own flexibility, stamina, and organizational skills. She coupled this with the use of generalized and balanced reciprocity with family, friends, and neighbors, and honed her urban foraging skills by taking advantage of the discounted and cast-off products of our economy.

Elicia's organizational skills were impressive. She managed to schedule and perform a great deal of work as earner, parent, and head of a household on a daily basis. However, she herself acknowledged that this lifestyle was not desirable or sustainable over the long haul. Her efforts as a worker were not leading to the accumulation of assets she wanted to maintain herself and her family. In addition, she struggled with the working-mother dilemma: trying to provide for her small family required her to be apart from home and child much of the time.

SUGGESTED READINGS

Brodkin, Karen, ed. (1984). *My Troubles Are Going to Have Trouble With Me: Everyday Trials and Triumphs of Women Workers.* Piscataway, N.J.: Rutgers University Press.

Ehrenreich, Barbara. (2001). *Nickel and Dimed: On (Not) Getting By in America.* New York: Metropolitan Books.

6

Sunday Dinner at Hanka's

Julianna Acheson

Green Mountain College, Poultney, Vermont

Slovakia, a country in Eastern Europe, has for most of the twentieth century been under the control of various people: Hungarians, Czechs, Germans, and Russians. Since the end of World War I, Slovakia had been part of the communist nation of Czechoslovakia. A nonviolent revolution in 1989 that threw off the mantle of communism was followed in 1993 by the breakup of Czechoslovakia when the "Slovak Republic" emerged as one of the world's newest nations.

Socialism is the term used in Slovakia to describe the economy that prevailed under the Iron Curtain. In this economic system, the government plays a heavy role in extracting taxes from individuals and distributing social welfare programs, including the subsidization of government-sponsored enterprise. In the case of Czechoslovakia, the government played one of the most significant roles in shaping the economy of all the countries in the Eastern Bloc. The government organized, regulated, and dictated the vast majority of aspects in this command economy. Slovaks also use the term *totalitarianism* to refer to the period between 1945 and 1989.

As an economic anthropologist, Acheson wanted to understand what life was like in villages for people living in this new Slovak republic. After a year of fieldwork, she learned that for most villagers, life was filled with the challenge of coping with grave realities. There were drastic reductions in employment, maternity benefits, and cheap transportation. There was also a threat of ending the government-sponsored free universal medical care. Even with new political and religious freedoms, the vast majority of villagers wished for the return of the "old regime" and an end to "democracy" as they were witnessing it today. Living in a newly independent state was cause to fear what the future held for them. In the village where Acheson worked, *democracy* and *free-market capitalism* were not the symbols of free will and opportunity as the new Prime Minister Vaclav Havel had promised and the youth of cities were experiencing, but rather signs of tragedy, despair, and real economic hardship.

As you read, consider the following questions:

1. What are some of the advantages that the communist (socialist) government supplied for rural women in Slovakia?
2. Why were women such as Hanka worried about the end of communism?
3. How were women coping with inflation when Acheson arrived in the field in 1993?
4. In your opinion, what are some of the economic possibilities for women such as Hanka? What would you do if you were in her situation and needed to make ends meet?
5. What caused tensions among the family members at the dinner table and what do these signify in terms of cultural and economic change?
6. What might sauerkraut, vegetables, meat, hens, noodles, and soup symbolize to Slovaks?

Life has been much more difficult for us since the Revolution," Hanka said to me at the end of a long interview. "We cannot afford to buy all kinds of things that we used to enjoy when we lived under socialism. I don't think that capitalism is all it's cracked up to be. I used to think that everybody in the West had everything anyone could ever want or need. But now I am questioning that assumption. Now I am not so sure if life wasn't really better before the 1989 Revolution."

Hanka, who lives in Laska (not the actual name), a village in eastern Slovakia, is faced with higher inflation and greater economic instability than she has ever seen. Coping with these new burdens has significantly altered her already busy day: she is even thriftier and more self-sufficient than ever. She had been working full time as the head of the kindergarten and is in charge of the family's finances. Shopping, cooking, cleaning, and sewing are responsibilities she shares with no one. Higher inflation means less purchasing power for women like Hanka, but the family's appetite for her goods and services does not diminish. To make up for household losses she simply works harder—a lot harder.

She said, "I've canned more berries, fruits, and vegetables than ever." This year she preserved 468 jars of delicious berries, jelly, juice, pickles, wild mushrooms, and even her own homemade ketchup. A few years ago she canned hardly anything, but now she wants to be prepared. Prices in Slovakia, as in all of the postcommunist countries, have been rapidly rising. Hanka's new means of coping with higher expenses involves more canning, more berry gathering, more mushroom hunting in the forest, and more self-reliance. Marianka, her neighbor, has started to breed rabbits, and Slavka breeds hogs. Each woman has become more and more efficient at producing what they can, and more and more afraid of what the future might hold.

For 40 years under socialism, price inflation was so slow that net household revenue barely shifted from decade to decade. Until 1993 Slovakia had been part of Czechoslovakia, whose citizens had many social benefits: a guaranteed place to live, health insurance, education, old-age security, and day care. Best of all, everyone worked and could depend on a monthly salary. "The state took care of us from the day we were born until the day we died. And now, no one cares," said Hanka. Four years had passed since the Revolution when I arrived in Slovakia in February of 1993.

Before communism, women in rural Slovakia had worked with the men, farming small private holdings. Their life consisted of heavy labor associated with intensive agriculture and keeping domestic animals. They cared for and educated the children, gardened, milked cows, and fed pigs, rabbits, chickens, sheep, and goats. They did the washing, ironing, cooking, and household cleaning. In the evening women spun, wove, knitted, and sewed. Those work-filled days have returned since the demise of communism, which many women remember as fostering relative relaxation.

Communism brought the village women the right to work with secure wages. Women were potentially equal comrades in forming a new society—a postwar, postfascist, postempire, multiethnic, multinational Czechoslovakia that ideally knew no sexism, racism, classism, or any other social evil. While I think no social observer would claim that women had become equals with men in communist Slovak society, one cannot overlook the fact that women did have advantages, not only because they were women, but also because they were comrades.

Some programs enhanced the romantic myth of the "virtuous mother." Maternity leave was paid, and day-care centers were built in every village. Mothers received stipends to support themselves and their children. At the birth of a child, a woman received a bonus from the government for special needs: to buy a crib, diapers, or bottles. Best of all, the burden of shopping and cooking was reduced through a program of national dinners held at the workplace. These work and school cafeterias saved thousands of hours for women each year. Their need to shop and stand in lines was reduced to buying food for the weekend meals and evening lunches. Moreover, the town bakers baked bread and delivered it every other day to even the tiniest villages.

The Revolution in 1989 threatened to end the welfare system and impoverish women and families. It resulted in massive unemployment for many, more in Slovakia than in the Czech lands, more in rural areas than in urban areas, and more for women than for men.

In the region of Slovakia where I studied, one-third of the people who had been working under the socialist regime were laid off. One day Hanka came home from work in shock. She had been told that she would be retiring early, next month, with no warning or discussion. That would be the end of her career as the principal of the local preschool.

Nowhere are the changes, hardships, uncertainties, and hard work more visible than at Sunday dinner, when Hanka's canned goods are brought to the table and shared with her family members, each of whom has his or her own problems, concerns, and ways to cope. A common practice throughout Slovakia, each week Hanka's children come home to spend Sunday, if not the entire weekend, with their parents. Sunday dinner at Hanka's house is a microcosm of contemporary life in Slovakia, highlighting pressing issues for families and emphasizing the differences between young and old, rural and urban.

In Slovakia, the profits of work are copiously displayed at mealtime. Dinner is a pageant where the produce from the garden and the proceeds from formal labor blend into a creation entirely cultural, and intrinsically historical. It was at mealtimes that I experienced some of the most rewarding and fruitful encounters with rural women and their families.

Hanka always leaves church in a hurry. Along with most of the other Laska women, she needs to rush home to continue preparing Sunday dinner and have it ready promptly at 1:00. My husband John and I relished dinner with Hanka and her family. It was not only delicious, but Hanka and her husband Vlado are my relatives. Vlado is my paternal grandmother's first cousin.

When we arrived, the dining room was ready to receive Hanka and Vlado's customary Sunday gathering. Two large beer bottles stood at one end of the table, like conductors to an orchestra of food. Vodka sparkled in tiny crystal liqueur glasses at each adult's place. A white tablecloth added a sense of formality to the otherwise simple room. A pitcher of raspberry syrup mixed with tap water waited at the opposite end of the table.

In the kitchen Hanka worked fervently. Every burner simmered with one if not two layers of pots, and lids were scattered everywhere. Two daughters-in-law, Petra and a younger Hanka, stood nearby ready to be put to work in an instant. Grandchildren squirreled underfoot. Zuzka, Hanka's daughter, ran here and there. The men had kept themselves well occupied elsewhere, but as mealtime got nearer, they started to hover around the kitchen door to smell the intoxicating aroma of good food. Traditionally, men do not cook in Slovakia, but they do love to eat.

Hanka called out, "Someone fetch some compote from downstairs."

My husband and I volunteered. The passage leading downstairs from the dining room was as cold as the mountain air outside. We carefully crept down the hand-woven woolen rugs that lay across the stairs, dangerously loose and covering the bare concrete. At the foot of the stairs and to the left was a dark room where some 700 jars of canned goods and syrups sat waiting to be chosen for a day in the dining room. Jars of fruit and pickles sat beside jars of meat that were hidden away for a day when the family could no longer buy meat at the marketplace. Jars of red and black currant jelly and syrup indicated that Hanka had devoted a lifetime to cultivating the currant bushes lining her front yard.

Each jar is precious, for it is impossible to buy jars in Slovakia. Canning jars are not produced in factories, despite the majority of women who use them this way. One must first buy a full jar (considered not only pricey, but mysterious and risky since one never knows what is inside) and reuse it for home canning. A good woman cans her own vegetables, fruits, and berries to ensure that the quality is fit for her family. The contents of these many jars reflect hours and hours of collecting berries, cultivating currant bushes, fertilizing fruit trees, hunting for wild mushrooms, or planting and harvesting vegetables. This past year Hanka and Vlado produced hundreds of pounds of vegetables. Slovak families have always grown gardens, but there is urgency in today's gardening. Homegrown carrots mean security.

Hanka's canning closet was particularly exciting for me since she had penciled in the numbers of jars she had canned in the previous years: 30 jars in 1988, 45 in 1989, and then huge amounts—300 in 1990 and up to 460 in 1993. Hanka used them very sparingly. Each jar was treasured as a small safety net in a risky world of unexpected politics and uncertain supply.

John and I selected cranberries from the closet and ascended back to the dining room, where the soup would soon be served. Soup, which must always be served exceedingly hot, is the first course at any noontime meal in Slovakia. This Sunday's soup, popular in most of Slovakia, was made from the finest ingredients from Hanka's kitchen garden.

This particular soup is not complete without a meat-based stock. Today it was cooked with a hen that Hanka bought frozen at the tiny privately owned butcher's shop in Laska. She was lucky to get it, even frozen, because many times there are no hens in stock at the butcher's. Although this particular bird had been bred and raised in the Laska agricultural collective, the chicken still had to be sent to a distribution center in Spisska Nova Ves, where it was slaughtered, dressed, and frozen. Then it came back to be sold in Laska. Hanka could not purchase anything directly from the collective farm in Laska or from any of the other neighboring villages in the collective unit because of an inefficient centralized transportation and marketing system left over from the socialist system.

This soup also requires noodles. Noodles, like most of the staples in Slovak village recipes, are made from scratch with ingredients that are almost always accessible in the village. Early Sunday morning, the noodles began as a tough mixture of flour and eggs. Hanka kneaded, rolled, and cut the dough. She then set aside the fresh-cut noodles, speckled with flour, for about two hours to become firm. During this interval, Hanka dressed and went to church. Later she would boil the noodles in a great pot and stack them high in a bowl until dinner. They would be served cold alongside the soup and added to each bowl by the diner.

Zuzka ladled out a bowl of soup for her sister-in-law on her left, Hanka-the-younger. (My husband and I designated her "Hanka-the-younger" to distinguish her from "Hanka-the-elder," her mother-in-law.) The younger Hanka was a meek woman who had arrived in her Sunday best, but changed into "house clothes" soon upon arrival to her in-law's house. She looked comfortable in a faded pair of stretch pants and an oversized sweatshirt. Nina, her 15-month-old daughter, bounced contentedly on her knee.

Jakub, Hanka and Vlado's second son, sat next to his wife, Hanka-the-younger. He too was young and clad in house clothes, having changed out of his gray dress pants and chic Italian shirt. He was unemployed at the time. He had worked at a factory in the town of Pokoj along with thousands of other men and women. He explained to me more than once,

When Havel came into power and promised to quit supplying the world with armaments, it meant that Slovaks would suffer. Czechs produced very few of those arms. But here in Slovakia we had tank and weapons factories that employed thousands of people. We made tanks where I worked but Havel closed down the whole factory. Of course, this was a moral act—I can understand that. But to simply close down factories, without having anything with which to substitute our production is ludicrous. The whole town of Pokoj is out of work now.

Petra, with dark hair and huge dark eyes, sat to the left of Jakub. Although she never wore makeup, she was an Avon lady in Košice, the largest city in eastern Slovakia, where she lived with her husband Milos, Hanka's oldest son. Petra had worked at the largest state-run department store before and after the Revolution. When Kmart bought the old department store and applied Western concepts of good business, employment was not guaranteed. When taking her year-long maternity leave, she lost her job. Although Avon products were extremely expensive by Slovak standards, the products were high quality. So Petra quietly made her way through a list of friends and neighbors and started a small Avon business. She claimed more than once to me, "I'm just not cut out for this." She felt odd and ridiculous asking people if they would like to buy makeup when she knew many of them hardly had enough money to keep their families well fed. She knew that many people still believed that working for a private company that made a profit off the common person was licentious. Petra apologetically sold Avon, reminding her potential clients that the products were overpriced and frivolous.

Petra's husband, Milos, was bold, brash, and happy to sell. He considered selling Avon to his neighbors a service—offering them something they had never before had the opportunity to buy. Milos was the only one in the younger generation sitting around the dinner table who was formally employed. He worked for a foreign-owned clothing company and made twice the average pay of workers in Slovakia. Milos also earned the right to gather imperfect goods for his own use, resale, or as gifts. He took advantage of capitalism every chance he could.

Vlado sat at the head of the table. He was Hanka's husband of 30 years and had been a fairly devout communist—that is, as devout as a villager and teacher could be in the face of a changing world. Vlado was still a communist as far as Milos was concerned. Vlado couldn't abide the new democracy in Slovakia. He hated to see all of the wealthy get richer and the poor get poorer. He subscribed to *Pravda*, the previously communist, and still leftist, newspaper. He simply could not embrace capitalism. He was the headmaster at a "nature" school, used under socialism to improve the quality of life for city children. The cost of running the school was rising and some of the costs were being

transferred to parents. Fewer and fewer parents were able to pay for the nature school, and Vlado feared he would lose his school and his job.

We soon finished our soup. Zuzka jumped up with Petra behind her. Hanka had already disappeared into the kitchen, and they were well on their way to filling the dinner plates before I could offer my services. Zuzka passed around the food, served on Hanka's finest china. Each plate had a carefully placed slice of roasted pork, three slices of homemade Czech yeast dumplings, and a large dab of homemade sauerkraut. The cranberries my husband and I had picked from downstairs in the fruit cellar were served in a pretty dish.

The meat represented an entire day's work—one hundred krowns—the equivalent of $82 for a middle-class family in America. The meat was tough and needed a great deal of pounding, marinating, and cooking before it was really delicious.

The dumplings nestled next to the pork present the Czech face of Slovak society. These raised yeast dumplings, *knedliky,* are inherently Czech. Sunday dinner with its Czech dumpling signifies the union of Czechs and Slovaks, two separate but very similar ethno-national groups. They formed one nation just after WWI and had been sharing many traditions, a common government, an army, a monetary system, and a cuisine for the last 90 years.

Hanka's sauerkraut (*kysla–kapusta*) was one of the most practical uses of cabbage in a land where fresh vegetables are hard to come by in winter. Cabbages are bought by the sackful (100 kg at a time) and transformed into sauerkraut in bathtubs all over Slovakia. In Hanka's case, this meant over 200 pounds of cabbage grated a head at a time, mound by mound, into the plastic-lined tub and if one is lucky and the cabbage is good, the proceeds for a year to come will be a blessing.

We ate our meal and talked. The only tension at the dinner table was between Vlado and his oldest son Milos. Petra always gave her husband a look of disapproval when Milos coerced his father into an argument. Milos has decided quite vehemently that the Revolution in 1989 was a great boon for himself, his family, and the nation:

> The Revolution was the best thing that ever happened to us. If you are smart and not lazy, you can do anything today. You have to be willing to work, though. Communism taught people to be lazy. That was one of its greatest faults. Communism also taught people how to cheat from their workplaces and bosses. It was terrible.

Vlado was not about to let his son's provocation pass—especially in front of John and me, two Americans who needed to understand the benefits of the "way it was before 1989."

"Totalitarianism," Vlado began, "had some unfortunate consequences. It's true that some people got lazy at work. But it had many more benefits than this horrifying system today. Everybody was equal, we could all eat, go to school, our children could all go to the university if they studied hard."

Milos interjected, "Okay, Dad, you know that everyone did not have equal access to the university. You know that having parents in the communist party gave some people an unfair advantage over others. If it was so great [for everyone], then why did you join the communist party?"

"I joined it because I liked it. And to this day I like it. Of course, it did have some problems, but that just doesn't make up for the advantages it gave everyone. Not like those stupid idiots who only think about themselves and who just want to get rich fast!"

Hanka jumped in, "Yes, those people who just want to make a profit on everything are disgusting. They are disgusting people; they buy something for one cheap decent price and then they sell it here to the people for a much higher price. They make a profit on everything they sell. It is immoral."

"Immoral was the past!" Milos retorted. "Immoral was when you joined the communist party just so you could keep your job and be teachers. Immoral was when you didn't go to church, the thing you love the most, Mother, because you would have lost your job if you had gone, even once! That is immorality."

Hanka explained to me, "I couldn't go to the church or I would have lost my job. You don't understand this, I'm sure, because in America this would not happen. But I could not have been a teacher and been religious. Teachers were the ultimate servants of the state. I don't know why. But we couldn't go. All those old women who work in the forest or on the collective farm, they always went to church. They always were religious and didn't stop for anything. But I was young and if I wanted to keep my job as a teacher, I had to abide by the socialistic doctrine. That is just the way it was."

Milos was not satisfied. "Yes, Mother, they forced you to abandon the most important thing in your whole life. And if you wanted to become the head of the kindergarten, you had to do everything they told you. Give up the thing the most dear to you. And the second there was a Revolution, you and Zuzka started running to church every chance you got. That's what capitalism has done for you. Do you really want it back the way it was?"

Hanka said this was a ridiculous question. "Julka (a nickname they called me), don't believe that it was as bad as you hear in the news. There was good too—before. We all had jobs. That was the most important thing. We could all eat and we all had a place to live. Now there are people who are homeless, and many people can't afford anything to eat. The prices are so high right now! Until now, we have been fortunate enough to still eat good meals and buy our dinners at the work cafeterias, but you know that a lot of people can't do that. The quality of the food that we can afford to feed the children at school is so much worse than it was." John and I knew this because we ate our main meal each day at a cafeteria, too: watery soups and white dumplings with butter and chocolate on top, no vegetables, no meat, no dairy products.

Unemployed Jakub retorted, "The entire town where we live was built around the factory where I used to work, and the town's very heart and soul was the factory. People had good jobs there. They weren't rich but they all worked and they had good schools there too. Now there is a great deal of frustration. The local businesses can't keep all of their employees because they don't get as much business. Everything is crumbling."

Hanka-the-younger agreed with Vlado and with her husband. It was families like her own that were suffering. Her husband had lost his job as a machine operator three months ago, and her job as a clerk had vanished. She and her husband both worked in the potato fields doing seasonal labor for two weeks during the fall. They made the equivalent of one month's salary (3,000 krowns) between the two of them and came home with ten 50-kg sacks of potatoes that they traded, gave out, and sold to family members and neighbors.

As I ate that meal, I knew that it was certainly a reflection of some hard times and a lot of hard work for this family. There was no question in my mind that living under the new capitalist economy would include even higher unemployment, rising prices, and more tension between family members. I also knew that this meal required an enormous amount of work at an enormous cost and I understood why Hanka served it with such pride.

SUGGESTED READINGS

Rkies, Nancy. (1997). *Russian Talk: Culture and Conversation during Perestroika.* Ithaca, N.Y.: Cornell University Press.

Verdery, Katherine. (1996). *What Was Socialism, and What Comes Next?* Princeton, N.J.: Princeton University Press.

PART III

Changing Political Realities

Photo by John Walbridge.

Political organization, according to anthropologists, refers to the means by which a society maintains order, manages its affairs, and deals with outsiders. Unlike political scientists, anthropologists studied societies in which the political system was not a separate institution but was embedded in other aspects of life. In such cases, "politics" was enmeshed with religion, economics, kinship, and so forth. Political anthropologists found, for example, that a hunting-and-gathering society such as the !Kung might not have a separate political structure, but people still needed to concern themselves with allocating water resources, organizing hunts, and determining where groups could forage for food. All societies have strategies to defend themselves from outside attack or encroachment on their territory. For anthropologists, such activities and concerns fell under the rubric of political organization. Anthropologists studying political organization traditionally focused their attention on small-scale societies.

By studying small-scale societies in far-flung parts of the world, some anthropologists classified them into bands, tribes, and chiefdoms. **Bands** are groups of approximately 25–100 people who are grouped into nuclear families, are usually nomadic, and rely on wild foods. **Tribes** consist of a number of small units among which authority is distributed. These separate units are loosely unified through a web of individual and group relations. (In some cases tribal groups, because they have come into contact with each other, with settled peoples, and with central governments, have formed into larger confederacies, with a more hierarchical political structure, such as was the case with the Qashgai and Bakhtiari people of Iran.) **Chiefdoms** are found in areas where populations are denser and where there is growing specialization of labor, development of trade networks, surpluses of goods, and some degree of centralized authority with a chief as a leader.

But most of the world's peoples do not live in small-scale societies. Rather, they are integrated into large, highly complex political units called **states.** The state has a central government that exerts control over a particular territory. Thus, anthropologists have had to find ways to study these complex political units and the people who live in them. Anthropologists often distinguish between a "nation" and a "state." They use the term *state* to refer to centralized political organization and the term *nation* to refer to cultural identity. Considerable focus has been given to the study of the **nation-state,** which consists of a group of people who share the same culture and language and whose leadership is recruited from the same group. France, where the majority of people see themselves as sharing the same culture and language, is usually considered a nation-state, despite the fact that it is inhabited by many immigrants. Canada, on the other hand, is better described as a multicultural, multilinguistic state. Many of the world's conflicts today have to do with the idea that each nation should have its own state. For example, the Palestinians of the West Bank and Gaza and the Kurdish people of Iran, Iraq, Syria, and Turkey are fighting for the right to have a state of their own, a process referred to as **nationalism.** In the past 20 years, several multiethnic states have split into smaller nation-states, based on cultural identity, including Czechoslovakia, now the Czech Republic and Slovakia.

Some thinkers believed that in a postindustrial society, **ethnicity** would cease to be a major factor in a group's identity, that the world would become a more homogenous place. But anthropologists have found that **ethnic identity,** that is, identity based on a group's cultural characteristics, continues to be a strong force in the world and, in some places, appears to be growing even stronger. European **colonial powers** often tried to suppress ethnic identity. One means they used to achieve this goal was to force people to stop using their native language and to adopt the language of the colonial power. This suppression of language and other cultural markers sometimes leads to **revitalization movements,** movements that attempt to fight off the vestiges of colonialism and to construct cultural patterns that the group believes reflect their true cultural heritage.

Other sorts of struggles can be found throughout the world as well. While the peoples of the world might live in states, they do not necessarily experience full membership in the system. More often than not the indigenous peoples of any given state—Native Americans, the Aboriginal peoples of Australia, the Indians of Mexico and Central America—constitute minorities who lack political and economic power. They are less integrated into the larger society in which they live and often experience extreme forms of discrimination, either officially or unofficially. Under certain circumstances these people might be in a position to actively oppose their government—sometimes through warfare—in order to gain either autonomy or new economic and political rights.

Occasionally, large portions of a population rise up to overthrow their entire system of government. The Soviet Union was formed out of a **revolution** against the Russian czarist regime. The peoples of Iran during their revolution overthrew the United States–backed Shah of Iran. He was replaced by a government run by religious clerics. Revolutions are marked by times of extreme upheaval in society. They bring about not only changes in government but also dramatic changes in the way people live.

As the following articles show, the world has gone through and continues to undergo dramatic political changes. In some cases, life improves through change; in others, life can become very precarious indeed. E. Moore Quinn shows us how important native languages are to issues of political identity, sovereignty, and resistance in Ireland. The fluctuating political climate in Mexico, and the Zapatista movement, has a profound effect on a family in Chiapas in Jeanne Simonelli's story. And Mary Hegland shows that in Iran, religious and political revolution received impetus from women, who used their own networks of communication.

Other articles that touch on the topic of changing political realities:

Sunday Dinner at Hanka's by Julianna Acheson

Tears for the Saint, Tears for Ourselves by Linda S. Walbridge

The Death of Omar by Frances Trix

Aurelio's Song by Barry Lyons

7

The Irish Rally for Irish

E. Moore Quinn

College of Charleston

Ireland, lying off the northwest coast of Europe, is divided into two sections: the Republic, an independent nation comprising approximately 27,000 square miles, and Northern Ireland, a British colony roughly one-fifth that size. Of late, the Republic has emerged from "beggar of Europe" to "Celtic tiger." As a result, people who left Ireland in decades past to go to America, Australia, and England are returning to take their place within a thriving economy, and to reclaim an understanding of what it means to be Irish.

Two "official" languages are spoken in Ireland: Irish, a Celtic language, spoken in Ireland for over 2,000 years, and English, introduced in the twelfth century by Anglo-Norman invaders. Despite British attempts to "Anglicize," the vast majority of people spoke Irish until the early nineteenth century. But from 1845–1850, when the Great Famine reduced Ireland's population drastically, a rapid shift to English occurred. Children were taught that English was the language of prestige and culture; Irish, of backwardness and indolence. "Ethnic pride" was at an all-time low. During the first few decades of the 1900s, the situation improved when national cultural revival got underway.

Elsewhere around the globe, other groups struggling for autonomy or nation-state status insist that their own mother tongue provides a charter for distinction and rights. They struggle against colonialist dictates, globalization, and related forces that threaten linguistic diversity. Of the world's 6,000+ languages, 20–30 percent of them are no longer spoken by children. Approximately 300–400 languages were lost in the twentieth century and it may not be long before that same number are lost every 10 years!

Many applied (or activist) anthropologists have joined ranks to call attention to these figures and to suggest governmental policy changes. The majority of the world's people speak, along with their mother tongue, at least one additional language. On a global sphere, the monoglot is the oddball. English, however, is the single largest linguistic market in the world, and its ideological forces (i.e., television, radio, the Internet) represent formidable challenges to those attempting to preserve their linguistic birthrights.

In this article, linguistic anthropologist E. Moore Quinn reveals her personal involvement with language revitalization in Ireland. She takes us to the valley of Gleann Cholmcille in northwest Donegal in the divided province of Ulster, where she introduces several individuals who have been instrumental in keeping Irish alive.

As you read, consider the following questions:

1. How does the article illustrate "culture in the making," or the processual, or dynamic, nature of culture? Why is language important to any understanding of a culture?
2. What features of linguistic revitalization can you distinguish from this account? What factors would you deem essential in terms of preserving a linguistic and/or a cultural heritage?
3. What were the power dynamics that influenced the decline of the Irish language? What aspects of language make it fearful to those in positions of authority?
4. What actions of a priest (Father McDyer) and a prisoner (Bobby Sands) directly or indirectly affected the learning of Irish?
5. Many anthropologists who work in the applied areas or research often face a tough dilemma. As scientists, they are trained to be as "value free" as possible. Yet, as humanists, they are taught to be concerned with critical issues that affect their informants and their worlds. How do you think this dilemma can be resolved? What are the dangers of being too "value free"? What pitfalls await those who become too committed to a cause?
6. How does this article affect your own attitudes toward the preservation of your ethnic or linguistic heritage? Do you feel that an ability to speak one's language is crucial in terms of identity? Why or why not?

Liam leaped to the top of the desk, his arms flailing in wild gestures of enthusiasm. From our position on the floor, he seemed crazed, like a madman. "*Tír gan teanga, tír gan anam*," he bellowed in the most robust of voices, and we, trying to imitate his intonation and his passion, repeated in unison, "*Tír gan teanga, tír gan anam.*" A country without a language is a country without a soul. Yes, we believed him, and yes, we would follow.

The weather was heavy with water that summer of 1985, and it was cold, but we were having so much fun that few noticed. We bought extra sweaters from the local knitting factory, asked for another blanket from our *bean a tí* (woman of the house) at our bed and breakfast, and rushed back to our places in the dusty old classroom. A makeshift photocopying machine in the hall made a meager supply of handouts possible, but Liam was encouraging auditory, not literary, skills. "'*Eist*," he gestured with his hands cupped behind his ears, "'*Eist, agus labhair.*" Listen, and speak. Although most of our faces were hot with shame when we failed to produce the word or phrase he wanted, he smiled his toothy grin, patted our backs, and taught us another expression. "*Is fiú agus is féidir.*" It's worthwhile and it's possible.

What was worthwhile? What was possible? That we 20-odd souls from Belfast, Dublin, Boston, Sidney, Liverpool, and Paris could come to this poverty-stricken Donegal *Gaeltacht* (an Irish-speaking area) on the outskirts of the Republic of Ireland and become fluent in the Irish language? We all had far to go, but we received only encouragement from Liam. When we "*bhuail an mballa*" (hit the wall) and became unable to utter another word without going mad ourselves, he provided a night of dancing, a banquet with music, a night in the pub, even a chance to weave the tweed. We sang "*Níl 'n lá*" (It is not yet day), about the adventures of a man in a pub, and "*Trasna na dTonnta*" (Across the Waves), detailing an exile's dream of home. There were fiddle tunes of the famous harpist, Turlough O'Carolan, and those of us with instruments negotiated the notes as well as we could. For beginners, the age-old questions, "*An bhfuil tú go maith?*" (Are you well?), and answers, "*Tá mé go maith*" (Yes, I am), reinforced the basics. Those with more prowess learned the legends of Deirdre and Finn Mac Cumhail, or we debated whether the fairy faith still existed next to Christianity. Some came for two weeks, others, for four. The experience was exhilarating, frustrating, sobering, rewarding. Every new gain in freeing our tongues was met with Liam's praise. "*Maith thú*," we heard over and over again: "Good for you." It was exhilarating to be complimented so much in a learning situation—none of us had come prepared for that.

THE LEGACY OF REVIVAL

Liam wasn't the first to try to revitalize Irish. Rather, he followed a long line of language activists. One hundred years earlier, as thoughts of nationalism swept Europe, it was said that if people had their own language, they could exercise their right to become a nation. In Ireland, Douglas Hyde founded an organization known as the Gaelic League, and pioneered a movement. He and his contemporaries promoted the belief that Irish should be the language to sing in, play music in, fall in love in. Most of all, it should be the language that would help Ireland liberate itself from Great Britain. Many nooks and crannies of the countryside held singing contests, rhyming games, ballroom dances, and football matches. Soon, as women and men met at various events, they did indeed dance, sing, play ball, fall in love, and speak Irish. Some deliberately abetted Ireland's move toward freedom; most did so unconsciously. The Gaelic League's vision took a number of twists and turns, but a few decades later, when the Republic of Ireland issued a Proclamation of Independence, politicians expounded their hopes that generations of children would grow up speaking Irish. After a revolution, Ireland was divided North and South, and the constitution of the southern Republic declared Irish its "first language." A future Irish-speaking nation-state seemed secure.

However, "*Ba mhór an focal é*" (That was a lot of hot air), as we were soon to learn. Despite the national policy, Irish continued to decline. Most of the Irish-speaking areas, located on the far edges of the island, shrank in size, for despite the politicians' rhetoric, many urbanites ridiculed the "Culchie-Dans"—"hicks from the sticks"—who spoke nothing but Irish. Each generation produced fewer and fewer speakers who had learned Irish at mother's knee, heard it spoken in school, or communicated in it daily. Predictions were that it would go "the way of all flesh" and succumb to the pressure of English. The name-calling, the ridicule, and the lack of employment pushed young people away from home; death claimed elders who were fast becoming the last repositories of a once-rich culture. After a number of generations, there were no monoglots—people who spoke only Irish—to be found.

LIAM TAKES THE REINS

Angry and frustrated at what he was witnessing, Liam, with a bold spirit and flamboyant personality, attempted to turn the decline around, to do whatever he could to effect a revival. A native-speaker of the Ulster (Northern) dialect and a schoolteacher by profession, he was a bachelor, the only child of Irish-speaking parents. His father, a reporter for the *Donegal Democrat*, knew how to make and break news. His mother, a *bean uasal* (noble woman) who deserved honor, encouraged him to leave his post in Dublin to embark on the teaching of Irish in his hometown. It was she who reminded him that, as a member of the community, he knew personally every singer, every storyteller, every fiddler in the village. If he asked them to perform music or verbal art, they would not refuse. They would recognize his undertaking as one that would restore respect for their cultural forms and put money in their pockets. Moreover, they would do it for her. So, Liam mortgaged his home to launch the project. He began to work tirelessly, traveling to all parts of Ireland, America, Australia, New Zealand, and Canada, showcasing his method, accentuating his style.

His strategy was to teach Irish to adults and to introduce material that could be understood in the wider context of life. He made the language come alive through wordplay and antic. As course participants, we gesticulated our way through the village, fitting new phrases to new friendships. When we found someone on our own speech level, we spouted, "*Aithníonn ciaróg, ciaróg eile*" (It takes one to know one!). Funny expressions such as "*Is minic a bhris béal duine a shrón!*" (Many times a man's mouth broke his nose!) were incorporated into the warp and woof of our lives. As *sean nós* (old-style) singers entertained, we heard about shipwrecks, fairy mounds, changelings, and bride abductions. Soon we could tell the difference between a *piseóg* (superstition) and a *seanfhocal* (wise saying). Some of us preferred *dinnsheanchas*, the lore of the land, which could—and often did—preserve pre-Christian tales and legends. For example, tombs built 2,000 years ago were called "Diarmuid and Grainne's Bed" because folklore revealed that, as two hunted lovers ran the length and breadth of Ireland, those ancient megaliths provided refuge for them. Others of us favored political materials that helped us relive Ireland's history. We learned how the song "Johnson's Motorcar" was written, and where the story *An Gadaí Dubh* (The Black Thief) originated. As for myself, I liked the triads, the pithy riddles in triplicate that seemed to convey fundamental truths:

Trí galar gan náire:

Three troubles without shame:

Grá, tochas, agus tart.

A love, an itch, and a thirst.

As we returned year after year, season after season, and as thousands joined ranks, our mentor Liam rallied and motivated all the more. He told us how Irish had deteriorated into its present state. It wasn't lost willingly, he cautioned; rather, it had been taken away piece by piece, bit by bit. The Great Famine, which occurred between 1845 and 1850, accounted for a huge loss, because over three million people, mostly Irish-speaking, had died or been forced to emigrate when the one crop they lived on, the potato, failed. Liam argued that there was plenty of food around, but "the contempt factor," the constant devaluing of a people, meant that only certain members of the society were entitled to partake. He suggested that Irish forebears had been reluctant to admit that they spoke Irish for fear of political and religious reprisals. From an early age, Liam told us, many children were taught that they were English. He showed us a poem that had hung on classroom walls in the 1800s:

*I thank the goodness and the grace
That on my birth have smiled,
And made me in these Christian days
A happy English child.*

It wasn't long before a composite picture began to form, as Liam the motivator, with his *caint spreagtha* (enthusiastic talk), shaped our image of what those in Ireland, and especially those in the Irish-speaking regions, had endured. By means of mini pep rallies, he created images that came into clearer focus with each songfest, each debate, each interactive opportunity to speak. We not only wanted to learn about the language, we wanted to learn about him. Who motivated the motivator, we wondered? From whence came his inspiration?

By the early 1990s, displayed for all to see in a newly built cultural center, were a score of newspaper clippings chronicling Liam's success. Father McDyer, a priest in the village in earlier decades, had promoted self-reliance and the people's ability to shape their own destiny. Mastering the media with slogans like "Knock at the half door [of the poor] as often as you do at the brass knocker [of the rich]," McDyer battled for basics such as electricity, running water, and a chance to develop a trade. At that time in Ireland, a priest's word was gospel, and many throughout the country took up his hue and cry. For Liam, a young altar boy with a quick and eager imagination, clerical oratory made an indelible impression; he was imbued with the promise for a better future, not only for family and village, but for the Irish language.

ACTIVISM OF ANOTHER SORT

Even while McDyer advanced his schemes in the southern Republic, creative resistance was occurring on the other side of the border in the North. Civil rights marches, modeled on Martin Luther King, Jr.'s nonviolent demonstrations, stirred minorities to action. Most demonstrators were Catholics who for centuries had been relegated to second-class status. Like their brethren in the Irish-speaking areas, they had suffered economic hardships; like them, too, they had encountered rejection and discrimination. Efforts to resolve peacefully their demands for better housing and decent employment had not succeeded, and the situation deteriorated into violence. Northern Irish Catholics and Protestants defended "home turf" (neighborhoods and designated sectarian territories) with guns and bombs. At first, British soldiers who were introduced to restore order were welcomed, but British prejudice against the Irish soon came to the fore. The troops failed to distinguish warring factions; they either saw all parties as troublemaking Irishmen, or they singled out Catholics for abusive treatment. The period known as "The Troubles" ensued. It was street warfare of a most unrelenting, savage kind, and as the death toll climbed, hundreds, representing all sides of the conflict, died.

Catholic Republicans and those who favored a united Ireland were arrested for infractions against the State. Although the British government referred to these mostly young women and men as terrorists, in their own minds they were political prisoners struggling to maintain the unfinished business of revolution that had brought earlier independence to the south. For some time, those arrested and jailed enjoyed Special Category status, a designation that ensured that they could wear their own clothes and receive frequent visitors and parcels. Housed with their fellow comrades, they were exempt from work as well; in short, they were the equivalents of prisoners-of-war. However, in the early months of 1976, British officials revoked the Special Status category; Prime Minister Margaret Thatcher declared, "Crime is crime is crime." No longer would any distinction between common criminality and political activity be recognized. The results of this decision escalated tensions enormously. In defiance, Republican prisoners "went naked," refusing to wear anything but their blankets. To make matters worse, they chose to fast until death until their rights as political prisoners were restored. The hunger strike stretched from days to weeks to months; no side was willing to give in. By October of 1981, 10 prisoners lay dead from hunger. The first to die was Bobby Sands, a young Irish-language enthusiast who had been elected to Britain's Parliament while he was behind bars and starving to death.

Sands, a fluent Irish speaker, appealed to Liam's imagination, even as he captured headlines around the globe. Just as Liam would do in his makeshift classroom, Sands bolstered spirits through word and song. He said that the "mother tongue" for which he fought was not the language of *An tSasanach* (the Englishman). *"Tiocfaidh ar Lá!"* ("Our Day will Come!"), Sands shouted to his fellow inmates from the confines of his prison cell. On scraps of toilet paper that he hid in different parts of his body, Sands wrote secret notes, even a prison diary, in Irish. Other prisoners joined him, and day by day, expression by expression, they communicated back and forth in Irish. They would not be prevented from speaking the ancient tongue of the Gaels.

Few in Ireland, north or south, remained disconnected from what was happening. Word of Sands's practice spread beyond prison walls. "What, they're speaking Irish in the H Block? In the Maze of Long Kesh Prison? Why, that's absurd! Everyone knows that the language is forbidden, taboo, rejected, denied. How dare they? That's ridiculous. They'll only get in more trouble. Why can't they be model prisoners, so that their jail time will be reduced?" Remarks of naysayers, members of the press, and loyalist politicians had little effect; regardless of pressure to desist, Sands and other prisoners stayed "on the blanket," remained on their hunger strike, and continued to exchange verbal and written messages in the Irish tongue. As more and more of those behind bars joined the effort, Irish became a conduit, a symbol of solidarity, a movement spreading to the outside, into living rooms of family, friend, and sympathizer. Many thought, "They're in prison becoming fluent Irish speakers. Maybe I could show my support for their efforts by speaking it, too. *'Tiocfaidh ar Lá!'* Our Day will Come!"

Thus it was that Liam became inspired, as did so many others in Ireland, with the verve of a priest and a prisoner. Thus it was, too, that once he put the wheels in motion and attempted to establish a language school for adults in his home town, those from parts north, from Belfast, Derry and Portadown, joined with those from parts south, east, and west. Dubliners poured in, as did Australians, Americans, Germans, and Canadians. They came *"feabhas a chur ar a gcuid Gaeilge"* (to improve their Irish). To expressions like *"Tír gan teanga, tír gan anam"* (A country without a language is a country without a soul), they added *"Tiocfaidh ar Lá!"* (Our Day will Come!).

THE GLOBAL STRUGGLE FOR LANGUAGE RIGHTS

As I reflect on the changes that have occurred in the little village in southwest Donegal where a handful of hopefuls launched a language movement 15 years ago, it strikes me that we were a rather tame bunch compared to the thousands who come from all over the world today. While some are still being spoon-fed, many more are conversing at advanced levels, using new words like *acid rain* and *nuclear disarmament* that pour from their lips with confidence. The school where we sat so long ago is still standing, although sessions are no longer held there. The pubs and the dance hall have undergone major renovations, and the tea shop now abuts a museum built in honor of Father McDyer. The legacy of Bobby Sands continues to unfold throughout the island.

More to the point, however, I became aware of how Ireland's struggle to maintain its linguistic heritage dovetailed with similar movements around the globe. There are historical revivals, epitomized by the efforts of Ben Yehuda, who inspired families to speak only Hebrew. As a result of his activism, Hebrew began to be heard on the streets as well as in the classrooms. In addition, there are current movements, exemplified by the work of Jessie Little Doe Fermino, who teaches her native tongue, Wampanoag, to tribal members in Mashpee, Massachusetts. Scholars and researchers Ole Henrik Magga and Tove Skutnabb Kangas devote untold hours to the preservation of Saami, a member of the Fenno-Ugrian family of languages. Legally enforced assimilation to English is fiercely resisted by those who work among the Navajo in Arizona, where a recently passed proposition sounds the death knell for the bilingual education of Navajo children and substitutes English immersion in its place.

Each of these situations is complex, unique. For some, the narratives of revitalization are as dissimilar from the Irish case as A is from Z. In others, however, a study of historical particulars reveals remarkable similarities, demonstrating familiar patterns well-attested in the Irish example. These include

- A force for change, an individual or individuals with charismatic leadership who believe in the cause espoused.

- A rejection of colonial representations and a disavowal of the dictates that the language of imperialism should be used as common parlance.

- An attempt to assert, via ancient words and traditional texts, a people's sense of autonomy and sovereignty.

These comparative aspects, striking and analytically rich, are coupled with the salient fact that, regardless of from whence the linguistic data emerge, each has, at its core, the names, and in many instances the faces, of people engaged in struggle. They share a common belief that what they have linguistically is worth preserving and defending. For the Irish, Douglas Hyde and Bobby Sands boiled the linguistic sap so that it flowed long enough to be imbibed by others. In the present day, Liam's adage, *"Is fiú agus is féidir"*—it's worthwhile and it's possible—provides the lens of analysis by which to observe how the motivational process for Irish linguistic revitalization is nourished and sustained. In addition, it renders a glimpse into the type of rhetorical strategies employed for these purposes.

To date, no fully developed theory of language maintenance and shift exists, albeit there is consensus among linguists that no successful language revitalization movement has been capable of accomplishing its goals without activism (be it via idealism or protest). Considering the imminent projections facing minority languages, and in order to curb what could be the very-near approach of significant language death, it behooves the student of linguistic revitalization to study and observe these motivational processes and negotiations cross-culturally, and to think radically, if not drastically, about what they mean.

SUGGESTED READINGS

O'Hualláchain, Colman, O.F.M. (1994). *The Irish and Irish: A Sociolinguistic Analysis of the Relationship between a People and Their Language.* Dublin: Irish Franciscan Provincial Office.

Quinn, Eileen Moore, ed. (2001). "Endangered Languages, Endangered Lives: The Struggle to Save Indigenous Languages." *Cultural Survival Quarterly* 25:2 (Summer), pp. 4–58.

8

The Scent of Change in Chiapas

Jeanne Simonelli
Wake Forest University

Chiapas, an agrarian state in southern Mexico, has experienced escalating political tension and violent strife for decades, culminating in the Zapatista uprising on January 1, 1994. Coinciding with the signing of the North American Free Trade Agreement (NAFTA), the rebellion responded to long-standing patterns of exploitation and discrimination in this region of rich land and poor people.

The fall in the price of oil in 1982, the subsequent collapse of the peso, and the international financial bailout that followed laid the groundwork for a decline in living standards for the indigenous and *campesino* (rural) peoples of Chiapas. As the Mexican government sought more foreign loans in the beginning of 1986, they agreed to remove food subsidies and to retreat from social programs in order to comply with economic reforms mandated for continued international funding. Declines in social programs parallel the escalation and expression of guerilla activity in the most marginal areas of the state, eventually coalescing at the moment of the signing of NAFTA.

The purpose of NAFTA was to open economic borders between the United States, Mexico, and Canada through "free trade." Though free trade should benefit all producers in Chiapas, it has allowed business interests to bypass local governments in decisions concerning use or sale of resources. A precursor to NAFTA was the reform of Article 27 of the Mexican Constitution, which allowed for the private sale of communally held *ejido* land.

The Zapatista uprising began with 10 days of fighting in 1994, followed by a cease-fire that led to stillborn peace accords in 1996. Since that time, low-intensity warfare has continued, peaking with the massacre of 47 women, children, and men in the village of Acteal in December 1997. A massive military presence and a harassment policy against foreign scholars and activists have characterized the war.

In July 2000, Vicente Fox defeated the candidate of the *Partido Revolucionario Institucional* (PRI), becoming the first opposition president of Mexico in 71 years. One month later, the PRI also was defeated in Chiapas as a coalition candidate was elected governor. Though Fox vowed to end the war in Chiapas "in 15 minutes" and the Zapatistas traveled to Mexico City in March 2001 to address the Mexican Congress, little has been accomplished. A new Indigenous Law was approved by a majority of Mexican states in July 2001, but Chiapas and other states with high indigenous populations refused to ratify the document. The full peace agreement has not been honored and the law does not recognize indigenous autonomy. In spite of the continuing conflict, non-Zapatista and Zapatista communities-in-resistance try to live peacefully and autonomously in several areas of the state. Many, like those in Tecolotes (below), feel that they are in the eye of a storm, planting seeds of peace in the fields of war, as they struggle to develop their communities using their own models for change.

As you read, **consider the following questions:**

1. What are some of the forms that nonviolent resistance takes in Chiapas?
2. In areas of active political conflict like Chiapas, is it possible to carve out an existence in a political third space, one that is between conflict and capitulation?
3. Should anthropologists consider the impact of their studies on the communities in which they work? How does this consideration reflect the Code of Ethics of the American Anthropological Association?
4. Do governments have the right to restrict the activities of foreign researchers in their countries or is research a part of "free trade"?

"We are walking in the hangover of a seventy-one year long drunk."

—Unsolicited commentary by a *Partido Revolucionario Institucional* (PRI) bureaucrat

There are owls and there are owls, *pues*," said Don Antonio Sanchez,[1] leaning back on the short-legged wooden chair. He turned the brown-and-white-striped feather over and over in his wrinkled hand, murmuring quietly in Tojolobal. We were seated in front of the old man's two-room house, warm winter sun angling under the aluminum overhang.

"Yes?" said Duncan, my fieldwork partner, urging the aging Maya to keep talking. He shifted in his seat, trying to get comfortable.

"There are owls that are of this world, and owls that come from the other place," said Sanchez, handing the feather back to Duncan.

"And this one?" Duncan asked, rotating the feather slowly, massaging the silky shape of the round-tipped plume.

Antonio shrugged, reaching down to take a few ripe mandarin oranges out of a cardboard box. He handed one to each of us.

"I can't tell looking," he said. "You tell by the smell. Those underworld owls, they smell different."

Duncan moved to the edge of his chair. I began to peel my orange, trying not to seem unduly interested in a revelation that was not objective science.

"What do they smell like?" asked Duncan, adding a few words of Mayan to his perfect Spanish, encouraging the old man's reminiscence.

"Ah. You know," said Sanchez. "*Pedo de zorro.*" A little like fox farts.

We nodded knowingly. I searched my memory quickly, and tried to remember a moment when a wandering red fox might have passed gas in my presence. I caught Duncan's eye, and could see him retracing his own steps through rural forests, looking for a comparative scent. We hadn't noticed an odor when we encountered the owl lying face down and freshly killed on the road about five miles from a military checkpoint in southern Chiapas. Owls were thought to be messengers, so we were concerned with getting the big bird out of the road before the next line of Humvees and troop transports rumbled by the *mirador* (scenic viewpoint) overlooking the raging, azure river. Duncan laid

the bird to rest off the road and out of sight, while I created a diversion by shooting pictures of the view, an activity fully authorized by our Mexican tourist visas.

In truth, there were few tourists on this stretch of Chiapas highway. Neither highlands nor jungle, it looked immediately south to Guatemala, where the military from that country had streamed across the border 15 years previous, in murderous pursuit of their own Maya population. The Mexican army was less overtly aggressive, monitoring the flow of traffic along main arteries, maintaining an insidious war against its own people. They kept track of those like Antonio Sanchez, whose main offense was to remember the smell of fox farts and the colors of his Maya clothing, now replaced by polyester pants. It was these neglected, second generation Mexican-Mayas that I'd become interested in, working in the community of Tecolotes, in a section of Chiapas that many other anthropologists ignored.

My colleague, anthropologist Duncan Earle, knew the area well. He'd lived there two decades ago, willing to forgo fieldwork in the cool and colorful highlands in favor of the vacant hot country. He was a good research partner. He had instant rapport with the people and a great facility with languages and, when needed, could provide comic relief. On the other hand, I had good organizational skills, but tended to hit the ground running, driven by passion rather than common sense. Years ago I decided that I would never do fieldwork alone again, especially in a place like Chiapas. The usual problems of intellectual isolation and loneliness were complicated by the possibility of individual bad judgment in a dangerous situation.

It was summer now, and we were returning to Don Antonio's community for another short field stint, continuing our research concerning community-authored development in Chiapas. We'd left San Cristóbal de las Casas early that morning, driving south in a silver VW bug. These 10-day trips to the field were exhausting. I longed for the luxury of a graduate student's extended field period, but settled for several quick trips per year. It was a long time between sabbaticals. More important, since the 1994 Zapatista rebellion in Chiapas, getting visas for extended anthropological research had gotten really difficult. Perhaps all that would change soon. The ruling PRI party had just lost its first presidential election in 71 years, as well as the Chiapas governorship.

The tiny VW hit a mountainous *tope* (speed bump) and bounced me out of my seat and into the roof as we pulled up to a military checkpoint. Three green-clad men, very young and armed with automatics, leaned into the open driver's window, asking for our passports. Duncan reached into his pocket. As usual, I was

---

[1] The events depicted here are all true. With the exception of the names of the anthropologists, all people and place names have been changed. The author thanks the Archie Fund of Wake Forest University and the Carr Foundation for support of this work and the Tecolotes community. Special thanks to my *compañero de trabajo*, Duncan Earle, University of Texas–El Paso.

silent. Passing through military *retenes* and other official checkpoints, I kept my mouth shut, offered no papers or unsolicited information, and let Duncan do the talking. I learned early in our field travels that a conflict zone was no place for me to practice feminist assertion. We gave them the relationship they expected, the invisible woman, mute and innocuous. In part, this was because I had been expelled from Mexico the previous year with another colleague for "political activities" while on a tourist visa. We brought an immediate appeal and won in the courts less than nine months later. The victory was a minute indication that things might be changing. The Mexican constitution could be a powerful document when it was upheld.

"What's this about?" Duncan asked, his Spanish taking on heavy New York tourist overtones.

"About control," answered a dark-eyed soldier.

"Control? Are we out of control?"

"No. No. It's for the foreigners."

"Are the foreigners out of control?"

I handed my passport to the soldier and nudged Duncan.

The soldier shrugged and wrote down our information on a crumpled sheet of white loose-leaf paper.

"I just do what they tell me," he said, quickly handing back our passports. "Have a nice visit. Enjoy Chiapas."

The invitation was a first. He seemed truly disinterested and somewhat uncomfortable, as though thinking of a possible return to wherever it was he and the other 40,000 military stationed in the state came from. Another minuscule change.

Continuing, we climbed the last sharp incline before the road plunged down to the river and the pueblo of Tecolotes where Sanchez and his family lived. We were at the edge of the jungle, and yet the slopes were so devoid of vegetation that it might as well be Ireland. Farmed for almost 2,000 years, the last 20 had been an environmental nightmare. Beef cows grazed where there once had been trees; corn grew only in tiny *milpa* fields clinging to angular parcels of overworked land. I looked out across the hills, searching for signs of trouble. But the valley seemed peaceful, no sign of overt problems. No smell of fox farts.

We drove past the tiny *Escuela Autonoma,* an autonomous school established and staffed by the community in response to the deficiencies of the government facilities. Though the Tecolotes families with whom we worked were not flagrant, armed rebels or professed Zapatistas, they were openly in resistance. They were rebelling against inadequate or nonexistent services and blocked access to the markets and education that might make a difference in their lives.

We cut through the last hundred feet, through a thick grove of bananas and mandarins, with coffee growing in the deep shade, and parked the car. As we walked into the cluster of houses, a chorus of dogs began a haphazard warning call, a bark-over-bark announcement of our arrival.

"*Cáyate,* Cleenton!" a voice yelled out in response.

The dogs refused to shut up. The barking got louder as they broke through the brush. The first to emerge was Clinton, a gaunt long-hair with just the hint of golden retriever. I looked for his ragged son, Zedillo, named after the outgoing PRI president. He was nowhere to be found.

On arrival, the enclave seemed empty, but now family members began to emerge. I saw Sanchez's daughter Luz come across the cement patio where they dried their coffee, heading toward the kitchen. Luz had been my point of entry into this community, and we were working with her to help the women set up a cooperative bakery on a small plot of communally owned land. Her husband, Rodrigo, and the other men would supply the labor to build the bakery. Duncan also was talking with them about their plans to improve the quality of their organically grown coffee. During our winter visit they wrote a proposal that I took to a small U.S. foundation. My good news was that their dream had been funded. As anthropologists, we hoped to be able to document and analyze the entire process of community-determined development.

I patted Clinton as Luz joined us. We hugged each other.

"Where's Zedillo?" I asked her.

"*Se murió* Zedillo," she said. He died.

We all laughed. In the capital, the other Zedillo was politically dead, superseded by the new president, Vicente Fox.

We went into the cramped, smoky kitchen area and I sat at the rugged table. On the interior hearth, the ever-present pot of beans simmered. The *comal* was over the coals, heated and ready for new tortillas. Coffee boiled in an old bucket; water in a small pot.

"How are you?" I asked.

"Good. Things seem quiet," she said, an oblique response to the unspoken question lingering in the greeting. Then, more explicit. "The troop convoys come through with less regularity. There are *Guardia* in the village, the informal army; some we recognize and some we don't. These we fear more, since they don't know our faces." The rest of the sentence was understood. It is easier to harm those you don't know than those with whom you live side by side.

Luz took a cup of coffee. There was a blue plastic basin on the table filled with corn *masa*. She took a small ball and began to pat out a tortilla. It was automatic with her, the arrival of guests followed by the preparation of food. I could see her thinking about supper and a couple of extra *gringo* mouths to feed. I reached into my pack and took out a bag of shelled peanuts, some rice, and a kilo of white cheese.

I thought about the implications of our stay in their community. The paramilitary Guardia didn't know our faces either. All foreigners looked alike. All foreigners were a threat. We'd talked about this with Luz and Rodrigo.

My spring visit here had not been a happy one. Four months ago the leadership of the cooperative landholding *ejido* in Tecolotes changed hands. *Ejidos* are a product of post-revolution land reform dating back to the 1930s. Groups of campesinos came together and claimed large tracts of agricultural and forest land. They held title in common but worked individually designated parcels. An assembly governed the *ejido*, with periodic changes in official leadership. The new heads of the Tecolotes *ejido* were from the government side of the political conflict in Chiapas. They voted to expel the 15 families in resistance from their *ejido*-held lands and homes, in spite of the fact that Don Antonio helped found the land-holding body 40 years before. The PRI-affiliated ejido leaders said that refusal of community members to contribute labor to government-funded schools and health clinics meant that they were not fulfilling their obligations to the larger body. They were told that they must either participate in all projects or pay a yearly "tax" of 15,000 pesos ($1,600 U.S.). In essence, they must either give up autonomy and independence or get out. This type of intimidation and expulsion, based on political and religious animosities, creates a huge population of displaced persons in Chiapas. Often, political divisions replicate religious difference, including divisions between Catholics and Protestant evangelicals, or even between traditional Mayas and reform Catholics.

I'd found Luz alone in her kitchen, waiting for Rodrigo to return from San Cristóbal and a consultation with human rights lawyers. As we talked, her seven-year-old daughter Marta leaned into her lap, watching her mother's taut face. The child's hair was ragged and unkempt, her eyes ringed with raccoon-like circles.

"We can't talk in front of Marta," Luz said. "I can't have my children crying in fear, up all night, unable to rest, because of this conflict."

This was an uncharted effect of the quiet war in Chiapas.

"We have lived in peace in this divided pueblo since 1994," Luz continued. "We must come to some kind of accord." The fact that relative calm had prevailed in spite of the fact that part of the village of Tecolotes was PRI and the rest pro-Zapatista was a small miracle.

The group's 1994 declaration of resistance to government policy coincided with the Zapatista uprising, which brought into visibility the patterns of unre-solved exploitation and discrimination in Chiapas. The community gained inspiration from their relationship with catechist Catholics, whose liberation theology promoted nonviolent resistance. And though outside observers described the group as a Zapatista support base, the reality was that the Zapatista organization provided practical support for the community. In order to maintain autonomous schools and health services, Tecolotes sent young people to the Zapatista stronghold of La Realidad to be trained to educate. When they returned, they worked without salaries in substandard facilities. Yet the children of Tecolotes could read, while many of the government-schooled kids could not. This easily recognizable difference had been one of the unmentioned factors in the *ejido* dispute.

Now, Marta darted into the kitchen, her three-month-old cousin swaddled in a rebozo on her back. She looked bright-eyed and happy, her hair recently cut and falling neatly around her elfin face. I took the baby from her and marveled at the smiles all around me.

It was a Sunday morning, a lazy day of rest in the short dry spell at the heart of the rainy season. The crisis was over for now. A month before, with the assistance of human rights lawyers and adjudication by a PRI agricultural judge, the men of the community went before an *ejido* assembly to present their case. All over Chiapas, similar land-related disputes had ended in armed confrontation and expulsion, but Tecolotes had been determined to solve their problems peacefully.

Later that afternoon, there would be a community meeting, where we would announce the acceptance of the grant proposal and watch the community make the next step to realizing their dream. In preparation, Duncan and I asked to hear the Tecolotes story, an oral history that would help us begin to document the entire saga of this frontier region.

The men retired to a closed room to plan their presentation. Duncan was out under the ramada, whittling a piece of coffee wood, drinking sweet coffee with Don Antonio. The old man's reminiscences meandered through time, collapsing some events and keeping others current. The revolution that predated his birth moved close to the era of land distribution that triggered his own migration into the region from the other end of the jungle. It was a time when Tojolobal women still wore traditional *huipiles* (blouses), people were polite, and the kids had decent names like Caralampio.

Duncan elicited Tojolobal vocabulary from the depths of Antonio's memory, as I bounced the baby around the outskirts of the ramada. The women arrived to cook the feast that would accompany the afternoon meeting. In the distance, a grey rumbling

FIGURE 4   The author shares child care duties in Tecolotes.
Photo by Duncan Earle.

began in the sky, a mechanical sound that was not thunder. We all looked up beyond the rooftops, as a dark blue two-engined prop plane belonging to the State Security Forces began a low circle over the compound. *Seguridad Pública.* The blue meanies.

"Should I go put mud on the license plates?" Duncan asked. The plane pulled up and away, circling back a few minutes later.

The plane's visit was a way of letting us know that they knew we were here. We made no attempts to hide our presence and actively sought mechanisms by which the divided pueblo might work together with common goals. As anthropologists, we were trying to do community development within the existing power environment, rather than work against it. Though guarded, the community felt the same way. But the whole conflict was tricky, lying somewhere between war and not war. The overt conflict between the Zapatistas and the government forces made space for a covert war between communities like Tecolotes and the existing structure that marginalized and exploited them. The visible conflict diverted attention from quiet attempts to make changes on the level of immediate survival. This was the story we now waited to hear from the men.

Luz came out of the kitchen and tossed the inedible innards of two recently butchered chickens onto the dirt floor. Clinton darted into the ramada in a lightning raid, beating out the other dogs. With the soup simmering in big pots over the fire, the women sat easily around the little room. I still held the baby; Duncan cleaned up some of the debris from his whittling. I saw

Luz look quickly at the closed door where the men huddled in conference.

"What did you think of the whole experience with the *ejido* assembly?" Duncan asked, nonchalantly.

The women shifted in their seats.

"No one asked us. No one told us anything. We didn't know if they would come back from that last meeting. If it was a trap. What do they think, that this isn't about our lives, our children? These are family issues. We talk, the women. It's *our* cooperative."

She was referring to the corn-grinding mill, held jointly by the women, on the piece of land where the bakery was to be built. It was an interesting and unexpected commentary, especially in light of potential control issues once the money for the development project was turned over to the group.

Marta was popping marbles against the cement of the coffee-drying plaza, waiting in expectation for the closed door to open. When it did her favorite uncle, Diego, emerged first, patting her playfully on the head. He had been a political prisoner for 18 months. It was during this absence, unfathomable in the mind of a five-year-old, that Marta's agitation emerged. It was good to see her happy again.

Diego called to Duncan and me. I handed the baby back to Luz and followed the two men into the room. A circle of chairs was set in front of an old bureau holding an aged black-and-white TV. When there was electricity, its one channel kept the community appraised of the international news. They were better informed than most of the people I knew, and we had discussions concerning everything from floods and fires in the States to past massacres in Kosovo.

Diego began. "You know how it is here. The *Municipio* is in resistance, but half the *ejido* is PRI. We've lived together here for 30 years and we have one thing in common. We are all screwed. We are all poor. Look at us. Mayas who don't speak our language. Look at them, Mexicans who are really Mayas. Our children die of the same diseases. We are the true forgotten of Chiapas. In 1994, after much thought, we were looking for a path. Before then, the Catholic Church helped us, giving us some advice, but eventually we went to the Zapatistas seeking guidance. At first they wouldn't receive us. We were strangers, after all. Finally they met with us. We listened to what these brothers had to say, and we liked it. Because of our faith, we heard these words well. Finally, a year later, we made a declaration in the *ejido* council that we were in resistance."

It was Rodrigo's turn to tell the story.

"The *ejido* had said that they would expel Zapatistas, but we said that our resistance was nonviolent. We would do all the work of the *ejido* that related to agriculture and trails, but no other government projects. The *ejido* agreed to honor this arrangement, but here is where we probably made our mistake. We didn't document it. But it was respected by all, even through times when the area was invaded by the military, and some were arrested and put into jail."

I listened avidly to the narrative, while Duncan took notes. I would have loved to have taped, to capture the emotion, passion, and humor in the voices of the narrators, but it was not worth the risk to them. The story used verbs that described a level of life we seldom experienced:

to sell out, to hear well, to have faith, to get closure.

"It was February when we were summoned to a meeting," Rodrigo continued. "The new executive committee told us that we must contribute to cooperative labor on schools and clinics and roads. We said that the *ejido* was about agriculture and that was all that we were required to do. They presented us with a document signed by all the PRI *ejido* members. The leaders said participate or pay or go."

We knew the next part of the story. Not only did I read about it in the newspaper while in the States, but through friends Rodrigo kept me posted by e-mail. The quiet war was also a virtual war.

A second summons brought them to a meeting in which all evidence was presented before an ejidal judge.

"The judge listened to our story, and then to the charges of the commission," Rodrigo continued. "When he asked the Assembly if it was true that we didn't do our required work, no one agreed, even though they had signed a paper a month before. They had worked beside us for years. In the end, they couldn't lie.

"The judge, the PRI judge, ruled in our favor. But to save face he asked us to pay a 'reintegration' fee of 50 percent of the original amount. Seven thousand pesos. He gave us three weeks to decide."

to sell out, to hear well, to have faith, to get closure.

Rodrigo leaned back in his chair and sighed. "In the end, we decided to pay. To go right back and sign the agreement. To close it. Legally."

The men's faces grew somber.

"They didn't expect us to agree."

to hear well, to have faith, to get closure.

"How did you feel when you agreed to compromise?" I asked Rodrigo. I could see his attitude shift with his body, like a faint breeze ushering in four centuries of conditioned response. Yet the decision was not a sellout to past patterns of exploitation and interaction, but a tactical decision. The human species survived by picking its battles. Rodrigo knew it. Old Sanchez knew it. The women knew it. We

knew it. It was not capitulation. It was a step toward reconciliation.

The closed room was dark, the air was still. Suddenly, the door flew open. Marta came waddling in, weighted down by Diego's youngest baby. As she handed the infant to his father, the baby farted. As the sound and the smell wafted through the room, the air seemed to lighten. Marta giggled. Everybody smiled. This was what it was all about.

Dinner was almost ready. The women and men and children of Tecolotes gathered near the ramada waiting to hear the good news brought by the gringos. Towers of newly made corn tortillas and small bowls of salt and *chiles* waited on the long wooden tables. Yet I hung back for a few moments, marveling at their story. I wanted to cry, listening to them. I sucked hope from dreams like these. Their faith made my soul go limp and the air smell like owls.

What was I doing here? Was it research or advocacy or activism? Or was it a loosely disguised professional undertaking designed to revitalize my own life? It was time to examine my own values and agendas. Was I thinking through the implications of my presence in communities that would have to face the consequences long after I was gone? In the old days we anthropologists produced detailed community studies written as though we were sitting up in a tree somewhere, impartial observers. But it was clear now that the production of cultural knowledge was no longer an insulated undertaking. The work was open to multiple levels of public scrutiny, and the insights that made it valuable to some made it dangerous to others.

Chiapas was a political reality. My expulsion experience taught me a valuable lesson about intimidation, and tempered my undertakings with a healthy dose of fear. If I wanted to continue to be an anthropologist working in a conflict zone, I needed to be upfront with my own intentions, using good old-fashioned social scientific objectivity without positioning myself beyond the fray. It was important to separate out the fieldwork from the soulwork, but honesty in one realm led to honesty in all realms.

Outside the room, Duncan played with the baby while Don Antonio taught him new Tojolobal words. I walked over to the kitchen where Luz was still making tortillas.

"Luz, are you and Rodrigo comfortable with this project, with the bakery and the coffee cooperative? Suppose the Guardia comes after we're gone?"

It wouldn't be the first time. And it seldom took much of an excuse for the military to target and to destroy. The Sanchez family and the Tecolotes community did a delicate dance trying to navigate through a political third space, a space between conflict and capitulation.

to have faith, to get closure.

Luz stopped turning the tortillas for a moment and rubbed her fingertips together, working out the heat.

"*'Tabueno,* Juanita," she said, finally. "It's all right. The development people come and they go and they make promises and nothing happens and we feel burned and saddened and still we dream. With the elections, maybe this is the time for all sides to work together. We have nothing to lose."

It was true. With Fox, for better or for worse, the smell of change was in the air. *Pedo de zorro.*

I looked out at the patio and the hibiscus and red bougainvillea. One of Luz's sisters was sitting on the other side, nursing her baby. Marta was still outdoors playing with marbles, ignoring the television. Clinton was gnawing on an old chicken bone. The men were gathering their packs preparing to take Duncan to the edge of the jungle on a plant identification walk, as soon as the meeting was over.

I reached into the blue basin and took a handful of masa, rolling the ball around in my palm, feeling the sticky corn absorb into my skin. I thought about my daughters on the other side of the country, the insane pace of my life and my struggle to see my own dreams. It seemed like there was a lot to lose here, family and community and a way of life that fit within the landscape, but it wasn't my place to say. Even if we stayed a year, we'd still get to leave. For Luz, a risk seemed better than no dream at all.

to have faith.

"Trust," she said simply. "For all of us, there is nothing left but trust."

"Let's go plan a bakery," I said, taking the rest of the tortillas to the table.

SUGGESTED READINGS

Nash, June C. (2001). *Mayan Visions: The Quest for Autonomy in an Age of Globalization.* New York: Routledge.

Ross, John. (2000). *The War against Oblivion: The Zapatista Chronicles 1994–2000.* Monroe, Maine: Common Courage.

9

Talking Politics: A Village Widow in Iran

Mary Elaine Hegland
Santa Clara University

In 1978, Iran was wavering on the brink of change. An agricultural and trading nation, Iran was modernizing. Using oil revenues, the monarch, Mohammad Reza Shah Pahlavi, had built up the military, governmental bureaucracy, and educational and health systems. Although standards of living were rising, the regime failed to liberalize the political system. People who spoke out against the government faced severe punishment. In 1978, resentment was growing and Shi'a Muslim leaders and organizations began coordinating revolutionary activities. Under the umbrella of Shi'a Muslim symbolism, rituals, and institutions, diverse groups successfully cooperated to overthrow the Pahlavi government. Ayatollah Khomeini, the central resistance spokesman, returned from exile in France, and the Pahlavi regime fell on February 11, 1979. As revolutionary forces had operated under the aegis of Shi'a Muslim clerics, these religious figures enjoyed a superior position in the ensuing political climate. Although Iranians voted for an Islamic Republic form of government, many who had supported the revolution did not support clerics' monopolization of power and their imposition of their own values on the lives of all Iranians, including severe restrictions on clothing and spheres of action for women.

In retrospect, U.S. political support of dictator Reza Shah Pahlavi and the Shah's brutal repression of dissident political expression and organizing led to the emergence of a theocracy whose gender policy has harmed and restricted women. Further, Iran's religious revolution has stimulated Islamic fundamentalist movements and networks in other Middle Eastern nations where political dissent is likewise forbidden. Fundamentalist Islamic movements have become the favored political form of resistance to repressive Middle Eastern governments and to the Western political influence often backing these governments.

The 1979 Iranian Revolution was a major event of the last half of the twentieth century. Only now, more than 20 years later, are we beginning to grasp the ramifications of this Islamic-framed revolution. Since September 11, 2001, even the most insular Americans are aware of how effective and far-reaching can be political resistance couched in Islamic ideology—no matter how controversial the interpretation of Islam upon which it draws.

"Aliabad," home of the young widow in Mary Elaine Hegland's essay, lies not far from Shiraz, capital of the southwestern province of Fars. Aliabad men had been cultivators and traders, but by 1978 many men from this settlement had gone to work in Shiraz. There, they could interact with the religious revolutionary movement's supporters and join demonstrations. They passed on news and attitudes to their female relatives in Aliabad, who became active in verbal ways, informing and persuading others.

Women are usually excluded from influential formal political roles. Often they can be more politically active in the absence of a strong central government. Their informal verbal networking can have more impact when a political system is not highly formalized, as in a period of political flux or revolution. During the Iranian revolutionary period in 1978 and 1979, women participated in marches and behind-the-scene communication. Also, because leaders framed the revolution in religious imagery, devout Shi'a Muslim women, ordinarily careful to stay at home, felt encouraged to live up to their religious beliefs and participate in the revolution, covering themselves in black body veils that became a symbol of support for the revolutionary movement.

After the revolutionary turmoil, as the Islamic Republic consolidated its power and formalized its political system, women again became more excluded. The Muslim family and Muslim women's modesty became markers between Muslim Iranians and "corrupt, immoral, godless Westerners." Women's purity and separation from unrelated males became a matter of state concern, not just the concern of the family. Laws and social pressure dictated more careful veiling and sex segregation for women.

How might women like Esmat, the village widow, with strong religiosity but also a keen interest in public affairs, feel about policies pushing women further into the private sphere? Islamic Republic officials have insisted that Islam gives women equality, opportunities, and better treatment. Might resourceful women like Esmat or her educated urban sisters find ways to take advantage of such declarations to gain greater influence in the wider world?

As you read, consider the following questions:

1. Why are Aliabad women's communication activities and opportunities different from those of the men? In your society, are communication styles and activities of women different from those of males? Why?
2. Why are communication opportunities, access to public forms of discourse, and dissemination of perspectives and information important in politics?
3. Explain the character and the significance of Aliabad women's contributions in local-level political factionalism and in the Iranian Revolution.

4. How do gender constructions and characteristics of the political system in your society affect women's political communication opportunities, access to public forms of discourse, and dissemination of perspectives and information? In your society how does women's political participation differ from that of men's?
5. What influences do politics—local, national, and international—have on the lives of people in this story? In what ways do women try to use communication to influence political conditions and dynamics in Aliabad and in your own society? What do you think Esmat's life will be like in the next few decades from the time of this story? Why?

Attired in wedding finery, Esmat danced in the women's line, waving a handkerchief and gracefully stepping to the right in time to the music. While the small group of musicians from the nearby city of Shiraz played their instruments, men and boys, women and girls crowded around watching the circling lines of dancers. Even people unrelated to the groom and bride and not formally invited to the wedding perched on surrounding roofs, observing the dancing and commenting to their neighbors. And there, in front of all those men, Esmat danced, her arms and legs slowly waving and bending in rhythm with those of the women on either side of her. Her long, full skirt gleamed as blue metallic threads caught the sunshine. The dark, rich red of her long covering tunic glowed. Around her shoulders, a stiff, gossamer blue scarf, part of regional dress, poked out between her veil's folds. Like other village women, bowing to the newly instituted Islamic Republic, Esmat had put her *chador,* or body veil, over her head, crossing it over her chest and tying it in back. But the veil did not conceal her pretty, full-length wedding costume.

Esmat, as a pious Muslim woman, had always been careful to stay at home as much as possible, cover her hair and body with her veil in front of unrelated men, and even avoid situations where men outside of her family might hear her voice. Even though she had told me beforehand that she would be dancing at this wedding, I was taken aback to see her celebrating like this.

Although village women viewed weddings as their main recreation, as a pious widow, Esmat attended only the weddings of close relatives. She had danced at her brother's wedding a couple of years earlier, she told me. Duty to family here outweighed

her usual avoidance of public gatherings where she would be exposed to unrelated men.

But now it was May 1979, three months after the Iranian Islamic Revolution. The visiting mullah or preacher had said it was a sin to dance, Esmat had reported to me. Strangely, she did not seem disturbed by this pronouncement. She went on to inform me that she would be wearing regional dress at the upcoming wedding of her mother's sister's son. And she would dance.

Eventually, sometime after Esmat danced at her cousin's wedding, the visiting preacher from Qom, Iranian center of Shi'a Muslim theology and religious politics, left the village, partly in disgust over people who persisted in sinful dancing at weddings. Later, as the Islamic Republic government consolidated its power, villagers were not able to celebrate their weddings with music and regional dancing. All over the country, people gave up music and dancing at weddings, or risked celebrating as they wished behind closed doors, perhaps after bribing officials or Revolutionary Guards. Many people went to jail or paid heavy fines when apprehended at their illegal festivities.

ESMAT'S WORK—SEWING AT HOME

All women veiled in this Iranian village, even before the 1978–1979 revolution. They were to remain at home as much as possible and to avoid interaction with males outside of the family. It was all right for men to find ways to entertain themselves. Men could sit in the sunshine outside the village gate or in the spacious area just inside. Men could go to prayers and sermons at the local mosque, ride the bus into the city, take walks, travel by themselves, and see movies in Shiraz. Men go out and develop friendships and do things together, people told me, while women just stay at home and interact with their own close relatives and neighbors. Women could only visit their close relatives and maybe go to a women's religious ritual. Once in a while, with adequate chaperoning, some young women and girls might plan an outing to a shrine just outside of the village. A woman should even be careful not to visit close neighbors or relatives too much, or she would gain the reputation of being a run-around. Women should be at home, or if out of the house for appropriate reasons, should wear a veil—rather like a tent or portable enclosure—to cover themselves.

I had come to "Aliabad"—a village of some three thousand inhabitants half an hour by bus from Shiraz, capital of the southwestern province of Fars—to do field research in late summer 1978. Soon, as the only woman in the village who did not wear a veil or chador (the large half circle that women used to wrap up their bodies and shield themselves from male view), I began to feel conspicuous walking through the village alleyways. Even long, tunic-like shirts over my slacks did not cover me enough to make me feel comfortable. My landlady suggested I order a chador to be made by the local seamstress and sent a boy after her. This is how I met Esmat.

When Esmat came, I asked her to make me a printed cotton chador. Women wore these when walking through the village to visit a relative or when men other than their immediate family members were in their homes or courtyards. She would also sew several of the loose pants for me that women wore at home or when dropping in on a neighbor for a quick chat or errand.

Esmat and her mother, grandmother, and great grandmother all had been unfortunate enough to be widowed with small children. All of them chose to remain single and raise their children themselves rather than remarrying and losing their children. They had to find ways to support themselves and their children. The others had worked as cloth sellers. Esmat, using her electric Singer sewing machine, became a seamstress.

When the clothes were ready, Esmat sent one of her sons after me, asking me to come to her home to try on the chador and pants. We turned right after coming out of my landlord's gateway into the village and walked aways up the alleyway. Esmat's son led me to a door on the left, knocked on it, and called out. Esmat opened the door and welcomed me, for the first of many times, into the small, rather cluttered courtyard.

Esmat lived with her mother, who had been widowed long before, and her younger brother's family.

Esmat had two sons, both school age. The brother and his wife had a baby boy. Esmat, her mother, and her two boys slept in the smaller, less formal room, while her brother and his family used the larger room furnished with a carpet. Like other villagers, all of them rolled up their bedding in the morning, covered the piles with cloth, and stacked them against the wall. Rooms were multipurpose. With the bedding set aside, they turned into family, sitting, and work rooms. A plastic tablecloth spread on the floor converted them into dining rooms. In the winter, women cooked on an *aladin*, a small kerosene burner that also heated the room. In the summer, they took the burner outside to the courtyard for cooking.

Esmat brought me into her small room and took out the loose house pants and light colored chador printed with tiny blue flowers. Here Esmat worked at her sewing machine using cloth from piles and bundles stashed around the room. She worked hard, not even taking time off when she was sick.

Esmat's mother brought the material. She traded in cloth, traveling to Shiraz by bus and buying cloth to bring back in a large sack, she and sack both covered with her chador. Women ducked into Esmat's home, looked over the mother's goods, and chose pieces from which Esmat sewed veils, infant layettes, children's clothes, and women's and men's loose house pants. She sewed women's local ethnic clothing of long tunic over several full, long skirts, and multilayers of long, loose pants, gathered at waist and ankles with elastic bands. Older women and less-city-influenced women wore plain cotton local dress every day instead of a blouse or sweater over loose pants as the more modern young women did. All women dressed in ethnic costumes of synthetic, shiny, brightly colored cloth for wedding celebrations.

Past childbearing age, Esmat's mother could travel alone for her cloth business without damage to her own or her family's reputation. Younger women should be escorted by husband, brother, mother, or mother-in-law—a family male or an older female relative—when they went outside of the village.

In earlier times, quite a few women, especially widows, had worked as traders. They even took their goods out to nomadic Qashqa'i encampments during their spring and fall migrations, accompanied by one or more of their children. In the late 1970s, though, Aliabad women generally did not peddle or trade. Because of proximity to Shiraz, which offered jobs for men in construction, factories, and service, most people enjoyed a better standard of living. Almost all men could afford to support their female dependents. Failure to do so, as demonstrated by a mother, wife, or daughter who worked, signified that the man was incompetent. Urban religious culture now influenced village attitudes about women's place. Men should defend their womenfolk's modesty by supporting them and allowing them to stay at home.

Esmat and her mother did not have husbands to support them. Esmat's younger brother provided for his wife and baby boy on earnings from his tailor shop in Shiraz. Two extra women, plus Esmat's two boys, would have been quite an added burden. To bring in a little more income, Esmat's mother lent out small amounts of money to some villagers for interest, in addition to selling cloth which she brought from Shiraz.

ESMAT AND COMMUNICATION

Because women from all over the village came to Esmat's home to buy material from her mother and order articles of clothing sewn by Esmat, she knew village affairs. Women need not be related to Esmat to stop in at her home. They had good reason to visit her; they had to get clothes for themselves and their families. A small glass of tea and some harmless gossip would add spice to their errand, they knew. As Esmat's home was a legitimate destination for them, some women felt comfortable stretching it a bit and dropping in on her even when they did not have an immediate clothing need. Esmat was a good source of news. Bright and inquisitive, Esmat knew how to best question people to elicit information. As a widowed woman, she needed to be even more careful than other women to avoid talking to unrelated men except when unavoidable. Normally she was restricted to home or permitted only quick, purposeful trips through village alleyways. Her ventures into investigative talk freed her from some of these restrictions. Her verbal skills extended to interviewing children and male relatives about goings-on that she had not witnessed herself. Women could count on her to provide updated news about village dramas and—when the Iranian Revolution heated up in summer and fall of 1978—news about revolutionary incidents in Shiraz and throughout the country. Esmat's brother owned a tailor shop in Shiraz and joined other shopkeepers in studying revolutionary interpretations of Shi'a Islam and supporting the religious dissidents. Esmat stayed well informed through him as well as through radio news, tapes, and conversations with many others and passed on her knowledge and perspectives to others.

A gifted researcher and communicator, Esmat seemed a fine anthropologist. I told her how good she was at collecting, analyzing, and conveying social and political data. When she was young, she responded quietly, she had done as I did. She had an interest in customs and local history. She went around asking old people questions about the past. But then, when she became a little older, people told her not to do this, that it was not proper behavior for a girl.

ESMAT'S HISTORY

At school age, Esmat, like most other village women and older men, had not had much opportunity for education. Although she had attended classes for a few years, she could not really write. When she needed to write something, one of her sons served as scribe. Although functionally almost illiterate, she addressed her wish to learn by studying religion and village (and, later, national) social and political dynamics. Her home served as a women's social center, and she herself as an informal information and communications coordinator.

As was typical for Aliabad girls, Esmat had been married when very young. In the village, elders arranged marriages. Parents choosing spouses for their children wanted political connections and prestige. They thought about a husband to best financially provide for their daughter or a pretty wife to best raise children and keep house for their son, not about a companionate marriage. Couples should not spend much time together. People laughed at one man who spent his free time at home with his wife instead of sitting on his haunches just outside the village entrance conversing with other men. In public, wives and husbands stayed away from each other. Men celebrated in one room or house at weddings, and women in another. During dancing, which might take place in village open areas outside of private walled courtyards, females and males danced in separate lines. Married couples should not express affection to each other while others watched. Ideally, they should not even speak with each other but rather send messages with a child.

Esmat and her husband's relationship did not fit into the typical pattern, it seemed. Although she herself did not talk about her marriage, Esmat and her husband acted like lovebirds, other women told me, and were sweet and attentive to each other.

Her husband had worked for Post and Telegraph in Shiraz delivering telegrams by motorcycle. They lived in Shiraz. Esmat was 19 when her husband was killed in a traffic accident. Esmat had been cooking for dinner guests expected that evening when the terrible news came to her. Esmat was left with a two-year-old son and another "in her stomach." When I asked her why she had not remarried, she said, "For the sake of my two children."

Men here don't marry widows, people told me; they get a "girl," a virgin. Few women with children marry again when they become widows, Esmat told me, unless they marry their husband's brother.

When a father dies, legally, the children belong to their father's family. The dead father's family want to keep control over their son's property and therefore want the children who should inherit that property. To cope with these constraints, a surviving brother sometimes married the widow. That way, she could continue to mother her children, yet the father's family would not lose either children or property. But Esmat's brothers-in-law had not wanted her. She was pregnant at the time of her husband's death. Because she was thin, she looked weak and unattractive. Her husband's younger brother, who had not yet married, brought a city girl to the village to be his wife instead of marrying Esmat.

Lacking the opportunity to marry one of her husband's brothers, Esmat faced a dilemma. A widow must go to court shortly after the death of her husband, Esmat told me, and declare that she does not want to be the guardian of her children, as she wants to get married again. Then the children will be under the guardianship of the father's parents or some other relative of the father. Or she can declare that she wants to be the guardian, will not marry, and will care for her children till the end of her life. Esmat declared the latter. When Esmat's husband died, the children did not have a guardian in Shiraz, she said. After living in Shiraz for eight years, Esmat moved back to Aliabad to live with her mother and brother. In fall of 1978, when I came, she and her children had been back in the village for seven years.

Esmat's husband's meager pension could not provide for them. Without a second husband to provide for her, Esmat became a seamstress. From her sewing room, a favorite women's dropping-in destination, she served as a main link in women's networks.

ESMAT AND THE IRANIAN REVOLUTION

Because of her religiosity, and the influence of her brother and other relatives, Esmat was an early supporter of the Islamic revolutionary movement. As the religiously organized revolutionary movement swelled in 1978 and 1979, Esmat furthered her religious knowledge and grasp of revolutionary interpretations of Shi'a Islam. She listened to radio news and tapes of revolutionary lectures and chants, questioned her brother, and interviewed whomever came her way. She became conversant about the revolutionary movement as she had been about local goings-on.

Esmat had learned from her brother all she knew about religion, she told me. Her brother spent most of his time in Shiraz and did not get back home until 10:00 or so at night. Her brother had worked in the Shiraz University hospital emergency room before opening his tailor shop. He still marched with the university people in revolutionary demonstrations. Also, Esmat said, all sorts of people came into his tailor shop. He had contact with many, many people and learned a lot this way. He belonged to a regular Qur'an study group in Shiraz. Members took turns going to each other's homes where they read the Qur'an, translated it, and discussed its meaning.

Because Shi'a Muslim leaders framed the revolutionary movement as an Islamic struggle, Esmat felt able to do things she normally would not do. During the prerevolution period, some religious women in her section of the village started after-dark chanting in support of Ayatollah Khomeini. The night they progressed as far as her house, Esmat peeked out of her courtyard door. After seeing another woman known for her piety and modesty in the little crowd of women, Esmat wrapped her *chador* around herself and slipped out to join the other female demonstrators for a few steps.

After the Shah fled the country in January 1979, Esmat and I went to the Secret Police station in Shiraz, now open to the public, and with others stared in horror at the remnants of torture. In late January, Esmat began attending the nightly prayers and talks at the village mosque, sitting with her mother and friends in the women's section separated by a curtain from the men. She invited me to come with her. Covering her face except for the eyes with her *chador,* she hurried along to the mosque, keeping her eyes down like the other women did. Chaperoned, Esmat went into Shiraz to join revolutionary gatherings, putting her devotion to Islam into practice. She saw the Air Force personnel's demonstration and ate a meal donated by partisans of the revolutionary movement at the main Shiraz shrine. In early February, when she heard that three buses were coming to take people into Shiraz for a march, she rushed to join them. Coming back on the bus with several other village women, I greeted Esmat who was on the bus too, unaccompanied.

During the height of the revolutionary period, many women felt freer than usual to move about. Women could accentuate the political and religious merit of trips into Shiraz to attend political marches and mosque gathering. Buoyed by revolutionary fervor, males insisted that their revolutionary "sisters" be treated with respect. After the February 11, 1979, fall of the Pahlavi regime government, Esmat sometimes went into Shiraz, combining a visit to her younger sister who was married and lived there with participation in religious/political events. In June she enthusiastically reported to me she heard the then prime minister give a speech. After that, the son of an eminent local ayatollah spoke. A large army contingency had gathered for this event, to show their cooperation with the people.

ESMAT AND LOCAL-LEVEL POLITICAL CONFLICT

In 1962 the Shah had put into effect a land reform program, which ended up having an effect on Aliabad women's lives. The extended family of Askaris, who were then the landlord's village representatives, and their supporters had secretly bought Aliabad's irrigated agricultural land from the large landlord just before the land reform. The large landlord was not required to distribute that land to the troublesome peasants.

The peasant faction—the people who had actually farmed the land—resisted the Askari brothers and their takeover of irrigated village land during the 1962 land reform. When the peasants learned how they had been cheated, strife broke out. Several men from the peasant faction were killed or wounded before the Askaris, with brutal assistance from the rural police, consolidated their control over the village and its land. Because of the Askaris's government backing, peasant faction members could do nothing about it. However, they never stopped resenting this swindle and the subsequent violence.

During the land reform conflict, the Askaris and their cohorts succeeded in gaining ownership of village land and monopolizing political power. They put a stop to village factional competition and conflict.

Before land reform, Aliabad women had played significant, if unacknowledged, roles in the periodic factional conflict over control of land and the position of village headman. After land reform, the Askaris were able to hold on to their position of ruling local family and central government representatives. Backed by the rural police force of the now powerful central government, the Askaris were able to consolidate village power in their own hands and prevent competitors for land and political control from rising up. After their definitive victory during the land reform fray, together the Askaris and the rural police prevented any threat to their domination, until the February 1979 Iranian Revolution.

Some months after the revolution in fall 1979, members of the local "peasant" faction began noticing that the new revolutionary government did not automatically stand behind the Askaris in their dealings with Aliabad people. Under the ensuing conditions of chaos and insecurity, they noted, the rural police hid out in their stations and did not dare come out. Peasant faction adherents began to lose their fear that the rural police would crush any opposition to the Askaris. Members of the peasant faction began gathering at the mosque chanting revolutionary slogans against the tyranny and injustice of Askari rule in Aliabad, just as they had denounced the Shah's rule.

When the Askaris lost their government backing because of the revolution, Esmat and other village women took part in reemerging factional conflict. They became active again in local factional competition, just as women had been before land reform.

Esmat's husband had been from a family who belonged to the peasant faction in the land reform combat. Esmat's husband's father had had farming rights to land in Aliabad. He was in Shiraz when land was distributed, though, so he did not receive any. Therefore, his sons did not have land either. All of them had lived in Shiraz during the land reform distribution. Since Esmat's and her husband's relatives belonged to the peasant faction, Esmat counted herself among the opposition to the Askaris.

During peasant faction strategy meetings at the height of the local clash, Esmat, as the daughter-in-law of a main leader, served tea with other womenfolk. Because of her researching bent, she took full advantage of her presence. She gathered details and analyzed different persons' stances and the historical, kinship, or material interests prompting them. Esmat articulately expounded her theories and described village dramas to me or others so vividly one could imagine oneself watching.

With other women, Esmat played a significant communicating role in the local conflict, just as she had in the national revolutionary movement. She gathered, compiled in her mind, and disseminated information and arguments. She persuaded, conveyed emotion, and showed support for the peasant faction through her physical presence.

After several months of contention and some violence, the peasant faction ousted the Askari faction. The peasant faction took over land belonging to the senior Askari brother. They got him jailed. When he escaped from jail later on, we heard, he fled the country.

REVOLUTIONARY POLITICS AND EFFECTS ON A VILLAGE WIDOW'S SPHERES OF ACTION

The revolutionary period offered Esmat opportunities to get out of the house; share information with friends, neighbors, and relatives; attend daily mosque prayers infused with revolutionary rhetoric and spirit; and participate in dramatic marches and exciting religious/political events in the city. She could take part in valued activities and gain and share respected knowledge. Even as a scrupulously modest widow, Esmat could cover herself with religious zeal and fulfill her duty as a devout Muslim woman while lending her support to the Iranian Revolution, which she saw as inspired by Shi'a Islam.

When the local uprising developed, replicating the national-level revolution, Esmat could clothe herself in that same Islamic rhetoric and symbolism that the peasant faction applied to the struggle against Askari domination. Moreover, in attending peasant faction meetings and wielding her verbal skills to aid them, Esmat acted in fitting dedication to family. She was supporting the faction to which both her husband's and her own parents' relatives belonged.

In the short term, the revolution opened a wider world to Esmat and other women in her situation. They gained opportunities for mobility. Esmat's talk was politically valuable, both in the national revolutionary movement and the local-level postrevolution conflict. But as time went on and power and authority again became regularized, Islamic Republic officials and their local backers curtailed women's spheres of activity. Women's seclusion and modesty became a state matter rather than merely the concern of family, relatives, and community. Women's covering and separation from unrelated men became legally enforced as well as coerced by unregulated "Revolutionary Guards" and private zealots. Women's activities outside of religion were limited, whereas religion-related opportunities burgeoned. But rural, illiterate women did not have the opportunities for teaching and studying religion and participating in Islamic politics that urban, middle-, and upper-middle-class Iranian women enjoyed. In the decade after the institution of the Islamic Revolution of Iran, most rural women's lives and talk became more confined.

POST-REVOLUTIONARY IRANIAN WOMEN STRUGGLING FOR POLITICAL VOICE

I conducted the research on which this essay is based in the village of "Aliabad" between summer 1978 and December 1979. By the time my two-and-a-half-year-old daughter and I flew out of Iran in December 1979, separation of unrelated males and females was already becoming a concern of the religious central government. Many executions of persons believed to oppose the Islamic Republic had already taken place. The devastating eight-year Iran–Iraq war began in 1980.

Today, over 20 years later, in spite of severe restrictions, women are actively attempting to define their role in society. In sometimes subtle and unique ways, Iranian women have kept pushing for a say over their lives, society, and political system. Though women must cover themselves, many have assumed roles in public life; several even serve in parliament. Women's votes brought moderate President Khatemi into office in May 1997.

Changes are more dramatic in urban centers, but invariably ideas and attitudes from the cities filter into villages. Politics in Iran, as in other places, continue to change. Women's talk is one factor in bringing about these changes and, with these changes, come changes in women's lives.

In the intervening 20 years since my last research visit, Esmat and her family moved to a new home, her mother died, and her two sons married, her letters tell me.

Because of political relations between the Islamic Republic and the United States, I have not been able to return. However, now relations seem to be gradually improving. The American Institute of Iranian Studies has given me a small research grant and arranged for my visa. In 2002, I will return to Iran for at least a couple of months. I dearly look forward to seeing Esmat and other Aliabad friends and catching up on their lives.

SUGGESTED READINGS

Hegland, Mary. (1991). "Political Roles of Aliabad Women: The Public/Private Dichotomy Transcended," in *Shifting Boundaries: Gender Roles in the Middle East, Past and Present*, ed. Nikki Keddie and Beth Baron, pp. 215–230. New Haven: Yale University Press.

Hegland, Mary. (1998). "Women and the Iranian Revolution: A Village Case Study," in *Women and Revolution: Global Expressions*, ed. M. J. Diamond, pp. 211–225. Netherlands: Kluwer Academic Publishers. Reprinted from *Dialectical Anthropology* 15:183–192, 1990.

PART IV

Gender

Photo by Linda S. Walbridge.

Many people believe that biology is destiny; that, by being born male or female, our behaviors and roles in life are laid out for us. Anthropologists argue that this is not the case; that cross-cultural research shows considerable variability in what constitutes masculine and feminine behavior, or even what constitutes male or female. Over the past few decades anthropologists have found that it is necessary to distinguish between "sex," which refers to the biological markers of being male or female, and "gender," which is a cultural construction. In other words, gender refers to how "feminine" and "masculine" are defined in a culture and how these definitions affect the roles that men and women play in their societies. Anthropologists are interested in studying and analyzing how and why cultures construct these gender differences.

Before gender studies became a subfield of anthropology, many anthropologists assumed that women participated primarily in the private spheres of life, that they did not play an active role in shaping their societies. Because men have been more likely to be warriors and political and religious leaders, they were assumed to be the ones who determined how a society developed, utilized its resources, and so forth. But anthropologists began to realize that these ethnographies often came from a male perspective, and such a viewpoint could distort what was asked and how it was interpreted. Studying women's roles has given us a much broader and comprehensive view of the diversity of women's and men's roles within their own cultures and throughout the world.

61

This is not to say that anthropologists have found that men and women share equally in resources and power in cultures around the world. To the contrary, women are often relegated to a lower status. In many places couples prefer to have sons and, when given a choice, will elect to educate their sons and give them a variety of advantages over daughters. Girls and women are likely to be subjected to a variety of rules and prohibitions that they do not share with boys and men. But the picture is usually more complicated than meets the eye. Often gender discrimination is linked to "race," social class, or caste. In other words, in any given place we find that all women are not subjected to the same requirements.

In studying gender, anthropologists have had to question the concept of "power." For instance, in some cultures where women may live with their husband's families and lack access to substantial resources, they may nonetheless find ways to exert their influence, such as through bonds with other women. Or they might have a great deal of influence over their sons, often having considerable say about whom they marry. Thus, while we may, and often do, see notable differences between the status of men and women, more subtle mechanisms are often at work that give women at least some avenues of authority.

The subject of gender identity has become a subject of increasing interest to anthropologists. As we know, physical differences between males and females do not automatically determine one's sexuality; that is, the idea that an individual's identity is somehow tied in with her or his sexual partner preferences.

Gays and lesbians constitute a considerable proportion of the population and, at least in the West, have become politically active. How they construct a sense of community, how they cope with discrimination, and how they organize themselves for legal battles are just a few issues that anthropologists study. They also might study different subgroups in the gay population such as "drag queens," transvestites, and transsexuals to see how the people in these different categories differ and how they relate to one another. Most intriguing is the fact that, while transsexuals and others are largely marginal in the West, they may play important roles in other cultures. For example, in Pakistan, men who dress and behave like women dance and sing at weddings and other festivities where they are treated with respect. Yet, we also have to be careful not to assume that what Euro-Westerners call transsexual is conceptualized the same in another culture.

Just as anthropologists came to realize that they must pay attention to women in order to have a holistic view of cultures, anthropologists specializing in gender realize that they must rethink how men's gender and sex roles differ cross-culturally. Research has shown that there is not one pattern of masculinity that is found everywhere and that we need to speak of "masculinities." But everywhere some forms of masculinity—such as that associated with sports heroes in the West—are more valued than others. The different values placed on some forms of masculinity can be oppressive to those males who somehow "fall short" of society's demands.

The following articles clearly challenge mainstream Western views of "masculinity" and "femininity" and demonstrate the diversity of anthropological studies of gender. Sarah Lamb takes us to India for a look into what life becomes when a high-caste woman's husband dies. Carolyn Epple spends a day with a Navajo queen and breaks down the stereotypes that typify popular conceptions of homosexuality. Susan Peake's look into masculine identity in Australia also shows us the changes in self-image that accompany disability.

Other articles that touch on this topic:

10

Green Earrings: A Widow's Tale

Sarah Lamb

Brandeis University

West Bengal is a state of nearly 70 million people in northeastern India. In 1947, when India achieved independence from England, and the predominantly Muslim provinces of India broke away from the rest of India, the western half of the Bengal region became the Indian state of West Bengal and the eastern half became first East Pakistan and then, in 1971, the independent nation of Bangladesh. Although West Bengal is largely Hindu and Bangladesh is largely Muslim, the two halves of Bengal share a common language (Bengali) and cultural heritage.

Mangaldihi, where Kayera Bou lives, is about 150 kilometers from West Bengal's capital city of Calcutta. The village of some 2,000 residents comprises 17 different Hindu caste groups and one neighborhood of Muslims. In the caste system, each person is born into a particular caste or *jati* (literally "birth group") with a prescribed traditional occupation and set of social mores. Kayera Bou was a member of the highest Hindu caste group, the Brahmans. Not all widows in India face severe restrictions when their husbands die. In fact, many widows, especially lower-caste women who are young and childless, are permitted and even encouraged to remarry. Kayera Bou's story, however, reveals the austere set of practices traditionally prescribed for Brahman widows in West Bengal.

Most of the practices constituting the Bengali Brahman widow's code of conduct—such as shunning remarriage; avoiding all meat, fish, eggs, onions, and other "hot" foods; forbearing jewelry; and wearing white—are aimed at curtailing a widow's sexuality now that it is no longer contained by a husband in marriage. Widows are also commonly regarded as inauspicious, because of their connection to their husbands' deaths. In addition to safeguarding the widow's chastity, the widow's practices thus serve to keep her partly segregated from others, so that her inauspiciousness will not spread into their lives. Not all Brahman widows follow the prescribed practices to the letter, though. Some secretly sneak onions or fish, or move to an anonymous city where they may wear colored saris or even remarry, or—like Kayera Bou—find small pleasure in wearing green earrings.

We see in Kayera Bou's tale that although she feels pressed to comply with the widow's code of conduct, at the same time she challenges and critiques it and the Bengali society, particularly the upper-caste Brahman society, that has produced such unbearable conditions for women. We also see how important it is in rural West Bengal for women to be wives and mothers.

As you read, consider the following questions:

1. Why do you think Kayera Bou sought out the author, to tell her her life story? What did the telling accomplish? Do you think it matters that only the author, and now you readers, heard this story, and not members of Kayera Bou's own community? How and why are life stories revealing—for the teller? For the anthropologist? For later readers of tales?

2. What kinds of customs are Brahman widows compelled to observe in West Bengal, India? Why? In what ways do these customs reflect the local social structure?

3. What are some of the symbols surrounding the widow's prescribed practices? For instance, why does a widow wear white, and not red? Why should widows be "cool," rather than "hot"? Why are Brahman widows forbidden to eat warm, boiled rice (as opposed to dry, puffed rice) more than once a day? Can you think of any similar symbols in American society? For instance, why is an American bridal gown traditionally white? (In West Bengal, the favored color for a bride's sari is red.)

4. Based on this tale, what is your sense of the ways high-caste women in rural West Bengal find value and meaning in their lives? Why is it so important to Kayera Bou that she present herself as having experienced, at least during a period of her life, "a deep love between husband and wife"?

5. Anthropologists often strive to be culturally relativistic, by working to understand a cultural item within the context of its own culture, without applying value judgments. Can you be culturally relativistic in approaching the situation of Bengali Brahman widows? Or do you find yourself wishing that

you could condemn or change some things about the society?

6. In what ways does Kayera Bou resist what life has dealt her? If she could change one dimension of her Bengali society, what do you think she would choose?

....

When I first met Kayera Bou in a large verdant village of West Bengal, India, she had her thin gray-black hair pulled back in a tight knot and she wore a plain white widow's sari. She was a Brahman, a member of India's highest caste, who had been widowed, childless, as a younger woman. This meant that, along with having to wear white, she could not remarry and was compelled to eat a vegetarian diet, with hot rice (the Bengali staple) only once a day. She was pressed by her kin and community to strip herself free of jewelry and adornments and to stay apart from auspicious ceremonies such as weddings. Such are the restrictions Brahman widows in West Bengal have to endure. Widows from other high castes, emulating the Brahmans, follow these same customs in their search for higher status. Kayera Bou had remained in her marital home even after her husband's death, but she maintained there her own separate cooking and sleeping quarters. The family was fairly well off, with several acres of land and a general store to its name, and so Kayera Bou was provided for; but she felt she had suffered severely and unjustly in her life as a widow.

One day, after I had been living as an anthropologist in her village for several months, I was wandering down the dusty lane by her modest home, and Kayera Bou called out to me. She pulled me aside into her room and closed the door. There she asked me to return during siesta time when it was more private so she could tell me her life story. I returned that afternoon with my tape recorder, and I listened as her story poured forth in a flood of words, with eloquence, vividness, bitterness, and pathos.

"Well, when I was in my childhood, I mean, when I was in my father's house, then I was very happy." Kayera Bou opened with these words, describing her childhood as the happiest years of her life, when she was loved, surrounded by kin, fed by her mother, and encouraged to study and to learn to read and write in school.

But childhood did not last long. After Kayera Bou (or Aparna, as she was called in girlhood) passed her fourth-grade exam, her teachers and parents declared that she would no longer study. She was already thirteen. It was time to give her in marriage. Within a few years, during what she refers to as still the "beginnings of her life," her father arranged her marriage, and she left her natal home of Kayera to come to the village of Mangaldihi, some 20 kilometers away.

Kayera Bou told me about the difficult years of her married life and her frustrated quest to have children—both of which are central to her tale of her life as a widow. For the first eight months of marriage she recalls receiving "a little, a little happiness." Her husband would come to sleep with her at night. There was some affection, some of what husbands and wives do.

But just eight months after her wedding, everything suddenly changed when her husband's 18-year-old brother died of meningitis. Kayera Bou went to the hospital to nurse him for three days, and while she was putting ice on his forehead, he died. Her husband and his parents blamed her for the death, threatening to send her back to her parents, and calling her ill-omened and inauspicious—in the way that Indian brides are often blamed for misfortunes in their husbands' families.

She recalls: "My husband's head went bad. He would say, 'You came, and my brother died.' He wouldn't come near me. Even if I would lie next to him in bed he wouldn't say anything to me. And I'm a woman. I couldn't touch him first. What if I touched him and he reproached me? But I didn't tell anyone about it. I was embarrassed. And what would telling accomplish? But many people would ask me about it; they'd say, 'Doesn't he talk to you? [i.e., have sexual relations with you?]' But I wouldn't answer; I would just cry."

About five years passed like this. Then Kayera Bou tells that when he finally had a little mind to love her, *she* was the one who had become sick. She was afflicted with the *sucibai rog*, a mania for cleanliness and purity, an aversion to touching or mixing with other people and things, a felt need to wash constantly. This was an illness state that seemed to occur only among high-caste women who were experiencing strife with their husbands. "So," Kayera Bou narrates, "even if he called me to him I wouldn't go. I wouldn't touch him. And I got angry at him, 'You judged me unfairly. I didn't do anything wrong. I came and your brother died. What could I do? It's fate.'"

Then, to make matters worse, her husband became afflicted with a disease, which she describes as some kind of growth or scarring in "that place," his sexual organs, and he left for six months to have an operation in Calcutta. Later he had Kayera Bou have an operation as well, in case there was a fault in her womb. Her mother and father wished desperately for her to have children. Her mother would implore, "Can't we cut her stomach and put a child into it? My daughter *will* have a family, a household!"

But as Kayera Bou reached 30 and "the time for having children passed," her husband became sick and bedridden with diabetes. She goes to great pains in her story to convince herself, me, and later her psychiatrist that during this one period of their relationship there was "a deep love between a husband and wife." Although there could be no more romantic or sexual love between them, she would sit by his bed daily. "Just like I'm sitting by you now as you tape me, I remember sitting by him. He couldn't go anywhere, but he would tell me to dress up and sit by him, and to paint red dye on my feet. He would say, 'Let my mother do the work. You don't do it. Stay by me. Love, love . . .'"

However, Kayera Bou's "head had gradually gone bad" during this period from the stress of being childless and from the absence of a sexual relationship with her husband. Her parents and husband persuaded her to go to a mental health sanitarium in Ranchi, in neighboring Bihar, for "a rest." She wept as she left, bowing down to her husband over and over again. That was the last time she saw him.

At Ranchi, she began a therapy of psychiatric counseling and electric shock treatment, a sign of Western medicine's penetration into rural India. Applying shock therapy in this case reflects how we Westerners tend to locate affliction in the body rather than in social relationships. Yet, shock therapy could not touch the unbearable condition of being a childless woman. As such, she was barely a wife in a world where motherhood and wifehood were the key sources of fulfillment, intimacy, and value.

She tells of how her doctor would ask, "How is romantic, sexual love with your husband? Then why didn't you have any children?" But she didn't want to admit to him the many failings of her years of marriage. "I would tell the doctor that the love between a husband and wife is inside. No one else can know about it . . . My doctor would say, 'I think you were never really able to mix with your husband, and that's why you have this illness.' But I told the doctor, 'Doctor-babu, the kind of mixing that happens between husbands and wives in a Bengali house also happened to us . . . At night what happens happens.'" But she acknowledges that "the doctor still understood, even though I tried to hide it from him. He said, 'No, no, you didn't have that kind of love.'"

Her husband died after she had been in psychiatric treatment for only 14 days. Her doctor and parents kept the news from her at first, though, fearing her instability. Finally, after two months, her father and brother came to get her. She recalls with vivid detail how she dressed herself for the journey in married woman's garb, with the married woman's auspicious red vermilion in her hair, her married woman's bracelets, red dye on her feet, feeling that she had become so attractive, with a fair complexion, overflowing with eagerness to see her husband again.

Then, after she arrived at her parents' home, it gradually dawned on her what had happened. Her mother was sobbing. Their family's widowed maidservant came to take her to the water to perform the ritual of becoming a widow, where she had to break her married woman's bangles; wash off her red vermilion; remove her beautiful, colored sari; and don the permanent white of the widow. White for Bengalis is a "cool" color, symbolizing celibacy, sexual purity, and widowhood; whereas red is the "warm," attractive color of marriage, fertility, sexuality, and auspiciousness. She tells:

> When I understood what was happening, I began to sob. I beat my head and cried all night long. I had to be taken to the water, take off all those things and throw them away and be bathed. Then where was the red vermilion? And where were the ornaments? And good clothes? Where was anything? One after another they were all sunk in the water. Everything became surrounded with gloom. When he left everything became gloom. Sadness . . . I was weeping and shouting. I wailed over and over again, "I'll see him one more time! One more time! Why don't you show him to me again?"
>
> When you didn't get any letters from your husband for a long time [she said to me], I could understand how awful you must feel. A husband is such a thing. I abandoned everything else, and my eagerness was for one person only. I was coming back from Ranchi with such hope and expectation. I sobbed and sobbed thinking of all the hope I had come from Ranchi with, thinking that I would see him again.

Kayera Bou told me how her mother could not bear to inflict the widow's lifestyle on her daughter. Brahman widows in West Bengal can eat warm (ordinary) boiled rice only once a day, at the noon meal—a restriction aimed at keeping widows' bodies thinner, cooler, and less sexual. "So," she explained, "at night they began to take out some puffed rice (*muri*) to feed me. My mother was saying, 'I won't be able to give her puffed rice. How can I give her cold, puffed rice and eat hot rice myself?' But my father told her that she would have to. My mother said, 'No! I won't be able to. I'm going to feed her boiled rice. Society! Let people talk! She's *my* child. I'm going to feed her. Then later whatever happens will happen.'" But Kayera Bou's mother wasn't able to feed her boiled rice in front of everyone. She was too embarrassed. Kayera Bou tells:

> People would have seen and said to her, "Oh, you're feeding her *boiled rice?*" Perhaps my husband's sister [who was married into her parents' village] would see and say, "You're feeding her *this?*" and then she would go around slandering us and telling everyone that my mother was feeding me. That's the fault of Bengalis, isn't it? They go around talking about who's feeding whom what. While at the same time my mother was saying, "She's never eaten puffed rice in her whole life. I can't give her puffed rice now to chew. She'll never be able to eat puffed rice."

Several days had passed while Kayera Bou learned to be a widow in her parents' home, and her father declared that he wanted her to remain there with them. Many upper-caste childless widows do stay with their parents. But her mother said, "No, I'm going to place her in her marital home. It's the place of her husband." Kayera Bou's mother-in-law also said, "Bring my daughter-in-law here. I won't be able to live without my daughter-in-law." So she returned to her marital home, where there were then left only her mother-in-law, herself, and her husband's sister's son, who had been brought in to look after and inherit the family property and to be the male of the household, as there were no more descendants in her husband's family line.

Kayera Bou details the suffering of her life there as a widow: "Dry, puffed rice at night, and vegetarian rice in the day. How many kinds of pain we suffer if our husband doesn't live in our house! Just one pain? Pain in all directions! Burning pain—agony! Clothes, food, mixing with others, laughter—everything for us is forbidden." She tells of the way she was guarded by her husband's kin, who prevented her from even looking at another man, treating her as a dangerous "slut" (a derogatory term commonly hurled at young widows), reproaching her, saying, "None of that will happen in our house. You've come to our house. You won't talk to any man." She tells of how she could not wear colored saris or petticoats, jewelry, or even a little powder on her face, without being reproached by her husband's kin and teased by the neighborhood girls. How she had to eat an austere diet as a means to control her sexuality, making her thin and "cool," without sexual appeal or desire. How she felt herself to be utterly alone in the world of kin, how she cooked her food and ate alone (because of her special widow's diet) and had no one to really love her or care for her.

Throughout, she frequently criticizes "Bengalis" and "Bengali society" for all this, the plight especially of upper-caste Brahman widows. She strives also to remove *her*self from blame—although her community often blamed her, other widows, and other young brides for the calamities that happened in their households. She would say, "What did *I* do that was wrong? If I put a little powder on my face, or wear green earrings (which glittered as she spoke), what will happen? Let them say what they will. They can't reproach me. *I* didn't do anything unjust!" "We're still human, after all!" she said of widows, with bitter irony. "After our husbands die, we're no longer human?"

She ends by stating, "I received everything in this life, but not peace. Ever since I came to my husband's house after marriage this all began to happen, one thing after the next. *From what did it happen?*" Then she blessed me by hoping for me that *I* will have children, and that all my wishes will be fulfilled, and that she will be able to know of my fulfillments.

SUGGESTED READINGS

Chen, Martha Alter. (2000). *Perpetual Mourning: Widowhood in Rural India.* New York: Oxford University Press.

Lamb, Sarah. (2000). *White Saris and Sweet Mangoes: Aging, Gender and Body in North India.* Berkeley: University of California Press.

11

Queen for a Day

Carolyn Epple
Southern Illinois University—Edwardsville

The idea of gender appears in all cultures of the world, and underlies many of the social structures in a culture, such as kinship, living arrangements, and how a child is raised. Each culture makes sense of feminine and masculine, woman and man in its own way. In Euro-Western societies, we may think of someone as being either man or woman, but not both. In other cultures, however, the meanings of "man" and "woman" are not as rigid, and a person who is born male may have many social aspects that are "feminine," such as what she/he wears, what she/he does for a living, and what she/he is called by relatives.

The Diné (Navajo) are a good example of how this works. When a child is a hermaphrodite (i.e., her/his genitals are not clearly male or female), or is a masculine girl or feminine boy, many Diné describe the individual as a *nádleehí*. While Diné have only two genders, there is plenty of "give" in what they define as "man" or "woman." When a person is a *nádleehí*, then, people accept that a male can and will behave like a woman (and still be a man), and a female can and will behave like a man (and still be a woman). As such, the *nádleehí* fits within the Diné two genders and often has been well accepted in her/his society.

The following describes modern-day *nádleehí*, who call themselves "queens," for one day among the Diné Nation in the American Southwest. In reading through this, think about how flexibility in genders allows a male *nádleehí* to fit in as a woman in some instances and as a man in other instances. Think too about why some Diné may be changing their attitudes toward *nádleehí*.

As you read, consider the following questions:

1. How are Diné gender practices similar and different from those of your culture?
2. How would you describe a queen—what makes it hard to know who or what is a queen?
3. How do queens view marriage? What kinds of marriages do they contract?
4. How do the stories we tell vary in different situations? What implications might that have for meanings of man, woman, gay, straight, and so forth?

I cracked open one eye, and began to calculate the distance between the approaching ant line and my sleeping bag. Five, maybe ten more minutes of sleep. PK and MC lay on the cot, still spooning each other from their previous night's loving. I had heard their whispers, the occasional muffled giggle as they tried to enjoy each other undetected.

I resigned myself to waking up. Another sunny day. In the high desert's summer, the sun was not a warm friend smiling down on the good green earth. It was oppressive and, like a cloying odor, was relentlessly present. It would be a hot day in our one room, with its single light bulb. Maybe today we'd go to the spring and get more water, and pick up ice on the way back. PK also had promised to look at my truck, since it was the only working ride between the three of us.

How different this summer was than the previous one, when we had stayed at PK's sister's house, with its modern appliances, swamp cooler, and plumbing. That summer, PK and I had gone through all sorts of definitions about who is and is not a queen, what the term meant, how a queen was not really a Diné homosexual male. PK and others had been emphatic that queens did not sleep with each other; in fact, PK had sworn that she in particular did not sleep with other queens—to do so would "be like being lesbians." It was a joke aimed at me, but I figured I deserved it, given all the probing I did into other people's intimacies. It was also a statement, though, of how queens saw each other as sisters of sorts, and queens "did it" with someone different.

But here, in our single room, everything was looking different. I knew PK's sister's house was pretty plush by reservation standards, but I was just realizing that, for many Diné, our working light bulb would be a luxury and hauling water was an accepted fact of life. And then, just last night, in the cooling breezes following twilight, I had realized that PK's lover was another queen. I wondered, will this summer be an unlearning of everything from the previous one?

Damn. The ants were at the edge of my sleeping bag, forcing me up and out the door to do morning duties behind a sagebrush. None of us used the two-seater outhouse—I had spotted a snake just under the adjacent seat a few mornings earlier. Ah, MC and I had fun with PK on that one. "Girl, with you keeping that pet snake, no wonder you like it out here so much. I bet you've got some really special pet names for it. Are you selling tickets? Is that why you've got double seats?"

It was a particularly apt joke for PK, since she and others generally defined queens as the receptive partner in sexual practices. But if PK and MC were lovers, then active versus receptive was not going to define a queen or a not-queen. Cultural rules work that way, though. Even as they give us a kind of road map about general patterns, people will name and demonstrate for you just as many exceptions.

PK and MC stirred as I wiped up the spilled soda that had beckoned the ants into my early morning dreams. I glanced over at the sleeping pair and toyed with waking them up. Yeah, MC was definitely a queen. She was not as overtly "feminine" as PK, but did the sexual punning, talked about herself and other queens with feminine pronouns, hoped to finish a certificate in a profession more often associated with women than men, and, given a chance, could swish her hips with the best of them.

The sun was too low to have burned the air dry and a slight hint of sage still lingered. I yawned and realized the air lacked the most essential smell of morning. Coffee. Damn it, why didn't we get water yesterday? They'd bitch if I left without asking what we needed in town, or what they wanted for breakfast. I swung the screen door open wide and stepped back, well outside of its arc, to dump the dustpan of ants. I waited until it banged shut. "Good morning, girls."

After breakfast and errands, PK popped the hood on my truck. "You'd think you diesel dykes would know how to check the sparks," she bantered. "Oh darling, but I just know you love showing us your muscles," I answered. Actually, PK was very slight but had learned how to work on trucks from her first husband. When a queen settled in with a partner in a serious relationship, they were considered married. PK's first husband had been young when they met, and PK feared she would not be accepted. But her husband's family literally embraced her, and would call

PK daughter-in-law for the next three years. Their relationship had a caveat, however. The young man's parents stated that it was okay for him to be involved with PK, but when the time came for him to get married and have kids, the young man would be expected to do that.

And that is precisely what PK's former husband did. Yet other men continue to see their queen lovers after "settling down" and having kids. These men, with their generally masculine demeanor and serious relationships with women, were known as "straights" to the queens. Unlike Euro-Western categories of sexuality, Diné do not rely on sexual partner preference to define people. Even though both "straights" and queens may have preferred same-sex sexual partners, the "straights" were not considered queens. The label "homosexual" just didn't work so well on the Diné Nation.

I turned on the truck. "Your first husband taught you well, girlfriend." "Thanks, boyfriend." I, as a female, was "boy"; they, as males, were "girls." "The truck's fine. Let's go to Moon Shines." Nah, I thought, not there, even if it would be cooler. The summer before, we had frequently traveled just over the border to this bar. We'd grab some of the other queens and get beer on Sundays, since where we lived still had Sunday blue laws—you could buy a gun, but no alcohol or pantyhose. PA, a queen, was always game for a Sunday beer, and she'd often curl her eyelashes in the car mirror on the way over. I have never seen anyone put on liner with such a sure hand. Part of the fun for the queens was picking up straights; part of it was just surviving the bar.

The year before, PK and a few other queens had been at Moon Shines and gotten into a fight in the parking lot. Several of us went to the jail to bail them out, and by the next morning, a much sobered-up PK had regaled us with stories diced with double entendres. The cops had been teasing, "Where do we put you? We can't put you with the ladies; you're just too pretty, they'd get mad and beat you up. And we can't put you with the guys—why that wouldn't feel like jail at all." In booking and fingerprinting them, one cop had stroked PK's hand, "Oh, honey, let me just look at those beautiful fingers."

I was never really sure though that she had been okay, and how much of the joking was to hide the humiliation they no doubt encountered. Two summers ago, a queen momentarily left a large outdoor party to use the campground's outhouse. When she crawled back an hour and a half later, badly beaten, the queens had to loan her a shirt, a pair of pants, even shoes before taking her to the Indian Health Services emergency room.

But I had my own reasons for avoiding Moon Shines. I had been sick a few years back, and last year, my hair was growing in. It looked like an intentional buzz-cut, one-inch long all over, and nothing like the long hair I had in my driver's license photo. My baggy shirt had hidden the only other sign of femaleness. I sat down with my beer, and the owner disappeared into the back room. When she came back, she was pissed. "This here's a lady," she said waving my license at me, "and you're not that." The scene escalated quickly— several men circled around, and one or two said take it off and let's see what you are. I ducked out and grabbed my passport from the truck. The owner and I were both fuming, mostly at each other.

It was an odd scene. With the influx of Christianity, *nádleehí* have been less well received, and in the last century, there were a few, rare reports that some people let a hermaphroditic child die in infancy. Nowadays, many Diné feel that hermaphrodites are the only real *nádleehí*, and they are special, important people. But they dislike other *nádleehí*, the queens: these are scorned as "pretend" *nádleehí*, whose makeup and feminine mannerisms "went to extremes." To the owner of Moon Shines, I had been some Anglo version of a fake *nádleehí* with a fake ID.

When PK and MC got back, we iced down the beer for later that night. A blessed cloud had wandered overhead, and we imagined rain later. But this was mostly an excuse to leave our hot room. Still, if it did rain, we'd need to get over to PK's mother's house and back before the roads, made of fine wind-blown sand, turned to a slickness I had seen only in the Midwest's ice storms. Besides, she might have found the herb we'd need to get the snake out of the outhouse, and she'd definitely have something on hand for the ants.

I liked PK's mother. She was an herbalist and knew a wide array of the local plants, their uses, and how to prepare them ceremonially. Most Diné knew at least a few herbs, and at the flea markets on the Diné Nation, usually someone was selling their own packets of remedies. The herbalist is one of several kinds of Diné healers—there are also *hataalii*, or people that conduct the long ceremonials that can stretch on for days, and the diagnosticians. One of PK's aunts diagnosed by the trembling of her hand. It was a gift passed down along the female line, usually appearing in every other generation. In one family PK knew, a male queen was particularly talented at helping people figure out the cause of an illness by the ritual shaking of her hand.

When we greeted in Diné, PK's mother smiled at my Chicago accent. I continued, *"Diné bizaad bíhoosh'aah nahonitl'a,"* a convoluted way of saying, despite my efforts, I'm not very good at learning Diné. The statement was itself telling. I had to repeat it in En-

glish, and PK had to translate it, before anyone knew what I had said. PK's mother laughed and shrugged in a kind way that said, ah, well, we all try as best we can. She and PK talked a while, caught up. She asked PK about her first husband, the car mechanic, and PK said she'd heard that his marriage wasn't going so well. They were silent. PK's mother began again. "Remember what a good son-in-law he was?" "Yeah, I do and how you butchered that sheep for him when I first brought him to meet you." "We should do that again, maybe he would look at your dad's truck." PK smiled, but sadly. MC looked at the floor.

Later in the summer, PK and MC would split up, and PK would return to her first husband, while keeping two other "snags," or boyfriends, on the side. This time, though, the husband's family would not be so accepting, and the husband's younger sister would warn PK, "Remember that my brother is not your husband, even if his wife has left him." But having three lovers would work well for PK, and she and I would talk for hours about them, and whom she liked best that week.

We stayed and ate with PK's family, since the cloud was only a stray, lost from some larger storm up north. It would be months before any real rain would come. PK made the frybread dough, patted out the rounds, and cooked them in the lard, then helped her mother with the dishes. At a squaw dance the previous summer, PK had pointed out the queens at work with their female relatives. They were mixing the Bluebird flour with the baking powder, frying the dough, handing out the bread to the dancers and the families involved with the ceremonial. PK had warned me to stay in the car, since the squaw dance was part of the larger Enemyway ceremony. That night, the one-sung-over had needed protection from the ill-effects of Anglo influences, and I would be in the direct line of ceremonial power. Later in the evening, some of the queens had drifted away to the party beyond the fire's light, well outside of the ceremonial circle. I had sat in the car, wondering where PK was, wondering if she wanted me to leave so she'd have an excuse to catch a ride with some new guy. Maybe the concern about ceremonial power was just a way to ditch the anthropologist. Finally, though, I had waited for PK in the car; I'd heard enough stories about the power of ceremonials for healing and, for the unprotected, harm.

This land was PK's family allotment. The U.S. government holds all Native lands in a federal trust, meaning that the tribal governments can designate parcels for families, but these lands cannot be sold by the family or the tribe. PK had grown up here with eight brothers and sisters. When she was around eight years old, her parents had her sleep with her sisters instead of her brothers. She was recognized as a *nádleehí*—it didn't matter that she was not a hermaphrodite—because she changed back and forth between masculine and feminine.

PK began to learn what it meant to be a girl. She babysat her nieces and nephews, helped keep the house clean, cooked, and when her older sisters married and left, would help run the household. But unlike her sisters, she had a lot more freedom. When PK was about 12 or 13, her dad gave her $20 to enjoy a nearby intertribal powwow. She took off on Thursday with her brothers, hung out with friends, watched the dancers, snuck into a couple of movies, and by Monday, when the money had run out, hitched her own ride back home. There was no way that PK's sisters would have been allowed to do that.

Part of the difference between boys and girls lies with the responsibilities incumbent on Diné women. Not only will they birth the next generation, but they carry on their mother's clan, and with it the family's land allotment, grazing rights, and water usage. PK grew up knowing the weight of this, also.

Last summer, PK had told me about her relationship with a previous lover, and his wife. It seemed the wife had known all along about her husband and PK; in fact the wife and PK colluded to keep the husband/lover in line. She'd tell PK if any queens were over at the house; PK would tell her if he was eyeing other women. About a year after their wedding, the husband became fed up with the commitments of married life. PK had saved their marriage, though, telling the husband that he had to realize that girls are raised to fulfill a lot of expectations, to be there for the family, to make sure the kids do well, to make sure the clan keeps its property. She told the wife a story about a young kid getting $20 to go to the intertribal powwow. And that guys sometimes need to be 12 years old again.

Other queens, though, did not have this kind of familiarity with their husband's female wife. I knew this was an important relationship to PK, but it stood at such odds with others' experiences that I wondered what else this story conveyed. Was it, in part, PK's longing for her first husband, where the husband's wife would accept PK as part of their family? An ideal relationship pieced together in loneliness? Tough to know. Maybe this relationship was the exception; maybe, too, it was a way to reaffirm a *nádleehí*'s importance in society as a mediator between men and women.

In Diné Creation teachings, a *nádleehí* played a major role as an arbitrator, based in part on her/his ability to know both male and female sides. In the previous, lower world, a dispute had broken out between First Man and First Woman, and each had argued that his/her own gender was the more important. First Man grabbed the men and boys and headed over to the other side of the river. We'll see who's best, he'd yelled as they left. Yeah, we sure will, won't we, she had answered back.

Each side also had several *nádleehí*—on the men's side the male *nádleehí* took care of the male infants, the cooking, and so forth; on the women's side, the female *nádleehí* hunted and helped plant the corn. Most accounts say the men succeeded and the women failed. But those were accounts told by men to men; women tell the story differently. It's like the differences between PK's and other queens' descriptions: we tell our stories, in part, based on what's going on in our lives, on what gives us the most meaning at the time.

On opposite shores of the river, both First Man's and First Woman's sides held out for four years, but, finally, a *nádleehí* stepped in to mediate between the two sides. If they didn't reunite, she cautioned, there would be no more children, no one to carry on the traditions. Everything would come to an end. And the situation was grim. People were running into the river to get to a husband or a wife, and dying before they could get to their spouse on the opposite shore.

It was a story that many queens knew. It told them that they had a place in Diné society; it made sense of why a young child called "son" was more like her sisters than her brothers. The story also said it was good to know both sides, since without that, humankind was doomed. In the *nádleehí*'s role as a go-between, the queens could explain why they were the ones in whom female coworkers confided a recent heartbreak, or to whom men turned to confess an affair. And, to some of the older Diné, it confirmed that "real" *nádleehí* were both male and female, and that these were the *nádleehí* that mattered. The universe is a dance between the male/female pairs of sun/moon, sky/earth, day/night; because the *nádleehí* is this balanced pairing, she or he will make sure the dance continues.

I slipped away from the after-dinner conversation—they were chatting in Diné and probably wanted some privacy. I walked around the family place. The house was small; I wondered how they had managed with eight kids. A ways off from the house was the corral, where PK's mom had butchered a sheep for a son-in-law, and butchered again when PK was drinking too much. They too had done an Enemyway ceremonial to protect her from the destructive forces of Anglo society. Those years had been a hard time for the family. PK had left for college, hoping to get away from her wilder days in high school, and start again. She had shared an apartment with a woman; they had ended up in bed and become lovers, but eventually PK found it suffocating. It didn't matter that PK understood that a woman would expect a sense of responsibility from a lover. At that point, PK wanted to answer to no one.

She hooked up with a couple of guys; neither of them worked out. She dropped out of school, then life.

The ceremonial had helped, at least for a while. In the last year, though, PK had lost her job and wrecked her truck and was thinking of changing careers entirely. Maybe she'd continue to stay on the family land and work. But then again, maybe this coming home was part of the healing begun when her mother butchered the sheep for the *hataalii,* who would place a shield around her troubled child.

Before heading home, we hooked the truck up to PK's parents' battery to recharge their small generator. They had been without a refrigerator since their battery had died. We drove around for a while, charging the truck back up, talking about nothing in particular. We stopped for gas, and the usual sexual punning ensued. "Boyfriend, you fill it up, you lesbians are good at finding the hole." I thought of a reply, something about frigidity and getting the ice, but said nothing. By this time of night, the queens' sexual bantering had become tedious.

We drank a few beers outside, waiting for our one-room house to cool down enough to sleep. We swapped a few stories about our families. Of the queens I had met, only PK was actively encouraged to learn both masculine and feminine sides. Many of the queens had only partial support from their families, usually their mother, and some had been kicked out. PK's supportive home seemed to be the exception. The meaning of the *nádleehí* in the Creation teaching also varied among the queens; several felt it really didn't matter in the present day. It seemed that the identity of "queen" I had learned last summer just wasn't as consistent, particularly when you looked at it in the confines of daily life. There wasn't a single "queen experience" that would define all queens. Yet, the queens still knew who each other was.

Maybe definition was more of a concern in Anglo culture. Hadn't PK suggested as much the previous summer? "Out here," she'd said, "you don't have the groups you have in the Anglo [cultures]. Time and events and classification and categories, that's how you Anglos try to put everything. You get so caught up, you don't see people as humans responding to situations." The queens differed with each other, and I differed even further, yet the dominant society would group us as the same simply because we all preferred same-sex sexual partners. But our real commonality this summer was having enough water, gas, ice, and shade.

Next morning. We had left the herbs for the ants at PK's mother's house, but the ants had remained outside anyway. I caught the scent of sage again in the morning air and found a new sagebrush to substitute for the outhouse. We never made it to get water yesterday, so I'd have to wait again for coffee. Later, I figured we'd be off to the spring, and I would help wash PK's hair, and she mine. She would tease me about my unshaven legs; I would smile at her plucking her facial hair in the truck's rear view mirror. It was getting hot again. I looked for the broom and dustpan and swept up the sand that had drifted in during the night. I swung the door open wide again and, stepping out of its way, returned the red dust to the desert. It banged against the doorframe. "Good morning, girls."

SUGGESTED READINGS

Jacobs, Sue Ellen, Wesley Thomas, and Sabine Lang, eds. (1997). *Two-Spirit People: Native American Gender Identity, Sexuality and Spirituality.* Urbana: University of Illinois Press.

Nanda, Serena, ed. (2000). *Gender Diversity: Cross-Cultural Variations.* Prospect Heights, Ill.: Waveland Press.

12

Sitting on the "Outers" with the Girls, Watching the Boys Play

Susan Peake

University of Melbourne

Although division between the sexes is based on societies' recognition of sexual difference, gender is not so much based on physiology as on doing, being, playing, and looking the part of male or female. This is what anthropologists refer to as gender identity, and it varies from culture to culture.

The history of Australia is the history of a masculine country, where in its early European-derived origins, men were thrown together, to rely on each other without the company of women, who were in a minority. In Australia the dominant form of European-based masculinity in male adolescence and beyond is centered on the activities of sport and mateship. *Mateship* is a peculiarly Australian term that means more then friendship because of its association with masculinity and more than "buddy," which is often used to imply informality. The term is an integral aspect of Australian nationalism and today is probably reserved for male groups such as the football club, where the traditional values of dependency are crucial to survival of the unit. It is particularly important for the Australian male not to stand out in any way as this is what Australian mateship is founded upon—being a good bloke and feeling equal to, and not above, others. It is this ethos of the "equality of the group" that results in Australians celebrating the reluctant hero (Waltzing Matilda) and the failed attempt (Gallipolis).

There are other accessories in Australia that confer masculine status such as the peer group, the girlfriend, and the bright future. All this was taken away from Blue Boy as the result of a single event. He lost a leg in an accident and for him this signified a loss of masculine status and an inability to belong. He was no longer normal, no longer one of the boys. Although many biologists would argue that it is the sexual characteristics of a body that make one male or female and determine how one thinks or acts like a male or a female, it was the change to the *outside* appearance of his body and his inability to perform that made Blue Boy feel "like a girl." His sexual capacity as a male remained the same yet he still felt like he had undergone a "sex change." So it was a change in his body's appearance and what it could do that made Blue Boy change from an "active, fit, healthy, rugby player" to the parody of a "pathetic, lame, disfigured, scarred, (and) ugly" individual. Moreover, weakness, helplessness, dependency, vulnerability, and sexual passivity are characteristics associated with being female in this society. Blue Boy believed in his early years that you *couldn't* be disabled and be a man.

As you read the following story about the relationship between changes in the body and gender identity, consider the following questions:

1. From the text pick out as many ways as you can in which you think Blue Boy lost his masculine identity.
2. Do you think it is still accurate to say that it is mainly women who are overly concerned with appearance? What about in your country: do men also do things to make themselves look more attractive and visible? (For example, do your male friends also watch their weight?)
3. What are the dominant expressions of masculinity in your country or culture? Are they also centered on sport and mateship? Can you think of one that is not based on sport? What are the values of this group?
4. Do you think Blue Boy's relatives were correct when they said, "They can change you on the outside, but you will always be the same on the inside"?
5. What specific changes to the body would have an effect on gender identity and the sense of self? How would these changes differ for men compared to women? How might attitudes about changes in the body differ from culture to culture?

It is only in Australia, I reflected, that a stationmaster would deliberately mislead his frantic passengers as a joke, telling them they were on the wrong platform and that they would likely miss their train. I wasn't amused. Sitting in one of the comfy seats of the suburban train out of Brisbane, I thought of my meeting with Blue Boy. The sleepy bayside suburb I arrived at is only 40 minutes out of the city, but it seems like a century away in terms of facilities. At the station, I had to decide how to get to our meeting place. A polite but firm stationmaster gave me instructions: "There's no point in ringing for a taxi. The last person had to wait two hours for one. It is quicker to walk. It's only fifteen minutes away." Forty-five minutes later I arrived sweltering from the walk in the subtropical sun. I knocked at the single-story house with a characteristically large garden, an icon in Australia, and waited. On seeing Blue Boy, his natural beauty, calm manner, and fit physique struck me again. His family still called him by that name even though he was now almost 30 years old. Blue Boy, a young man who believes with a passion that he was born to play rugby, lost one of his legs in a motorbike accident at the age of 16. Along with his leg he lost all sense of his masculine identity and this is what this story is about.

THE ACCIDENT

Maneuvering around the small kitchen on crutches, he deftly made a cup of Earl Grey tea for me as we talked about the accident that changed his life. He talked about his rugby and the mates that formed his world in his youth. I could feel the anticipation he must have felt that Friday night as he set out to meet the other players for a night of "fun and cruising chicks" just like any normal 16-year-old who is just discovering girls. The next morning the school bus would pick them up for their regular Saturday rugby game for the second 15s.

"I was on a motorbike," he told me. "I was licensed but the licensing system was a bit raw back in those days where I walked into the transport department the day after I turned 15 and walked out with both my *Open Car* and my *Open Bike* license. And that was after I had taken the instructor round the block, went through a give way sign, and then did an illegal park. So I came out with both open licenses the day after I turned 15 but with no formal training. So it was your 007 License, a license to kill. And this (the time of the accident) was only 12 months after that, still with very limited car experience on the road. I had been on a bike all my life, on a farm, but on the road it's different . . ."

I felt I was there, watching, as he described the accident. He met up with his friends on the highway and seeing them on the other side of the road, he proceeded to do a "U" turn so that he could join them at the rest area on the other side of the road. It wasn't until he was half way across the road that he caught a glimmer of white out of the corner of his eye. It was a speeding car. The next thing he knew his right leg was caught between the wheel and the wheel arch and the bike was actually underneath the tires, which were slightly elevated. The driver panicked. Instead of getting out of the car to come and check on him, he struck in reverse and backed up, with Blue Boy still attached to the car. That was probably when most of the damage was done. People from roadside assistance arrived and cut off his clothes.

In the time immediately after the accident, Blue Boy told me he wasn't overly worried about his situation because he was accident prone; he had already had stitches and broken bones in almost every part of his body. In fact, when in the back of the ambulance he actually joked about his situation. "So, what's the story?" he asked. "What, have I got a little bit cut-about? How many stitches, about 20 or 30?" The person attending him replied, "Yeah, mate, at least that." That was when Blue Boy realized that he was seriously injured, that it wasn't just a matter of some stitches. I reflected on risky behavior and joking with the boys and other rules of young masculinity.

Blue Boy remembered little after that. The next morning he woke up and discovered that his left leg was broken in a couple of places, though they hadn't actually identified the places where the breaks had occurred. His right leg was broken in five places and he had a laceration from the hip to the ankle. All he could see were the pins stuck through the femur and down through his lower limb. His leg was suspended in a pulley system and a large metal cage surrounded the entire leg. Because of the bandages all he could see were his toes, which had no sensation. His upper body was untouched.

He had been in the hospital 11 days when someone from the hospital staff came and approached him with a consent form. They needed permission to amputate. He recalled the scene in the hospital: "The doctors came around that morning, you know how they do, and they have a lot of young doctors that they are showing, 'Look, this is our patient, and he can't wiggle his toes and we are going to cut his leg off,' sort of thing. It came out like that, and I am just absolutely shocked, tactless as hell . . ." This was the first time that he had been aware that amputation would be necessary.

Shortly after, he went through the operation and in the recovery room tried to come to grips with why he was there. He recalled the words of his doctor who had told him they would try to save as much of his leg as possible. He ran his hand down his leg to where it finished at his femur, the middle of his thigh. At that point he passed out.

Back in the ward with his parents, he had the curtains drawn around the bed. He recalls crying for a couple of hours. "Here I am," he told me, "16, lying on the bed, and all I can see is this big soccer ball at the end of my hand. And that's where my leg was. This gap—from here down to the end of my foot. It's missing and from there it is just like a big story of what I am not going to be able to do. Rugby's gone for me and even though I was playing softball and everything, rugby was still the main focus. There was the idea also, that flashed through my mind, that I am not going to be so attractive and I am not going to be as marketable in the workplace, like the careers I was chasing at the time as well. There were so many thoughts in such a short period of time."

In the aftermath of the operation, Blue Boy's relatives sent him cards with sentiments like "they can change your outside but they'll never change your inside. You are always beautiful on the inside no matter what you are."

I asked Blue Boy if he believed these sentiments.

"The more and more I got (cards), the more I started to turn towards that idea. And then someone brought in an article for me. It was about Brian Froggit. He is a Kiwi marathon runner and he is amputated at the hip and he was running with this prosthetic limb. It was about a five-page story in this glossy mag and I thought wow, there *is* opportunity. I didn't want to pursue it immediately, but it gave me relief to know that life really wasn't over yet. There really could be something down the track. I remember that I used to go to a pool nearby where I used to live and jump off the diving board and run around the pool with my friends and I remember dreaming, these things really stick in my mind. I remember dreaming while I was still in that hospital, I was on the diving board, wearing boardies (baggy shorts) that covered my stump and me fitting in with everybody else. Like there are no dramas and I am jumping off the diving board and hopping around the pool and being normal, so to speak. It was quite bizarre. I really do remember that."

"It was like a future vision," I commented.

For the next month the hospital prepared his leg for the prosthetic (false leg) that was to be part of his new body. They did this by filing the end of the bone and stitching up the stump to form the shape of a cone so that the prosthetic limb could be worn. It was at this stage that he decided not to go back to school because he didn't want to be the disabled one there. He didn't want to be the one who was the center of attention and the object of pity. Although he had support from friends, parents, and other family members, he felt it was not enough. He said he had developed "a complex" and was not yet able to overcome it.

"Your complex was about being different?" I asked.

"Absolutely! Absolutely!"

"About being noticeable."

"Yeah! Sticking out like a sore thumb."

THE AFTERMATH

As Blue Boy related his story to me, I tried to imagine what a devastating effect this all must have had on a 16-year-old who was just starting to form ideas of who he was. Becoming vulnerable to the stares, looks, and whispers of others, for example, must be a terrible blow to the masculinity of any recently disabled male. Women are the ones who are traditionally seen as living through their bodies and are thus used to being looked at and are used to practicing a sort of policing of how their bodies appear. However, awareness of being looked at and the need to be constantly aware of how one looks to others is a new experience for many recently disabled men, as it was for Blue Boy. In fact it was a totally new experience for him to have to pay so much attention to his body. Yet for Blue Boy, disabled people had always seemed somehow extra-invisible. He continued to explain to me:

> If I had looked around and I saw a group of people playing with someone with a disability, well, I just basically wouldn't see them. They weren't in my world. Also, being from an isolated town, I did have that attitude that people with disabilities were second rate. I was a staunch rugby union boy and I never gave it a thought about what they were going through or how difficult their life must be. It was just that they were leprechauns and (my attitude was) *leave them to their own devices.* You know, they don't come into my life at all.

SEXUALITY AND DISABILITY

I agree with Blue Boy that disabled people do have a kind of invisibility. They are also seen as sexually neutral, as having no sex at all. I have noticed that public buildings in Australia have three categories when it comes to providing toilets, male, female, and disabled. It's as if being disabled means to belong to one neutral and sexless category. I also have noticed that many movies that portray disabled men seem to suggest that being disabled is synonymous with impotence or sexual impairment. Just think of *Lady Chatterley's Lover* or some of the movies about heroes returning from the Vietnam War. Only last week we watched a rerun of the 1997 Spanish movie *Live Flesh,* which featured a paraplegic police officer who had been injured in the line of duty. It is a modernised portrayal of disabled masculinity as there are scenes where he actively plays wheelchair basketball and makes passionate love to his wife, albeit in unusual circumstances. Yet the movie climaxes with his wife's eventual succumbing to a man who has all his limbs intact.

Blue Boy and I were sipping our second cup of tea as we talked of the years following the accident, those years when he tried to normalise his life and become part of society again. He told me he had great difficulty with his new identity and couldn't allow people to know his "secret." It was in the aftermath of his accident that he felt he must "jump the fence," and, in the process, deliberately let go of his former mates. He was now disabled and could only "sit on the outers with the girls and watch the boys play." He thought of himself as unattractive, just as he thought of all disabled people that way.

He told me that he tried to hide the fact that he was missing a leg by wearing long trousers. He tried to "look normal," only letting down his guard when he felt that people were comfortable with disabilities. "Some women are not totally comfortable with disability," he added.

The issue of women and sex were of great concern. He had been a virgin when the accident occurred but lost his virginity "in the back seat of a Peugeot 404" soon after he had lost his leg. At this point he was still "blue line bandaging" as he called it. He refers here to extra-high-performance pressure bandages that would have been used to reduce swelling and fluid accumulation in his limb, before everything could heal over. It would have been a painful process to wear a prosthesis while still in this stage. One can only imagine the degree of pain it must have taken to feign normalcy. He told me that in losing his virginity and in meeting a number of women over a six-month period, he began to build his confidence. He came to realize that they perceived him as a more normal person than he perceived himself to be. "And the more women I was, er, meeting," he said, "the more confident I was becoming and confident not only about my disability but about my own beauty, as a person."

I asked how he let people know he was missing a leg. "Did you come straight out and say, 'I've got no leg, would you like a beer?' How did you do it?"

"Well," he chuckled, "it happened in many different ways. A lot of the time I wouldn't say anything and they would wake up in the morning and they would see a leg on the floor. Oh, it happened a couple of times. Other times, women are good at doing groundwork and even though I think I have just met a person—they've already done the groundwork on me through my friends, colleagues, or whatever."

RESTORATION

One of the transitional phases that helped him to go from "one spectrum to the other" was his parents' move from a colder climate to the beautiful, tropical town of Cairns on Australia's eastern seaboard. Cairns, situated in close proximity to the Barrier Reef, is very hot. In the warmer climate he was forced into wearing shorts and thus revealing his stump and this was a turning point for him. At first it caused him some concern, as he was worried about people's reaction, in case he "scared the heck out of them, looking at your stump." Instead he found that mostly the reaction was one of curiosity rather than horror. However, "in my mind I was a freak in a show."

It was at this stage that he was going to his first race meet in swimming. This was another turning point for him, as it forced him to take his artificial leg off in public. At the swimming meets he began to "meet all these other wonderful people with disabilities." He came to realize that his life was "pretty sweet" in comparison with the lives of others. This realization was brought home to him when he met a girl in a wheelchair whom he found very beautiful. He thought to himself, "If she's beautiful and she's in a chair, it gives me assurance that I can still be attractive with a disability." If he could be attracted to a woman more disabled than himself, then why couldn't an able-bodied person be attracted to him, a person with a relatively minor disability?

He came to realize "how lucky (he) was" and that his disability was not as severe as that of so many others. Seeing people with cerebral palsy, for example, who appeared to accept themselves and their bodies taught him to accept himself. From such people he learned to concentrate on his abilities and not his disabilities. He started to see things differently, which "brought (him) back into the paddock." He became part of a team environment, going from one side of the playing field to the other. He became part of the in-crowd as he repositioned himself and started to perceive himself to be "back up the top end of the scale." He saw himself as being "normal again . . . just one of the crowd." He became an extrovert, "using and abusing" his disability.

Blue Boy told me about the way in which swimming became more and more a part of his life. He was invited to tour on the lecture circuit, inspiring people with stories about how he changed his life around. He was awarded the title of Developing Paralympian of the Year. As he talked I reflected on my own experiences of seeing him in action. His story climaxes for me at the Paralympic Games in late 2000. I flew across to Sydney for the last three days of the competitions with my son, Josh. On our first visit to the outer Sydney suburb where the games were held, we walked through Kings Cross, an area of Sydney noted for its less respectable citizens. It was growing dark as we wove our way through myriad crowds to the specially built, double-decker trains that carried us off into the night. Darkness was an asset as the first object we became aware of as we neared the custom-built site was the Olympic Flame—an enormous structure that glowed like a beacon to guide us into the satellite city. The complex was huge but organized like a scene from Orwell's *Brave New World,* with loudspeakers directing its citizens to every corner of its little empire. It is hard to convey the atmosphere of a prestigious event like the games—excitement, electricity, awe, otherworldly, a sense of being there when important world events occur. And there was Blue Boy, in the midst of it all, in the impressive new swimming complex with the high-tech overflow system. I had the proverbial lump in my throat as I watched him swim to three Olympic medals. Josh stated that he is thinking of going in for the next games. He is not sure which event yet.

As we spoke, the focus of Blue Boy's story changed. He is no longer a youth of 16 faced with a loss of identity, nor a competitive athlete buoyed on by his own power and his ability to change his life around. His leg was giving him plenty of pain that day, and this was reflected in his somber tone of speech. As a young man of 30, he is now faced with some life decisions that any person of his age would have to confront. He is entering a promising relationship and a new job, but yet he still holds fears for the future. With an unreliable body, commitment to the needs of others, be it partners or bosses, causes problems for him:

> It is like signing an agreement where I am compelled to be doing certain things for the rest of my life when I know that when my leg buggers up I don't want to be going to work and I won't be able to provide for my family as in the case of working six days a week. I get really stressed out with it from time to time and it would be nice if down the track, if I don't want to get in a relationship with a lady and my leg has played such a part it's stressing me out to the max and I want, maybe, to leave this world and get away from everybody and go overseas and go to Amsterdam and shoot up and die happily ever after. I always want that escape avenue. It comes down to the physical, like it is pretty hard walking around on those things (crutches) all the time and I always want options. At the moment I am

working eight hours a day and it is painful for the whole eight hours. I don't want to be going through that for the rest of my life. You know, I would rather take the soft option, which is what I did at the very first part when I took the apprenticeship instead of going back to school. I still want to have a soft option in the background.

"So the soft option is literally opting for an easier life?"

"Exactly, I would like the option of just chilling out and maybe just going on the dole and smoking cones everyday and watching the midday movie. It would never be the fact that I am missing a leg that would stop me from getting into a relationship and living happily ever after. It comes down to the financial security—the whole thing. I am obligated to doing the nine to fives."

"So that's what being a man is?"

"Absolutely! Yeah, sitting on the sidelines with the girls watching the boys is a pretty good depiction of where I am. I don't have the openness and the mind-set to be part of the woman group and I don't have the masculinity to be on the man's side out on the field playing rugby and you know you don't belong to either group so where do you belong? It's a gray area. But you try and adapt and be part of both groups and different areas of people's lives. Well, in my talks in general, I tell them that what I have achieved through swimming, medals, rewards, scholarships, sponsorships, accolades, and the press and everything—I always say that I would give it away tomorrow to have my leg back and be on that football field for one more game of rugby."

"Why?"

"Because I still long for it. I watch it on TV and I put myself on the field. It's something that I was born to do—to play rugby. I feel that I've been cheated from it. I've been cheated out."

"So it's more than a sport for you. It's a way of being."

"Absolutely—a way of being. And rugby is not just about sport. It's about being one of the boys too. It's all about the aftermath, having a few beers with the lads and belonging—and making great friendships from that."

I couldn't help hoping his leg would be less painful tomorrow.

SUGGESTED READINGS

Connell, Robert William. (1995). *Masculinities.* Australia: Allen and Unwin.

Gerschick, Thomas J., and Adam Stephen Miller. (1995). "Coming to Terms," in *Men's Health and Illness,* ed. D. Sabo and D. Gordon, pp. 183–204, London: Sage.

PART V

Social Status

Photo © Michael S. Yamashita/Corbis.

When we talk about social status, we are usually referring to how much power and privilege people enjoy in society. Each individual in a society has a certain degree of access to resources and operates under a particular set of restraints based on where he or she fits into the social structure. This may be accorded on the basis of age, sex, wealth, or other criteria. The higher the person's status, the more likely he or she will be to take advantage of resources, whether they be economic or social.

The status a person enjoys in society can be either **achieved** through life's accomplishments or **ascribed** at birth based on characteristics over which a person has no control. These two sources of status can be found in societies both large and small, modernized or traditional. In traditional societies, status can be achieved via the recognition of ability or the attainment of age and knowledge, or ascribed on the basis of sex or kinship. In most modern societies, characteristics such as age, gender, ethnicity, religious affiliation, perceived sexual orientation, or perceived "race" might place limits on the status a person can achieve. Alternatively, in societies where ascribed status is the greatest determinant of a person's rank, we can increasingly find examples of people achieving a higher position through their own efforts or particular talents.

In modern industrialized societies, people are born into various **social classes,** large groups based on economic or other factors. The social class of one's parents will largely determine the neighborhood in which she or he lives, the schools she or he attends, the organizations to which he or she belongs. It may place severe restrictions on whom a person can marry. While many people will remain in the class to which they are born, there is often the possibility of moving to another class through one's educational or creative endeavors, or through personal achievements. The **caste** system, which is a form of class system found in India and other countries, provides an example of a system of ascribed status. People born into a particular caste can only live in certain places, do certain kinds of work, and associate with and marry certain people.

Societies with large populations commonly are organized in a hierarchical structure with many different social classes. Distinctions among these groups or classes can be based on occupational differences or on the ability of one group to control another, economically and sometimes even physically. The distinctions might be based on achieved or on ascribed statuses. Few societies in this world now are truly "classless," although occasionally societies do appear to be **egalitarian,** where members are accorded statuses based primarily on age and sex only. Systems offering basic social equality were once prevalent among hunting and gathering societies, and can still be seen in some herding societies where populations are small. In these societies great variation in power, prestige, and wealth generally do not exist.

Throughout the world, colonization, globalization, and the changing world economy have changed how social status is determined. While ascribed characteristics might still be very important for a person's power, prestige, and privilege, new opportunities for education and jobs might seriously affect the traditional order. In other words, a person of a lower social status might find opportunities that could cause him to outrank people who were of a traditionally higher status. Harsh economic conditions also might accentuate the differences between groups or even transform the way people are ranked in their societies.

In the following articles we see the wide variety of societies in the world, from the most complex, urban society with rigid social classes to more egalitarian societies that have made little distinction among their members. These articles illustrate that changing conditions in the world can certainly affect the place of individuals in the social order. We also learn that governments attempt at times to "reengineer" social status, as was the case in socialism when everyone, in theory, was equal. Government intervention in the ways of reckoning social status was not always successful. The caste system is still very much alive in the Indian subcontinent, and the great socialist republics of the communist era have disintegrated.

The first article places Riaz, a man who makes his living driving for visiting academics, in the caste and class system of Pakistan. Linda Walbridge shows the large social gaps that exist in Pakistan and how some people, such as Riaz, attempt to at least partially bridge these gaps.

Sherylyn Briller's article takes us on a visit to the tent (*ger*) home of a wealthy elder, Tsengel, in the mountains of Mongolia. Through the man's words and his demonstrations of hospitality, we learn about the growing social distinctions of a herding community in this post-socialist state.

In the final article, Lisa Cliggett shows us through the experience of a woman named Mutinda how extreme poverty has disrupted the social fabric of life in a community in southern Zambia. Those life accomplishments that once gave elderly women a high status in their society are of little consequence when people are struggling simply to survive.

Other articles relating to social status:

Eliasa and the Kwacha Video Coach by Pamela A. Maack

Sunday Dinner at Hanka's by Julianna Acheson

Green Earrings: A Widow's Tale by Sarah Lamb

Living the Chulla Vida by Jason Pribilsky

13

Driving the Memsahib

Linda S. Walbridge
Indiana University

Pakistan was created in 1947 when the predominantly Muslim provinces of India broke away from the rest of India, where most of the people are Hindu. Both India and Pakistan rid themselves of British rule, which had continued for about 200 years. Although the vast majority of Pakistanis are Muslim and believe in the equality of all people before God, they are still affected by the caste system that we associate with India. In the caste system, people are born into particular roles and places in society, and, as such, have to behave in ways prescribed for those roles. Superimposed on the Indian caste system was the rigid British class system, which had a strong racial component as well. A white woman in the Indian subcontinent (which now consists of India, Pakistan, and Bangladesh) had a very privileged existence, whether or not she came from a "high class" position in her own society and whether or not the person deferring to her was of high caste or not.

Today in Pakistan, people still do not marry and freely intermingle with people who have either higher or lower social stations. While these restrictions are not so rigid in Pakistan, we see in Walbridge's article that her driver, Riaz, a man born and raised in Lahore, a city of about three million people, was limited in his choice of occupation. His ascribed status also prevented him from mixing freely with people of a higher status. However, through personal initiative and talent, he has found a position of importance that professional drivers in Pakistan rarely achieve, by working for Western academics living in Pakistan. While to upper-class Pakistanis he remains simply "a driver," to his employers from the United States he is indispensable. Will his children, whom Riaz is determined to educate in the best possible schools, be able to escape the social confinement their father faced and achieve a higher status? If they do improve their lot in life, will they be willing to accept those at the lower levels of society as equals?

As you read, consider the following questions:

1. What evidence can you find that the caste system affects Riaz's life? What evidence is there that his life is affected by a social class system? How do these two systems interact?
2. How did the caste system affect the lives of Walbridge's students in Lahore?
3. Why was Riaz so concerned that his employers look good and behave well in public?
4. Overall, what things do you think Riaz and other members of this society value most highly? How do these values differ from those in your own society?
5. What is it that the Fulbrighters give Riaz that other employers might not. Why?

Riaz, my husband's driver, met me at the airport in Lahore bearing flowers. I was joining my Fulbrighter husband John in Pakistan after spending four months in Indonesia on my own Fulbright grant. Fulbright scholars from the United States receive grants that allow them to spend up to a year in another country teaching or doing research. Riaz was very familiar with this program, as he had already worked for other Fulbrighters.

On the way home, Riaz was silent, which surprised me since my husband's e-mails to me had been full of tales of Riaz. After the shooting of four Americans in Karachi, for example, Riaz had tried to convince John that the guards (*chokidars*) who stood in front of the house night and day should be carrying machine guns to protect him.

By the second day, Riaz was selecting clothes for me in a boutique specializing in beautiful, designer *shalwar qameez*, the national dress of Pakistan consisting of pajama-like pants and a long tunic. He had decided that I was, in his words, a "real" American— someone who looked upon him as an employee, not a servant. In a society where the Hindu caste system is still apparent in spite of centuries of egalitarian Islam, this was significant. Soon we were on joking terms—that is, when we were alone or just with his family or mine. When others were around, he was the epitome of the discreet servant. He always called me "madam." Odd, how I had never thought of myself as a "madam." Riaz considered "madam" to be a more modern expression than "memsahib," which is how I was more commonly addressed. The term *memsahib* came into use when British women joined their husbands in India during the period when the British ruled the subcontinent. The men were addressed as "sahib," sir, the women as "memsahib." Today the British occupiers are gone, but much of the old social structure remains. Thus, a European or American woman living in the subcontinent would automatically belong to an elite, and this elite—along with anyone else who had any extra money at all—was expected to employ people of lower status as servants. They are the people who clean and cook and garden. Servants and people on the street always use deferential terms in addressing those with higher social positions. The term *madam* could be considered as deferential as memsahib, but, often when Riaz used it, it had an ironic tone, as in "Madam, if you had listened to me . . ."

Riaz was born in Lahore to a family that had moved from the village a few decades ago. Riaz's father owned and operated a variety of shops over the years. A strict man and devoutly religious, he was keen on educating his four sons and three daughters and making sure that they all married "well." With 10 years of schooling and some knowledge of English, Riaz was better educated than his parents, and he, in turn, was going to make sure that his four children were better educated than he and his wife, Beena, who had nine years of schooling.

Riaz, his parents, his wife and children, his unmarried sister, and his two unmarried brothers live on a narrow brick street in a section of the city that spans the whole social class system. His home has a painted door leading into a pleasant courtyard with rooms surrounding it where the various members of the household live. Riaz, Beena, and their four children occupy one of these rooms. There is a large bed, a couple of cupboards for storing their belongings, and Beena's sewing machine. His next-door neighbors, whose lives are more typical of the neighborhood, have no such courtyard. To enter their house, you have to go through a rusted metal door that leads into a narrow hallway that is more like an alley. In the house itself are two small living/sleeping areas where grandparents, parents, and seven children make do. A couple of streets away are large new modern houses—referred to as "white houses"—the houses that physicians, lawyers, and more prosperous military officers have built for

themselves. Poorer neighborhoods fit in between the wealthier planned neighborhoods like tree roots twining among boulders. On streets such as Riaz's live the servants who work at the "white houses." Riaz lives on Street No. 1, only a couple of streets away from Street No. 7 where we lived. But the two streets seemed to be worlds apart. While our neighborhood was posh by any standards, the Fulbrighter house is the most humble of the homes in the area, which makes our status a bit difficult to calculate. It can only be explained on the basis that we are "Fulbrighters."

When Riaz was 21 years old, he announced to his father that he was going to marry Beena, a girl a year younger than he whom he had met in school and fallen in love with. Without waiting to win over the families, the two eloped. Riaz's father was not happy with this marriage because he had not arranged it and because he comes from the Syed caste; that is, he and his children are descended from the Prophet Muhammad. He strongly believes that a Syed should only marry another Syed and Beena does not come from this caste. While it took only about a year for Riaz's father to find enough forgiveness to be able to talk with his son again, Beena's father would have no contact with the couple for almost 10 years. Certainly Riaz was not a very promising husband for Beena. Pretty, talented in domestic arts, and with some schooling, she could have married someone of a higher status than Riaz, who, in those days, drove a rickshaw, a very inexpensive way to travel around the city. A rickshaw in Pakistan is a sort of three-wheeled motorcycle with a boxy little cab holding the driver and three passengers. The driver sits in the front seat and the passengers, clutching the bar that separates the driver's section from theirs, sit precariously in the back. In order to conserve petrol, the rickshaws, which zip around Lahore at all hours of the day and night, have no mufflers, and their roar can be deafening. But Riaz did not want to sit in a shop all day like his father and his elder brother. He liked the activity that came with providing transportation for others. However, driving a rickshaw did not provide enough income for his growing family, and he found himself sleepless from the ringing in his ears caused by the rickshaw's two-cycle engine.

Then, one day, his luck changed. He found a job as a personal driver when he was approached by an American Fulbrighter, Andy, who hired him on the spot. Andy commissioned Riaz to buy a car, and eventually allowed Riaz to buy the car on easy terms. This chance encounter changed Riaz's life. He was now a "permanent" driver, with his own car, a drastic improvement in his social standing. He soon began to identify himself as the "Fulbrighter driver." After Andy's year in Pakistan ended, Riaz showed up at the door of the rented Fulbright house to introduce himself to the newest occupants, handing his prospective customers the letters of recommendation he was accumulating. By the time my husband arrived in September 1997, Riaz was very much established as the head Fulbrighter driver, unofficially recognized as such by the Fulbright office in Islamabad.

TO BE A FULBRIGHTER DRIVER

Riaz's main duty was to safely negotiate his way among the cars, trucks, rickshaws, horses, donkeys, and brahma bull carts, herds of water buffalo, and the other wonders that clog the streets of Lahore to take his Fulbrighters to the libraries, universities, markets, and expatriate hangouts of the city. This meant that he must know every part of Lahore thoroughly and never forget where a place was after having driven to it once. But he became much more than that: an unpolished Jeeves who runs the lives of his wealthy, incompetent employers.

If the house's water pump was broken, which it frequently was, Riaz would be there to fix it. When he decided that we did not have an adequate television antenna on our house, he took it upon himself to install a new antenna, which he purchased on our behalf. He simply handed the bill for the antenna over to us to pay. He was always on time to take us places, except when he decided we were arriving someplace too early, in which case he would simply come for us later. He would insist that we not change too many dollars at once if the exchange rate was not in our favor and he would bargain ruthlessly on our behalf for even the most minor purchase. This latter practice annoyed the shopkeepers, who were in the habit of giving a commission to drivers who kept their mouths shut. But he would never take these commissions. He was a "permanent driver" and worked for the Fulbrighters, not the shopkeepers. This was a point of pride.

His status as permanent driver in addition to his extracurricular roles gave him the power to carry out additional duties; ones that he relished. For example, if our cooks or the housekeeper did not show up or did not do what he considered a satisfactory job, he chided them and ensured that they carried out their duties in a more acceptable fashion. After all, he was the one who had found them their jobs in the first place, so he saw it as his responsibility to keep them in line. If the security company had sent a new *chokidar,* he took it upon himself to interrogate the man to see if he understood his duties properly and then to check with the other *chokidars* to see if this man was honest. He told them where he wanted the guardhouse set up and in-

structed one of the *chokidars* to find a shotgun so that he could accompany me on one of my research excursions to a religious gathering that he considered dangerous. He was extremely protective of us and flaunted his role as protector, thereby enhancing his status in the eyes of those who were lower on the pecking order. We regularly found one of the local hangers-on in the neighborhood washing and dusting Riaz's car. When we asked about this, Riaz said that he was "training" the man. As payment for the car cleaning, Riaz would explain how "things were done."

In exchange for the multiple services he provided his employers, Riaz expected certain things in return. Among the reasons why he liked working for Fulbrighters was that they tended to be more generous in their pay than even far wealthier Pakistanis. But aside from his pay, which in fairness was not that great when one took into consideration that he paid for gas and maintenance, he wanted other things from us. For example, he wanted us to appear to be worthy employers. While he was particularly fond of my husband and the former Fulbrighter, Andy, who had helped him purchase his car, he shook his head in dismay at their appearance. While I dressed in stylish Pakistani dress, these two men wore their rumpled slacks and comfortable shirts, judging their clothes only on the basis of whether they contained enough pockets for all their pens and note cards. One day he told me that he had been embarrassed when he was escorting Andy around. Someone inquired who he was. "He's my boss," replied Riaz. "This poor man?" asked the questioner in some disbelief.

One day Riaz commented disapprovingly of the condition of my husband's dusty shoes. "Nazeera (the cleaning woman) should polish them every day," he said. My husband retorted that, since Riaz was responsible for transportation, perhaps the cleaning of shoes should be considered in his domain. Riaz was neither amused nor convinced. Each day thereafter Nazeera polished our shoes.

Having carefully polished and presentable shoes is important in Lahore. One evening my husband and I went to a colleague's home for dinner. I noticed that everyone was staring at my husband's feet. I was horrified to find that he had not had his shoes cleaned before we left home. He had breached the standards of proper dress. We in the West are often so casual about our attire that we do not think that we could bring offense by having dirty shoes or rumpled clothing. But this is not the case everywhere, and certainly not in Lahore. A person considered to be of high status is expected to dress well and, perhaps above all, to have clean shoes. Even an American diplomat friend of mine was chided one day by her servant for going out with dirty shoes. He told her that this was a bad reflection on himself.

Among other things that Riaz wanted from us was comradery and interesting work. During one of our later stays in Pakistan, Riaz regularly ate lunch with us in our home because we had moved to a house too far from his for him to go home. When my Pakistani students and friends learned that we ate lunch at our dining room table with our driver, they were aghast. Even a Pakistani anthropologist friend said that she could not do this—the caste barriers were just too strong. In fact, if we had guests in the house, Riaz would not eat at the table with us, regardless of our invitation for him to do so. He knew that this would be breaking the caste rules and I suspect that he also thought it would lower our status in people's eyes—something that Riaz was keen to avoid.

Riaz also wanted interesting work. This my husband could rarely provide. John's usual schedule involved going to the library every day and then visiting bookstores two or three times a week. The worst of it was the trips to the main post office so that he could indulge his collector's passion for the latest stamps. "Oh, Madam," I can hear Riaz groan. "John Sahib is a good man, a simple man, but so boring."

I, on the other hand, because of the nature of my research, often expected him to drive me to more varied places and sometimes to even dangerous ones. Although he good-naturedly complained sometimes that I gave him too much work—and in Pakistan's brutal heat, this is quite understandable—he was always ready for a new adventure. One of my research ventures led me into a protest demonstration that the police eventually attacked. I had slipped away before the trouble started, but Riaz did not know this. He waded

FIGURE 5   Linda Walbridge, Riaz, and the car before setting off to to work. *Photo by John Walbridge.*

into the mob, frantic to find me. I realized I was paying him for being much more than a driver.

LEARNING ABOUT LAHORE

As time passed, I became increasingly aware of the social cleavages in Pakistani society and the difficulties that peoples of different castes and classes have in understanding one another. I taught a course in Urban Anthropology at an exclusive university in Lahore. As part of the course, my students—almost all children of the "white houses"—were expected to select a neighborhood in which to do research. Since this was a new experience for them, I decided to take them on a couple of field trips to help them get their research projects underway. I talked to Riaz about this. He suggested that I bring the class to his home to meet his family. The students were courteous and extremely interested in every aspect of Riaz and his family's life. It was as if I had brought them to a foreign country. They wanted to know how Riaz and Beena had met, how Beena spent her day, and what their relationship was with their neighbors. They were intrigued that this extended family lived under one roof. Except that they all spoke a common language, Urdu, I felt as if I had been taking a group of American students to Riaz's home. Afterwards they talked about how fascinated they were by the experience and that they, as Pakistan's elite class (as they refer to themselves), never came to know someone like Riaz except as an employee. One student went back to Riaz's home repeatedly for her research. She was amazed at the warmth with which she was received on each visit, yet she knew she could not reciprocate their hospitality.

When we visited Riaz's street, the students, Riaz, and I walked to a neighbor's home so that Riaz could introduce us. As we walked, we were surrounded by a group of young children. I had long since been accustomed to being stared at on the streets of Lahore. There are few Western foreigners there and I rather stand out. But it was the students who interested these children, one of whom asked, "What are you educated fools doing here?" Indeed, my students were strangers in their own land.

When our 20-year-old son came to visit, Riaz was delighted since it became part of his responsibility to usher this young man around and to expose him to life in Lahore. Lahore is a place where everyone seems to have hobbies. For the literate, writing poetry is a favorite pastime. During February the sky is a fantasia of bright colors as people fly kites for the great Lahori holiday of Basant. I met numerous people who raised pigeons. People also love to stop what they are doing just to talk. On the streets of Lahore, people are often clustered in groups, chatting away. I took up horseback riding shortly after arriving in Lahore. When I rode, people would approach me to find out who I was, where I was from, what I thought about Pakistan, what I thought of American foreign policy, how many children I had, and on and on. This was not done in a discourteous manner. It simply seemed quite natural. Everyone stopped and talked to everyone else. One day I was riding in the car with Riaz—I always rode in the front seat, a source of pride for Riaz because it showed that I did not put too much social distance between myself and him—and pointed out a man on a bicycle in a beautifully embroidered *shalwar qameez*. Riaz looked and announced delightedly that this was his friend. Passing through the traffic light and barely clearing the intersection, he stopped his car, leaving me to wonder when we would be rear-ended. He leaped out and embraced his friend, who had gotten his bicycle across the busy road. He later told me that he had not seen this friend for some years. "He used to be a very bad man," explained Riaz. "He was a *dacoit* (robber), and he killed many people. But now he is a very good man who lives only for God. He prays five times a day (as a devout Muslim should), does not fight with anyone, and does not care about money."

But perhaps even more than kite flying, raising pigeons, and socializing, people seem to love the game of cricket.

Thus our son John, known as J-J, would be expected to know how to play cricket. It fell to Riaz to organize the *chokidars* on the street for a cricket game in the middle of the day so that J-J could have cricket lessons. (This, of course, was much more pleasant than driving my husband to the bookstore.) The fact that this young American man was playing cricket on the streets with Riaz and other servants bemused our friends and acquaintances of higher status, but it apparently delighted the *chokidars*. The young *sahib*, they told me, *needed* to learn to play cricket. It was seen as an essential part of life.

RIAZ'S VALUE SYSTEM

It is true that we paid Riaz rather generously by Pakistani standards, yet he could be making more as a driver. His reputation has spread to certain corners of the expatriate community, particularly to the American Center in Lahore. He probably would be paid more if he worked for a foreign consulate, and certainly he would be driving a better car—something that he obviously longs to do. He also could work for an American or European company in Pakistan, again being bet-

ter paid and driving a better vehicle. Yet, he shuns all of this. He calls himself "the Fulbrighter driver" and has no interest in pursuing any other occupation.

Why is this? For Riaz one of the most important aspects of his work is the social equality that comes with it. He told me repeatedly that he enjoys the informal relationship with his employers, but he also can leverage this equality with his Americans into status in his own neighborhood. He very conspicuously showed up at our door some evenings with his youngest child and his wife, Beena, who sewed most of my clothes. The pleasure of the visits, I believe, was at least partly to be found in the impact they have on the neighborhood *chokidars*. These visits are a reminder of Riaz's relatively high standing. Occasionally, we would hear the echoes of his intricate battles for social position in his neighborhood—a cricket grudge match, for example, that almost cost us our cooks. If Riaz worked for the American Center or for an American company, his role would be far more formal and he would have to be more deferential to his employers. This is not a trade-off he is willing to make.

This is not to say that Riaz sees his Fulbrighters as social equals. He does not and it appears that he does not aspire to such equality. He is a Fulbrighter driver—nothing more, nothing less. It became increasingly apparent to me that he not only sees us as his responsibility but that he also gives us his loyalty. If he thinks someone is bothering us on the streets, he shoos them away, showing anger if they persist. If he hears that there are threats against Americans in Pakistan, he comes by at night to make sure the *chokidars* are awake. He always varies his route home to make sure no one can follow us to find out where we live. He does not behave toward us in this way because we are "guests" in his country, something I have seen operate in Middle Eastern societies. Rather, he simply identifies himself with us, the foreigners who employ him. When J-J became ill from food poisoning in another town, I telephoned Riaz. He drove a hundred miles to fetch us home. But my son was not well enough to travel right away. Riaz sent me from J-J's room and sat by his bed until he was well enough to travel. He would not leave his side.

Perhaps only in a society that is so thoroughly caste-based could such a relationship between employer and employee prevail. People have "their place" in society and it is not considered commendable to reach too high. It is certainly acceptable to bask in the "glory" of one's employers. Here I have noticed people brag about their employers, constantly comparing notes and ranking each one. We are openly compared with former Fulbrighters and other foreigners whom the servants have known. When one of our cooks showed a picture of me to a cousin, she said proudly, "This is MY memsahib."

This does not mean the system is completely inflexible. Riaz is ambitious for himself and for his children. A person who has an education certainly can better his lot in life. Someone who knows some English improves his or her job prospects considerably and, as a result, falls into a different sphere from those who don't. Riaz's English is serviceable and has given him a higher rank than a non-English-speaking permanent driver who also has worked for Fulbrighters. The mother of our cooks cleaned the house for us. She knows no English, while the daughters, who have received an education, do. As cooks they have a higher status than their mother. Sometimes, if their mother was behind in her work, the girls helped her. They did a beautiful job of cleaning but would not touch the bathrooms. I asked Riaz about this and he said simply, "They are cooks." Cleaning a bathroom is considered too menial a task for them. That is the job of the sweeper caste—one of the untouchable or scheduled castes—to which their mother and father belong. The girls will probably never know full equality in the society, yet they will have some respect because they are educated.

When we asked Riaz what he would do if no other Fulbrighters showed up in the coming year, he simply said he would wait for the next Fulbrighter to arrive. We asked if he might not want to explore the possibility of working for American academics in Pakistan on other grants. "I work for Fulbrighters," he replied. It is as if he has created his own caste. While some of his employers do not dress properly and do not pay him enough for a better car, they give him a good deal

of pleasure. He grows very fond of each one. A keen observer of people, he knows each person's eccentricities—something that academics have in abundance. He appears to have found all of us to be entertaining and interesting. Though we have not made him as prosperous as he might otherwise have been or given him the Land Cruiser that he so covets, we have given him a title and honor and influence both on his street and on ours. He believes that it is only Fulbrighters who would provide him with this sort of fulfillment. He has known many drivers who work for elite Pakistanis or for other foreigners and who must behave in a far more formal manner with their employers. He has seen drivers publicly berated for being late. Some have even had their wages docked if they didn't live up to standards. Thus, Riaz will play it safe and wait for the next Fulbrighters to show up.

Our final duty, ongoing after leaving Lahore, is to write to Riaz. The letters from former Fulbrighters he then shows around to both those who can and those who cannot read English. We know that, when we leave, the pictures of us that adorn his house will be shown to all who visit. We also know that memories of Riaz will adorn our lives forevermore.

SUGGESTED READINGS

Ahmad, Saghir. (1977). *Class and Power in a Punjabi Village.* New York: Monthly Review Press.

Weiss, Anita. (1992). *Walls within Walls: Life Histories of Working Women in the Old City of Lahore.* Boulder, Colo.: Westview Press.

14

Vodka and Dumplings for New Year's

Sherylyn H. Briller
Wayne State University

Many people in Western societies know of Mongolia only from a few sentences in a world history textbook, perhaps being most familiar with the Mongolian Empire's legendary 13th-century leader Genghis Khan. The modern country of Mongolia is a large land-locked country in Central Asia that shares a border on the north with the Russian Federation and on other sides with the People's Republic of China. Despite being a vast country (larger than all of Western Europe), Mongolia has a population of only 2.6 million people, making it one of the world's most sparsely populated countries.

Like many nomadic pastoralists, the Mongols have had a segmentary society for centuries. A bit like nesting blocks, they are organized into a hierarchy of families, clans, tribes, and confederations. The Mongolian social structure included nobles, herders, artisans, and slaves, but was never completely rigid and some social mobility was possible.

Among these nomadic herders, wealth was traditionally determined by the numbers of animals owned. Wealth and social status also could be visually expressed through other material objects. Since these nomads were always on the move, even valuable objects, such as decorative headdresses, clothing, horse blankets, saddles, and jewelry, tended to be portable.

In 1924, Mongolia became the second socialist nation established in the world after the U.S.S.R. During the socialist era, which lasted from 1924 to 1989, the traditional nature of the Mongolian herding society began to change as it developed a socialist ideology. With emphasis on economic and social equality, herd size and differences in wealth were greatly reduced.

After the U.S.S.R. disintegrated, there was a democratic movement in Mongolia that brought about the creation of multiple political parties and the beginning of a free-market economy. Some herders embraced the new entrepreneurial system, rapidly increasing the size of their herds and making them more profitable, while others failed to prosper and sank into poverty.

Many signs of increasing wealth differences can be seen in Mongolian communities today. While some people can now afford to purchase expensive imported goods from Western countries, others can no longer even afford to buy basic food products such as flour and tea.

Sherylyn Briller has written an account of a place she calls Altan Gazar, which means "golden place." Located high up in the Altai mountains, Altan Gazar is one of the most remote herding areas in Mongolia. This tale describes her visit to a Mongolian elder's household and the hospitality she received during Tsagaan Car, the New Year. She illustrates how Mongolians show politeness, entertain guests, and honor the elderly through rituals, rituals that reflect social status.

As you read, consider the following questions:

1. What are some important ways of showing hospitality in Mongolian culture? How does Tsengel show that he is a man of importance and status?
2. How does the celebration of Tsagaan Car display respect for Mongolian elders? Compare American and Mongolian New Year's celebrations. What features are similar and different in these societies?
3. What has changed in Altan Gazar from the socialist to the post-socialist era? What does Tsengel say about U.S.–Mongolian relations in the socialist and post-socialist eras? Were you surprised by his comments? Why or why not?

The post office is a hub of activity in Altan Gazar, a Mongolian herding community in the Altai mountains. Most of the 5,000 or so people who live in Altan Gazar are nomadic herders who move with the seasons so that their animals can enjoy the best grazing. Because Altan Gazar herders are often traveling, I was always happily surprised to run into someone at the post office whom I had not seen for a while. The post office was also important because it had the only long-distance telephone in Altan Gazar.

On a rainy spring day in March, my assistant Barsbold and I met Tsengel, a 62-year-old herder, who had come to the post office to call his younger sister who lives in the capital city Ulaanbaatar. We had not seen each other for almost two months, and he greeted us enthusiastically and invited us to come to his home to visit. Tsengel lives with his wife Ayush, his 20-year-old unmarried daughter Oyuntsetseg, and his 11-year-old son Dorj in a round felt tent known as a *ger*. Since it is made of folding wooden walls and felt coverings, the family can simply collapse their *ger* and load the parts onto the backs of their pack animals or stack them onto the back of a truck. Then, when they move to a new site, they can reassemble their *ger* in about an hour's time. Even I learned how to assemble one. The heavy felt outer coverings of the *ger* helped keep us warm on those blustery winter nights when the temperature got as low as −50 degrees Celsius.

Adjacent to Tsengel's *ger* was the *ger* of his 33-year-old eldest son Ganzorig. Seven people lived in this *ger* including Ganzorig, his wife Badam, and their five young sons. For centuries, Mongolian sons have set up their households in a common herding camp with their fathers. While some families today prefer other living arrangements, Tsengel still likes living next to his son's household and sharing the work. After all, the two households together owned more than 200 herd animals: sheep, goats, yaks, horses, and camels.

WORK OF HERDING HOUSEHOLDS

For Tsengel and his family, the work they do every year is pretty much the same. For many centuries men have done some kinds of work and women others. Traditionally, men were primarily responsible for herding and slaughtering animals, hunting, and maintaining animal shelters. Repairing carts, tools, and weapons also were considered men's work. Women were mainly in charge of housework, milking animals, making dairy products, cooking, washing, sewing, and caring for children and the elderly. Some tasks that were shared by men and women included setting up and breaking camp, loading carts for a move, driving the animals to a new location, making felt, and tanning hides.

Socialism brought some drastic changes in the way people lived and worked. For example, while women's work has always been valued, under socialism, they were granted legal equality and girls were given the same opportunities for education as boys. Thus, herders' daughters as well as sons often left Altan Gazar seeking education or employment in larger cities where they believed they could better their lives.

When the free-market economy was introduced after the fall of communism, some herding households such as Tsengel's prospered and their herds grew. But now they had to worry about how to care for the large numbers of animals that they now owned. Before and during socialism some households always moved and worked together. Others only camped together at certain peak labor times of the year and then moved on to different pastures. These days, some prosperous herders have more animals than they can manage and have to hire others to help. But this isn't as simple as it sounds. These wealthy herders had to decide who to hire. Should they be distant relatives or should they not be family members at all? How should they be paid? In one case I heard about, a poor cousin was working for a wealthier one. He received animals as payment so that he could build up the size of his own herd. In a second case, a young unmarried man who had recently returned from school in the provincial capital city was working for a wealthy herding family and was receiving a monthly cash payment. A third instance involved one entire herding household working for another and receiving payment in food such as meat and dairy products. When I asked Tsengel about these arrangements, he told me that they were still pretty new but were becoming increasingly common in Altan Gazar. I asked him whether he would ever consider this strategy and he said, "Right now I don't need to because we have a large family and lots of hands to help out but there could come a day when it would happen."

While the daily lives of herders revolve around safeguarding, caring for, and growing their herds, visiting with family and friends is also considered to be one of life's pleasures. I always enjoyed making the rounds to see different families in Altan Gazar and hearing about how they celebrated various holidays. The most special time of the year to welcome visitors and show hospitality is Tsagaan Car, marking the beginning of the Mongolian New Year.

MONGOLIAN HOSPITALITY TRADITION

Tsengel's *ger* was located in a high steppe area (grass-covered plains) strewn with rocky boulders where it was not unusual for patches of snow to remain on the ground as late as May. There was not a tree in sight. Traveling in Altan Gazar, I often was struck by the rugged beauty of this landscape and how big and empty it truly is. It's the only place that I have ever been where I could actually imagine still seeing dinosaurs.

Although there were a few lactating animals with their newborns tethered near the *ger*, Tsengel's sons had taken the majority of the herd farther away to graze. Upon reaching Tsengel's *ger*, we entered it carefully because the *ger* should be treated with great respect. According to an ancient Mongolian legend, the *ger* represents a small-scale universe with the spherical ceiling symbolizing heaven and the hearth standing for the earth. Thus, we guests needed to be careful not to step upon the door threshold or soil the hearth.

Inside Tsengel's *ger* were wooden beds and brightly painted red and yellow storage chests. Tools and bags with food supplies lined the walls. In the center of the *ger* sat a metal stove fueled with *arghal,* dried patties of animal dung. When we entered, Ayush, Tsengel's wife, was making milk-tea in a large metal cauldron specially designed to fit on top of this stove. The milk-tea contained tea leaves, milk, salt, and a generous spoonful of rancid butter. Not exactly Lipton's.

While a battery-operated cassette recorder from China played a tape of Mongolian folk songs, Tsengel motioned for Barsbold and me to sit on small stools near the fire. Since we were guests, we sat on the stools to the left of the doorway. On a low table, Ayush immediately placed a hospitality bowl that was always offered whenever neighbors or other visitors arrived. The bowl was heaping with various homemade cheeses, flour pastries known as *bordzig,* sugar cubes, and wrapped hard candies imported from Poland.

In the socialist era, Mongolia's main trading partners were the Soviet Union and other socialist nations at that time. Thus, most local herders could purchase luxuries such as Polish candy, Bulgarian jam, and Russian tobacco from which they rolled their own cigarettes. After Mongolia established a free-market economy in 1990, increasing wealth differences quickly emerged among herding households nationwide. In just a few years' time, prosperous households had significantly increased their herd sizes while poor households struggled with animal losses, debts, and unemployed household members. Since social etiquette dictates that visitors should be offered the finest food available, the contents of the hospitality bowl as well as the furnishings in the *ger* told how the household was doing financially.

Tsengel's household seemed to be getting on quite well since his *ger* contained a new carpet, the cassette player, and a number of other imported things, mainly from China. Ayush showed me a pile of beautiful silk and cloth fabrics that she was planning to use to make new *dels,* the Mongolian national robes, for the family. Tsengel's *del* was already in progress. Ayush had cut out the fabric for this knee-length garment and had selected a warm sheepskin for its lining. She explained how when the *del* was finished, Tsengel would wear it belted with a wide silk sash, in a bright contrasting color. She also showed me the heavy silver buttons that would be sewn on to fasten the *del* at the neck, shoulder, and waist. Although Ayush did not comment

upon it, I remember thinking to myself that wearing such fine clothes would remind others of the family's prosperity.

Tsengel was an excellent Mongolian host. When he sat down, he immediately took out a silk pouch containing an agate snuff bottle, which he handed to each of us to examine. This is a custom that has been practiced for centuries. I knew from experience that I should loosen the top and sniff the opening of the bottle, but I didn't have to inhale the snuff. I carefully handed the snuff bottle back to Tsengel and then he poured Russian vodka to the brim of a small porcelain shot glass and passed it to me ceremoniously. I did the courteous thing: I took the cup with my right hand extended and my left hand positioned under the elbow of my right hand. Being left-handed this maneuver took some getting used to but I managed. After I sipped the vodka, I returned the glass to Tsengel using the same gesture. He then refilled the shot glass to the top and passed it to Barsbold. Next he drank from it himself. Then he repeated the process, passing the shot glass to his wife, Ayush.

After returning the glass, Ayush got up and put out a large metal bowl filled with hunks of boiled mutton and several large knives. She then busied herself preparing soup made of homemade noodles, pieces of mutton, and chunks of sheep fat. Mongolian herders detest lean meat and would never serve it to a foreign guest. As a good host, Tsengel carefully searched for a bone with a suitably large chunk of solid fat attached and, with a big smile, presented it to me. Due to this particular aspect of Mongolian hospitality, I postponed my cholesterol level testing for almost a year after returning home.

MONGOLIAN NEW YEAR

Although courtesy and expressions of warm greetings to visitors are basic to Mongolian life, hospitality is especially important at Tsagaan Car (pronounced *Tsagaan Sar*), the New Year festival. This celebration is the most important festival in Mongolian culture, and has been for centuries. Because the Mongolians use the lunar calendar, the time of the festival changes each year, but most commonly falls in late January or early February. The official line these days is that the festival should last for three days; however, in rural areas such as Altan Gazar the festivities sometimes go on for as long as several weeks. This is a time when people visit their parents and eldest relatives and many travel thousands of miles to do so.

Tsengel was eager to find out how I had enjoyed Tsagaan Car. I assured Tsengel that I had thoroughly enjoyed celebrating Tsagaan Car, which I had done with Barsbold's family in a different region of Mongolia. I was interested to learn how Tsengel's family celebrated the holiday in Altan Gazar. Tsengel began by saying, "As you have learned from spending time in Mongolia, traditionally the first day of the first month is considered to be the most auspicious day of the year. So there are numerous rituals that all Mongolian families perform on this day. Like people throughout Mongolia, my family arose at dawn and bowed to each of the cardinal points, beginning facing east. Then we performed a ritual of sprinkling mare's milk toward heaven in hopes of a year filled with good fortune."

He drank some tea and continued, "Once we had completed these annual rituals, we returned to my *ger* because I am the oldest member of this family. Ayush and I sat at the top of the *ger* (rear section opposite the door) and all of the family members came up to pay their respects to us first." He paused and then said, "Tsagaan Car is a great holiday for older people like myself because it involves gathering the whole family together and honoring the elderly. All of my children and grandchildren were here. My 30-year-old daughter Soyolmaa is married to a man who has an office job in the provincial capital. Of course, they traveled with their three children to Altan Gazar for Tsagaan Car, which is about a four-hour trip by jeep through the mountains. It's very important to have your family all gathered for the New Year." He cleared his throat and went on, "After these greetings, I made a speech blessing the whole family and wishing them good fortune in the New Year. At that point, the sun had risen and we spent the whole day receiving visitors and feasting."

Ayush smiled broadly as she presented us with steaming bowls of soup. The smile suggested that she well remembered the scene her husband was describing. Tsengel sipped briefly from his soup bowl and then proceeded with the account of how his household had prepared for Tsagaan Car.

"Economically, you should know that this is by far the most expensive time of the year for Mongolian families. There are so many things that you have to do. Every household must make a big hospitality display. Ours was very nice. We spent weeks before baking these special brick-shaped cookies that form the layers of the hospitality display. On these layers, we piled sugar cubes and hard candy—it was a very beautiful display."

Following another round of vodka, Tsengel resumed his story. "We also served some of the finest food to our guests. It's important to show good hospitality by serving the best food available during Tsagaan Car or if you are hosting another important event like a wedding or a child's haircutting ceremony (the ceremony which celebrates a child's survival past the dangers of infancy). For instance, we slaughtered one of our fattest sheep for this occasion. The tail from this sheep was the centerpiece of our hospitality display. Because I am the head of this household, I personally carved pieces of meat from this tail for the guests to eat. Along with this meat, we also made *buuz*, meat-filled steamed dumplings. Since we knew that many people would be visiting us during the New Year's celebration, we spent the week before making hundreds of *buuz* to serve them."

Tsengel took out a large round metal tin of tobacco and then carefully rolled and lit a cigarette. After a few puffs he emphatically stated, "Everywhere in Mongolia, *buuz* are considered to be the most traditional and respectful food that you could serve to guests. I'm sure that you ate many *buuz* during Tsagaan Car as well." I confirmed that I had eaten large quantities of the steaming hot *buuz* with meat juices running out of them during this festival time. Actually, during the rest of the year, I as a foreign guest often was served these special dumplings in the households that I visited. Tsengel nodded and then remarked, "Yes, Mongolians are a very hospitable people and we know how to treat visitors properly. I think it comes from our heritage as nomads. After all, on the steppe visitors may have been traveling for many days and so it's very important in our culture to extend the best hospitality possible to visitors."

He added with a twinkle in his eye, "Of course, part of this hospitality has always included *nirmalike*." He was referring to the homemade milk-based vodka that the herders like so much. I had already learned about this. Nowadays, depending on the prosperity of the household, the host had a choice as to whether to serve store-bought vodka or the homemade *nirmalike*. Indeed, it was important to serve multiple rounds of vodka "shots" to visitors. Tsengel, like other good hosts, served vodka when his guests arrived, while they were eating, and periodically during a visit.

Of course, there also had to be a final one "for the road." Tsengel and his family had purchased seven bottles of vodka for Tsagaan Car alone. He also served substantial amounts of the home-brewed variety.

We didn't just talk about food and vodka. I was interested in what Tsengel thought about the condition of the national economy now that the socialist era had ended. And we talked about the large number of herd animals that had died in a harsh storm during the past winter in Altan Gazar. Then there was the matter of where Tsengel's family would camp in the summer.

It grew dark and we realized that we should be going. Tsengel poured another round of vodka for everyone in the *ger*, including his son Ganzorig and daughter-in-law Badam who had come in while we were talking.

As Tsengel was pouring the vodka he remarked, "When I was describing why Tsagaan Car is the most expensive time of the year for Mongolian families, I also should have mentioned the costs of giving gifts of money and goods to relatives and friends. As you have heard, even in poor families it is expected that you will give gifts to your elders—even if it is only a few *tugriks* (Mongolian currency unit). This year, for example, our household alone gave money and other gifts including clothing, fabric, candy, and other gifts to more than 50 people."

I was interested in knowing more about how poor families dealt with these expectations about hospitality and asked Tsengel specifically about this issue. He stated, "Yes, I think this is a major concern now. This problem didn't exist under socialism when households in Altan Gazar had more or less the same things and could all celebrate in the same way. It's very hard for families now where there is just not enough money and if they don't have any animals that they can sell to get what is needed for Tsagaan Car. It's especially difficult for poor older people since everyone will still be coming to visit you to pay their respects—and there must be food to serve and vodka to drink. These problems didn't exist in socialist times and I don't know what will happen in the future." He began smoking his pipe and pulling on his beard at this point. It was very quiet in the *ger*.

After we drank the vodka and were preparing to leave, Tsengel commented thoughtfully, "I'm very happy to be able to share news about my family's New Year's celebration with you. For a long time under socialism, Mongolians didn't know much about Americans because we were partners with Russia. And Russia and America were not friendly nations at that time. So people like us in the countryside didn't ever know any Americans. The only things that I had ever heard about America was that it was a capitalist country with bad practices like allowing poor people to starve and live on the streets—even in the wintertime.

It all sounded very inhumane to us, so, of course, we had a bad impression of your country. Those were different times. It's only very recently that Americans have started coming to Mongolia and visiting with Mongolian families like we did today. When you go home and tell other Americans about Mongolian society—I think they should know that we are a polite and hospitable people. We always treat guests well in our homes and we are eager to celebrate this new friendship between our countries."

He went on to say, "Of course, we are now going through a big time of change in Mongolia. As you can see, there are many good things going on but there are also some very serious issues that must be dealt with. But you should keep in mind that Mongolians are a strong and resilient people. We live in an extremely difficult climate and we can survive many things. You will see that Mongolians will find a way to go on."

With a big grin he continued, "Personally, I hope that you will be here next year and celebrate Tsagaan Car with my family in Altan Gazar. You can be sure that we will have lots of *buuz* and vodka and you will have a wonderful time here celebrating the New Year." I thanked him and said that I hoped to be able to celebrate this holiday with them.

As circumstances turned out, I was not able to be in Altan Gazar for Tsagaan Car the next year. But I wrote a letter to Tsengel's family telling them that I hoped the invitation would remain standing for my next trip to Mongolia. I like to think of Tsengel going to the post office in Altan Gazar and finding my letter waiting for him. And I like to imagine drinking vodka and eating dumplings in his *ger* on New Year's.

SUGGESTED READINGS

Goldstein, Melvyn C. and Cynthia M. Beall. (1994). *The Changing World of Mongolia's Nomads*. Berkeley: University of California Press.

Major, John S. (1990). *The Land and People of Mongolia*. New York: Harper Collins.

15

Ambivalence of Grandsons
and Rescue by Daughters

Lisa Cliggett
University of Kentucky

The Gwembe Valley cuts a narrow swath approximately 120 miles long and 10 miles wide along Lake Kariba in Zambia's Southern Province. The Gwembe Tonga people constitute the majority of the approximately 150,000 Zambians living in this escarpment valley. The region is notorious throughout the country for its difficult living conditions. There are annual hunger seasons when the villagers depend on wild foods collected from the forests and bush areas. Over the last century the region also has experienced several severe droughts of a few years at a time. Zambia's declining national economy also has had an adverse impact on the Gwembe Valley.

As Lisa Cliggett's article demonstrates, despite the prosperity that many Gwembe Tonga experienced in the 1960s after their relocation from their old homes on the shores of the Zambezi River, these days their lives focus more on daily survival. The creation of Lake Kariba in 1958 transformed the Tonga farming system from intensive planting in small gardens along the flood plain of the Zambezi River—sometimes giving more than two harvests a year—to expansive rain-fed farming in large fields, giving only one harvest a year. Under these difficult circumstances, social relationships can become severely strained and people's lives increasingly insecure. The story emphasizes that economic change does not always progress in a linear fashion toward a better life. Additionally, even though the Tonga are a matrilineal society, tracing social identity through ties to women, women are dependent on men for material well-being. Although women may feel emotionally close to their female relatives, the men play a crucial role in providing for matrilineal relatives, particularly old widows who are best cared for when they live with a married son. The story emphasizes that while respect and care for elders is a common norm in many societies, actual support for elders is not a given. Although elders hold a high social status within Gwembe communities for their knowledge and experience, and old women gain status from raising children well and playing important roles in community ritual activities, such social positions do not guarantee a comfortable old age. Tracing the story of this elderly woman reveals complex social relationships between generations and genders. It also points to the individual adaptations that people will sometimes make, particularly under conditions of resource scarcity.

As you read, consider the following questions:

1. During economic hardship, how might social relations change between family members? Between neighbors and community?
2. Why would food scarcity and a poor economy challenge norms of "support for the elderly"? Why does doing research on social support systems in a region of food scarcity make sense?
3. How does the payment of cattle at marriage influence a girl's relationship to her family? In what ways would cattle payment solve an instance of illegitimate pregnancy? Why might parents encourage daughters to have affairs before marriage?
4. How do the different generations represented in Mutinda's story participate in the social obligations of support for the elderly? What role does gender play in support systems for the elderly? What kinds of justifications can each generation, and gender, offer for how they behaved?

Mutinda was married long before the American missionaries set up the Pilgrim Wesleyan Church Station next to the lakeshore and long before the Irish Catholic missionaries established their church halfway down the mountainside toward her village. Her wedding took place even before the British Colonial officers had visited the region where she lived, and certainly before the dam was built on the Zambezi River. It was that dam that forced Mutinda, her family, her community, and some 70,000 other Gwembe Tonga people of Zambia's Southern Province up the valley escarpment away from their fields next to the river. After that they had to grow their food in marginal soils and depend on rains that were never reliable. In that new location Mutinda and her people had watched their fields go to ruin and their gardens lose their rich fertility. And they watched their prosperity vanish in the 1970s and 80s. But by this time Mutinda had lived much of her life. Her busiest farming days had passed; these days she relied on other people's farming for her survival.

I met Mutinda in 1994, over 70 years after she had married the man her family had chosen for her. I had been living in Sibamba village for about a month when I learned that the oldest woman in the village was living just up the hill from me. Since I was interested in support systems for the elderly, I was eager to meet this 80-something-year-old woman who would surely have valuable stories to tell of life in the Gwembe Valley.

She was long, lanky, and very slender, her sinewy muscles protruding through her fragile skeleton, and stretching her tissue-papery skin. When she saw me walk through the doorway of her house, she jumped with excitement. She eased herself from her reclining position, finally coming to rest crouched on the edge of her bed, her arms and legs folded on top of each other, reminding me of a baby bird just hatching from its shell. I couldn't tell if her ashen color was from ill health or simply from the dry and cold air of the June to August cold season that caused skin flaking for everyone, and bloody noses for me. Her small, round, thatch-roofed house was made only of branches and trunks salvaged from nearby trees, and couldn't have been more than five feet in diameter. Usually, mud would be smeared between the poles to keep the wind and dust out. Mutinda had lived in this house almost two years waiting in vain for her grandsons to mud the walls for her. Her grandsons had enough work to do, trying to provide for their wives and children with no hope of employment, and with repeatedly poor harvests. The grandson Mutinda lived with, Mister, had a particularly difficult situation. He had two wives, and five young children, and he didn't have the help necessary to grow enough food to feed everyone, let alone to build houses for his growing family. However, about a year after I first met Mutinda, a local church group got together and mudded her walls, helping to keep the house slightly warmer during the cold winter months.

I hunkered down inside the house on a miniature wooden stool. A small fire burned in the center of her home. Her narrow bed, which took up about a third of the round living space, was made by planting four poles into the ground, and then lashing together longer poles to serve as a mattress. The poles were then tied to the "frame." A small pile of threadbare graying fabrics lay on top of her bed. These fabrics doubled as padding for the mattress, and also her "winter ware." As we talked, Mutinda periodically took a piece of this cloth and draped it over some part of her body that felt chilled. Her few articles of clothing hung on the wall above her bed, perhaps for decoration, or possibly to cut the wind. In an effort to keep the chill away Mutinda kept the fire going—as long as someone brought her firewood. Unfortunately, the smoke of the fire only irritated her chronic eye infections.

For a decade or so after the forced relocation from their homelands, many Tonga people actually had steel bed frames and real foam mattresses. They had formal clothes that would have put me, the "rich American," to shame. One man who ran a local shop even bought a Land Rover truck during the 1960s, which he used to generate income as the local public transportation service. But the carcass of the truck sits on the edge of his son's homestead now, with bits and pieces of the vehicle appearing in surprising places: the metal headlight frame has morphed into a window for one house, and the radiator makes an excellent shower pad that keeps your feet clean as you bathe.

Those days of a booming economy, when people could sleep on spring beds, own cars and bicycles, and dress up like urban American socialites on a Saturday night are now gone, along with the abundance of fish that came with the construction of the dam that created Lake Kariba. The officers who planned Lake Kariba included a fish-stocking program that they hoped would generate a new industry for the local people. The plan worked for about the first six years. After that, when the nutrient-rich feeding grounds for the fish were tapped out, the fish population declined rapidly, and the local people's opportunities to cash in on the fishing industry were over. Since that time, the well-being of the Gwembe Valley and the Tonga people has been continually declining.

Mutinda herself used to sleep on a steel frame bed, but these days she rests on branches and rags. As she extracted one of the rags from her mattress, she explained to me that this was now her most valuable possession—a blanket she had inherited when her brother had died four years ago. These days it was the warmest garment in her collection of old clothing and fabrics.

Mutinda stored a few other valuables under her bed, where she could reach them easily. These possessions included a gallon container for water, only partially full because of the gaping hole half way up the side; a small blue plastic bowl with what looked like yesterday's *nsima* (corn meal porridge) and a green slimy sauce; her water pipe made from a gourd, lying empty on its side; and a few baobab fruit that her grandchildren had collected for her. The sweet and sour powdery fruit helped to cut hunger and thirst during this season of scarcity.

DAYS OF FLIRTATION

Mutinda told me the story of her wedding. She took particular delight in describing the beaded skirt that she wore, and how it swished from side to side as she danced. It sounded like she was quite a flirt, using all the skills she had learned from the older women who advised her on how to be a good wife, one of the primary ways women gain status in this society. Although some Tonga groups living on the plateau above the Gwembe escarpment seclude adolescent girls as a formal way to prepare them for marriage, the Gwembe Tonga are more informal about the matter. Aunts, older sisters, and other relatives simply tell them all they need to know without hiding the girl away. Mutinda spoke of the lessons she learned from her elders when she was young, particularly the need to "behave morally," which she explained to mean not becoming pregnant before marriage. So, while the older women encouraged her to dance and even be seductive, moral codes of the time dictated that girls should avoid illegitimate pregnancy. "These days," she complained, "parents are no longer proud of their daughters because of the pregnancies that force families into legal disputes." Legal disputes are indeed common these days. Now, when a girl becomes pregnant prior to marriage, her parents seek "damage payment" from the man who impregnated her in order for the girl to maintain respectability in the community. One or two cattle usually serve as payment. There is another twist to all of this. Poverty has driven parents to depend on the income they gain from their daughter's premarital affairs, sometimes actually encouraging repeated affairs to gain continual income. The days of expecting a girl to remain chaste until marriage are not much more than a memory.

Mutinda remembers those days fondly, especially since she could still flirt and dance during the courting period. Mutinda told me that she was happy to marry, although she had little choice in the man who became her husband. "Families based marriages on the clans preferred by the parents. That's why young girls were chosen for marriage even when they were little, and when they grew up they were ready to marry that man," she explained. She knew she had been lucky. Her husband treated her well and wasn't jealous of her, like so many other husbands were. Even though she was married, she continued dancing the popular styles of the day with other young women, without her husband accusing her of trying to seduce other lovers.

While Mutinda shared her memories of life before the creation of Lake Kariba, she interjected a running commentary on her current life, particularly about her constant hunger, her lack of tobacco to distract her from her suffering, and the pain in her legs that prevented her from attending the many funerals of her relatives during the past year. In the Gwembe valley malaria, tuberculosis, and malnutrition rob people of their lives. People have noted that over the past 40 years, when there is a bit more cash and food available, fewer people die. But when these things become scarce, death knocks on the door of old and young and anyone in between. Severe droughts bring "hunger years," and funerals become even more commonplace.

Tonga funerals usually last for five days, with people staying for the duration of the event. Older women, especially, are expected to attend funerals because they play important roles in the funeral rituals, an important part of women's social status as they age. Tonga will tell you that "you can't have a funeral without old women." Indeed, old women must perform the important funeral rituals of "opening" the funeral on the first evening with a ritual cleansing of the homestead, and they "close" the funeral in the wee hours of the morning on the last day, by pouring a ritual porridge and smashing ritual pots on the grave, as a way to send the deceased into the afterlife with nourishment. As sad as a death might be, the funeral itself gives people a chance to socialize and catch up on each other's lives. Mutinda, isolated as she was because of her physical weakness, felt the loss of that social contact and role of respect. Even funerals were denied to her.

As she expressed her disappointment in not attending the funerals, I felt sorry for her, even though I myself had mixed feelings about these events. As part of funeral festivities, women sell maize beer at the edge of the funeral homestead, so, to reach the central funeral site, a guest must traverse the gauntlet of belligerent drunks, an intimidating experience for any newcomer. Once this torment is over, however, and when safely within the boundaries of the funeral homestead, the atmosphere changes considerably. There I could feel a powerful fusion of family, community, and beliefs. I also took pleasure in seeing the funeral as a time when women, particularly senior women, are valued. Mutinda's frail health deprived her of this sense of importance and social status in her community.

I visited Mutinda frequently, and I paid close attention any time she was mentioned. I liked her spunky personality, and the image of her as a young girl flirting and dancing provocatively appealed to me. My interest in her was also academic: she was a living example of what too often happens when poverty grips an area and food becomes scarce. Such difficult conditions force people to make hard decisions about who will get food and other valuable resources. They also undermine "traditional values" of communities. Among the Tonga, as among so many other African peoples, respect for elders has been a spoken norm. But during times of scarcity in particular, practical decisions and behavior overpower norms of support. People will use such times as an opportunity to "trim down" family expenses, including elders who do not add to the household "communal pot."

FAMILY AND SUPPORT

Mutinda lived in the homestead of one of her grandsons, Mister, with his two wives and five children. Mister's homestead was nestled at the foot of the boulder ridge that separates Sibamba from the next village. Among the Tonga, mothers are often called "mother of" with the oldest child's name usually added. Bina-Mister, that is, the mother of Mister, lived within a 10-minute walk of Mister's homestead, in the homestead of one of her other sons. Mister's "other mother," that is, his mother's sister, BinaFosten, lived in the homestead just below with her own son Fosten. Thus, Mutinda had two daughters (both widows living with married sons) in the immediate vicinity to help her. BinaFosten brought firewood to Mutinda every few days so that she could keep a fire going. BinaMister brought vegetables from her garden every so often. Both of them brought small dishes of cooked *nsima* (corn meal porridge) and relish two or three times a week.

Mutinda could also get other people to help her from time to time. Occasionally I took a small bag of sugar or salt on my interviews, to give as a small gift of thanks. Mutinda gently explained to me that she preferred sugar, so that she could use it to bribe one of her great-granddaughters to bring water for her to drink and wash with. Normally, an older woman such as Mutinda could expect her daughters-in-law to bring her water. But Mister's wives refused. Perhaps it was because they feared Mutinda. While the Tonga respect the elderly, they also believe that very old people can sap the energy from their younger relatives and can make children sick.

This belief deeply concerned Mutinda. I once asked her where her food came from. I was surprised to hear her reply, "I only think I shouldn't cause any trouble to someone before I die, so I don't ask for anything, whatever they give you, you just say thanks. It's only my daughters who give to me." Though Mutinda's daughters were good to their mother, Mutinda could not live with them. According to strict custom, old widows should live with married sons. Mutinda

did have a son, but he lived in the bush, and suffered, as she said, from "problems in the head." Other villagers agreed that her son was indeed mentally unstable. He was not married, and certainly could not care for his aging mother.

Even though Mutinda did not have a reliable son, she still could not depend solely on her married daughters. When a girl marries, her family receives cattle. Once a man's family has paid the agreed number of cattle to the wife's family, her family can no longer make claims on her. To bring an old woman into her daughter's husband's homestead would be seen as too great a burden on the man's family. So, when an old widow has no son to look after her, she must turn to brothers for support. When all the brothers have died, as Mutinda's had, a widow needs to rely on her grandsons. These grandsons are members of her matrilineal clan and are thus her "proper family"; that is, they are the ones who can be called upon for assistance.

Mutinda's two daughters made arrangements for their aging mother to live with Mister. But it was never clear to me just how agreeable Mister was to this arrangement. I began to suspect that Mutinda's grandsons, while they provided fairly well for their own mothers, did not include their grandmother in their notions of "respect for the aged."

During one of my visits with Mutinda we were sitting next to her house in the small garden of bulrush millet that she had planted. Mister had decided that he would clear an even larger area in the same vicinity as Mutinda's garden. Throughout our conversation, Mutinda turned to Mister, making comments about the trees he was cutting and threatening him with what she would do if one of those trees fell on her millet and crushed it. Mister responded with sarcastic chuckles, and teasing pleas for some of her tobacco. Among the Tonga, it is a practice for grandmothers and grandsons—or any people of alternate generations—to joke with one another. But this seemed a bit different to me. Mister seemed truly unconcerned with the damage he caused when a tree fell and crushed a section of Mutinda's crop.

Mutinda's other grandson, Fosten, an active and vocal leader of the local Seventh Day Adventist church, rarely visited his grandmother or gave her assistance, although the meals his mother brought to Mutinda came from his food supplies. However, he did make a trip to her hut on one occasion—one that I would hear about later through the gossip mill.

Before leaving the village one day, I had left a gallon jug of water for Mutinda, thinking that she could use this new jug in addition to her cracked one. About an hour after I left the jug, Fosten arrived at Mutinda's doorstep and took the jug back to his own homestead. Mutinda, almost blind and physically frail, could not defend her rights to the jug. It was added to Fosten's collection of property in his homestead.

It was painful for me to watch Mutinda's grandsons ignore and mistreat her even though I understood that poverty was bringing out the worst in them. Still, worse was yet to come and I was quite unprepared for it.

THE CRISIS

By August 1995 there had been no harvest. Severe drought had plagued the place for two years, and there was no grain for even the season of eating well. This led to another crisis for Mutinda. Without any warning to his mothers or brothers, Mister packed up his homestead, including both wives and all the children, and moved to their gardens on the lakeshore. Such a move was not uncommon, especially in hunger years, and especially during the time when many hands are needed for weeding and for scaring hungry birds away from the crops. People build temporary shelters in the gardens so that they can sleep in the fields at night to scare away hippos and intruding cattle. However, when a man has two wives, and dependents in the village homestead, one wife usually stays behind to keep house.

This time, the whole homestead was abandoned, leaving Mutinda alone to fend for herself. Because her daughters, BinaFosten and BinaMister, were also living at their river gardens, neither they nor anyone else knew of this abandonment for three or more days. Mutinda ate nothing, and drank the few drops of water left in her cracked jug. Once word of Mutinda's plight reached her daughters' ears, they tried to decide what to do. BinaMister, because she had a particularly successful garden even during "the hunger," went to rescue her mother from the abandoned homestead. BinaMister carried the few possessions Mutinda owned, while Mutinda, weak from hunger and thirst, struggled the few miles to BinaMister's garden. A 40-minute journey took Mutinda close to five hours.

When I found Mutinda at her daughter's garden a week after she had been abandoned by her grandson, Mutinda was cleaner and more animated, more mobile and clear headed, than I had seen her in 16 months. She was now eating regularly and had water to bathe. Her daughter had rescued her and saved her from starvation.

AGING AMIDST SCARCITY

The people condemned Mister for abandoning his grandmother. They said it was wrong to leave Mutinda alone in his homestead with no food and water. Yet people only gossiped. They did not even reprimand him to his face. They understood that he had five young children to feed and protect. Why deprive them in order to feed Mutinda, who has already had more than her fair share of years? Perhaps this is why Bina-Mister, also an old woman and living alone in her garden, could care for her very old mother. Two old women living on their own and feeding themselves were not a threat to the youngsters of any homestead.

Mutinda was still living with BinaMister when I left Zambia in October 1995. She survived the drought of 1994–95, despite her daughter's predictions that "this hunger will kill Mutinda." When I returned to Zambia the following year, I learned that Mutinda had died in February 1996, during the rainy season. Although the rains had come that year during the planting season, they had come too heavily and flooded the fields, so there was yet another poor harvest. The rains also left breeding grounds for water-borne illnesses. Mutinda didn't live to see whether the crops survived or not. Some people said that it was the hunger of the previous year that caused Mutinda's death; she was just too weak to carry on. Some said that it was her grandsons who killed her, either with witchcraft or simple neglect. Others said that is was just old age. I suspected that it was a mixture of all these circumstances.

Many other old women and men died during the year of my residence in Sibamba, and also during the following years when better times continued to elude Gwembe people. Some people said that one old woman died because of the greed of her husband who was "too in love" with his new, and younger, wife. The man and his young wife lived in their lakeshore field, leaving the older wife to beg from house to house in the village. Back in the 1960s when people slept on softer beds, wore spiffy clothes to weddings and funerals, and ate regular meals of fish and meat, it might have been hard for them to imagine a time when they would refuse food to an old woman in need. Now those days of "luxuries," such as food, are the foggy images of an elusive time.

SUGGESTED READINGS

Cliggett, Lisa. (2001). "Gender, Subsistence, and Residential Arrangements for the Elderly in the Gwembe Valley, Zambia." *Journal of Cross Cultural Gerontology* 16(4).

Colson, Elizabeth. (1971). *Social Consequences of Resettlement.* Manchester: Manchester University Press.

PART VI

Medicine and Healing

Photo by Alan R. Sandstrom.

As the articles in this section show, medical anthropologists are interested in a wide array of issues relating to health and health care. They study how wider cultural, economic, and social issues, such as poverty and access to adequate nutrition, affect health and the choices people make about treatment and medical services. A long-standing interest in anthropology is the study of "traditional" concepts of illness and healing. Anthropologists have found that people have definite ideas about the causes of illnesses and their treatment. In some societies, for example, people believe that evil spirits are to blame for particular illnesses and that intervention by a healer is needed to remove the invading spirits. In other societies people believe that social disharmony or unresolved anger can cause illness. In such cases the involvement of a healer or some resolution of the situation can be a cure for the symptoms of the illness. Alternatively, illness could be caused by imbalances of energy in the body. Peoples in many cultures have a highly developed knowledge of herbs and treat specific maladies with specific herbal remedies.

Modern medicine has now been introduced all over the world. It was originally assumed that with its introduction, traditional healers of all sorts would vanish; that people would see the value of Western medicine and find no need for local curers. Indeed, this generally does not happen. Often we find people using both forms of therapy. Sometimes the two compete, but at other times they are used in

95

a complementary fashion. People who have tried Western medicine often assess its strengths and weaknesses and incorporate what they like into their traditional healing strategies. We also find, though, that individuals might resist the use of hospitals and modern clinics because they feel they are not being seen as entire human beings but only as examples of certain symptoms. Anthropologists also have found that practitioners of modern medicine often share society's stereotypes about ethnic and racial groups. A person of a marginalized ethnic group is less likely to visit a medical doctor if he or she feels that the doctor harbors ethnic prejudice.

Anthropologists are continually expanding their areas of interest. These days patterns of alcohol consumption and sexually transmitted diseases, especially HIV/AIDS, have gained considerable attention among medical anthropologists. Alcohol is the most widely used psychoactive drug in the world with a history of use that dates back thousands of years. Modern medicine has long associated excessive alcohol consumption with illnesses such as cirrhosis of the liver, brain dysfunction, heart problems, and certain kinds of cancer. Anthropologists have been interested in the role culture plays in shaping alcohol consumption and the behavior of the people in different societies when intoxicated. In some societies, for example, alcohol is consumed only during rites of passage and during festivals. Some anthropologists in their case studies have noted extreme aggressive behavior resulting from drinking binges, while others have noted more subdued behavior. Anthropologists also are interested in how alcohol consumption has been affected by changes in the global social order. How, for example, do advertising, economics, and social inequality affect drinking? Also, how do conflicting attitudes toward alcohol affect drinking behavior, especially among young people?

Perhaps the greatest health challenge facing today's world is the spread of AIDS (acquired immune deficiency syndrome) caused by HIV (human immunodeficiency virus). The societal and economic impact of this disease especially in some of the world's poorest nations is staggering: orphans left to fend for themselves, a shortage of adults to carry out even basic tasks necessary for survival, an overburdened health care system. These nations often lack access to drugs that can slow down the progress of AIDS, drugs that are available in wealthier nations. Sexually transmitted diseases, and especially HIV/AIDS, are viewed with charged emotions shaped by cultural and religious conceptions of morality and causes of disease. A disease as harrowing as AIDS, some people claim, must be the result of divine punishment for sexual behavior. Such beliefs, along with other cultural attitudes, can cause discrimination and stigma of those living with this disease. They also can prevent dissemination of important information about how to avoid its spread. Anthropologists have found that ideas of shame, especially as they relate to sex, actually help to increase the likelihood of people contracting and spreading sexually transmitted diseases including HIV/AIDS.

Anthropologists must always be concerned about **ethical** issues, trying particularly to ensure that their work does not have a negative influence on the people they study. The anthropologist must first of all be sensitive to how powerful he or she is seen by the sick person and his family. The anthropologist, though well-intentioned, may exert undo influence in determining what course of action a person should take. He or she must consider, for example, the social status of the person, how that person's place in society might expose him or her to different health risks and perhaps prevent a person from responding to a particular treatment. In other words, the medical anthropologist must avoid the sometimes overwhelming tendency to insist that a particular treatment is the only—or even the best—course of action. Too many societal factors can influence the outcome.

In the first of these articles, Elizabeth Cartwright shows her involvement in trying to save a tiny baby, only referred to as "Little Dove," whose life is in such jeopardy that her Mexican migrant farmworker mother has not even permanently named her. Cartwright learns that modern Western medical treatments are not always well received by these indigenous peoples who have their own approaches to healing.

Vaughn Koops' research on alcohol consumption shows us the role alcohol plays in the social life of people on the Cook Islands in the Pacific Ocean. By "hanging out" in homes and bars where people are drinking, he comes to appreciate the toll that heavy alcohol consumption takes on the people's health and well-being.

West of the Cook Islands are the Solomon Islands where Holly Buchanan-Aruwafu has conducted research on sexually transmitted infections among young people. Through the experiences of one young woman, Kayzy, we see how traditional religious values and ideas about sex actually hamper people from taking the necessary precautions that could help prevent the spread of disease.

Other articles relating to medicine and health:

Eliasa and the Kwacha Video Coach by Pamela A. Maack

Healing the Body, Healing the Soul by M. Ligaya Hattari

Death of an Irishman by Kathleen G. Williamson

The Shaman's Art by Alan Sandstrom and Pamela Effrein Sandstrom

Swamiji: A Life in Yoga by Sarah Strauss

16

Little Dove

Elizabeth Cartwright
Idaho State University

The Amuzgos Indians come from the Southern Mexican states of Oaxaca and Guerrero. These states are among the poorest and most remote of any region in Mexico. There are approximately 19,000 Amuzgos Indians residing in Mexico. In the village of San Pedro Amuzgos, Oaxaca, where about 4,000 people live, approximately two-thirds of the residents identify themselves as "indigenous" (Amuzgan). The Amuzgos work in the northern Mexican state of Sonora on large agricultural farms because the poverty of southern Mexico forces them to search for work outside of the region where they live.

Migrant farmwork in Mexico is extremely low-paid, but it is one of the few options that the Amuzgos have to enter into the cash economy. While working in Sonora the migrant farmworkers live in small crowded sheds that house 10 or 15 people where there is rarely electricity. The drinking water often comes from agricultural ditches that are polluted with pesticides. Illnesses of all kinds are rampant in this setting.

In this chapter Elizabeth Cartwright explores Amuzgan ideas about illnesses and healing, especially focusing on what happens to these individuals when they are living away from home and working as migrant farmworkers in the camps of Sonora. In both their home village and Sonora, the Amuzgos have very little access to the medical care provided by doctors, nurses, and other hospital personnel.

Instead, the Amuzgos rely on traditional remedies and local experts such as *curanderos* (healers) and *parteras* (midwives). The story Cartwright tells explores the Amuzgan logic of healing by focusing on the illness of one young Amuzgan girl.

As you read, consider the following questions:

1. When is it appropriate for anthropologists to intervene in the culture that they are studying?
2. How does the issue of intervening in people's health care decisions relate to the ethical considerations that an anthropologist has to live by?
3. What was the reason that Lupita could not use the *Suero Oral* to rehydrate Little Dove? Can you think of any forms of healing in your own culture that people don't like to use even though a doctor or a respected friend might tell them they should?
4. What kinds of choices do Amuzgan mothers have to make when seeking medical care for their families? What factors cause them to choose one type of care over another?
5. How is Lupita's life similar to working women's lives in different sectors of the our own national economy?

My first impression of my research site in northern Mexico that summer of 1996 was one of heat and sun and dust. The large agricultural area of La Costa Hermosillo, Sonora, was in the midst of a two-year drought with no end in sight. The usually lush Sonoran desert was crispy dry and even the large saguaro cacti were brown and desiccated. With temperatures soaring close to 120°F (49°C) and the irrigation sprinklers working overtime, the heat made even the smallest of tasks in the migrant farmworker camps seem overwhelming.

The heat affected everyone in the area, but those who were young or sickly were especially at the mercy of the blazing sun. This is the story of one little girl who was desperately ill during that long, hot summer and how her mother cared for her while living in the migrant laborer's camp.

LITTLE DOVE

The little Amuzgo Indian girl lying on the small bed in the tin shack was terribly sick. She was six weeks old and had been ill ever since her birth. Her tiny face was sunken in and her huge eyes were ringed by deep black circles. Flies covered her face and walked across her painfully thin legs that stuck out of a tattered diaper. Her skin was bunched up at her elbows and she hardly moved. All these things were signs that she was very dehydrated and in danger of dying. Her mother quietly answered my questions as I asked about the fragile little baby in front of me.

"Does she have diarrhea?"

"Yes."

"How long had she been sick?"

"For a long time, ever since she was born."

"Was she breast-feeding?"

"No."

"Why not?"

"She doesn't want it"

"Well, what is her name?"

"She doesn't have a name."

"Don't you call her anything?"

"Well, we call her *kitoo;* it's an Amuzgan word."

"What does it mean?"

"Little Dove."

Little Dove's mother was obviously wearied by my barrage of questions.

First as a medical anthropologist and second as a registered nurse with many years of experience, I was seriously concerned about the severity of Little Dove's illness. That her mother had not yet named her was a sign that she thought the baby might not live. Dehydration from serious diarrhea such as Little Dove had is the leading cause of death in infants in the developing world. My panic at the situation increased as I realized that the infant was not getting any liquids and had been ill for several weeks. I felt sure she would soon die.

How had this mother let this happen, I wondered? Why didn't she go to the hospital that was located in the nearby town? What should I do? I pondered these questions and, while I did so, I looked back at some notes that I had written a year earlier about this area. Doing so helped clarify the issues in my mind.

From my fieldnotes, summer 1995

This area is pure desolation. Huge, flat expanses of fields crosscut with irrigation canals. Miles and miles of dirt roads isolate each farm. The camps are usually composed of the owner's house, barns, equipment sheds, and several rows of corrugated tin and tarpaper shacks where the workers live. Depending on the time of year and the labor needs of the camps, anywhere from 20 to 500 people would live at a camp like this. Now I see a few people huddled in the tiny shelters, the sun beating down outside. It is eerily quiet. Inside the shelters, the sweltering heat of the smoldering cooking fires makes them more like ovens than living quarters.

Faces peer out of doorways as we pass. The workers' bodies are whitened by ash from the fires. Five, 10, or 15 people live in each of the five-meter-square sheds. Shafts of light reflect the smoke and the ashes swirling in the wind that comes through the walls.

I sat in the dirt, talking to the eldest girl in one of the shelters and I wondered how I would ever learn about these people. How could I enter into their lives and make some sort of connection with them, I wondered?

As it turned out, Little Dove's mother, Lupita, was more than willing to talk about her perspective on things and about her life. I'd walk from the nearby building where I was staying and in the early mornings Lupita would do her chores and chat with me as she worked. Lupita was often the only worker left in camp during this time. The rest had gone off to other farms in search of day labor to hold them over until the upcoming grape harvest began when they would stay and work at the farm where Lupita was living.

Lupita and I often sat at the table outside the family's shelter, under the shade of a corrugated metal porch roof, cleaning vegetables, sorting beans, or doing the dishes. The old 55-gallon drum made over into a stove was also on the porch. Every day around eleven, just as it started getting really hot, Lupita began making kilos and kilos of corn tortillas for the workers to eat when they came home for their midday meal. The smell of wood smoke and baking corn tortillas will always remind me of those mornings I spent with Lupita, learning about her life and the lives of the other workers.

The first morning that I really got a chance to talk to Lupita, I asked her to describe Little Dove's birth. Lupita's face became tense with the memory. She recounted how she was at home in the camp with only her three-year-old daughter, Laurita, for company. Her husband was off in the fields moving the irrigation pipes, as he often did at night. Lupita knew she was going into labor because this was her fourth child. She told me she felt three strong contractions and then just pushed as hard as she could and tiny Little Dove was born.

According to Lupita, Little Dove's throat had been "swollen" ever since she was born and she cried whenever she nursed. Over the last six weeks her stomach had swollen up and she had endured multiple bouts of diarrhea. Little Dove wouldn't nurse and, most seriously, she wouldn't "ask to be fed."

Lupita remained at the camp as a cook, instead of quickly returning to work in the fields as she had with her other three children, because of the difficult delivery of the placenta after Little Dove's birth. Lupita had been taken to the nearby state hospital (IMSS) where they had "cleaned her out" very roughly. She felt that the doctors and nurses had "treated her like an animal." She vowed to never go back to this hospital, where the medical staff were among the more privileged *mestizos* (non-Indians) from northern Mexico. They looked down on people like her who were Indians from the south, Lupita said.

The pile of tortillas grew higher and higher and the sun grew hotter as we talked. I went to get some water from the spigot across the yard. The water came from the fields, and it smelled and tasted heavily of the pesticides that were being applied to the crops. Pesticides, herbicides, and fertilizers permeated the water and the air because the workers' housing was located in the middle of the fields that were constantly being sprayed with these agro-chemicals.

I brought the pan of water back to the table and we started washing the dishes. I asked Lupita what she planned to do about Little Dove's diarrhea. She said she planned to perform an egg cleansing, a *limpia de huevo*, if Little Dove was not better the next day.

THE EGG CLEANSING—*LIMPIA DE HUEVO*

The following day when I came over to see Lupita, it seemed that Little Dove was not feeling any better. I had decided the night before that I needed to intervene, so I had gone by the IMSS hospital and they had given me 20 or 30 packets of *Suero Oral*—oral rehydration powder that is similar to Gatorade. Because children with diarrhea don't die from the diarrhea itself, but rather from the dehydration that comes along with it, the most important thing for anyone with severe diarrhea is to keep them hydrated. The sugars and salts in the *Suero Oral* would allow Little Dove to absorb the water in the breast milk and anything else she drank. Oral rehydration solution has saved many thousands of children and adults from the more severe consequences of dehydration.

I spoke with Lupita about how important I thought it was for Little Dove to get an adequate amount of the *Suero Oral*. She, however, was not won over to the idea. Down in the Oaxacan village where she came from, many people would not use the *Suero Oral* because it was seen as a Hot entity—one that would interact with what was causing the diarrhea from their perspective, which was anger or *coraje*.

The Amuzgan Indians see the anger (*coraje*) between a husband and wife, or between any two people, as a disease that can manifest with many signs and symptoms. Diarrhea is one of the symptoms of *coraje*. The *coraje* comes off the individuals who are fighting and "falls" somewhere on a vulnerable person's body—babies are especially vulnerable. If it "falls" on their stomach they get diarrhea. If it "falls" on their lungs they get pneumonia. If it "falls" on their heart they could die.

The *coraje* also can get on a breast-feeding baby through the breast milk. Lupita said that Little Dove was "drinking her angry blood," in her breast milk. She wasn't sure which way Little Dove had gotten the *coraje*, but to be on the safe side she had stopped breast-feeding her. This, in turn, was exacerbating Little Dove's dehydration.

Because *coraje* is Hot, according to the Amuzgan way of classifying illnesses, it must be treated with Cool medicines like the *limpia de huevo* that Lupita was about to perform. On the other hand, the *"suero"* (which in Spanish means "intravenous solution" although it is consumed orally) is considered Hot. In fact, all things associated with modern medicine and hospitals are considered strong and Hot. As far as Lupita and her people were concerned, the life-saving *Suero Oral* was *not* considered to be a treatment option for diarrhea caused by *coraje*. A Hot illness and a Hot treatment were actually considered to be a dangerous, even fatal, combination.

Lupita listened to me as I spoke about the importance of using the *Suero Oral*. I had been doing research for the past six months in her home village in Oaxaca. As a medical anthropologist, I almost never intervened in what people were doing. If they asked me what I'd do in a particular situation, I would tell them. Other than that, I saw myself as their guest who was trying to learn their ways. Usually anthropologists are observers and there are ethical considerations that must guide us if we do take action. Before we do anything, we need to consider what ramifications our actions will have on the people we are trying to help. But the gravity of Little Dove's situation made me leap in and go beyond my normal hands-off approach. I really tried to get Lupita to give Little Dove the *Suero Oral*. As I finished my attempt to convince her about what to do, Lupita looked at me, smiled, and said we'd carry on with the *limpia de huevo*. Lupita reiterated that the egg cleansing would take away the anger that was causing Little Dove's diarrhea.

Lupita set to curing Little Dove. She gathered leaves from the lemon tree (*hoja de limon*), alcohol (*aguardiente*), and roots (*ruda*). With these herbs chopped up in a pungent smelling mixture she took an egg, dipped it in the mixture, and rubbed the egg and the curative mix all over Little Dove's body. Starting at the baby's head, she rubbed the mixture into her hair, then spread it over her arms, her legs, and her stomach, as well as over the soles of her feet and the palms of her hands. Little Dove lay on her back as her mother rubbed her down. The electricity was working that day (it often did not work), and a fan was blowing over her little, emaciated body. Little Dove looked calm and happy during the entire procedure.

Every time I saw a child get a *limpia de huevo*, I was struck by how happy and relaxed the whole procedure made them.

I never knew if Little Dove got any of the *Suero Oral*. In the days that followed she looked better. She was less dehydrated, was eating more, and was wetting more diapers—all signs that she was getting more liquids and nutrients. The young male farmworkers made up the packets of *Suero Oral* for themselves to drink out in the fields. Since they weren't sick, the *Suero Oral's* Hot qualities were not an issue, and they felt that drinking it would make them stronger during the long, hot days out in the fields.

GETTING READY FOR THE GRAPE HARVEST: NEWCOMERS IN THE CAMP

The days and weeks passed and many more workers started showing up for the grape harvest. The camps were swelling to capacity as hundreds of workers arrived for the harvest. This rapid influx of people stressed all the available resources and resulted in cramped living conditions, overflowing latrines, and periodic shortages of water. It was also a time when one could make new friends and enjoy the company of a wide variety of individuals from all over Mexico. For a while, people forgot the hard work and had some fun.

One hot afternoon we were relaxing after lunch when a family arrived from Guanajuato. Each time another family came into the camp they had to stake their claim on one of the rooms in the housing sheds. The father of this particular family had a big bundle tied up with string slung across his back. It was the family's belongings, their clothes and cooking utensils.

We were sitting on the benches outside the shelters swatting flies and talking a little bit after a lunch of watery beef soup and mounds of tortillas. A quiet came over the group as the newcomers walked in. All of a sudden the father of the new family started singing, "Things for sale! Clothes, shoes, blankets!" Everyone laughed at the joke of selling the clothes off their backs. He kept up the joke, deadpan, till the whole camp was laughing very hard. He pantomimed trying to sell us each something. He offered to lower his prices. He even pulled off his own shirt and tried to get one of the young girls to try it on. She giggled and hid behind some of the smaller children who had flocked to see what the commotion was about.

Laughing, Lupita got up and showed the newcomers where they could put their possessions and sleep. Then she invited them to the table for a cold drink. The father had eased his family into the camp and gotten a rather prime room with a good porch for his humorous performance.

PICKING GRAPES

The farm where Lupita and her family lived and worked was planted almost exclusively in grapes. When the harvest began, I went out with the workers and picked grapes alongside them. In this way I came to know them better.

By the time we were going out into the fields to pick grapes, Lupita was feeling a bit stronger and she left Little Dove in the care of one of the younger girls who had just recently come up from Oaxaca. She paid the girl 10 pesos each day to care for her. Since a person could earn about 30 pesos a day (about $3) if she worked really hard, her outlay for child care was considerable. Like working mothers everywhere, she was working a good part of her day just to pay the babysitter. The young babysitter had rigged up several little child-sized hammocks from corn sacks under the porch awning of the workers' quarters. In the dense heat of the day she'd swing the babies back and forth in the hammocks, trying to keep them quiet and as cool as possible in the oppressive climate.

Only the smallest children stayed behind with the babysitter because by the age of six or seven the farmworkers' children were out in the fields helping their parents bring in the grape harvest. Without the help of everyone in the family, fieldwork like this didn't pay enough to make ends meet. Indeed, a couple of families who didn't have any young children to help them out in the fields told me that they wouldn't be coming back the next year because they had spent more on travel and food than they were making as laborers. About half of the fieldworkers, like Lupita and her family, came from southern Mexico. They referred to themselves—and others referred to them—as Indians (*indigenas*). The other half were the poorer, *mestizo* (non-Indian) families from the northern Mexican states of Sonora and Sinaloa. Many of the children in these families experienced infectious illnesses such as diarrhea and dehydration as well as work-related injuries and pesticide exposures.

Little Dove's three-year old sister, Laurita, became ill with a fever during this time. Lupita believed that it came from a fright (*susto*) because a large dog had chased her and tried to bite her just before the fever started. Lupita had given her cooling baths, but did not want to take her to the hospital. Even if she had wanted to do so, she would have had to pay for transportation (about half a day's wages) and would have lost a day's wages from her work. Instead, Lupita opted to take

Laurita to the herbalist who lived within walking distance of the camp.

The herbalist had prescribed several things, but one of her treatments had caused little Laurita even further problems. The herbalist had placed a couple of cloves of garlic into her vagina, and they had caused a severe local irritation and infection. When this began, Lupita was compelled to take the little girl to a doctor, who removed the garlic and gave her some ampicillin for the infection. Trying to save time and money hadn't worked in this case. Migrant farmworking women such as Lupita are always forced into difficult decisions about health care for their children. Losing wages and paying for transport have negative consequences for the entire family. Yet, it is also dangerous if a mother ignores the needs of a sick child. These mothers face very difficult options.

FROM LITTLE DOVE TO LILLIANA

A few weeks after the *limpia de huevo* treatment, Lupita brought Little Dove by for me to see. Lupita had pierced the baby's ears and placed red strings through the holes that would protect her from illnesses as well as allow her to sport sparkly little earrings in a few months. Little Dove had on a new dress and little white socks. She was looking much better, although she still probably weighed less than 10 or 12 pounds. I mentioned to Lupita how delighted I was at Little Dove's progress and how she seemed to be over her diarrhea.

She then explained what had really happened. A few days after the egg cleansing Little Dove had taken a turn for the worse. I had been absent from the camp for several days visiting another farm. Late one evening, during that time, Lupita and her husband thought that Little Dove was going to die because she had another severe bout of diarrhea that drained her body of what little strength she'd managed to build up.[1] The couple had gotten a ride into town and, con-fused about what to do next, made an emergency phone call back home to Oaxaca. By phone they talked to one of the traditional medicine people, *curanderos*, in the village. The *curandero* had instructed them on how to do another sort of egg cleansing, this one involving more powerful herbs. It seems this cure had been the answer to Little Dove's problems. Lupita spent two weeks' wages on the cure, but she was satisfied with how things had turned out.

I, too, was pleased. During my period of research, I felt it necessary to try to intervene in health matters on very few occasions. I had given Lupita my opinion and I had respected her decision to ignore it. Little Dove had gotten better and Lupita and I still had a good relationship.

The long, hot summer was drawing to an end. It was September and I was getting ready to go back down to Oaxaca to spend time in Lupita's home village. On the last day before I left, I stopped by to say good-bye to Lupita, Laurita, and Little Dove. I was delighted to learn that Little Dove was now being called Lilliana. She had been given a real name. The little girls were swinging in one of the hammocks. Their laughter filled the air. Laurita tickled her sister every time she'd reach for the orange slice that Laurita was teasing her with. All of a sudden, in one quick move, Lilliana grabbed the piece of orange and stuffed it into her mouth. Far from the listless little baby I'd first met four months earlier, Lilliana now had the look and the humor of a real survivor.

SUGGESTED READINGS

Wright, Angus. (1990). *The Death of Ramón González: The Modern Agricultural Dilemma.* Austin: University of Texas Press.

Scheper-Hughes, Nancy. (1992). *Death without Weeping: The Violence of Everyday Life in Brazil.* Berkeley: University of California Press.

---

[1] It is the repetitive nature of severe diarrheal episodes that can be so dangerous. Over weeks and months the individual becomes progressively weaker, and it becomes more difficult for them to recover from subsequent illnesses.

17

A Virgin to the *Vaka*

Vaughn Koops
University of Melbourne

The Cook Islands are an archipelago of 15 small islands scattered over 1,800,000 square kilometres of Pacific Ocean, between Tonga and Samoa to the west, and French Polynesia to the east. Formerly annexed to New Zealand, the Cook Islands achieved independence in 1965.

Rarotonga, lying to the south of the group, is the largest of these islands, although it is just 32 kilometres in circumference, and has the largest population of all the islands at about 8,000 people. Rarotonga is the island through which most trade in the Cook Islands flows and is where the Cook Islands government sits when in session. It is the only island in the group with an international airport. Since the airport opened, in the mid-1970s, the number of tourists visiting the Cook Islands has increased markedly, as has the emigration of Cook Islanders to other countries. Although the per-capita consumption of alcohol is high in comparison to other Pacific nations, it is quite similar to that of New Zealand and Australia. In recent times, people have noticed that more Cook Islanders are prepared to stop drinking after just one or two glasses; however, binge drinking remains the norm in Rarotonga.

Noncommunicable diseases are becoming more prevalent as causes of morbidity and mortality in the Cook Islands. This is associated with more effective communicable disease control, and particularly with changes in the diets of Cook Islanders, with an increasing reliance on imported foods. The Cook Islands have high rates of diabetes, coronary heart disease, high blood pressure, and gout. High alcohol consumption is an associated risk factor with many of these. In addition, 55 percent of vehicle accidents are reported as alcohol-related. It is likely that this underestimates the proportion of accidents that are alcohol-related.

Alcohol was unknown in Rarotonga before the arrival of Europeans. Rarotongans did drink *kava*, an intoxicating beverage prepared from the rootstock of the kava plant (*Piper methysticum*), but the consumption of *kava* was rapidly discontinued following the arrival of the first missionaries in the 1820s. It was not until the 1850s that techniques for brewing "orange beer" were introduced from Tahiti, much to the missionaries' disgust and censure. Originally this alcohol had to be consumed in secret, because its use was prohibited. Rituals associated with the consumption of this "bush beer" were, in a number of respects, similar to those previously associated with the consumption of *kava*. However, nowadays most people living in Rarotonga do not practice these rituals when drinking alcohol. Only since independence was granted have Cook Islanders been legally permitted to drink alcohol, and only since 1985 has it been legal to produce alcohol within the Cook Islands.

The following discussion demonstrates, in part, how drinking practices in Rarotonga are intimately bound up with wider processes of globalisation. Many aspects of drinking practices found in contemporary Rarotonga are similar to those found in other places, and, consequently, differences are more subtle than profound.

A vaka is a district, of which there are three in Rarotonga. As you read about the vaka, consider the following questions:

1. What are some aspects of drinking alcohol that may affect the health and well-being of Cook Islanders? List the health problems that arise from drinking.
2. Are there any ways in which the meanings of alcohol and drinking in Rarotonga differ from your own experience, or knowledge, of alcohol and drinking?
3. Do you think it is appropriate, from a Cook Islander's point of view, to regard alcohol consumption as primarily a medical, or health, issue?
4. Do you think that this kind of research would encourage drinking? Is it ethical to conduct any such research?

It was about four o'clock on a Friday afternoon when Tony rang me from next door to see if I would like to go over and have a drink with him and a few of the boys. Work this week had been particularly long and difficult for Tony, and as far as he was concerned the best way to relax and "stop going crazy" was to buy some beers, maybe a dozen or two, sit down with some friends, and drink them all up. For Tony, and many other Cook Islanders, the drinking would start at four o'clock every Friday, and continue throughout the weekend—although it wasn't uncommon to have a few drinking sessions during the week as well. After saying goodbye to my wife, Sarah, I put on my sandals and walked next door, which was just on the other side of the coconut and chestnut trees that grew around our house.

Walking across the courtyard I could see Tony and Henry seated at the picnic table, each leaning forward on their elbows, Heinekens placed in front of them. Henry was a quiet man in his mid-30s who sometimes worked for Tony's family in their trucking business. Tony was approaching 40, but worked at another job around the island, rather than for the family. Although Tony's family were from Atiu, one of the "outer islands" of the Cook Islands group, his immediate family had lived on Rarotonga all his life, and this house was now known throughout Rarotonga (and was listed in the phone book) as the Plumber Family House. Although the Plumbers held other leases around the island, this house was thought of as their home—Tony's father was buried at the front of the house, in a white-washed concrete grave that stood above the ground, with a small roof to shelter it. Graves like this are a familiar sight in Rarotonga, and you often will see children playing chase in their yards, on and around their ancestors' graves. Sometimes Tony would sit beside his father's grave and "talk to the old man" about things that were troubling him, or the latest island gossip. His dad used to be a heavy drinker when he was alive, and died from kidney failure quite a few years ago now.

Henry smiled and said hello as I walked over, and Tony opened the deep freezer, hauling out a Heineken for me to drink. There were a couple of cartons (boxes of two dozen cans) stashed in there. A Deep Purple CD was playing on the stereo.

We talked for a while, catching up on who was doing what, how work was going, and what were the latest scandals to hit the island. Recently there had been rumours circulating that the Prime Minister was going to lose his job, and that a new coalition government would form. I added my two cents' worth, commenting on what, in my opinion, were the nefarious deeds of one high-profile politician. Tony, however, would rather not talk about this particular public figure:

"Why not?"

"He's my uncle, you know."

"Oh, of course, you're both from Atiu, eh?"

"Yeah. Uncle is alright; he treats us well."

Politicians in the Cooks do tend to look after their extended families and political supporters well. Very often, in fact, a politician's extended family and political supporters are the same people. So we talked about other politicians, ones that Tony and Henry weren't related to. Judging by the cans now stacked up on the table, Henry and Tony had drunk about five each—this was especially obvious because Henry, who was normally very shy, and didn't say much around other people, had started giving us a detailed account of the intricacies of production-line car manufacture. He used to work in a factory in New Zealand a few years ago, before the vehicle industry was deregulated, the factories closed down, and Henry was made redundant. According to Cook Islanders, one way to tell when shy people are drunk is when they start talking, talking, talking. Sometimes, people who you only ever hear talking Cook Islands Maori will suddenly start speaking English when they are drinking.

Tony's older brother, Max, came out of the house, said hello to me, walked to his car, and drove off. Tony and his brother hadn't been on good terms for a couple of weeks, since they were both drinking and had an argument. I think it was over a girl, but it was hard to say because Tony only told us they argued—about what, he would not say. Although Tony never fights when he is drinking, his brother sometimes has a very bad temper. During this argument Max picked up a chair and threw it at Tony, which hit him in the forehead and cut him quite badly. Tony kept out of his brother's way and called some friends for help. They drove over and took him to the hospital to have some stitches put in. The scarring was still quite obvious. To my thinking, he was quite lucky not to have more visible scars. In the past 20 years or so, Tony had seven motor vehicle accidents, three in cars and four on motorbikes. But, as he took care to point out, only five of them had been after "serious heavy drinking" when he shouldn't have been driving. For the other two he thought he was sober enough to drive.

At about five o'clock or so, stereos in the neighbouring houses started up, one a little way past our house, and another over the back hedge, through the bush a little way. They were loud, and I was sure I could feel the tropical air shuddering with the thump of the bass. A curious mix of Venga Boys and Dire Straits drifted over the village. Tony looked at me and smiled:

"He's the brother of the Minister over there. . .," nodding toward Dire Straits.

"Brother of the Minister and he's making home brew!"

I flicked my eyebrows up and down, the Pacific signal of acknowledgement, or at least it seemed to work that way for me. We chuckled for a bit, talking some more. Tony told me the house on the corner of Te Ara Metua (the ancient road, now tar sealed, running around most of Rarotonga) was another home brew house, and there the proprietor was an elder of the Cook Islands Christian Church. This warranted another chuckle.

"Hey, Tony!"

We turned toward the road to see Ta'i shuffling toward us, smiling and waving. Ta'i was a slight man of about 50, eyes glazed and a bit yellow, always with a happy look on his face. We shifted around the table and made room for him. Before Tony could begin moving toward the deep freeze, Ta'i asked him if he could have a beer. Tony opened a Heineken and handed it to Ta'i. We asked Ta'i how he was, where he'd been, but he was a bit vague and was happy just to listen to us talk, smiling and laughing occasionally. Tony tried to include him in the conversation:

"Ta'i almost played for the All Blacks (the New Zealand rugby union team), you know, Vaughn; he was really quick, eh, Ta'i?"

"Mmm," Ta'i smiled.

"So you used to live in New Zealand, Ta'i?" I asked.

"Yes, yes," nodding and smiling.

"They're not letting you in the homebrew house today, eh, Ta'i?" said Tony.

"No, no, they say I need money, eh." Ta'i looked at Tony, his expectation clear.

"How much do you owe? Here, here."

Tony handed Ta'i some money—I couldn't see how much. Ta'i sat on for a while as we talked, sipping his beer, then rose and said thank you and goodbye, smiling all the time, and left. When he had gone, Tony filled me in. Ta'i worked for the family company every so often when he needed money—just for a few days until he had enough saved, and then he'd go back to drinking again. Tony gave Ta'i some money because he knew the company owed Ta'i some pay, and also because Ta'i was a friend and Tony wanted to help him out. Apparently he had diabetes, and he was an "alcoholic," which is why he looked so skinny.

"Alcoholics, are there a few of them around?"

"Yeah, in this village, and that's the real down side of things—that they do sort of walk the roads at six o'clock in the morning looking for another dose of alcohol."

"What does the village do? Do people in the village do anything about that?"

"Yeah, I think the village leaves it up to people like that. I mean, you're gonna get the rich and the poor, so

you're gonna get the healthy and the ill and, of course, people don't disregard them totally; there is a lot of advice given to them but it's up to them whether they want to take it and sort of give up drinking."

In the Cook Islands, relationships between people and their families, and other people of the village, are an important part of everyday life. Given these strong ties and relationships, I was often surprised at how willing Cook Islanders were to let individuals within the village make their own decisions, and live their lives as they chose.

There were a few other "alcoholics" in the village. Tony told me about a man who looked like a skeleton, apart from his swollen stomach, "like those children in Ethiopia." Doctors said that his liver had been damaged by drinking, and this caused his stomach to swell. Despite advice to the contrary, he kept drinking—and died as a consequence. There have been many cases of disease associated with chronic heavy alcohol use in the Cook Islands.

I asked Henry and Tony if they drank much homebrew. Their unanimous answer was no!—only when you have run out of kava papa'a (imported alcohol) do you drink kava maori (homebrew). Most mapu (younger adults, very loosely aged 16–35 years) felt the same way, that kava maori tasted horrible and was unhygienic. You only drank homebrew when you had no money, or all the shops were closed and you couldn't get anything else. Most of the time though, if you knew the shop owner and woke him or her up, you could get kava papa'a anytime you wanted, as long as you had money. Just about every grocery shop in Rarotonga sold alcohol nowadays. Homebrew cost just a few dollars for a big bottle, just a few mouthfuls were enough to get you feeling drunk, and homebrew houses were open all hours. It used to be that homebrew was made from local fruits—oranges, bananas, even pineapples—but nowadays most of the brewers used commercial brewing kits, imported from New Zealand, producing malt-and-hops beers.

Now it was getting on to six o'clock, and the Assembly of God congregation in the hall across the road had cranked up their sound system, competing in gospel with the Venga Boys and Dire Straits. I was feeling hungry so I asked Tony and Henry if they would like to come home for dinner. They both declined—they'd rather stay where they were and continue drinking. Later, Tony told me:

"I never eat while I'm drinking."

"Why not?"

"It makes you tired and sleepy, and then you don't want to keep drinking anymore; you just want to go to sleep."

"And then you miss the party?"

"Yep, or if you do eat, it's always at the end of the night and you go get some takeaway from Just Burgers and that's greasy food, heavy, you know? Better to just wait until tomorrow and get some *ika mata* (raw fish) and drink some *nu* (coconut milk), then you feel much better. . ."

By about 8:30 the air had cooled, so I changed from shorts and sandals into jeans and hiking boots and walked back over to the Plumber Family House. A few more people had joined Tony and Henry by this time—Vira, a plump, happy woman who lived just down the road, and Roy, a wiry young man who lived over toward the west of the island, up in the Avatiu Valley. Someone had brought along some Victoria Bitter, an Australian beer, and there was a mixture of empty Heineken and VB cans piled up in one of the Heineken cartons from earlier that evening. Roy had brought along some fish that he dried a few days ago, and everyone was tearing off pieces and chewing as they drank, laughed, and talked. Tony passed me a can as I sat down, listening to Roy's story about how he and his friend trapped a shark in the lagoon up at Manihiki, another island in the Cooks group.

It was getting dark when a motorbike pulled into the driveway, and we looked to see who had arrived. The rider was an older woman, maybe in her mid-40s, dressed in a short black skirt, with plenty of makeup on. She had a black eye. Tony and Roy called her the Black Widow, and when I asked them why, they laughed and said it was because "she creeps in your window at night." She got the black eye from a fight with her boyfriend, after they had been out drinking one night. He thought she had been flirting with another man, which, to be sure, was probably the case. She called out to Tony, asking him if Okota'i, one of the company workers, was still there. He wasn't, so she got back on her scooter and drove off.

In Rarotonga, it wasn't uncommon for spouses to have fights after one, or both, of them had been drinking. Tony's sister, Sera, was often beaten up by her husband. After a particularly bad fight, Sera called the police and they took her husband away to the cells for the night. However, the police would not press charges until Sera made an official complaint. Consequently, her husband's extended family put a lot of pressure on her not to make a complaint, demanding that she keep things in the family. She was afraid that if he was prosecuted or put in prison, she would be unable to find enough money to feed and clothe her children and pay for their school fees. She had considered leaving him, but Rarotonga is a small island with relatively few people, and it was difficult to find anywhere secret to stay without being discovered. Ultimately she dropped her complaint, as she had done all the other times before.

Legislature required the police press charges for all episodes of domestic violence, regardless of whether the spouse made an official complaint, yet often they did not prosecute. Tony speculated that a number of police officers are reluctant to press charges because they too are known to have beaten up their spouses.

By about 11 o'clock, we decided it was time to go "outing," which is a term meaning to "hit the town." We were going to the Banana Court, or BCs as it is known in Rarotonga. By now the Orama Dance Troupe would have finished their performance for the tourists and curious locals, and people would be gathering at BCs to party. BCs used to be the only nightclub on Rarotonga, but now there are a number of other bars and nightclubs scattered around the island.

Henry had started up his scooter and Vira sat behind him. Roy had his own motorbike. I asked them if they were OK to drive, and they said yes. Roy offered me a ride, but I decided to walk into town with Tony—after all, BCs was only five minutes' walk away, at the most. We walked down Happy Valley Road and on to Te Ara Metua, passing the monument to Pape'iha, a Tahitian missionary who was the first to introduce Christianity to Rarotonga. Tony said to me:

"I'll probably have an afterhours later, if you want to come over."

An "afterhours" is a party, after the bars have closed.

"So, it's going to be a big night then?"

"Yeah."

It's not unusual for "afterhours" to go through the whole weekend. Usually, Tony says, if he starts drinking after work on the weekend and he's still going at, say, five or six in the morning, then his mind starts telling him, "whoa, you've been going a long time, you've gotta take a rest or something," so he'll probably have something to eat, drink lots of water, and take a nap.

"So how long would you nap for?"

"Oh, an hour, two hours, and then if the party's still happening get back into it; I don't want to miss out if it's still going."

I knew that Tony's parties didn't always make his family very happy, particularly now that his niece also was living in the family home with her newborn child. Some of them (the ones who didn't drink) thought Tony drank too much, and said so:

"They used to go, 'oh, Tony, man, you drink quite a bit,' and I'd go, 'hey, I can stop when I want to.' Just to prove it I used to go without drinking for six weeks before my birthday, just to prove to everyone I could do it, but when it comes around to my birthday, of course, right, I'm gonna have my first drink, yay!"

"So, when was the last time you did that?"

"Well, I've done it so often it's become boring so now I just set other challenges instead. . ."

By the time we arrived at BCs, tourists were already streaming into buses waiting to carry them back to various resorts around the island. Some tourists had hired scooters, and they wobbled down the main road, accidentally flicking indicator lights and struggling to find gears. A couple of them were strapping on helmets, which was a sure sign they weren't from around here. We walked into the Banana Court. A mixture of Cook Islanders and tourists danced on the sunken dance floor, and people crowded around the walls and the bar, on the far side of the room. On the right I spotted Vira and Henry, leaning on the wall with drinks in hand, Henry with a large bottle of Steinlager, Vira with a lemonade and vodka. There is a locally made commercial beer, called Cook's Lager, but most people drink alcohol imported from New Zealand and Australia, even though it's a bit more expensive. It just tastes better.

Tony asked me what I was drinking, his shout. When someone "shouts," they are buying drinks for the entire group, with the expectation that later on everyone else will take turns to "shout" until it is the first person's turn to "shout" again. The favour need not be returned that night, however, and need not be returned in kind. So, for example, when Tony came over a few days before to see if he could borrow my motorbike, I was happy to let him take it. People do keep track of favours though, even if it is in an informal way—if you don't pay back favours sooner or later, people stop inviting you to go out with them.

Beer was fine, so I followed Tony to the bar to help carry bottles back for all of us. At the bar he ordered the drinks and told the barman to put it all on his tab. It came to about 30 dollars. Thirty dollars (not to mention the shouts that come later) is a lot of money when your weekly pay is just NZ $180. I knew this was certainly the case for Tony. Like a lot of people, if he spent too much money drinking, the bills would go on hold for a week or so, and any necessities he might need this week he would get with *kaio'u* at his local store. *Kaio'u* is credit—pay you back later. There were limits to *kaio'u* though, especially in a small community where shop owners often knew that if you weren't paying them back this week, it was because you had spent all of your money on booze for yourself and your friends, again. None of this worried Tony, however. He liked to shout people because he liked to see people being happy, and, as far as he was concerned, people were happy when they were drinking, although sometimes the bar tab could be a bit of a shock at the end of the week.

For single people, spending too much money on booze was not considered a real problem. But relatives and neighbours feel sorry for the children who have no dinner because their parents have spent the money on alcohol, and will make sure these children are fed, calling them next door at meal times. Sometimes, a husband will spend the food money on alcohol, and then come home and argue with his wife because there is no dinner ready. But how can you cook dinner when all the food money has been drunk?

Henry joined us at the bar and took some bottles back to the others, so I was left with just mine to carry back. Someone tapped me on the shoulder; it was Pita:

"Pita, hey, man, how are you?"

Pita was a young man who I interviewed a few months before, he worked around the island at Titikaveka:

"Oh, I'm good; yeah, I'm alright."

"Just drinking orange juice tonight, huh, Pita?"

Pita smiled, "I have to; I'm on the antibiotics."

"Antibiotics, how come?"

He had a jacket on, and from beneath it he produced an arm. It wasn't the same arm I saw him with the last time we met. This one was in a cast. But it was his hand that made the impact. It was swollen, very swollen, and kind of yellow-purple in colour, obviously infected. The ends of some wires poked out from beneath the skin.

"How did that happen?"

"Accident. Fell off my bike."

"Man, that's no good, it's pretty swollen, eh?"

"I'm going to New Zealand on Friday, get the operation."

It turned out that his arm had been operated on twice here in Rarotonga, but it still hadn't come right. So, as with all critical cases, Pita was flying to Auckland, New Zealand, so the doctors there could sort it out, if it was not too late already. Pita's arm was broken when he drove into a tree. The first operation failed to set it properly. So did the second, and this time it was further complicated by infection. He didn't tell me then, but I found out later, by putting two and two together, that Pita was drunk when he drove into the tree. Pita's family was being put under pressure by the hospital to pay for his travel to New Zealand, because he was drunk when the accident happened. His family was struggling to raise NZ $2,000 the hospital demanded.

"I have to learn how to write with this arm, eh?"

"That must be pretty hard."

"My writing looks like a kid's again (laughs)."

"But you'll be right when it's fixed up."

"Oh no, no, I won't be using this arm again. . ."

More complications—nerve damage. Pita was 21 at the time and had been drinking for just two years. Until now, he had "only" had one accident. The other time, he was drinking vodka with some friends when they decided they would like to go downtown. Although he didn't remember any of it, his friends told him that he got on his bike and drove straight across the road and off the other side, cutting his face quite badly. They took him home and put him to bed, where he awoke at three in the morning to find the bed soaked with blood. He had a shower and used some ointment on his cuts for the next few weeks, until they finally healed up. When I spoke to him about this first accident, he thought it was "funny." All his friends were laughing the next day when they told him about it.

I stayed and talked to Pita for a while, and then to some other friends standing around one of the small tables next to us, all joking, laughing, and dancing. A girl swept up and grabbed Pita, pulling him on to the dance floor. He followed, carefully shielding his arm from the other dancers. A lot of people said that they were normally too shy to approach people they liked, and only had the confidence to do so after a few drinks. In fact, Tony once told me that of all the relationships he had been in, only one began when there was no alcohol involved. We watched them dance for a while, until the girl accidentally walked into a stool and fell over, taking a few patrons' drinks with her. Pita gathered her up with his good arm and led her toward the door. She was unsteady on her feet and staggered along beside him. Just before they stepped out the door, Pita looked at me, grinned, and rolled his eyes. I waved him goodbye.

It was getting close to two o'clock, closing time for a Friday night. I weaved my way back through the crowd to find Tony. Tony was talking to a large man, standing with a beer hovering below his chin, surveying the crowd. Tony introduced me to the man, whose name was John.

"Hi, John, my name's Vaughn."

"Pleased to meet you, Vaughn. So what brings you to Rarotonga?"

"I'm a student, studying drinking here in Rarotonga."

"Oh, you're the one; my brother was telling me about you. So what do you actually do?"

"Well, I'm seeing what people do when they drink, what they think about it, that kind of thing."

John laughed: "That's simple mate; we drink, we get pissed, and we fall over."

"Yeah, well, I want to see how people feel when they're drinking and . . ."

"You don't know how it feels?"

He was shaking his head now.

"Well, I know how it feels but . . ."

I was beginning to sense that I wasn't going to get far with this. Time to change tack: "How does it feel?"

"Mate, you're just a virgin; you're just a virgin to drinking."

John continued in this vein for a while, and I slowly disengaged from the conversation. Sometimes people took exception to what I was doing, which was understandable. A lot of people said they drink to relax, and some of them didn't want to feel as though they were under scrutiny when they were drinking. I made a point of telling people what I was doing in Rarotonga, and if they didn't like it, I left them alone. Most of the time people didn't mind.

A little after 2:15, the music stopped, side doors to the Banana Court were opened, and people started leaving. Tourists, ex-pats, and Cook Islanders found their cars and scooters and started their short journeys home. "The best thing about living in Rarotonga," a barman once told me, "is that you can get pissed and still drive home afterward." When I was in Rarotonga, the police did not have breath-testing equipment, and most of the time they didn't lay charges for drunk driving unless an accident had occurred. By now it was now time for the "afterhours." Tony and I started walking back home.

At the Plumber Family House we were soon joined by some Cook Islanders Tony had bumped into at BCs and invited to the "afterhours," and a few more who had heard the music as they drove past and decided to gatecrash. The beer from earlier that evening had long run out, and now vodka and fruit juice were the favoured drink. I grabbed a juice, figuring it was as good a time as any to stop drinking. Among the crowd were a couple of boys visiting Rarotonga from Ma'uke (another one of the outer islands) and a gatecrasher called Angelina, who loudly announced that her husband was elsewhere on the island and that she was looking for a man. Tony was constantly having to turn the stereo down, as one of the boys from Ma'uke had obviously decided that loud music was good music, and kept on turning the volume back up. The other boy from Ma'uke was showing an interest in Angelina, and they had started cuddling in the corner. I looked over and was surprised to see his hands cupped around Angelina's breasts—public displays of intimacy by Cook Islanders are usually very rare—in fact it is often said that you can tell the Cook Islanders who have lived in New Zealand, because they're the only ones you will see holding hands with their spouses in public.

The "afterhours" continued through the early morning, with most of the drinkers becoming progressively more drunk as time wore on.

It also was getting very late now, or early, depending on your perspective. I decided it was time for me to make the trek home. Tony said I was welcome to stay, that soon they were going to go to the beach and watch the sun come up, but I declined the offer. I stood up, said goodbye, and walked home past the coconut and chestnut trees. Venga Boys were still echoing around the bush. As I crept into bed I wished, and not for the last time, that they would buy another bloody CD.

AFTERWARD: MY PLACE IN FIELDWORK

All of the major churches and medical organizations, such as Public Health, are opposed to the excessive consumption of alcohol by Cook Islanders. Some religious organizations encourage their members to abstain from drinking alcohol entirely. However, not all persons of high social status are against the consumption of alcohol. Nevertheless, because of the stance of these organizations toward alcohol, many of the people I met when I went "outing" assumed that as I was researching their use of alcohol, I also would be opposed to drinking and, consequently, would view them in a negative light. The fact that people could observe me drinking alcohol with them implied that I was not necessarily opposed to drinking per se, and that I had not decided that all drinking was bad drinking, as indeed I had not—although clearly there are some potentially serious consequences associated with alcohol consumption. Had I not participated in drinking, it is unlikely that I would have gained as much insight into people's drinking practices. That being said, I did not encourage anyone to drink, and only participated in drinking initiated by other people. For example, I did not hold a drinking party for my farewell, although a number of people encouraged me to do so. Finally, although my participation in, and observation of, drinking practices was an important part of my research, I did not stand by in situations that I felt warranted my intervention. I drove people home who were obviously too drunk to drive themselves safely. I also diffused a few arguments that were about to blossom into fights. However, as in all social situations, my ability to intervene was tempered by the strength of the relationships I had built with people. The irony is, of course, that these relationships probably would not have developed if I had not been there, drinking with them.

I continue to be in contact with Tony. He still lives in Rarotonga, and still drinks most weekends—and the occasional weekday. He still eats *ika mata* for hangovers, and recently got a pay rise, but remains shocked by his bar tab.

SUGGESTED READINGS

Lemert, Edwin M. (1976). "Koni, kona, kava. Orange-beer culture in the Cook Islands." *Journal of Studies in Alcohol* 37 (5): 565–585.

Sherratt, Andrew. (1995a). "Introduction." In *Consuming Habits,* ed. J. Goodman, P. Lovejoy, and A. Sherratt, pp. 1–10. London: Routledge.

18

Trae Had: Kayzy's Reflections

Holly Buchanan-Aruwafu

Key Centre for Women's Health in Society
University of Melbourne

Best known to many people for their role in the Battle of Guadalcanal during World War II, the Solomon Islands consist of hundreds of culturally diverse islands that stretch over a vast region northeast of Australia in the South Pacific. The peoples who live on these islands have been steadily migrating over the past 50 years to the capital Honiara. By 1999 Honiara had a population of just over 49,000 people and was becoming a rapidly growing Pacific city.

Young people are attracted to Honiara in the hope of finding cash work, an education, a place to buy or sell goods, and specialized health services. They come to visit *wantoks* (relatives or people of the same language group) and friends; attend religious, sporting, or cultural events; or catch travel connections. They also are attracted to urban life and want to experience the freedom of being away from family obligations and control.

Honiara is undergoing rapid social, cultural, and technological change, and young people participate in bringing about these changes. In the 1999 census, 72 percent of the population of the Solomon Islands was under the age of 30. While changes can be seen in fashion, music, Pijin language expressions, and technology, increases in sexually transmitted infections (STI) and teenage pregnancies indicate that changes are occurring in sexual mores.

During the 1990s, steady increases in the number of cases of sexually transmitted infections and teenage pregnancies indicated to the Ministry of Health that young people were having unprotected sex, which put their health at risk. Among their greatest concerns was that these young people would be catching HIV and AIDS. Holly Buchanan-Aruwafu, through the story of Kayzy, explores some of the factors that affect young people's sexual health in the Solomon Islands. While not using condoms and having many sexual partners make young people more likely to have sexual health problems, *kastom* (cultural traditions and beliefs), social change, religious values, secrecy in relationships between young people, and lack of employment also can make young people at risk of catching HIV.

As you read, consider the following questions:

1. What are some of the changes occurring in Honiara and what has contributed to these changes?
2. In the Solomon Islands, what are some of the reasons why young people hide their sexual relationships?
3. Why do some young people prefer to use *kastom* medicine when they have a sexually transmitted infection instead of going to a clinic?
4. What cultural, social, economic, or other factors do you think make young people in the Solomon Islands vulnerable to sexually transmitted infections, including HIV?
5. In what way are young people's lives in the Solomon Islands similar to young people's lives in the United States?
6. What are some examples of different *kastom* discussed in this article?

As I stood and waited for the bus near Chinatown, the humid tropical breeze and the lushness of the trees seemed to disappear into the dry dust blowing off the road into my eyes. This and other sections of the main road had been turned into a construction site as it was being made bare for the insertion of water pipes, the repair of potholes, and tarring.

A van pulled up with a Point Cruz sign in the window. I moved forward with a young girl and maneuvered around a bunch of dried coconuts and plastic bags full of cassavas, slippery cabbage, and bananas to grab one of the last seats. The folded seat that opened into the aisle was torn, the backrest precariously tilted to the side.

FIGURE 6   Mendana Avenue, Point Cruz, Honiara. *Photo by Holly Buchanan-Aruwafu.*

The van hummed with the lively talk and laughter of teenagers, dressed in light-blue uniforms and just out from school. In spite of the overpowering heat, the bus windows were pulled shut against the dust. The radio blared as the young driver swayed back and forth to the music of Lucky Dube. A Brazilian soccer flag and a piece of wood with a marijuana leaf burned onto it dangled from the rearview mirror; a sticker with the words "Trust in God" was partially adhered onto the dashboard.

My last stay in Honiara was in 1997 when the first FM radio station, ZFM 100, was launched. Now two other FM radio stations sent pop, rock, reggae, and soul music to urban and village areas across the islands. I had been away for 18 months and access to music, technology, and global images had increased; things had changed.

In 1997, few houses had televisions with video machines, so it was common to see living rooms full with people, or people sitting outside houses peering through open windows to watch a movie. In 1998, televisions and antennas sold out in the capital when the World Soccer Cup became the first broadcasted television ever viewed in Honiara; now there was daily Australian television broadcasting. The number of video stores providing new releases had increased, with a wider selection, cheaper memberships, and more competitive prices for videos. Underground loans of illegal *blu muvi* (pornographic videos) could be negotiated quietly. Most recently, the start of an Internet café provided cheap and easy access to e-mail, opening up the world of the Internet to more Solomon Islanders.

I heard the call for the main market stop and responded with a tissing sound to indicate that I wanted to get off the van; I passed a dollar to the young boy collecting money on my way out. I could see Kayzy in the distance, tossing her hair and laughing with some other girls near the betel nut vendor. She sat on the edge of a large tree root, breaking open the skin of a be-

tel nut, with the half-corked bamboo stick filled with lime, a handful of leaves, and a rolled cigarette all balancing on her knee. While her skirt was well above her knees, she sat with her legs folded in a careful manner, showing her discretion. As Kayzy laughed, I could see her lips were already stained red from chewing betel another time that day.

Kayzy was one of many young people in Honiara who work hard to hide their drinking, night-clubbing, smoking marijuana, and sexual activities. But it is difficult for them to hide increasing teenage pregnancies, single parenting, and the increase in sexually transmitted infections such as gonorrhea and syphilis that the town clinics were reporting. Young people who find it hard to go to school and to get jobs tend to hang out and get involved in organized gangs, sex work, selling of marijuana, and theft. As a medical anthropologist doing research with the Ministry of Health in Honiara, I was interested in how economic and social changes were affecting the lives and especially the sexual health of Kayzy and other young people. I also was interested in how *kastom* contributed to how secretive they were about their lives.

A lot of young people also chew betel nuts (*Areca catechu*), which are the acorn-shaped seeds from a tropical palm tree. But unlike marijuana and alcohol, chewing betel nut is generally a part of *kastom* and social life in the Solomon Islands. It is used in some traditional medicines for stomach pain, diarrhea, gonorrhea, and other complaints, and it also can transfer bad magic, *bua*.

Betel nut is chewed with lime made from ground coral and the leaf or the drooping fruit from the *Piper methysticum* plant. When chewed, the combination creates a reddish color that stains the lips and over time blackens teeth. The mouth feels numb and the chewer feels like spitting the excess red saliva. Betel nut as a stimulant has a similar effect as a beer drunk quickly. Chewing it gives people a feeling of being refreshed with renewed energy, and it can depress hunger.

As I walked closer to Kayzy, the ground under the tree looked like it was splattered with reddish paint. There were some areas of town where chewing and spitting betel nut were prohibited, but despite sporadic crackdowns by council authorities to fine unauthorized vendors, selling betel nut on the street was hard to stop. Kayzy saw me and in one movement of her arm, she motioned me forward and began to move herself away from the group.

She had left work early so that we would not miss our chance to get a free membership at the new video store, Millennium Movies. She had telephoned that morning to let me know that it was opening and if we were one of the first 100 people to get memberships we would save the $80 charge.

"Hey, Holly, OK, let's go negotiate!" she said emphatically.

"Do you think there will be any left?" I asked.

"Don't you worry, I know how to get something I want. I rang them and told them that we were late because we had just come back from gardening in the bush," she said smiling.

I laughed and let Kayzy go ahead with her witty remarks until we walked away with our free memberships in hand, leaving everyone smiling in the shop. After all, it was more than curious for a "Missus," as all white women were called, to be out in the bush carrying *kumara* (sweet potato) back from her garden.

The first time I met Kayzy was in 1997. I went to visit Salomi, who made *kastom medisin* (traditional medicines), and Kayzy was playing with her six-month-old son on a pile of pillows behind their store. I was told that Kayzy had had a child and that she was not married. "That's the way young people are these days. They do not listen to their parents or respect custom," Salomi lamented, but she also made it clear that the child was definitely part of their family.

Meeting Kayzy that day had led Salomi and me into a discussion about *kastom*. What would be the social consequences for young people from the island of Malaita to have sex outside of marriage? Salomi explained that in *kastom,* sexual activities are restricted and controlled through bride price, requests for compensation, and retaliation through violence. If it is discovered that a young girl has had sex and she is not married, she could be beaten by her brothers and then forced to marry the boy. The boy could also be beaten by her brothers and made to pay compensation to her family.

This compensation could be five *tafuli'ae* (red shell money) and sometimes cash as well. Each *tafuli'ae* is made of 10 strands of ground shell beads, usually of white and red colours, joined together with flat wooden or tortoise shell pieces. "These days," continued Salomi holding her arms straight at shoulder length and reaching, "they are usually between 6 and 10 feet long."

If a girl is not a virgin before she is married, the amount of bride price that her family can ask for to reimburse them for the loss of her labor is reduced. Bride price is affected by other things as well: the wealth of the family, the character of the girl, and even how much was paid for her mother when she was married. The kinds of social relationships or ties that are created when bride price payments are made between the families of the groom and bride need to be considered.

When Christianity was introduced in the 1850s, the principle that premarital sex was forbidden became strengthened for Solomon Islanders, even though the missionaries did not necessarily support bride price or the violence and demands for compensation when

FIGURE 7 Tafuli'ae—red shell money. *Photo by Holly Buchanan-Aruwafu.*

people broke the rules about sex. Bride price practices have changed only to a degree. Some churches such as the Seventh Day Adventist, South Sea Evangelical Church, or the Anglican Church do not allow more than five *tafuli'ae* and $2,000 to be paid, but the Catholic Church does not place a limit on bride price. These days bride prices range considerably. It could be as high as 10 *tafuli'ae* and $5,000, in addition to goods such as rice, pigs, taro, yams, and so forth.

Traditionally, because of the importance of bride price, young people in Malaita could be killed because of premarital sex. These days, young men and women still fear compensation and beatings, and as Kayzy explained, "We young girls have to try to keep our reputations as virgins. We fear compensation and violence, as well as the shame and stigma caused by social gossip and school and church sanctions. We have to try to hide everything."

It was not long after I met Kayzy that I left the Solomon Islands. I never asked her about the father of her child or about more personal details of her life. She was overloaded with a new child and working, and I believed at that time it was not appropriate for me to ask her. After I left, I sent her a letter and a pair of shoes for her son. When I returned in 1999 we began to spend more time together. We became friends and she started sharing her life stories with me, as well as her understanding of how life worked in the Solomon Islands.

After we got our video memberships, we decided that we would walk and sit near the ocean at a local hotel, the Kitano Mendana, and have a drink. As we walked along, young people moved in and out around us, some in groups together, some standing alone or leaning against the storefronts. The numbers of young people hanging around to socialize had become more visible.

I reflected in my field notes about youth fashion on Honiara sidewalks—"coiled or *nudol* hair (small braids with or without colored elastics on the ends); dreadlocks; shaven heads; dyed hair; makeup and fingernail polish; tortoise shell rings; shell money necklaces; chains with dangling crosses or skull and crossbones imported by the Chinese shops; tattoos; Bob Marley and African freedom t-shirts; hood hats sporting red, green, yellow, and black colors; brightly colored flowered island shirts; and the influx of second-hand clothing from Australia generating shorter and shorter hemlines that challenge cultural mores of female modesty. Army hats and trousers are increasingly being worn by male youth as ethnic tension between the groups from two islands is increasing. . ."

As Kayzy and I continued to walk towards the hotel, I smelled the distant wafting scent of marijuana. If a person listened closely on a particular area of the street, they could hear young boys advertising what they had for sale and customers looking to buy marijuana.

Seller: *Mi sutim iu?* Do you want me to shoot you?

Buyer: *Sutim mi. Iu garem eniting fo sutim mi?* Shoot me. Do you have anything to shoot me?

Kayzy later told me that she thought marijuana smoking had increased with the influence of reggae music and that people coming back from Papua New Guinea in the middle of the 1980s had first taken the seeds into the country and started to grow it. It was only in the 1990s that it became more obvious when more plants were being harvested. Although it is illegal, it is being grown, it is cheap and easy to buy, and young people are smoking it. It is popular for young people to make bongs out of Schweppes plastic soda bottles.

The Mendana was like an oasis from the heat and dust of the city streets. We sat on white sunbathing beach chairs at the end of the pool looking out at the sea, talking and having a drink in the late afternoon breeze before the sun went down. Here Kayzy told me about her life.

Kayzy had gone to a Catholic boarding school. At boarding school if girls were even suspected of being with boys, they were suspended. The first time she was suspended was when she was in Form 2 (about the equivalent of an American Grade 8). She and some other girls had been picking flowers for a Form 5 graduation and when they returned, they found their water tank empty because everyone was using the water to get ready for the ceremony. She and two other girls took their towels and went to the river to bathe and on their way back they met two boys inside the plantation. They all walked back together. They went to the dorm, changed, and went to the graduation. She was later suspended for four weeks because someone had reported that she had been in the plantation having sex with Form 5 boys. She explained her side of the story, but the principal had already written her suspension letter. She was the only one suspended and after her suspension she returned to school angry.

Kayzy: So after I had finished Form 2 exams and reached Form 3, I started to dislike school. My grades were good but I started to be naughty. *Mi trae had nao;* I was trying my luck with men.

Holly: How was that?

Kayzy: At that time I started to have sex. Having sex, running away at night to go to the nightclub was big, and it was at that time I started to act like that. We would go to a nightclub, then go and drink by the sea, and then we would be dropped at the road near the plantation and we would go through the coconut plantation and then creep up to the school when people were at early morning prayer.

Holly: How old were you then?

Kayzy: I think I was 16, 14, 15 or 16.

Holly: Did you ever use condoms?

Kayzy: Absolutely not. I didn't even know what a condom was.

Holly: Did you ever get any infections?

Kayzy: No, not even when I had two boyfriends in town and one at school. But another student got gonorrhea.

Kayzy had taken home economics classes where they talked about sexuality and reproduction as part of the curriculum, but only superficially. It was taboo for her to talk about sex with her mother and she was never told about menstruation before she had her period. When it happened, she thought she was dying. In this class she did a project on gonorrhea, but they were never taught how to protect themselves as this went against Church teachings. "Most young people do not have information about sex and infections or how to protect themselves. I did not even know what a condom was then."

Young people learn about sex and sexually transmitted infections, including HIV, from their friends, magazines, *blu muvis,* and other videos, as well as from the radio, health workers, teachers, and the newspaper. Young people get advice about some *kastom* treatments to use for STI and about abortion from their peers. Kayzy explained that if young people contract a sexually transmitted infection, they are afraid to go to a clinic because the nurses could write their name in a book, tell one of their relatives, or talk to them in a way that makes them feel ashamed. Because of these reasons, many young people took antibiotic tablets that other friends gave them, or they used *kastom medisin* from their friends or from *kastom* healers.

After she had reached Form 4, Kayzy was suspended again. At her school, if a student is suspended twice for a similar incident, she or he is expelled and a disciplinary committee meets to discuss the case. This time, Kayzy said, "I was wrong. I had gone out at night and when I came back in the morning the man dropped me off beside the classroom and some boys saw me. Later that week they reported me to the principal."

Kayzy: My parents were tired of my behaviour that time. I was at home and mom and dad said that they did not know what to say and they were angry with me. They said "We talk to you but you do not hear us. The first time you were suspended it was from a boy and now this time again; it is too much. Now you will marry and not go back to school."

Holly: They wanted you to marry the boy?

Kayzy: They went and told the boy's family and when I heard this I ran away. I ran away and went to my uncle's house. I told my parents that I would not get married. They said, "Well, you hang around with this boy and not go to school, so you might as well just marry."

Kayzy refused to marry. Then the disciplinary committee agreed that she could go back to school because her grades were good and they were concerned about girls' educations. This was the first time that the school had ever allowed a girl to come back after two suspensions; the first time they had ever given someone a second chance.

Kayzy cut down the numbers of her partners and said she "started to discipline herself" when she was in Form 5. "But one weekend, my boyfriend saw me in town when I was playing sports. Later, when he came to school looking for me, he was drunk. I was then indefinitely suspended, but I could take my exams somewhere else. My mother tried to arrange it all for me but, when we went back to the school to get my things, my books and notes were all gone. Other students had taken them. I felt so bad about the loss of all my hard work that I refused to take my exams."

Kayzy went through a rough time over a period of months looking for work and dealing with the anger of her parents. She would run away, then come back. They told her to leave, and at that point she even thought she would have to do sex work to make money. But she went back to her parents and *mi trae had nao*—"I worked hard, and tried my luck to find some work."

One morning, after cleaning her parent's house, Kayzy saw a newspaper notice from the week before that a company was looking for a secretary. She applied and got the job. It was at this company that she later met the father of her child, who was from another country.

"At that time I still had sex and I didn't use a condom. It is not easy to get condoms and the nurses tell young people that family planning is for married couples." After she found that she was pregnant, her boyfriend wanted her to run away with him to his country, so he bought her a ticket and then flew before her. She had her passport and ticket, but just before she was to go, her father died. She felt sorry for her family and felt she could not leave them now. Her boyfriend rang to find out why she had not come, and she told him that she would raise the child on her own.

Kayzy did not tell her mother that she was pregnant but eventually it became apparent. She had been afraid that they would want to know who the father was so that they could ask for compensation, but no one said anything. "I think they felt sorry because our father had just died, so they did not do anything." After her son was born, her mother told Kayzy that her grandson was hers and that if Kayzy were ever to marry that Kayzy's son would not go with her.

So Kayzy worked and stayed with her family and her son. After two years, Kayzy started to have an interest in a man but hid her relationship from her mother. One day her uncle saw her having lunch with him, and he reported this to her mother. "When I came home that day my mother was angry with me, so I left and stayed the night with him. The next day, my mother hit me and then my brothers went and asked for $1,500 compensation from him."

He paid the compensation and then he asked Kayzy's uncle if he could marry her. Kayzy's mother set the bride price at $10,000 and 10 red shell money. Kayzy's mother had said that she would not stop her from marrying, but the price was too high so that Kayzy knew she would not be able to marry in the Anglican Church. She had conflicting feelings about this relationship and she did not want to lose her son or her family. So she told him that he had to wait for her to make up her mind. Weeks had passed since he had again asked her to marry him.

The sun disappeared beneath the horizon and the mosquitoes were beginning to bite. Kayzy and I had been sitting talking for so long that the night had arrived. Today Kayzy had talked about how difficult it was being a single mother and that it was hard to make all the right decisions. She struggles between getting married and staying single, but she wants to have her child with her. *Mi trae had.* That afternoon she had told her uncle she would not marry the man who had been asking her. She was sure that her mother had already heard of her decision and was wondering why she was so late coming home from work. We walked quickly from the hotel to catch a bus, as we were both late and had to get home to make dinner.

I later thought about Kayzy's story. For me it illustrates the many factors that affect young people's sexual health in the Solomon Islands. Cultural taboos, religious teachings, and a nurse's negative attitudes all can limit discussions about sexuality and condom use. Thus young people do not have clear information about STI, family planning, or how they can protect themselves. Condoms are not easy to get. Because of the fear of the consequences of *kastom* for premarital sex and the harsh words of health workers, young people protect their reputations by creating secrecy about their sexual relationships and they do not always go to clinics when they have an STI or are pregnant. Like many young people Kayzy lost her opportunity for further education, but she was lucky to find

work despite high unemployment. Others in her situation might have to turn to sex work, drug and alcohol use, or involvement in gangs and theft because there aren't many job opportunities for them. Kayzy, like most young people, juggles choices between the expectations of her family, *kastom,* and how she wants to live her life in the changing world around her.

SUGGESTED READINGS

Sex and Youth: Contextual Factors Affecting Risk for HIV/AIDS: A Comparative Analysis of Multi-site Studies in Developing Countries. (1999). UNAIDS, Geneva. http://www.unaids. org/publications/documents/children/99sandy1.pdf.

Pacific Youth Profile. In *The Pacific Youth Strategy 2005: Directions for Pacific Youth towards 2005 and Beyond,* Secretariat of the Pacific Community, New Caledonia. http://www. spc.org.nc.youth.

PART VII

Religion and Belief

Photo by Linda S. Walbridge.

For anthropologists, religion is a social phenomenon. Anthropologists approach religion much differently than do theologians since the "truth" about a religion is not of concern to them. Rather, anthropologists want to know about the ways people understand and relate to the supernatural. They record and study the myths that societies pass down through the generations to explain their origins. They observe and analyze the symbols and rituals that societies use to express their religious beliefs and feelings. They seek to understand how religion serves to unify and to divide societies.

Religion involves communication with the world of spirits: angels, ghosts, demons. It involves the belief that some objects are **sacred**—set apart from ordinary use—or that even ordinary objects may have symbolic value or sacred elements. Religion tells people that some behaviors are forbidden, while others are prescribed. What these objects and behaviors are differ from religion to religion. An ordinary-looking pile of stones might, in the eyes of believers, be endowed with great supernatural powers or **mana.** While one religion might forbid sexual intercourse outside of marriage, another might encourage extramarital sex as a spiritually meritorious behavior. One religion might forbid mind-altering drugs; another might encourage their use as a means to communicate with spirits.

Religious activity often is associated with healing. Before the advent of modern medicine, people had to rely heavily on manipulating the supernatural. In traditional societies, people turned to healers—**shamans**—for help. The shaman would use his powers of divination to discover the cause of an illness and communicate with the spirit world to remove the cause of a person's suffering. But we do not have to look to traditional societies to see the role of religion in healing both the body and the soul. Educated people from highly industrialized societies turn to the supernatural in times of illness, especially in cases that even state-of-the-art medical treatment cannot remedy.

Throughout much of the world today, people adhere to what we refer to as major world religions: Christianity, Islam, Buddhism, Judaism, Hinduism, and others. Over the past several centuries, Christianity and Islam in particular have spread throughout the globe. They often spread to peoples who believe that nature is animated by supernatural powers (**animism**). Spreaders of Christianity and Islam also found themselves teaching their religion to people who had a pantheon of gods, goddesses, or spirits to whom they turned for help. Converts to these religions did not automatically turn their backs on their previous beliefs. Frequently, they made God and the saints of their new religion fit into their already-existing hierarchy. For example, a person might light candles in the church before a statue of the Virgin Mary to ask her intercession with God, but this will not necessarily prevent him from seeking help from a traditional god as well. Often people incorporate symbols from one religious system into another system. For example, an object or a place that traditionally was held sacred might be imbued with a new significance after a people have been converted. Throughout the world, societies have creatively blended religious ideas from the old and the new. This process of blending, which we call religious **syncretism,** continues to produce new rituals and ways of interacting with the supernatural.

Religious beliefs and practices are also affected by the process of globalization, a process that allows for increased contact among peoples and the sharing of cultural practices and ideas. But other factors also have promoted subtle and not-so-subtle changes in religious traditions and practices. Revolutions and civil wars in far-flung parts of the world often have enhanced the role of religion in politics. They also have been the impetus for the migration of millions of people, many of whom have fled to the United States, Europe, and Australia in hope of having a more secure life. They often bring with them religions with which the West has been largely unfamiliar: Buddhism, Hinduism, and Islam, for example. Adaptation to a new homeland inevitably brings about changes in behavior, religious and otherwise. But these new religions also have an impact on the receiving society as well. Their members add their voices to the formulation of new conceptions of the role that religion plays in society.

Ligaya Hattari's account of her mother's battle with cancer is a spiritual journey that takes the reader through a variety of religious paths. We see in this article how her mother incorporated the practices of her Catholic upbringing with those of Javanese traditional beliefs, as well as those of Islam, the majority religion in Java, Indonesia.

As a young research assistant and friend to Larry Kuznar in Peru, Manuel illuminates the complexities of Aymara religious belief. An unlucky encounter with the law leads Manuel to take a dangerous journey up a mountain to make a sacrifice to Andean spirits, spirits that Manuel believes do not conflict with his belief in Catholicism.

Linda Walbridge introduces us to Seyed Moustafa, a Shi'ite Muslim "priest" in a turban and robes, who has fled with his family from the oppression of Sadam Hussein's Iraq. Seyed Moustafa now finds himself in the United States as a preacher and counselor to Muslims, using the centuries-old story of the courage of the hero-saint, the grandson of the Prophet Muhammad, as a way of helping people adjust to their new lives in America.

Other articles related to this topic:

Talking Politics: A Village Widow in Iran by Mary Elaine Hegland

Death and Hope: Syrian Stories by Anne Bennett

The Shaman's Art by Alan Sandstrom and Pamela Effrein Sandstrom

Swamiji: A Life in Yoga by Sarah Strauss

19

Healing the Body, Healing the Soul

California Institute of Integral Studies

....

The current Indonesian government formally acknowledges the practice of five main religions within its borders: Islam, Protestantism, Catholicism, Buddhism, and Hinduism. Historically ancient Hindu-Buddhist influences underlie the ceremonial rituals of these major religions, while more distinct practices are evident among the informal indigenous spiritual traditions.

Ligaya Hattari gives an account of a Western-educated Catholic Filipina. It tells of her spiritual reality in Java, Indonesia. The woman is Hattari's mother. She was a woman who lived in a variety of cultures and experienced religious "syncretism." The term *religious syncretism* is normally defined as a process where various elements of differing religions and traditions are assimilated so that new, revised spiritual tenets emerge. However, such a definition, the creation of something "new," is too simplistic an explanation for this case study. Rather, syncretism should be viewed as an ongoing cultural process, not a final end. In this account the reader can clearly identify the dynamic relations that result from interactions among different hybridized traditions—Javanist mysticism, Islamic ritualism, and Catholicism. Each of these traditions sustained Hattari's mother through her battle with cancer.

In this article, the reader can see how actions, dress, symbols, and so forth subtly reflect meanings of spiritual being in everyday life. This story also shows how religious feelings and ideas intensify during periods of life crises.

As you read, you'll want to consider the following questions:

1. How might Hattari's account of her visit to the shamans differ if she had visited them only as an anthropologist and not as the daughter of a dying woman?
2. Do you think that Mom's choice to immerse herself in religious syncretism was determined by her terminal illness alone? Explain.
3. In what ways do you think Mom's wake and funeral reflected many cultures? Explain.
4. Do you think that Mom's family and friends viewed her death as the end of her spiritual process? Explain.

....

Indonesia has long been the home of many cultural practices. As a Javanese, my father hailed from the most densely populated, and the most politically and economically prominent, of the 13,677 islands in the Indonesian archipelago. While most Javanese are Muslim, you do not have to look far to discover evidence of daily Hindu-Buddhist influences since these practices flourished in Java and the surrounding islands for many centuries prior to the introduction of Islam. In fact, traditional Javanese music and dance distinctly reflect these ancient Indian religions.

My parents were married in a Catholic church in Berkeley some years after they first met at a student gathering at International House. The fact that she was Filipina and he Indonesian was not viewed as an odd pairing, and both found communicating in English quite natural given their Western academic training. Much later he would convert to Islam and marry a Muslim Indonesian woman.

I was an undergraduate, halfway around the world from my mom, yet, I felt "connected" the way mothers and daughters do when they are far apart and find time to catch up on every little detail of their lives during long-distance telephone chats. I was wiping away some tears during a lull in our conversation, my jaw aching from so much laughter after an especially good story, when mom nonchalantly blurted out, "Oh, and, by the way, I found a lump on my left breast about, oh, I'd say 9 or 10 months ago."

Mom probably sensed my inability to respond to her surprise announcement, so she candidly proceeded to explain that the lump was the size of a large walnut and was probably nothing serious and, no, she had not thought of seeing her personal physician nor sharing this information with any other family members. I was dumbfounded with shock. Eventually I found my voice and insisted that she visit an oncologist, immediately! She gently told me that I was overreacting.

Some months later, she finally agreed to come to the United States, stayed with me, met with an oncologist, and had her breast surgically removed. Afterward the surgeon told me that the spread of cancer had been "... a total mess ... it was everywhere."

For the next two years, mom traveled to and from the United States and Indonesia, subjecting her body to several sessions of chemotherapy, radiation treatments, and occasional bouts with various traditional Indonesian "alternative" healing methods. Always, she never complained, made extra efforts to mask her fatigue, and continued to be active in her many professional activities as an educator. I followed her lead, confident that she would heal, my judgment dependent on the assurances of the medical profession that progress was at hand. Whenever I faltered, she would joke, "Don't worry, I'm indestructible!" And, looking at her, my logic told me that she was right. After all, she still looked and acted the same as before. Whatever could go wrong?

That winter break we met in Japan. I was taken aback at the drastic physical transformation she had experienced since just the previous summer. Somehow she seemed so much frailer and exhausted than before, even smaller the way elders become after a while. It was rather strange that our holiday activities consisted of my dad, my sister, and I accompanying mom to the health clinic. Yet, it was the first time in a long time that our nuclear family had been together and mom appeared pleased and beamed with pride.

A month later, my sister was back in the United States, my dad had resumed his busy work schedule, and I had decided to take some time off from school and stay home with mom in Jakarta. By now I had received the numbing verdict of the Japanese cancer specialists that mom had only a few more months to live before her trachea would narrow so much, due to the spread of the cancer, that she would lose the ability to breathe.

During the next few months, on my mom's insistence, I visited many a special shaman who had been recommended by either a relative or a family friend. Everyone seemed to have a solution for mom's ailment, indicating the unique powers of a particular shaman. I wondered why she even bothered to follow up on these suggestions for a holistic approach, but her response was simply, "We must respect each effort to help. Meeting with the shaman whom they feel can heal me can do no harm."

She appeared calm, yet I detected a tinge of fear in her soft whisper—fear that the lump in her breast had been put there by another shaman, one working for another intent on destroying her life. More than a few people had put that idea into mom's mind to the point that her Western analytical skills faded into the backdrop of her daily pattern of activities. Life in Indonesia was very much one of Javanist mysticism and Islamic rituals of protection and blessing.

Each shaman was located in a different region of Java, and my trips became adventure quests of sorts. After each excursion, I would return home bearing various natural medicines and healing symbols, enthusiastically explaining to mom their different functions, and sharing with her my story of how the shaman had presented himself. She always listened attentively to my descriptions and patiently prodded for my perspectives as well.

On one journey to a small village in East Java, the driver of the rented car I had reserved became comfortably animate as we deeply inhaled our aromatic clove cigarettes and exchanged pleasantries. I explained the urgent purpose of my visit and he, sympathetically, reassured me that the shaman we were going to visit was a powerful and wise man with a long history of distinguished, satisfied clients.

That road trip was quite similar to others before it, the sights, smells, and sounds drawing me deeper into the context of its provincial world. Two-way traffic sped precariously close to the sudden drop of the road's bumpy asphalt, dangerously skimming past bystanders who were waiting to cross to the opposite side. I looked out on rectangles of cultivated rice paddies that dotted the surrounding lands whenever the road emerged from the shade of a local rainforest. Bulging green stalks of rice, ready to be harvested, swayed gently in the warm breeze, creating emerald waves atop the still shimmer of the rice paddies' shallow waters that linked it to the earth's life force. There I could see women of various ages diligently working side by side in the knee-high waters of the fields, deftly cutting the stalks and then tossing them into individual back containers. Each had pulled up her *kebaya* sleeves to her elbows and fastened her *kain*, sarong style, higher up to her knees in order to better accommodate her labors. Batik cloths wrapped into a headdress or inverted cone shaped rattan hats diverted the sun's rays, creating a soft personal shade.

It was night by the time we reached our destination. The driver had directed me toward what appeared to be the largest structure in the village, and I left my shoes outside its front doorstep as had others before me. "Assalamualaikum!" I called out. A group of smiling young girls appeared. In unison they responded, "Mualaikumsalam!" then ushered me into the front receiving room of the home. I was the lone female in the audience waiting to meet the shaman, and I respectfully sat apart from the others, defining the difference in gender. I settled into as comfortable a position as possible on the rattan mat that covered the cold dirt floor, trying my best to not cross my legs, rather, to keep my knees and ankles together. The soft sputter of a kerosene lamp and the sounds of the night outside were barely audible above my companions' chatter. Occasional nods and friendly smiles were directed to me, acknowledgment of my presence that I gladly reciprocated. I took a sip from a glass of freshly brewed coffee that had been set down in front of me, its coarse grains floating in the rich mixture.

Without notice, the shaman rushed in. A slight man, middle aged, his dark and rough skin revealed years of outside manual labors. He was barefoot, as we were, and was wearing a clean, white, short-sleeved shirt and dark pants. Barely glancing at us, he promptly seated himself atop the only chair in the room and closed his eyes. Everyone became silent. I noticed thin lines of smoke, originating from the lighted insect repellant coils placed near his chair, rising up behind him, its synthetic smell intruding upon the sweetness of the coffees.

His body started to rock to the left and then to the right, while his hands clenched the undersides of the wood chair he was seated on. Suddenly the rocking stopped and he slouched into the back of the chair, his arms hanging limply at his sides; his eyes appeared to be clouded, seemingly focused on his inner self. A deep voice escaped his lips, announcing that he was an entity from the past. His body and head remaining static, he pointed to the nearest seated man and ordered him to ask one question. The question was succinct, the answer even briefer. Then he proceeded on to the next person and so on. Such was the process of our consultation.

Afterward the shaman's body shook vigorously, as though to rid himself of the ancient spirit that had possessed him, then, once again, he slumped back into his chair. Moments later he had fully recovered, returning from his spiritual journey, and he adopted more of an observer's role in the ensuing group discussion about how best to interpret each question–answer set. More glasses of coffee and additional packs of clove cigarettes accompanied the dialogue until sunrise.

Though by this time I had been present at a variety of like consultation sessions with other shamans, the extent of the others' faith still surprised me. For instance, some of the men seeking the shaman's advice were highly successful, educated professionals. They sought answers to a wide array of life crises: Should I accept my creditor's request to give my daughter to

him in marriage? Is the closure of my business wise? Should I sell my lands this month?

As for me, I acted out my part, presenting my mom's case and respectfully requesting the shaman's advice and healing power. Privately, I found myself unable to put aside my objectivities, subconsciously resisting the answer that he provided. I had to remind myself that I was there for the specific purpose of fulfilling my mom's wishes. Only then was I able to retain the detailed explanation that I was to relay to her.

I returned home with a large plastic container containing a yellowish liquid that the shaman had presented to me. His last instructions had been to have Mom drink a glass of this liquid, once a day, at midnight. Then, wearing no clothes or jewelry, not even her wedding ring, she was to go outside the confines of her home, under the open sky and stars, and reach her arms to the heavens. She should allow her soul to speak with the ancient spirits to assist her in her healing process. I do not know if Mom ever exactly followed the directions of the shaman. But I did notice that the container of liquid emptied over time, and Mom still kept her scheduled chemotherapy treatment dates at the hospital and continued to meet with other traditional healers.

Yes, there were plenty of success stories of people who were on their dying bed, people on whom mainstream medicine had given up, people who had been delegated to an inevitable death. Many, it was rumored, had become ill due to the interference of an evil shaman working for a rival, yet, given the "appropriate" assistance, it was not impossible for a terminally ill person to miraculously recover.

Different shamans used a variety of methods. Some said that magical powers were contained in symbolic objects (e.g., a miniature curved dagger, a silver amulet) that were to be kept near a person's body at all times to ward off the advance of evil spirits. Others claimed that their herbal potions cleansed the body's system, ridding it of polluting Western medicines. Then the healing ritual would include prayers that called upon the healing powers of ancient spirits and either the prophet Muhammad, Jesus Christ, or some other holy deity. All of the shamans insisted on the patient's complete trust in order for the suggested alternative healing method to be effective.

My dad and sister had just left the hospital for home when I arrived to take my shift to watch my mom. There were now only three of us in the room: my mom, her private nurse, and me. I sat on the hospital bedside as she finished her dinner and we exchanged news about her latest set of chemotherapy treatments, the condition of the household, and my day's activities. She mentioned that she was happy my sister had been able to come home for spring break. We recited the rosary together as a warm evening breeze wafted through the room's small windows and she closed her eyes, clasping her rosary beads to her breast, wisps of hair framing her face on the piles of pillows. I watched her, my lips mouthing the prayers, my fingers keeping count, wishing she was well.

By now most of her hair had fallen out and her face had become discolored, dark blotches staining her complexion. Her chest and neck appeared to be more like flaky reptile scales than human skin and, when touched, felt as solid as a hard wood. The doctors had told us that these were normal side effects of the radiation treatments. Besides these "normal" side effects, her legs had become mere sticks from lack of exercise while her left arm had bloated like a water-filled balloon. Her head was forcibly jutted forward, held at a constant angle by the combination of the hardened skin and an additional growth on the back of her neck, so that her chin rested on her chest, unable to move. I had become accustomed to seeing her this way, yet could not fully believe that she may not return to her "old" self.

As we closed the rosary, she appeared tired and eager to sleep. " I love you, Mommy," I whispered. It was the first time I had ever verbally expressed my love for her. I felt weary and helpless. "I know," she replied with a sad sigh, her lips pouting at her predicament. "Please, get well," I heard myself pleading.

She smiled and motioned for me to kiss her and leave the room. I had just moved to the foot of her bed when her body jerked upright into a seated position—her arms outstretched toward me, her eyes filled with despair, her mouth wide open, desperately gasping for air, her voice incomprehensible . . . I think she was screaming for help. I froze, watching death wrench her life away. She flailed at her invisible assailant and I heard the private nurse hysterically crying out for the staff in the hallway. At that moment, I felt that nothing could save her. I watched, entranced, her dance of death until there was no more motion.

After the crowds of nurses and doctors had dispersed, I approached her and held her hand, kissing it gently, letting her limp fingers stroke my cheek. It seemed to be the right thing to do even though I knew that Indonesian tradition disallowed physical contact between the living and the dead.

Later that day, my mother was transported home. She arrived in a bare, simple coffin, her skin pale, her body still dressed in the hospital robe. There was great confusion as to where her coffin should be placed.

We decided to place the coffin atop a low platform in the living room. The stench of death permeated into each corner of the house. I recalled that, during her illness, Mom had requested to be dressed in a traditional Javanese costume, though untraditionally all white, at her funeral. I ransacked her closets for the appropriate outfit. I proceeded to cleanse her skin, change her clothes, make up her face, and fix her hair. Someone placed a rosary in my mom's hands, another slipped a small Bible underneath her clasped fingers.

Burning incense was discreetly placed under the platform to nullify the fetor. Female relatives and friends assisted in the labor-intensive task of weaving and then attaching chains of *melati*, a delicate, fragrant, white flower, around the coffin. Female family elders quietly arranged different trays in the kitchen, making extra sure that all was complete in the offering to the spirits of our ancestors: three colored puddings, a saffron rice plate molded into the shape of a cone and sprinkled with shavings of fried shallots, tiny potato fritters, different small servings of entrees and other side dishes, cups of sweetened coffee and tea, a glass of water, desserts wrapped in banana leaves, a pack of clove cigarettes. These offerings were placed upon a small table near her, next to a framed black-and-white picture of Mom, beside a Bible, rosary, and three white candles.

I remember watching my dad walking back and forth in the garage, isolating himself. He kept calling to my sister to meet still another guest as relatives and family friends continued to arrive. I felt rather sorry for my dad. He seemed unable to cope with my mom's death on his own terms and reverted, it seemed, to acting out what he deemed others would expect of him in such a situation. I sensed that his displayed grief was his optimal effort to maintain his self-dignity. I switched my attentions to an annoying stranger who was meandering between guests with a huge strobe light and video camera, capturing each nuance of grief. Yet this person, too, was part of the process of grief and I noticed "normal" reactions as the limelight paused at different groups of mourners. A long line formed as people took turns paying their last respects to Mom, and there were demonstrative signs of the cross by Catholics and upturned hands of Muslims and simple bowed heads of those less flamboyant in their prayer.

All said she looked beautiful, even in death, and they were correct. That night I lay myself on a straw mat on the floor next to her and fell asleep, oblivious to the huddled groups of horrified relatives and friends. It is believed that on the first night following a person's death, the spirit is set free and, thus, should be allowed to discover its appropriate path. My close physical presence was viewed as a deliberate attempt to "meet" Mom and, perhaps, convince her to stay or take me with her.

I looked up and saw my dad standing with my stepsiblings, his arms embracing them. Next to them I saw my sister, sheltered from the day's heat and sudden rain shower by an umbrella held over her head by close family friends, staring intently at mom's coffin. There was a wall of silence from those present at the funeral. After mom's coffin had been lowered into the ground, we each gathered a handful of petals to throw into the gaping hole that held her. Planks of wood had been positioned around the grave so that our clean shoes would not get muddy.

The following prayer gatherings at home, which consisted of a simple mass and praying of the rosary plus offerings to the ancestors, held for Mom on the third, seventh, and fortieth days after her death, brought news of her "appearance" to different family members and friends. Everyone told me that she looked well and happy. Some even told me that she sent her love to me. A few months later I returned to the United States to complete my studies. I lost track of when the hundredth and one-thousandth day of prayer for her should be. But every year, on her birthday and on the date of her death, I light three candles and prepare a simple offering of food and flowers. We will always be connected, the way mothers and daughters are when they chat.

SUGGESTED READINGS

Beatty, Andrew. (1999). *Varieties of Javanese Religion: An Anthropological Account*. Cambridge Studies in Social and Cultural Anthropology. Cambridge, UK: Cambridge University Press.

Smith, Wilfred Cantwell. (1991). *The Meaning and End of Religion*. Minneapolis, Minn.: Fortress Press.

20

Manuel, Apprentice *Yatiri*

Lawrence A. Kuznar

Indiana Purdue University Fort Wayne

The Aymara people are one of the largest surviving Native American groups in the Americas, with more than two million people living in the Andean highlands of Bolivia, Southern Peru, and northern Chile. They are descended from the Tiwanaku Empire, which reigned from about A.D. 600 to A.D. 1000 in northern Bolivia and southern Peru. The empire centered on the southern shores of Lake Titicaca, the world's highest navigable lake at 12,500 feet in altitude. Consequently, most of the Tiwanaku's Aymara descendants live in high valleys and plateaus up to 15,000 feet. The Tiwanaku Empire declined and eventually the Inca Empire conquered the remnants of the Tiwanaku people during the 1400s. Despite centuries of Inca and later Spanish rule, the Aymara maintained their cultural distinctiveness in dress, language, and belief. These differences live on today in the modern ethnic distinction between the Aymara of the Lake Titicaca basin and their Quechua neighbors to the north.

We hear much these days of globalization and the homogenization of world cultures. While Western technology and its associated consumerism are spreading rapidly to all parts of the world, they have hardly overwhelmed indigenous people like some cultural juggernaut. Non-Western people, while comparatively weak against Western economic and political forces, do exercise some control in resisting and choosing the elements of Western industrial culture they encounter. Such active selection is apparent in the Andes of South America, where indigenous Aymara continue to practice age-old herding techniques and ancient religions while coping with the modernization of their world.

In this article, Lawrence Kuznar describes how a young Aymara man used his religion to deal with a personal tragedy and threat to his security.

As you read Manuel's story, consider the following questions:

1. How does Aymara religion differ from Western religions in terms of a person's relationship to the supernatural?
2. Reflect on some of the things that Kuznar describes as having symbolic or sacred importance to the Aymara. What characteristics might make otherwise "everyday" things special? Can you think of anything from your own culture that serves both a mundane and a symbolic function?
3. What is the economic logic of Andean sacrifice? Are there parallels in how people use religion in your society?
4. Explain what Manuel meant when he said that different deities were the same. Can you think of other religions that contain similar ideas?
5. Why has Aymara religion persisted in spite of many centuries of conquest and other social change? In your own culture, do you see elements of religion changing? Are some elements persistent?

I met Manuel while conducting fieldwork in the southern Peruvian highlands as part of a large project that incorporated archaeology, geology, ecological studies, and ethnography. I was to study contemporary Aymara land use patterns in order to provide archaeologists with ideas about how the land may have been used in the past. Manuel was a single man in his early 20s who was hired as an assistant to the project. His duties ranged from excavation to odd jobs, to translation, to keeping me out of trouble. In addition, Manuel helped me to understand why so many Aymara have retained their ancient beliefs.

Manuel lives in the Andean highlands, known as the *puna*, situated between 12,000 and 15,000 feet in altitude. The climate is bitterly cold and oxygen is not readily available to a person's body at these altitudes, resulting in hypoxia, or high-altitude sickness. The symptoms include dizziness, nausea, and headache. Although most of the symptoms are relieved as the body adjusts to the lack of oxygen, there is no adjustment to the cold. Frequent frosts prohibit most agriculture in the *puna,* so many Aymara depend on herding native domestic animals such as the alpaca and the llama, New World cousins of the camel that provide wool, meat, and transport. Other Aymara who live in the lower altitude sierras (8,000 to 12,000 feet) raise goats and grow potatoes, quinoa (a leafy, grain-producing plant), broad beans, maize, and some uniquely Andean root crops.

In addition to eating food plants, the Aymara chew the leaves of the coca plant (the unrefined source for cocaine). Coca is a key and indispensable element in traditional Andean religion and life. Aymara and related Quechua people claim that coca chewing alleviates the physical stresses of high-altitude life including cold, fatigue, and hunger, and some medical research supports this view. The amount of cocaine released while chewing is small, but it soothes feelings of nausea and minimizes the headaches that accompany high altitude. Aymara like Manuel also consider coca to be a powerful medicine and a ritually sacred plant. They use it as medicine to sooth many ills including infections, coughs, and colds, and they offer it as a sacrifice to deities. Aymara also toss the leaves into the air and read the patterns made by the fallen leaves to foretell the future. Manuel knew about and used these practices.

Traditional Aymara families consist of a married couple and usually two to three unmarried children who live in a complex of small stone and thatch huts called an *estancia* in Spanish. Vegetation is scarce in the *puna,* and vegetation that animals can eat is even scarcer. Aymara *estancias* are therefore located on the margins of marshes known as *oqho* in Aymara. *Oqho* not only provide necessary forage for a family's herd, but also provide other scarce commodities in the arid Andean highlands, including water, fish, and edible algae.

Aymara dress continues to be distinctive. Manuel and other men typically wear trousers, sweaters, and perhaps a jacket to shield from the cold and wind of the high Andes. Woman's clothing is more colorful, serving as an emblem of their ethnic identity. Women wear wool leggings, covered by several layers of skirts and topped with a colorful blouse and often a sweater. Their ensemble is completed with a wool bowler hat. Most people go barefoot, or at most wear sandals fashioned out of old tires, no matter what the weather.

Aymara religion is a complex affair, incorporating elements of both traditional Andean beliefs and Christianity. There are a number of deities in traditional Aymara religion. The most immediate in any person's life are the *achachila* who reside in, or perhaps are, the high mountain peaks of the Andes. Since every Andean community is near an impressive peak, jutting into the sky, every community and its residents deal with a local *achachila* regularly. *Achachila* were especially important in my research since they also often are considered the supernatural owners of livestock on which peoples' lives depend. *Pachamama* is another important deity recognized throughout the Andean world by both Quechua and Aymara. *Pachamama* is female, or at least female-like, and is important in issues of fertility, whether it be of the land, animals, crops, or people. Important Christian deities include Jesus Christ, the Virgin Mary, the Catholic saints, and lastly the Christian God, who many Aymara typically regard as distant and unconcerned with their affairs.

The extent to which Andean and Christian religions are blended or kept apart varies from community to community. For Aymara like Manuel, the specific features of each religion, such as deities and rituals, are quite distinct and separate. However, at a deeper level, Manuel and other Aymara view a more fundamental connection between these religions. This connection ironically enables the two religions to retain their distinctiveness, and many contemporary Aymara practice both religions side by side.

As with any culture, Aymara is a complex tapestry of technology, behaviors, economic activities, social organizations, ritual practices, and religious beliefs. How had Aymara culture changed after 1,500 years of Inca and Spanish persecution? What elements predate the Spanish conquest? How have the Aymara remained culturally distinct? Answering these questions would require an intimate and lengthy contact. In my case, this contact came through Manuel.

FRIEND AND COMPANION

Manuel had a keen understanding of anthropology, and we became not only companions but also collaborators in the fieldwork. He introduced me to foods, attitudes, preferences, and places that would help me acculturate. In turn, he relentlessly grilled me on details of American life. We became one another's cultural teachers, struggling to translate the elements of our respective societies in a way the other could understand. As I asked, "What deities exist for Aymara?" and "How do you harvest quinoa?" he countered with "How much money do Americans make?" and "How much does it cost to live in the United States?"

When I first met Manuel, I was still single and considered a *joven,* or a young (and somewhat immature) man in Peruvian society. Like *jovenes* around the world, our conversations often turned to the opposite sex. Manuel enquired, "What are American women like?" "What does it take to marry one?" and playfully (I think) "Bring your sister to marry me!" In turn, he let me in on the courting practices of Aymara youth and stressed the importance of public events, such as Saints' festivals, for seeking sweethearts. Our mutual interest in one another's culture provided a bridge between our worlds and the foundation of a friendship. The particular issue of the opposite sex was to play an unforeseen, yet unexpectedly dangerous role in Manuel's life.

BREAKTHROUGH

Many dimensions of Aymara culture that chroniclers recorded nearly 500 years ago have persisted into modern times. The continued use of Aymara as a language and the continued reliance on livestock such as alpacas are obvious and fundamental. Other elements serve as distinctive ethnic markers. For instance, it is popular to raise and especially eat *cuy,* or guinea pig, in the Andes. Aymara keep *cuy* in their houses where the animals freely roam about, devouring bits of food and other organic litter, acting as small vacuum cleaners. The price paid by the *cuy* is that, occasionally, one of their number is relished for dinner. Some restaurants serve nothing but *cuy* for the benefit of Aymara and *cuy*-loving anthropologists who do not keep their own. The *cuy* is prepared by casually gutting the animal, singeing off its hair, flattening it between two stones, dredging it in some corn meal, and frying. A proper *cuy* meal is washed down with copious amounts of beer.

Another ancient practice is making traditional corn beer, or *chicha.* Women make this ancient drink by chewing corn kernels to begin the breakdown of carbohydrates in the corn. They add hot water to the chewed and ground corn, and set it aside to ferment. This frothy brew is essential for traditional religious ceremonies and social occasions, and it can be found in any Andean market where an older woman will purvey her product from an open pot and a communal glass. While herding alpacas, eating *cuy,* and drinking *chicha* are distinctive and colorful aspects of Andean Aymara life, there are ideological dimensions to these material facts that bind the elements of Aymara culture together. Alpaca, *cuy,* and *chicha* not only sustain the living, but these are the most essential sacrifices offered to sustain supernatural forces that, in turn, give humans life.

Philosophers and theologians ponder the meaning of the universe and its relation to the supernatural. Aymara are no different, and they have their own class of philosophers and religious specialists known as *yatiri,* or knowledgeable ones. As luck would have it, Manuel hoped to one day become a *yatiri* and had studied his own culture from a very philosophical and theological point of view.

Traditional Aymara assumptions about the supernatural differ from Judeo-Christian principles. A paradox (to me at the time) that I encountered during my fieldwork was that Aymara would simultaneously invoke traditional Aymara deities as well as the Christian saints and God, and that they would practice both Aymara and Roman Catholic rituals. At first, practicing two seemingly different if not opposed religions did not make sense to me. Manuel eventually succeeded in helping me to understand.

One day, driving along a treacherous high mountain road, we started to discuss Aymara religion. Perhaps the lofty road put us in the mood. I pressed Manuel on the differences among *achachila, pachamama,* the Virgin Mary, Jesus, and God. My friend patiently tried to explain the subtle differences among them and how they fit into an Aymara person's worldview. I gradually began to understand, and to be sure I continued with my line of simplistic questioning, which probably seemed unsophisticated and boorish to my more enlightened companion. Finally, in frustration, Manuel tersely replied, "Don't you understand? They are all the same thing!"

With that one outburst, Manuel helped me get a much clearer view of Aymara religion. The reason that Aymara see no contradiction in practicing their ancestral religion alongside the religion of their Spanish oppressors is because an Aymara view of religion and the supernatural can be far more abstract than a Western view. For Aymara, an abstract, vital force permeates the cosmos and constitutes the supernatural world. The Aymara do have a tradition, perhaps thousands of years old, of a male sky god, a corresponding female deity of the earth and fertility, and local deities associated with mountain peaks, lakes, and springs. But according to Aymara philosophy, these are merely manifestations of a greater underlying force.

This force is the same power that gives all things life, including potatoes for human consumption, maize for *chicha* beer, *cuy* and alpacas for meat and wool, coca for medicine, and all other things humans need. This force also brings rain to fertilize the land and luck to ensure the right combination of rain, sun, and fertility so that all things may prosper. In turn, people sustain this force by "feeding the mountain." Sacrifices of the very things it generates feed the supernatural so that it may continue to prosper. In this way, the living and the supernatural are inextricably connected and dependent upon one another.

When the Spanish brought Christianity in 1532, Andean people could incorporate it with little contradiction to their own religion because all systems are mere manifestations of a greater supernatural entity. This notion, that the supernatural permeates everything and that deities are merely representations, has been recognized by anthropologists in a variety of Native American religions, including Aymara. However, if all religions are mere aspects of a greater force, why have the Aymara tenaciously held onto many of their beliefs in the face of 500 years of persecution and execution by Spanish and Peruvian nationals? Why did the Aymara not simply adopt a new system and avoid the hassles? Manuel demonstrated some of these reasons as his life took a turn for the worse.

A DANGEROUS LIAISON

Manuel was a *joven,* unattached to any young woman, and always eager to meet potential new girlfriends. This eventually got him into trouble. A Peruvian family had a maid whose virtue and welfare they guarded. The head of the household was a retired military officer and had close ties with the Peruvian police. Manuel became acquainted with the maid and began a clandestine relationship that in time became quite serious. Unfortunately, for Manuel anyway, the officer's wife did not approve of Manuel and planned to take him out of the picture.

One day, the wife reported a necklace stolen, and, under pressure, the maid was urged to implicate Manuel, her lover. The retired officer decided to act on his own and Manuel was taken off the street, thrown into a car trunk, and eventually incarcerated—he disappeared. Archaeologists who employed Manual made inquiries (I was not there at the time), and he was eventually found and released on his own recognizance.

Perhaps Manuel's real agony began after his release. He was threatened with charges, a trial, and jail. His situation was serious, as Peruvian prisons are known for their harsh conditions. Once Manuel descended into the Peruvian penal system, he might never get out. Also, Manuel had no resources that might improve his chances with the Peruvian legal system; he was a young, relatively poor, Aymara Indian. Indigenous people occupy the lowest rung on the Peruvian social ladder, and being called an *indio* (Indian) or *cholo* is considered an insult. A *cholo* would stand little chance of beating a rap leveled by an official of the Peruvian government. Manuel's situation was very much out of his control.

ANCIENT RELIGION IN THE MODERN DAY

Could Manuel appeal to the supernatural for assistance and thereby gain some control over his fate? In Aymara religion, there is no clear hierarchy between the living and the supernatural; they are thought to be dependent upon one another. The living need the supernatural to bring luck, rain, crops, and animals, and the supernatural needs sacrifices for its sustenance. This equality between the supernatural and the living creates a reciprocal relationship. When people want something, they sacrifice objects, such as blood, fat, and sometimes living animals to supernatural forces. In return, the supernatural is obliged to return the favor by granting the living what they desire. Aymara expect to exercise at least some control over the supernatural, and consequently have some supernatural control over their lives. Perhaps Manuel could manipulate the supernatural in his favor.

The reciprocity between the supernatural and the living is also governed by an economic logic: the larger the request, the larger the sacrifice. The impoverished Manuel was in a lot of trouble, and he would have to make a big enough sacrifice to enlist the supernatural to his cause. Manuel chose the two courses of action that he had available. He could divine his fate and at least know what awaited him, and he could offer a sacrifice of his own labor by making a tortuous trek to an Andean holy site. He could go to *Cerro Baul.*

Cerro Baul is the giant basalt core of an extinct volcano that juts dramatically, 2,200 feet above its valley floor. There is virtually no way to get to the top, since the basalt core has shear cliffs all the way around it. Over thousands of years, pilgrims and even armies followed one route. A long trail winds its way along a knife ridge of debris that has fallen from *Cerro Baul.* Then a vertical climb greets a pilgrim (or anthropologist) as one encounters the rock face of the monolith. Here, ancient people carved and wore steps into the stone. At one point, an abrupt turn requires a climber to hang briefly over a 2,000-foot drop to the valley below. Finally, a trail on loose gravel, hill on one side, precipitous drop on the other, guides pilgrims to the

FIGURE 8 *Cerro Baul*, the sheer butte that Manuel climbed to make offerings to the spirits. *Photo by April Sievert.*

summit. At the top there is an altar, called an *apacheta,* made of a pile of stones. Andean people pilgrimage to this place to make sacrifices on the *apacheta,* to pray, and to conduct both traditional Andean and Christian rituals. Manuel made the arduous trek to the top of *Cerro Baul* and cast coca leaves, divining his future in the pattern of fallen leaves.

What did Manuel see in his leaves? That was a personal matter he did not share. Manuel returned to the mountain—his fatigue substituting for the material sacrifice he could not offer—and cast his coca leaves. In the end, his efforts appeared to pay off. An official investigation determined that the necklace had not been stolen and actually uncovered the wife's devious plot. The matter fell out of the public record, no blame was assigned, and Manuel went on with life. Manuel eventually married and moved to another part of the Peruvian *puna.* Manuel's words, actions, and companionship have given me much to consider over these intervening years. In particular, he was the person who most forcefully impressed upon me the character of Aymara religion, and his wisdom has been reinforced many times by other Aymara people and *yatiri.*

THE RESILIENCE OF AYMARA RELIGION

In 1532, Francisco Pizarro arrived in central Peru. In a matter of months, he and his men effectively took control of the Inca Empire, which contained perhaps nine million ethnic Inca and their other subjects, including the Aymara. As the Spanish consolidated their control over the Andes, Catholic priests set up monasteries and proceeded to exterminate Andean religious beliefs and practices. They were brutal, thorough, and unforgiving. The Spanish sought out every religious icon and temple they could find and destroyed it. They slaughtered Inca priests and nuns and replaced them with their own. Since then, traditional Andean religions have been persecuted at every level. Given such harsh treatment, how could indigenous people continue to practice their religion? A better question is, "Why?"

Manuel's wisdom regarding Aymara philosophy and his behavior in crisis illustrate why traditional Aymara religion persists in a modernizing Peru. Aymara religion would not necessarily cease to exist because of the Andean idea that different religions may provide access to the supernatural. More important, Aymara use religion pragmatically, and traditional beliefs still serve people's needs. Everyone desires at least some level of material wealth, bounty for one's crops and livestock (or bank account), love from an admiree, and freedom from incarceration. The prevailing message in the Western, Judeo-Christian tradition is that rewards will come in the afterlife. Given the here and now practicality of Aymara religion, the Western import could never attain the appeal of the Aymara's own religion. Christianity does not contain a way that necessarily influences the supernatural on one's material behalf. Sure, a person can pray, and many Christians pray for material things, but such manipulation contradicts the unconditional worship of an all-powerful God. In contrast, Aymara want and expect to manipulate the supernatural, and traditional Aymara religion provides a means of doing this.

Because Aymara religious concepts and practices have an underlying pragmatic and economic rationale, and given the increasing penetration of a worldwide, materialistic, consumer-targeted capitalism, Aymara religion could conceivably flourish instead of disappear. Of course, other intervening variables such as persecution of indigenous religion, bigotry against being Indian, and progressive loss of the Aymara language may work in the opposite direction. In the end, Manuel and his fellow Aymara will determine whether or not Aymara religion survives. For my part, I am only thankful that I had Manuel to help guide me into the complex world of the Aymara.

SUGGESTED READINGS

Allen, Catherine. (1988). *The Hold Life Has: Coca and Cultural Identity in an Andean Community.* Washington, D.C.: Smithsonian Institution Press.

Bastien, Joseph. (1985). *Mountain of the Condor: Metaphor and Ritual in an Andean Ayllu.* Prospect Heights, Ill.: Waveland Press.

Bolin, Inge. (1998). *Rituals of Respect: The Secret of Survival in the High Peruvian Andes.* Austin: University of Texas Press.

Kuznar, Lawrence A. (1995). *Awatimarka: The Ethnoarchaeology of an Andean Herding Community.* Fort Worth: Harcourt Brace.

21

Tears for the Saint, Tears for Ourselves

Linda S. Walbridge
Indiana University

In Iraq, the vast majority of people are Muslim. Unlike most Arab countries, which are predominantly Sunni Muslim, Iraq has a slight majority of Shi'ite Muslims, who live mainly in the southern part of the country. One of their holiest cities is Karbala, a shrine city dedicated to the veneration of one of the most holy saints of Shi'i Islam. Karbala and other cities in southern Iraq are home to some of the greatest schools of religious learning in the Muslim world. These schools train scholars who then teach Shi'ism throughout the world. Some of their students specialize in dramatic recitations that recount the stories of the suffering of a central figure of Shi'ite Islam, the Imam Hussein.

Because of political and religious persecution in Iraq, many of the Shi'ite religious scholars have had to flee the country or face imprisonment, torture, and even death. At the end of the 1991 Gulf War, when the Shi'a rose up against Saddam Hussein, the Army brutally attacked Shi'ite civilians. Tens of thousands of Shi'a fled on foot to Saudi Arabia, where they were reluctantly given refuge. Since then, countries throughout the world, including the United States, have divided up the responsibility for taking them in. These refugees often don't know English, don't have the proper job skills, and frequently have major health problems; they are virtually destitute. They rely more than ever on their religious faith to sustain them. While their physical needs are great, it is important to them to have spiritual assistance from their religious leaders, especially those who recount the story of the Imam Hussein, who was killed in the desert of Iraq 1,400 years ago. This ritualized storytelling links the Iraqi Shi'ites to the larger Shi'ite community and gives people hope that their suffering has meaning and purpose.

As you read Seyed Moustafa's story, consider the following questions:

1. How are religion and politics linked in the lives of the Iraqi Shi'a community? Can you think of cases in your own experience in which religion and politics are linked?
2. Reflect on what it would be like to be a refugee, and especially on what it would be like to be forced to flee one's homeland to escape religious persecution. What types of support would you need in a new community?
3. Why would it be especially important for the Shi'ite refugees living in the United States to have their mourning ceremonies led by someone like Seyed Moustafa?
4. Why would Seyed Moustafa and other Muslims from the Middle East be nervous about living in the United States?

My friend Moustafa's job is to make people cry. I spotted Seyed Moustafa standing alone at a reception at a scholarly conference in Washington, D.C. He was hard to miss in his turban and robes, which easily distinguished him as a Shi'ite Islamic cleric. We greeted each other nervously over our little plates of food. Somehow, though our lives were worlds apart and in many respects divided by centuries, we became friends. My research among Shi'ites enabled me to understand the world from which he came. And his personable style, his interest in people, and his openness to new ways helped him overcome our cultural differences.

I learned that Seyed Moustafa was from Iraq, where his family had deep roots. They were among southern Iraq's elite class of religious scholars, who were trained and, in turn, trained others in the beliefs, laws, and rituals of Shi'ism. In the schools, or *madrasas,* turbaned men sit on the floor explaining ancient texts, surrounded by students eager to learn. Through long hours of the night, these young men review and study what they learned the previous day. Some, such as Seyed Moustafa, also learn rhetorical styles so that they can be effective in reaching the ordinary layman. Seyed Moustafa's education centered on the preservation of the memory of the Shi'ites' greatest saints and martyrs, who are buried in the cities of Karbala and Najaf in southern Iraq. These cities are considered so sacred that, throughout the centuries, Shi'ites have had the remains of their loved ones transported any way possible so that their bones can be interred in this sacred land. Seyed Moustafa's education might not have been "modern" in the Western sense, but, refined and articulate in several languages, he is a learned man and one who knows a great deal about human nature.

Such a life sounds peaceful enough. Yet Saddam Hussein and his regime had been busy rooting out anyone suspected of being a dissident. His prisons were full of Seyed Moustafa's friends and relatives, whether dissident or not. Few prisoners have lived to talk about the horrifying tortures inflicted upon them.

Seyed Moustafa was a teenager when Saddam Hussein came to power in Iraq. Like many of the Shi'a, especially those who were clerics or priests, Seyed Moustafa's father viewed Saddam Hussein as someone determined to destroy the religious institutions of the Shi'ites. Late one night someone came to his home and warned his father that the Iraqi police were about to arrest him. Seyed Moustafa's father awoke his wife and sons and daughters, and they fled across the desert to the safety of Kuwait. Seyed Moustafa's father was fortunate. Other clerics arrested at that time have never been seen again.

In Kuwait, Seyed Moustafa met others fleeing the persecution of Saddam, others who wanted this tyrannical leader overthrown. Their chance seemed to come when Ayatollah Ruhollah Khomeini rose to power in Iran, Iraq's neighbor and a Shi'ite country. Ayatollah Khomeini was fighting the despotism and corruption of the Shah of Iran, a ruler backed by the United States. To the shock of the entire world, he won his battle, transforming imperial Iran into an Islamic Republic.

Though the Iranian Revolution did not directly affect Iraq, many Iraqis, both pro- and anti-Saddam, saw the revolution as a threat to Iraq. If the Iranian Shi'ites could overthrow the mighty Shah despite his American backing, couldn't the same thing happen in Iraq? So Moustafa's family was uprooted again, going to Iran to help establish a new Islamic society. They were jubilant at first. The revolution gave them a chance to show how an Islamic government could succeed, how it could transform the lives of people and free them from oppression.

But it did not work out. One day Seyed Moustafa visited a prison and found it full of young girls and women. Women, he had always been taught, were to be respected and honored in Islam, not abused. This was not the Islam he wanted. This was not what he wanted for his own country of Iraq.

Seyed Moustafa's parents, three of his brothers, and three of his sisters packed up their bags again and headed for the United States, a land that was completely alien to them. The United States has several million Muslims, but they are scattered and little known to most Americans. What would it be like walking the streets of America in a turban and robes, as Seyed

FIGURE 9 Seyed Moustafa leads prayers. *Photo courtesy of Seyed Moustafa.*

Moustafa and his father and some of his brothers do? How would they be able to observe the laws of Islam? Would they be taunted, harassed?

Growing numbers of Shi'ite Muslims have been arriving in this country since the 1970s. There were the Lebanese, for example, who fled in large numbers during the prolonged war with the Israelis in southern Lebanon. There were Iranians who had supported the old regime of the Shah and were at odds with the new Khomeini regime. Many of the Afghans who had fled their own civil war were Shi'ites. Finally, there would be the Iraqis themselves, refugees from the uprising supposed to overthrow Saddam Hussein after the 1991 Gulf War. They all needed help—help in practicing their religion, help in adjusting to this new world. All of these people would need mosques or religious centers to practice the rituals of Shi'ism. For it is these rituals that have bound the Shi'a together for centuries and made them a distinctive community. Seyed Moustafa and his family are specialists in conducting these rituals and have gained some fame since arriving in the United States.

MOURNING FOR THE IMAM

In a Shi'ite religious center, or *Imambargah,* Seyed Moustafa sits cross-legged on a platform in front of a congregation. Men and women sit on opposite sides of the room. They are all dressed in dark clothes, the Iraqi women wrapped in black *abayas,* all-encompassing robes that cover them from head to toe. The Lebanese women are more likely to wear simple head scarves. When Seyed Moustafa starts talking, the people are not necessarily quiet. They continue to chat among themselves. But as he progresses, silence falls on the crowd.

Seyed Moustafa is dramatically relating the story of the martyred grandson of the Prophet Muhammad, the Imam Hussein, from whom Seyed Moustafa himself is descended. In A.D. 680 Imam Hussein and his family and a small entourage were killed in the desert of Iraq when they stood their ground against a government that they believed had betrayed the Prophet's mission of establishing a just society.

Imam Hussein's family and close followers were trapped in the desert. Surrounded, they could not go forward or backward. With no provisions to sustain them, some of the men risked their lives in order to find water to bring back to the women and children. One by one they were mowed down. Some engaged in battle with the enemy, fighting valiantly until the end. Each one of these heroes is remembered during a period of 10 days each year.

For 10 days people come to the mosque or the *Imambargah* to hear the tragic story of that day's occur-rences. The story reaches a crescendo when the Imam's infant son is killed in the Imam's arms and then, finally, when the Imam himself is killed in battle and be-headed. It is the courage and defiance of the Imam's sister that keeps the Imam's other son from being executed. As Seyed Moustafa reaches the climax of the story, the crying begins—not silent tears, but loud sobs. No one is ashamed of the tears he or she is shedding.

In the same way they have over these many centuries, Shi'a today mourn the loss of their leader who died 1,400 years ago. Each person who died with Imam Hussein is as familiar to them as their own neighbor. The audience listens to the entire story. Often they see these events dramatized, usually in the streets. Something else is happening, though, through this ritual. People are reliving their own traumas and tragedies. They too had seen loved ones killed before their eyes. They too had known thirst in the Saudi Arabian desert where they lived in refugee camps after the Gulf War. They too knew what it was to be maimed for life or to have one of their kinsmen tortured into an unrecognizable state. The rituals of their religion thus serve as symbols for the suffering of their own lives.

The grief that people feel for Imam Hussein is genuine and Seyed Moustafa knows exactly how to tap into it. He knows how to link the experiences of the people today with that of their saint. The people come expecting to cry, but how heartfelt their tears are is determined by the skills of people such as Seyed Moustafa. It is important to cry for the Imam Hussein because his suffering encompasses all the sufferings of his people. Through him and his ordeals, the world can be redeemed. If they forget him, they forget everything that has meaning in their lives.

While Shi'ites from various parts of the Middle East and Central Asia have suffered deplorably in the past few decades, the case is especially poignant for the Iraqis, whose lives revolved around the shrines of the Imam Hussein and his father, the Imam Ali. Their dream is to return to their own country, a country rid of Saddam Hussein and his tyranny, and to return to the land sacred with the blood of their beloved martyrs.

It is not just major tragedies that recall the sufferings of the Imam. He is called to mind on many occasions. Whenever I have faced a problem, my Shi'ite friends reminded me of one whose sufferings were greater than all others were. Once when my younger son was going through a crisis, I confided in Seyed Moustafa, telling him about my concerns. He responded by relating my suffering to the women who had suffered with the Imam Hussein. This was not an impersonal response. These women were his physical and spiritual ancestors, and he had lived with their stories all his life. All suffering had meaning and that meaning was linked to deep, spiritual experiences.

For all of this, Seyed Moustafa is still a performer. His voice cries out the grief of those who suffered in the desert during those awful days. His facial expressions reflect the pain they suffered. Though he has had to learn skills to ensure that his words have an effect on his audience, this does not diminish the religious aspect of his role. He performs because it is his job to remind people in the most poignant way possible of the sufferings of the Imam and his family. His talent for performing also can be seen in his everyday encounters with people. He doesn't limit himself to making people cry. I told him once that I had had a dream about the Imam Hussein, dreams being something that many Shi'ites, like other peoples, take very seriously. Before this, I had told a Shi'ite woman about the dream. She looked at me and said with some exasperation, "Linda, I cry every year for the Imam Hussein and he has not come to me!" I passed on her comments to Seyed Moustafa. His response was immediate: "Linda, every year I MAKE the people cry for Imam Hussein and he has not come to me either!"

SEYED MOUSTAFA OUTSIDE THE *IMAMBARGAH*

Seyed Moustafa has had to adjust to life in America. Some of these adjustments are major life changes; others are minor. Snow, for example, falls into this latter category. One snowy cold night he and another cleric were to attend a conference in upstate New York. As it grew late, I became worried when they did not arrive. Since I had invited them, I felt responsible. Finally, they burst in through the glass doors, wet from the heavy snow that had fallen on them. His first words were, "It was horrible!" He then burst into laughter. Normally, when an Iraqi, and especially one with the polished manners of Seyed Moustafa, greets someone, he beseeches God to bring peace on that person and inquires about his health, and the health of his family, and makes other polite conversation. The abruptness of "It was horrible" made me laugh because it was so out of character. For Seyed Moustafa, making people laugh is almost as important as making people cry.

Seyed Moustafa has watched as other members of his family have ventured out into new lives in the United States. His sisters, growing up in Iraq, had lived a segregated life. Except for their father and brothers, they would have socialized only with women. To some extent they still live this way. Part of Seyed Moustafa's extended family lives in a large house in a Los Angeles suburb. There are two main parts to the house, one where male guests are entertained, the other the place for the women of the family. Because of my research, I am always ushered into the men's quarters, but being a woman, I also have access to the women's part of the house. The women of the household, all being descendants of the Prophet and women of clerical families, must maintain strict rules of modesty. Whenever any man, even a brother-in-law, walks through their quarters, they make sure to draw around them their black robes, their *abayas*.

However, two of Seyed Moustafa's sisters were attending college. At the university they simply wore long coats and head scarves. It had to have taken a great deal of courage for these young women to venture out among strangers, yet, by the time I met them, they seemed to be women of great poise and self-confidence. It was quite revolutionary for the daughters of this family to attend a university, but it was something that Seyed Moustafa, at least, seemed very proud of. His wife, a multilingual woman, also defies the stereotype of the oppressed, sequestered Middle Eastern woman. Black *abaya* or not, she is a woman of intelligence, sophistication, and presence, and someone that her husband relies on.

Seyed Moustafa clearly wants to pick and choose those aspects of American culture that he finds admirable. He has learned that education for women—even secular education—does not have to lead to their corruption and to the breakdown of the family, something that the religious Shi'ites fear. With his insatiable curiosity about American culture, he is always mentally calculating what he wants to borrow from this society and what he wants to avoid. Intelligence and learning in women were something he saw worth fostering.

Life has changed in other ways for Seyed Moustafa as well. Now, he is in an office, answering his phone, arranging meetings, and, above all, counseling people. Back home, Seyed Moustafa's role would have been confined largely to leading the mourning rituals. In the United States, he has become a pastor, very much in the tradition of the Christian minister. The Iraqi refugees came with a vast array of problems. They were virtually penniless when they arrived. These people were farmers or herders back home. How are they expected to have the skills for a job in an American city? These problems are compounded by the fact that at first few spoke any English. What is a man to do when he has no job? Iraqi men are not expected to sit around their houses, keeping their wives company. They are expected to be out working and living among men. Being uprooted and separated from home and family, often living in substandard housing and not having the wherewithal to afford even the basics of life, worrying about those left behind in Iraq—all these factors and more lead men and women to experience depression and suffer from marital problems. People such as Seyed Moustafa must now play a role among their congregations in a way they would not have had to back home. He also has a whole new array of questions to answer.

In Islam, as in Judaism, religious law is very important. In theory, every action of a pious Muslim is covered by Islamic law: food, dress, manners, marriage, family relations, money, as well as religious rituals such as prayer and fasting. Now that Seyed Moustafa is in America, he has to deal with the issues of Islamic law in a new way. He has to ask if it is wise for an older man to marry a young girl, especially in view of the fact that Iraqi men living in the United States have been arrested for marrying young girls. These men are perplexed by the fact that young American girls are allowed to be pregnant, unmarried, and unprotected but that they themselves can be arrested for marrying a girl!

Should a man shave his beard in order to find a job? If a woman's husband is beating her, what should she do? And what should an Islamic leader do to protect her? How can he persuade poor families to abandon the demand for large payments for brides (bride wealth) when they see such payments as a chance to escape the pangs of poverty? How does he explain to them that bride wealth should not be an obstacle to their sons' and daughters' marriages? He's faced all of these problems and many more, involving himself in the lives of his congregation far more than he ever would have in Iraq. There, family and tradition take care of most of these problems. But the United States is different. People are on their own, fighting their own battles. New immigrants don't have the old support systems. They lean on Seyed Moustafa and others like him. He is their counselor, their helper in a strange, new world.

Seyed Moustafa did not come to the United States in any formal role. He is not like a Catholic priest assigned to a parish. He came as a free agent, defining his own role in the United States. This is not always easy. To make a living, he must find acceptance among a group of Shi'ites, many of whom he will not have known previously.

He also will have to deal, to some extent, with American society. Islam might be the third largest religion in the United States, but it is still deeply misunderstood. The image of the wicked Arab terrorist is one of the last stereotypes that Americans have been permitted to keep. It does not help that most Americans do not know the distinctions among nationalities in the Middle East or among the various groups of Middle Easterners within a country. Threats or acts of violence toward Muslims residing in America are not uncommon, and thus a man appearing in robes and a turban needs a certain amount of courage and resilience. Seyed Moustafa himself marvels at his new life and the challenges he faces, at the many Americans with whom he has become friends and associates. Had he remained in the Middle East, he would be both respected and ordinary.

But one thing is the same. He is still reminding his fellow Shi'ites of the suffering of the Imam Hussein—suffering that people can relate to and that gives them hope and meaning in their own lives. Most of all there is the hope—the belief—that some day, the Imam will return to this earth and all will be well.

SUGGESTED READINGS

Mottahedeh, Roy. (1985). *The Mantle of the Prophet: Religion and Politics in Iran.* New York: Simon and Schuster.

Walbridge, Linda. (1997). *Without Forgetting the Imam: Lebanese Shi'ism in an American Community.* Detroit, Mich.: Wayne State University Press.

PART VIII

Death and Dying

Photo by Pamela Keech.

While death is a biological process, it is also very much a social phenomenon, one that involves the living and the dead. Mourners in every society have to adjust to the loss of a loved one as well as dispose of the body. Since most societies believe that the deceased lives on in some new way after death, mourners also give attention to aiding the transition of the deceased on that new path.

Anthropologists have documented that the cultural meanings associated with death vary from society to society and from religion to religion. Views of death reflect strongly how people understand life and their place in the universe. In societies across the world we find an extraordinary array of beliefs and rituals associated with the process of dying, the disposal of the body, and the remembrance of the deceased. As soon as it is clear that a person faces death, the ritual process usually begins. The devout Catholic receives the sacraments or Last Rites from a priest. A devout Jew recites the words of the Final Confession. Traditionally in India a woman who saw her husband dying would prepare for her own death by self-immolation. How and when a body should be disposed of is also determined by beliefs. Muslims bury their dead no later than the second day after death. The Hindu Balinese first bury their dead and then, after decomposition, cremate the bodies in an elaborate and colorful ceremony. People in the United States conduct viewings at specially designed funeral homes, so that friends and relatives may say goodbye and offer condolences to the bereaved.

Death, no matter where it occurs or what customs prevail at the time of death, has an intense emotional impact on the survivors. It involves separation from a loved one, the realization that the deceased will no longer share with them in life's joys, and a heightened awareness of their own mortality. Not surprisingly, crying is a common occurrence at funerals, but even this emotion can be culturally conditioned. In some societies, for example, only the women may weep at funerals, no matter how intensely the men also feel the loss of a loved one. Alternatively, we might find the most dramatic weeping being done by those least affected by the death. Anthropologists refer to this as ceremonial weeping, a display that has more to do with strengthening the bonds of the community than it does with expressing grief. In some cases, grief can be displayed by creating artistic expressions or memorials in a public setting. While some mourners may wear black and behave in a somber fashion, we can find peoples for whom dancing, singing, and even flirting are obligatory at funerals.

What happens to the loved one after death? Does the spirit go to dwell in another world? Does the deceased lose contact with the living or continue to interact with them? In societies as far apart as Africa and Melanesia we find what is commonly called "ancestor worship." In such societies, ceremonies aid the person in becoming an ancestor, someone who continues to play a vital role in the society. "Caring for the ancestors," perhaps by leaving food for them, is an important part of life and reflects and affirms the obligations that children have to their parents, obligations that do not cease at death. In contrast, Buddhists believe that the essence of the person—feelings, thoughts, and consciousness—continue on after biological death, but that the total identity of the person is not maintained. In some forms of Hinduism and in Buddhism there is a belief in rebirth or reincarnation. A Hindu experiences a good rebirth as a reward for performing his or her ritual and ethical duties associated with his or her caste during a previous life.

Regardless of who we are or what we believe, we all must confront death. At some time in our lives we will find ourselves coping with the passing of relatives and friends, of helping make sure they are put to rest while trying to continue to celebrate and affirm life. The following articles show us different ways in which this is accomplished.

In the first article, Kathleen Williamson takes us to a home in Dublin, Ireland, where the family has gathered to await the death of Williamson's Uncle Paddy. The conversations we become privy to give us a window into how the Irish view death and reveal the importance of family in sustaining the dying, as well as the living.

While Frances Trix was teaching in a southern Lebanese village, one of her students, Omar, the first in his family to go to school, died suddenly from a bleeding ulcer. How the villagers responded to this young man's death and how they behaved toward Trix in the process reveals much about the values and concerns of these people.

Anne Bennett's friendship with Amal, a Syrian woman, reveals to her the role that reincarnation can play in the life of members of the Druze religion. When a five-year-old girl claims to be Amal's deceased mother, Amal's family must come to terms with this child's claim and find a way to both accept and assist her.

Other articles that touch on death:

Green Earrings: A Widow's Tale by Sarah Lamb

Ambivalence of Grandsons and Rescue by Daughters by Lisa Cliggett

Healing the Body, Healing the Soul by M. Ligaya Hattari

22

Death of an Irishman

Kathleen G. Williamson

University of Arizona

Dublin, Ireland's capital city of over a half million people, commands a prime port on the western shores of the Irish Sea. For well over 300 years, Irish people set sail from Dublin to find prosperity and opportunity across the sea, to England or the United States or beyond. Most Irish families are now widely dispersed because of this immigration and welcome reunion with family members who have moved away from Ireland. Reunion is often tinged with sadness, however, as distant family members most often convene when someone is gravely ill or dying.

The Irish have long-standing traditions regarding illness, medical practice, death, and mourning. Religion, always central to the picture, governs how different members react to grief, to changing social dynamics within the family, and to attitudes about the future.

As you read, consider the following questions:

1. Why was it important for all of Paddy's siblings to be there at his death?
2. What similarities do you see between the way that Paddy's illness, death, and funeral were handled and the way this might be done in your own culture?
3. How do the Irish appear to regard the medical profession?
4. What was the role of religion in helping to improve Paddy's medical condition? In seeing him safely into the next world? In helping the family cope?
5. What effects has immigration had on Irish family structure?

Paddy Gavin died in the late summer of 1995 after months of sickness in a Dublin hospital. The presence of all of his siblings at the midnight deathbed was an unusual occurrence in Ireland, a nation of families historically dispersed by emigration. Seamus held vigil, having walked over from his Dublin house. Bridee drove from rural County Mayo in western Ireland, during the intense time of hay harvesting. Eamon had flown in from England. From "across the wide ocean," as it is typically depicted in Irish emigrant songs, Mae, who is my mother, was also there. As it coincidentally happened, Mae and I were researching her ethnobiography. During that summer, Mae experienced daily life with her family for the first time in the nearly 50 years since she had emigrated alone as a young woman.

The siblings grew up in a Catholic home during the 20s and 30s in a provincial, remote part of West Mayo. Their school curriculum resurrected Gaelic language, culture, and history. Their world consisted of a poor but socially close-knit, thatch-roofed community, the physical borders of which were decided by how far one could travel by foot, bicycle, or horse. Their mother was born and raised in Meath, a county known for its

rich soil and bourgeois economy in the east of Ireland near metropolitan Dublin, a place none of the siblings would see until they arrived there to live and work as youthful laborers and servants for their uncles.

At 14 years of age, Mae was the first to leave for Meath because she was a girl and her labor was less valued on the farm. Her brothers, Seamus and Paddy, moved to Meath when they were in their early 20s. Like his brother Seamus and most of the western Irish men of his generation who were not destined to inherit the farm, Paddy migrated to Dublin as a young husband and father after a few years sampling life in England. There, he reared his children, worked as a carpenter in the local construction industry, and spent the rest of his life. The brothers always visited home and relations in the West of Ireland. However, in 1947, Mae, bored with domestic service, crossed the Atlantic by boat to the land of opportunity, from where seductive images of fashion, wages, and modern amenities composed an America that was magical for her and millions of Irish women before her. It also evoked a place of permanent exile. Indeed, even in Mae's time, 27 years passed before she could return home to visit.

When Mae did return, her siblings and other relatives greeted her warmly back into the family fold. They extended the same warmth to me, even though most of them I had never met.

"Going to funerals is an Irish hobby," one Irish cousin told me. In Ireland, people renew and strengthen their family and social connections by gathering around weddings and funerals. "She was robbed!" was one Dublin woman's shocked response when told that Paddy's was Mae's first Irish wake.

Paddy's death could have happened far removed from Mae, like on that sad summer day in 1966 when she was living in New York City. Mae had received a letter with an enclosed newspaper clipping reporting that her mother, whom she had not seen in nearly 20 years, had unexpectedly passed away and was already buried in the graveyard near their rural family church. Although her grief was staggering, no one in the United States could wake this loss with her. In 1980, she could afford a weekend flight to the Dublin hospital to say goodbye to her dying father. As Mae entered the hospital room, he jested in the melodic tenor of 19th-century Mayo English, "The Yanks are here! The Yanks are here! My daughter has taken a notion to cross the ocean to see her father." He died within days after she left.

Usually, numerous family members greet the "Yankee" at the airport. Photographs are taken to memorialize these family reunions and partings. Our visit in the summer of 1995, however, began ominously. Paddy was conspicuously absent for Mae's arrival. Angela, Paddy's wife, told us that he was "not well" and was home resting and waiting for Mae. Thus began the long summer's worth of reports about "tests": a "test for the blood," "the camera down the throat," a "test that will make you roar," tests for the "fluid on the lungs" or "the glands," and the ongoing struggle to extract their meanings.

The doctors, priests, nurses, and nuns of Ireland seemed to hold out comfort, explanations, cures, and miracles. Discussions about how confused the doctors seemed to be, what the tests would show and mean, how dedicated and hardworking the nurses were, and litanies of medical testimonials about the recovered and the dead were told and retold. Simultaneously, as a desire for either a miraculous cure or the spiritual acceptance of "God's will," Paddy's situation permeated every rosary, Angelus, mass, communion, and visit to graveyard or shopping mall chapel.

Prayers to St. Anthony for a "happy death" tempered one's anticipation of not receiving the miracle cure requested from St. Rita. A battalion of saints, Our Lady Queen of Peace, and deceased miracle workers queued up for Roman beatification were all employed through the use of religious relics, matrix medals, and a purse full of prayer cards. Angela would place a row of religious items on the hospital bed and prayerfully touch Paddy with them. One afternoon near the end of Paddy's life, while Angela was laying out her relics on him, Paddy turned to Mae and sadly said, in contradiction of his lifelong religious character, "It's funny, isn't it, you don't feel like praying in a hospital."

Throughout the summer, Paddy was revered as both a "good patient" and "a saint." It was often said that he was "too good" (especially after he had died and his chair and recent photos became sacred icons). During the hospital experience, he typified the highest of "Irish" ideals in suffering. He never complained or questioned the doctors or his circumstances. People commented that, when asked how he was feeling, his response would be an ever weakening, "Not so bad now." His few words were only of praise for the staff. "Look at that nurse now. Isn't she gentle, like a swan, the way she moves around the ward?"

Paddy was a very religious man and said the rosary every night. Angela was also a vigilant force for daily piety at home. She attended mass every morning and administered the sacrament alongside the priest. Their home's interior decoration is mostly sacred art, from the nationally common Sacred Heart of Jesus over the gas hearth, to the holy water container in the doorway. A 3-D picture of Pope John Paul II hovering over the Vatican adorns the wall over the sitting room couch. They were inclined to visit weeping Mary statues and to take pilgrimages to Lourdes. Neither one of them had ever tasted alcohol.

Even though Mae and Paddy were closest in age and enjoyed a favored bond, within 24 hours of Mae's arrival, they were delicately advancing their positions concerning abortion, divorce, and euthanasia. Paddy and Angela exemplified the soft-spoken holy Catholic Ireland, troubled by increasing threats to their beliefs, while Mae represented the progressive Democratic American Catholic who disagreed strongly with the Pope on these issues. Her siblings had little real-life understanding of Mae's life as a divorced mother of four heading a single-wage household on waitress tips in Manhattan.

While the siblings marked each other's politics and manners, no love was diminished. This summer, the need to address any disharmonious opinions between the siblings would be postponed or suppressed due to the portentous nature of Paddy's medical condition.

Paddy was failing, coughing more frequently and violently. Within a few weeks, he was admitted by ambulance to the local hospital, the same one in which Mae had visited her father years earlier. As the eldest sibling, he was sorely disappointed to be missing any part of Mae's visit. However, he did not return home until the funeral motorcade crept by the house nearly two months later.

During those summer mornings, a single magpie was frequently seen through the large kitchen window. Because of the impending tragedy, ever present in our minds, no one would verbalize the common expression we associated with that sight: "One for sorrow, two for joy." When two magpies appeared, however, there would be a hopeful comment. Deference to Paddy's anticipated situation was the spoken and unspoken variable guiding our schedules.

"Will ye have the dinner early tonight?"

"I don't know. If Paddy is doing well, I may go to hospital."

"Shall we climb Croagh Patrick on Reek Sunday?"

"We'll wait and see what happens with Paddy."

"Are you going to Mayo next week, Mae?"

"It depends on Paddy's tests. We don't know how he's going to be."

"Shall we go to the church at Knock and say a prayer for Paddy?"

"Let's."

"Angela, what have the doctors said about the swollen legs?"

"They're waiting for the results from the camera down the throat."

"How long are ye home, Mae?"

"'Til September, but we don't know with Paddy now—"

One afternoon, we waited in the hospital corridor until after the rounds were done. A young male Irish doctor approached us (Angela, Mae, Paddy's son Joseph, and me). He made a superficial gesture of giving Angela some privacy but loudly said, "There's no change today. He's the same. There's no progress." After the hospital, we went to the shopping center to get our "messages" for the evening meal. On the way over, Mae pursued her previous suggestions to get the family to consider what in America is called a "living will," the legal document Paddy would have to sign to ensure that he wouldn't be artificially sustained on medical machinery.

Joseph, Paddy's son, tersely injected, "He won't need that," and abruptly ended the discussion.

When the siblings differed over medicine and health, Americans, such as Mae, were perceived as pedantic and pushy. Paddy would suffer a setback and seem upset if anyone by his bedstead questioned the medical treatment or asked the nurses to get water or provide bedding and care that would prevent bedsores. Mae would not question a doctor directly but would rather follow preventative health care and would prescribe the same to everyone else at any op-

portunity. That summer, she told Paddy daily to "drink plenty of water" in contradiction to the doctor's orders and suggested other natural remedies. Angela, Seamus, and Bridee would respond to Mae using "ye," the plural, instead of "you," the singular, meaning that they perceived Mae's voice to represent that of the "Yanks." In response to Mae's suggestions, an irritated Bridee at one point complained that Americans are often telling the Irish what and how to do things. Despite the strangeness of it, Mae did manage to get her sister and sisters-in-law to take raw garlic, vitamin C and vitamin B and drink lots of water. Seamus had negative class-related feelings about Americans and associated them with strangers who undeservedly inherited the farms of childless Irish uncles or aunts. He did not hesitate to contribute, "They think they are smarter than us. They can be arrogant, can't they?" into such a discussion about Americans.

In August, Angela's older brother Sean was visiting from Sligo, also in the West. Such visits from afar were weighted with the unspoken understanding that people might be saying goodbye to Paddy. Over tea in the family sitting room, Angela said something about Paddy still being on the "heart thing." Mae and I asked for a clarification. Angela said, "You know, the, uh, drip thing, to make his heart stronger."

"Oh, what's in it?" we persisted innocently.

"The drip," she responded in a suddenly exasperated voice, as if it was unnatural to know any such thing. She stressed, "I mean, you've got to trust the doctors. They know what they're doing, don't they?"

Sean chimed in, "Aye, sure the doctors know what they have to do. There isn't any use in questioning them, and he mightn't tell you anyway, or he mightn't know himself," he said, with no tinge of irreverence or irony.

Whereupon, Joseph piped up from the kitchen, "They know what's in it," but didn't go on to challenge any notion that they wouldn't tell you.

Sean and Angela went into an anxious and lengthy lecture about how "you have to let the doctors do whatever they think they have to do, and it's no use, what use would it be, to ask them such things." To them, it was not to be questioned that "they have the knowledge and we don't know anything about it."

Every night at Paddy and Angela's house, we said the rosary together on our knees in the informal sitting room. Mae conformed immediately to her past religious childhood regime. She chanted the prayers with the same quick tempo and rhythms as those who had continued the practice all their lives. The evening ritual of the rosary is a throwback to her own time of innocence, which she reflected in a soft girlish tone. Angela knew all of the "mysteries" and led the sessions.

One Saturday morning, instead of going straight to the hospital or mass, Angela drove into Dublin's city center, to St. John's Priory, to attend the "Petitions to St. Rita." In this weekly gathering, St. Rita is supplicated by an audience, mostly women, who light electric votive candles and engage in donations, prayers, and the "One Hundred Petitions for Miraculous Recoveries." The priest read some petitions directly from notes that were sent up to him. According to Angela, the same priest may have been transmitting the petitions to St. Rita since the practice started there over 20 years ago. "That priest had a tumor last year," she added. Paddy's petition was brief: "And pray for Paddy in Beaumont Hospital suffering with fluid on the lung."

We spent the last day of August at the hospital. A steady stream of people wove in and out from the hall to Paddy, who by then was little more than yellowed skin and bones struggling to breathe. Five-year-old Julie obstinately insisted that everybody was "getting to say goodbye to Granddad" and she was being "kept out," which made her "hate them all, even the nurses." After much deliberation among the family, the grandchildren came in for a brief time.

The staff moved Paddy from the large ward with its rows of beds to the private room near the nurses' station. Seamus said he heard something, which he expressed with a gesticulation of his hand around the upper lung area to indicate the familiar sound of life on the wane, the gurgling of fluids in the top of the respiratory system. Angela commented in hushed tones about whether Seamus was "sure to have had some brandy before he came over" and that he'd "probably have a pint when he got home . . . What can you take when you get such a shock? What about some tablets?" Angela sought an answer for her blanketed panic. She said, "The drink might be good for some," but her tone belied that she was more curious about how she was going to cope emotionally than that she was approving of alcohol. Mae predictably suggested prayer and brewer's yeast.

The rhythms of the day were set by Paddy's struggling spasms and rests. For most of the day, only two or three family members were allowed in the room at one time but everyone took turns. After a long pause, each time the breathing began again it was a surprise. Everyone was waiting for Eamon to arrive from England. Abruptly, at one point, Paddy looked up to Angela standing over him and said with alarm, "Mae's not going back tomorrow, is she?"

Suddenly, near midnight, Paddy began breathing violently. Bridee, Seamus, and Annie came into the small room from the hall. We were all touching Paddy soothingly. In his struggle, his eyes opened wide and searched Mae and Angela's faces, bent closely together over his head. Both women desperately stared at the cryptic red numbers blinking on a digital monitor next to his bed. The breathing stopped and Paddy relaxed. The heart monitor confirmed that peace had come over Paddy.

Angela was urgently yelling into Paddy's seemingly deaf ears, "Wait, Paddy, wait. Eamon is coming! Wait, Paddy!" Indeed, as I stepped out of the room to call in the others, Eamon was running down the hallway in his heavyset lumbering manner, wearing the mussed gray bachelor suit he wore in airports or hayfields. He seemed to have been running since he got off the plane. Alert eyes on his ruddy face signaled recognition as his body followed my gesture to the room. "Hurry," I said solemnly as I played my part in the family story that was constructed at that moment, as it will be retold forever: that Eamon got there just moments *before* Paddy died.

A large crucifix appeared at the foot of the bed along with the hospital's resident priest dressed in a brown hooded gown and oversized rosary beads hanging from his waist. Paddy's body was straightened out from the pained and bent cramp it assumed only minutes earlier. The medical apparatus and personnel were quickly evacuated from the room as Paddy passed from medical to religious jurisdiction. Several candles were lit on one of the stainless steel tables near the head of the bed. Paddy's hands were sculpted into a clasp of prayer.

The priest led us through the rosary. After a long silence, Angela commented that Paddy had lived to see exactly one year of peace in the North. Some marveled that "he's still warm." The priest explained twice that he wouldn't become "stiff" for hours.

That observation continued into the next night at the private family viewing of Paddy in a Dublin funeral parlor. Several noted how "soft and warmish" and "nice looking" Paddy still was, evidence that confirmed that "he was a saint." For the first time all summer, Paddy and Angela's parish priest came to the house, just before the wake got under way. Everyone stopped the sandwich and tea preparations to sit with him in the living room. The 29th anniversary of the siblings' beloved mother's death was within two days of Paddy's. She was enrolled into the gathering of predeceased souls who would greet Paddy at heaven's entrance. Unlike many Irish, Paddy had no descendants living overseas. Regardless, the priest spoke irrelevantly about "long-distance" relations and grandchildren and their limited knowledge of the Irish world and its dead. He talked about "how it's different when the death occurs far away" and "that it's not the same when the relations are in a different country far away; maybe they never even knew their grandparents." I reflected on the day that Mae had received the newspaper clipping about her mother's death. Her grief was amplified by the distance and lack of rituals that she needed for closure. When the priest left, before the wake got underway, he stopped at the door to ask about Paddy and what kind of a man he had been. This was despite the fact that Paddy had been active in that church and had religiously attended mass there for over 30 years. Indeed, he and Seamus had been on the construction teams that had built that church.

Thus began the two nights of waking at Paddy's house. Unlike during the generation before his, Paddy's remains were in the funeral parlor rather than at home. While we were waiting for the guests and other relations from all over Ireland to arrive, someone made the highly unusual sighting of a single swan flying slowly in a line directly over Paddy's house and toward the graveyard to the north. The story of this unusual sighting was told and retold throughout the evening. Teresa, Paddy's sister-in-law from Sligo, said a robin had been inside their home earlier that summer. A Donegal who was known to be a "person whose dreams came true and no one wanted to know what she was dreaming" had told them, "When a robin flies into your home, it means someone will die." Jimmy Malloy, Paddy's brother-in-law also from Sligo, said, "The swan was a symbol of purity with the old folks in the country . . . If it flies over the house, there will be a death," or it meant that there had been a death; he wasn't at all sure. Mae insisted on finding a swan knick-knack and placing it in Paddy's open casket at the public gathering at the funeral home the next day. Another night of waking ensued, with more opportunity for comforting, laughing heartily, some singing, reminiscing, and social reunion.

The funeral and burial were held on Monday. In a break with family tradition, the modern and urban Paddy had purchased his gravesite in a commercial graveyard. His parish in the city did not have a graveyard of its own, as did the churches back in Mayo. The new graveyard is across the street from the Dublin International Airport. Years ago, he had joked once that it would be a convenient place for the Yanks to visit

him. Airplanes monotonously take off and land directly overhead. At the burial, folks from the West commented disapprovingly, mumbling from the rear fringe of the crowd, "That's not the way it's done in the country."

On Tuesday morning, Angela called her doctor to the house and became a severely depressed widow. The doctor commenced a "tablets" regime that lasted for over a year. Mae took her flight back to Arizona. At the airport, everyone kept saying, "It's great that you were here" and perceived as destiny that the ticket she had purchased in the spring had a return date that coincided with the day after the then-unforeseeable September funeral.

The usually elusive Eamon stayed after the funeral and also was present for Mae's airport departure. It was the last time Mae and Eamon saw each other. The aging bachelor died alone in an English hospital a year and a day after Paddy's death. Mae, the "Yank," commented disapprovingly, "He wouldn't even die in an Irish bed."

On the way to and from the airport, we said prayers for Paddy as we passed the nearby graveyard. Early that morning, I saw hundreds of gulls on a distinct path inland from the sea. They performed an elaborate dance in the sky above Paddy's house for about five minutes. Then the leaders turned around and the flock followed, streaming in single file southeast on the same skyway back toward the River Liffey and the Irish Sea. Angela announced, "Well, now you know the weather is going to change."

SUGGESTED READINGS

Crozier, Maurna. (1987). "'Powerful Wakes': Perfect Hospitality in Ireland from Below." In *Social Change and Local Communities*, ed. C. Curtin and T. Wilson. Galway: Galway University Press, pp. 70–91.

Heaney, Seamus. (1990). "Correspondences: Emigrants and Inner Exiles." In *Migrations: The Irish at Home and Abroad*, ed. Richard Kearney. Dublin: Wolfhound Press, pp. 21–31.

23

The Death of Omar

Frances Trix
Wayne State University

In ancient times Lebanon was the homeland of the Phoenicians who sailed from its port cities of Sidon and Tyre. It early became a refuge area for persecuted Christian and Muslim sects, and its religious diversity remains to this day a dominant feature of its society. Located at the eastern end of the Mediterranean Sea, Lebanon is a densely populated country of coastal plain and mountainous interior, only 4,000 square miles in total territory. When it became an independent country in 1943, its population was roughly half Muslim and half Christian. Among Muslim Lebanese, there are members of the Shi'ite, Sunni, and Druze religious communities. Among Christian Lebanese, there are Maronites (an Eastern Rite Church allied with Roman Catholicism whose patriarchy is in Lebanon), Greek Orthodox (liturgy largely in Arabic), Greek Catholics, and Protestants. Its modern political history has been characterized by power sharing and disputation among the different religious groups. Complicating this is the presence of almost half a million Palestinian refugees who live in poor conditions in refugee camps in Lebanon.

The Lebanese village in the article by Frances Trix is located in southern Lebanon, one of the poorest regions of the country, on the northern border with Israel. Shi'ite Muslims and Maronite Christians are the main religious groups there, with Sunni Muslim, Greek Catholic, and Protestants also represented. But as noted in the article, at certain times, like the death of a young man, people of these different groups came together. Culturally they have much in common. However, the events of this article took place shortly before Lebanon's Civil War (1975–1990). During this war 150,000 Lebanese died and a quarter of the population left the country. The southern region suffered acutely from internal fighting, from the politicization of the Shi'ite Muslims in response to the Israeli invasions, and from the Israeli occupation. The Israeli troops finally left southern Lebanon in 2000, and there was hope for greater stability and development. But the long civil war and longer occupation had polarized many of the different religious groups, disrupted the economy, and affected the lives and culture of many of inhabitants of the region, particularly those who came of age during the war.

As you read, consider the following questions:

1. How do practices surrounding Omar's death in south Lebanon differ from practices surrounding death in your country or culture?
2. What high schools in your country would be most similar to the village school in Lebanon? What schools in your country would be most different?
3. Why do you think the villagers thought that foreigners don't cry?
4. Why do you think Omar's classmates were so skilled in honoring him symbolically after his death?
5. Many of Omar's classmates were killed in the civil war, but were not mourned by the broader community the way Omar was. What aspects of cultures are most affected by civil wars?

The first time I saw Omar he was rhythmically destroying a pink stucco statue of the Virgin. The priest and several men stood impassively off to the side, just far enough away to avoid the cloud of dust that rose with each blow of the sledgehammer. Omar was covered with dust; his hair and his face and the maroon of his shirt were gradually becoming one color.

I noticed his man's body and the thinness of his bandy legs. Later I would recognize in others of my young students this same early oldness, probably the result of much physical labor and a diet of tea and bread. But then I didn't speculate on Omar's identity. I'd only been in the village in southern Lebanon one week and everyone was new.

Rather I watched with pleasure the destruction of the statue. It had already caused me some grief in the short time I'd been there.

On the second day in the village, I'd been walking with one of the younger daughters of the priest—a Maronite priest and therefore allowed to marry. We'd walked by the bend in the road where one of the three stores of the village stood. As we'd turned past the church and the statue, she'd asked me if I knew al-Adra. I hadn't a clue and shook my head. Then she'd stopped and turned to me. Certainly I knew Yasua? No again. She shook her head and from her eyes I knew something was wrong. "How then are you a teacher?" she demanded.

Ah, in my Arabic training, I'd learned the Muslim term for Jesus—Isa, not Yasua. "You mean Isa," I said brightly, hoping to redeem myself in her young eyes. She started to smile. "And Maryam," I added. "Yes," she said, "al-Adra," that is, the Virgin.

I wasn't the only one who'd had trouble with the statue. A car had come from the east, from the inland hills, through the village, headed toward the Mediterranean, and from there north to Tyre, Sidon, and Beirut. Or maybe it'd just come to the store in the village. Whatever, it hadn't negotiated the almost 90-degree bend and had slammed into the statue of the Virgin. Better that than running into the church, I thought.

The crash had happened sometime before my arrival in the village. How long before—days, weeks, months? In any case the priest must have decided that it didn't look respectful to have a partially smashed statue, even if it was mostly the podium that had been damaged. In truth the virgin herself had survived unscathed, as had the grill in front of her and the little coin box with a padlock as big as the box.

But probably people weren't putting much money in the Virgin's box anyway. Not many in the village had extra money, and if they were going to give, let it be publicly appreciated. Or, if someone was to give privately and it was seen by another, all sorts of gossip would result.

In the village everyone was interested in everyone else's business. What privacy there was was jealously guarded. That was why people refused to go to confession. Why, if they went to confession, the priest's wife would have it all over the village by the next day, they insisted. Only if a priest came from a faraway place would they consider going to confession. Unfortunately no place in Lebanon was really far away.

OMAR AND HIS CLASSMATES

The next time I saw Omar was in the *brevet* or intermediate diploma class on the first day of school. The school itself had been started by the priest and was located in the basement of the church. It was attended by boys and girls from the village: Maronites, Greek Catholics, and Protestants, as well as by boys from the surrounding Muslim villages and towns, both Sunni and Shi'ite Muslims. The Lebanese YMCA had assigned me—a foreign volunteer teacher—to teach English and biology to 7th through 10th graders in the village school. My favorite class soon became the seventh graders, the "class of five Muhammads," many of whom were as new to the school as I was. They even took to the book we'd been assigned for English instruction, a simplified version of Dickens' *David Copperfield*. "Just like Muhammad Hammadi's sister," they'd commented partway through the book when a young woman unwisely left home with a young man. The human relationships and the poverty of 19th century England were not distant to them.

The older class, the *brevet* class, were the veterans of the school. They were in their last and most serious year, at the end of which they had to take the nationwide *brevet* exam. For their English instruction we had been assigned *The Tempest*. The priest made the usual joke about the playwright being an Arab—Sheikes-Speer—but it would be a major feat of teaching and learning, I thought, to make the text intelligible.

I watched the older students look at their book. One of the Muslim boys looked particularly ill at ease as he sat there in his maroon shirt. Now I knew his name. It was Omar. Full of optimism on that first day, I announced to the class that by the end of the year they would all be more comfortable in English. Why, Omar would be "the friend of Shakespeare."

Mercifully for me, school got out early in those first few weeks. It was Ramadan and the Muslim students were fasting, meaning that they had no food or water during daylight hours. In recognition of this, school let out in early afternoon. This extra time eased my adjustment to village life and to my classes. In particular I wanted to learn more about my students.

My grade books had been prepared for me beforehand, with the students listed alphabetically by first name—alphabetically, that is, according to the Arabic alphabet. I soon learned to adjust for the differences in alphabets. And the listing by first name made sense. There were very few last names. For example in the Christian village of some 700, there were only four last names. I was told to count my blessings though. Until three years before, grade books had all been listed alphabetically according to the first name of the fathers of the students.

A problem with listing students by first name, however, was that it took me awhile to learn who was related to whom. This was especially important when I assigned people to help one another. Early on I made a mistake and assigned a student who was a Shi'ite Muslim to help a Sunni Muslim. Better to have picked a cousin.

In general it took me longer to get to know the Muslim students because they lived in surrounding villages and towns, and I didn't see them or their families much outside school. Except for Omar. Besides that first week when he'd finished off the statue, I saw him several times, always doing physical labor in the village.

Gradually I learned that Omar lived about two miles from the village on land owned by the Maronite Church and managed by a Maronite family. Omar's Sunni Muslim family had been Bedouin or desert nomads until his generation and worked for the Maronite family. They lived in a ramshackle place near the larger home. Omar was the first in his family ever to go to school, and to earn money for tuition, he often did odd jobs for people in the village. That's what he'd been doing that day I first saw him with the sledgehammer.

As it turned out, I mastered the students' names fairly rapidly. They always sat in the same place, separated not only by religious grouping but also by family in that girls sat next to their brothers. Among the Muslim students this caused no problem as no Muslim girls came to the school. (Throughout Lebanon this was not at all the case. But in the smaller, poorer villages like those of the south, money for schooling was scarce.)

Furthermore, the students always wore the same clothes. This too helped me learn their names. For example, Omar always wore the same maroon shirt. Only after his death did two of his cousins get new shirts. Meanwhile the year moved slowly as years do in places where people walk wherever they need to go, where everyone knows each other's second cousins, and where news comes not from outside, printed in columns on paper, but rather from neighbors sitting on short reed stools around low tables sipping thick dark cardamom-scented coffee.

Yet in this village where people still took donkeys with metal cans down the long path to the well, my students knew about life in ways I had yet to learn. When asked to write an essay on what he was afraid of, 14-year-old Daoud wrote that he was afraid of dying for no reason. Saidie did poorly on my biology quizzes, but then I watched her skin a rabbit her brother had trapped and prepare it for cooking. And when asked to write on what they had done during a school vacation, many in my ninth-grade class wrote on planting wheat. Still, nothing could have prepared me for the actions of the *brevet* class the first day of Lent.

FIRST DAY OF LENT AND OMAR'S LAST

Religious holidays stood out in the village. Certainly they were numerous, what with Muslim holidays and both Eastern and Western Christian holidays, not to mention national holidays. But perhaps it was the daily celebration in the Maronite church that made any change for a holiday stand out. Unlike in America and other Western societies where holidays have to be worked into schedules, there you could even feel their approach. And so Lent arrived.

Not to be outdone by the Muslims with their fast of Ramadan, many Christians were also fasting for Lent. Even I walked off to school that spring morning with little in my stomach. The first hour went as usual, but by the second hour it was clear something was in the air. Two boys who normally remained respectfully in their seats on the long hard wooden benches kept standing up to see out the high basement window. Twice I told them to sit down. I looked over to see what was out there, but all I could see was the dusty road in front of the old garagelike store. No traffic, no people, nothing. But the third time they stood up I had the sense not to call them on it. Suddenly they ran out of the school. At once the other students began talking and in a growing tide poured out of the school. Again I looked out the window.

There on the ground in front of the store I saw a girl writhing in the dust. What had happened?

No one had time to explain to me. I picked up only phrases from the students about an engagement party up in the hills and blood and the hospital in Tyre. Finally one of the other teachers stopped to tell me.

It seemed that Omar had been dancing the day before at an engagement gathering up in the hills. All of a sudden he'd begun throwing up blood. They'd brought him by car down to his house where he'd insisted that he had homework to finish. But then he didn't get better, and in the evening someone had gone for a taxi to take him some 40 minutes to the hospital in Tyre. Apparently several years before he'd had what sounded like ulcer problems but what care he got, who knew? The next morning his sister had waited by the store in the Christian village, for that's where there was a telephone. She'd been waiting for news from the hospital. The boys in my class who'd been jumping up to look out the window had been Omar's cousins. They too were waiting for word.

School was over, as the students and teachers and priest had all left. The students seemed to be headed for the end of the village nearest the sea. I followed.

There, at the very edge of the village they waited. Soon we heard suras from the Qur'an, the sacred book of Islam, filling the air and there came into view a small white ambulance with a loudspeaker on its roof, rotating to send the incantations in all directions. It stopped at the edge of the village. The boys from the *brevet* class, Omar's class, gathered at the back of the ambulance. What were they doing?

Then I saw they had the stretcher, with Omar's body on it, hoisted up on their shoulders. They carried him at a pace through the village and we all followed with the ambulance slowly bringing up the rear.

Down into the school for the last time they carried Omar on the stretcher. As we waited outside the school

I happened to glance over across the road and see soldiers of the United Nations International Peace-Keeping Force, blond Scandinavians in their cerulean blue berets, watching us by their jeeps. I felt a gulf of more than the road between us. How could they understand what was going on?

His fellow students then carried Omar back out of the school and down the road to the other edge, the eastern edge of the village where the ambulance was waiting. They slid the stretcher in the back and the ambulance set off into the hills, again with the Qur'an blaring.

And we followed. Not just students now, but adults as well. A raggle-taggle group, we walked the dusty road toward where Omar had lived. Cars now joined the procession. The priest in his old white Plymouth stopped to pick me up. It was good to sit even though we were squashed together in the car. The sun, the lack of food and drink that morning, and the events had taken a toll.

Up in the hills outside where Omar had lived, they were already bringing out chairs for people to sit on from the nearby house of the Maronite landkeeper. People passed around cigarettes to the men. Omar's family didn't have money for this; it was done as a courtesy by those both Christian and Muslim who were better off.

I stood still in a stupor. Slowly I began to notice that some of the old women had begun to dance. I watched their weaving motions, confused. What was going on? Then I realized that I knew the women—they were all from the Christian village. Certainly they had gotten the news first and so had arrived first. But why were they dancing?

I saw the grandmother of a friend of mine, and taking up my courage asked. Without stopping her dance she told me she was doing a wedding dance. A wedding dance? With one arm lifted making gentle serpentine motions she added that Omar had never been married and so they were dancing him through what he had not had.

Over next to Omar's house there was more going on. A fire had been made and a kettle full of water was on the fire. From the shack of a house a young woman came out, her face beyond all of us there. She slowly dropped a maroon shirt and other clothes into the kettle and with a stick stirred it round. She was washing his clothes for the last time.

I remembered when I'd first seen Omar in the village going at the statue, then where he'd sat in school on the left side of the class. For the first time I was aware I was crying.

Omar's father, an older man, walked wordlessly among us, clutching the short legs of his youngest son who was seated up on his shoulders. Omar's sister, the one who had been on the ground outside the school,

FIGURE 10   One of the elderly women who danced a marriage dance for Omar. *Photo by Frances Trix.*

now sat alone by the door of the house, slowly rocking herself from side to side. The young woman boiling Omar's clothes turned out to be Omar's mother. As Omar himself was 15, she must have had him when she was less than 15. And still the old women danced to music only they heard while the men shuffled and smoked.

I think there was a meal, the men separate from the women. Somehow we got back to the village. Certainly women relatives stayed with Omar's body that night.

FUNERAL AND BEYOND

The next day was the funeral. It was held in the large Muslim town inland from the village. As with the day before, all other work had stopped, and people from the whole area had gathered. There were speeches full of Arabic rhetoric and premicrophone fire that I couldn't follow from in front of the mosque. And then Omar was buried. With his body were placed his schoolbooks, including Shakespeare. It was only fitting, people said. He was the first in his family to go to school.

The following day there was school again. The students respected Omar's place and it remained empty. Then one student stood up in class, and after I'd called on him, he asked if I remembered how I had told Omar that he would be the friend of Shakespeare. How could I forget? But then it seemed as if the students really had another question that they couldn't ask me.

Later I found out that the people of the village had been amazed that I had cried. We didn't think foreigners cried, they said. And even more strangely, the priest had later given me, not his family, Omar's final grade sheets. It seemed that as I had been looking at the UN soldiers when my students took Omar down into the basement school for the last time, the villagers had been looking at me.

But how could I explain that in America 15-year-old students didn't die like that? That ambulances took people to the hospital, not bodies back home. That ulcers could be treated.

And there was more. How could I explain that 15-year-old American students, all on their own, wouldn't have known to carry a fellow student who was dead into class for one last time? Or that school and work and whole communities didn't stop when someone died. Or that we didn't hear the rhythms of life anymore to know how we should dance when a young man died.

These events took place in south Lebanon in the spring of 1973. Two years later incidents and killings in Lebanon would escalate into civil war. With the Syrian and Israeli invasions, the whole region would be sucked in, and the large Muslim town where Omar was buried would be wiped off the map. As for Omar's classmates, they would grow into adulthood and many to early death during the ensuing 15 years of war, leaving my gradebook a meager memorial.

SUGGESTED READINGS

Gilsenan, Michael. (1996). *Lords of the Lebanese Marches: Violence and Narrative in an Arab Society*. Berkeley: University of California Press.

Munro, Gladys. (1994). *An American Nurse Amidst Chaos*. Beirut: American University Press.

24

Death and Hope: Syrian Stories

Anne Bennett

University of Arizona

Modern-day Syria came into being in 1946 after a quarter century of unhappy wrangling with French and other European powers after World War I. It is a country of approximately 17 million people and is comparable in size to the state of Arizona. Syria is a country of many religious and ethnic groups. Of the Arabs, Armenians, Kurds, and Turks that comprise the rich mix that is Syria, 85 percent are Sunni Muslims, and the rest are affiliated with various Christian and Islamic sects. The rhythm of religious practice marks daily life in Syria. Although there is freedom to practice one's religion in Syria, there exist a delicate balance and tension between religion and the state. The result is that Syrians hesitate to talk freely about what religious group or sect they belong to, or their ethnicity, unless they are among friends they trust. Regardless of religious or ethnic affiliation, all people experience certain universal rites of passage at birth, marriage, and death.

The capitol of Syria, Damascus, is a city of about eight million people and it lays claim to being the "oldest continually occupied" city in the world. One hundred kilometers south of Damascus is the provincial capitol, Suwayda, a mid-sized town of 50,000 lying between the breadbasket (grains and legumes) of Syria's southern plains and the basalt-black rocky hills of *Jebel al-Arab* ("mountain of the Arabs"). The vast majority of those who live in this southern region of Syria are members of the Druze sect. Until the early 1970s this region was called *Jebel ad-Druz* ("Mountain of the Druze").

In her article, Anne Bennett, who resided in both Damascus and Suwayda, explores the role that a belief in reincarnation can play in the Druze sect's attitude to-

ward death. The Druze belief in reincarnation is extremely unusual in Islam and as such it sets them apart; one could say it even marginalizes them.

Amal's family, who live in the southern Damascus suburb of Jeremana, dealt with the sudden loss of their mother several years ago when there were still six young children living at home. In this article about death and hope, we see how the Druze attitude toward death is partly informed by their belief in reincarnation. We also see beyond the specifics of Druze beliefs to what might be a universal need to immortalize, or hope for immortality, that this rite of passage inspires.

As you read, think about the following questions:

1. If a five-year-old child in your own society were convinced that she were the mother of children, what would the reaction be? How do you think people would have responded to her?
2. In your own experience, what are some ways that people who have died become immortalized? How are they "kept alive" in people's minds?
3. Where do you see similarities and differences between Syria and your own country when it comes to mourning and other rites of passage related to death?
4. In Syria, oral traditions that are traded as stories or poems serve to transmit ideas about death through time and across regions. Are similar traditions or customs used in your own culture? Compare the role of oral traditions about death among the Druze to oral traditions you are more familiar with.

T he first time I met Amal, she told me that her mother had been reincarnated. Amal was one of the first people I met when I went to Syria. At first she was my tutor in Syrian Arabic, but she eventually became a friend as well as an invaluable consultant during my fieldwork. She was from the Druze sect, which is considered Islamic but with elements from different reli-

gious and philosophical traditions, and a reputation for secrecy on religious matters. For many Muslims, the esoteric departures of the Druze, such as a belief in reincarnation, set them up for charges of heresy.

The longer I was in Syria, the more people I met who would tell me their personal stories about reincarnation. At the same time there were plenty of skeptics within the Druze community who did not easily believe in it. Because of her experiences following the death of her mother, Amal was no longer among the skeptics.

Both of Amal's parents died suddenly about 10 years ago, leaving behind six children under the age of 18. Amal's mother died at home as a result of a freak electrical accident. As the oldest unmarried child, my friend Amal became the de facto mother of the household. Some Druze say that when the soul is taken by surprise, as in Amal's mother's case, by sudden bodily death, it is not prepared yet to move beyond the earthly level of existence. The soul is still emotionally attached to the people it suddenly left behind. It has a burning sense of unfinished business. Amal told me that after her mother died, people were always saying, "God-willing, your mother is reincarnated. It's got to be the case that she's reincarnated."

"People said that?" I asked.

> Yes, because whenever someone dies in an accident and leaves behind young children, it is said that "God-willing, they are reincarnated." This is especially so when someone dies suddenly or violently in an accident. But it is not so much the case when someone dies naturally, from old age.

When I first heard her tell me this story, I naively thought that having her mother reincarnated like this would be a happy occasion and would make it easier for Amal's family to deal with their mother's sudden death. But over time, as the specifics of Amal's story emerged, I learned that reincarnation is a bittersweet experience for everyone involved.

REINCARNATION STORIES: ELEMENTS OF A GENRE

Reincarnation stories are a living oral tradition. They first come to life and perpetuate through word of mouth, rumors, and gossip.

> Approximately five years after my mother died, we started hearing stories that my mother was reincarnated [natiq] in a village in the district of Suwayda. There was a girl there who talked about the young children that she left behind. This girl would say to her mother, "I have a beautiful house, more beautiful than your house, and I have children."
>
> I was away in Nigeria for 11 years. After I returned here to Suwayda my sister told me about this fellow who had come by to see us while I was away, claiming he was our reincarnated brother.

As a story progresses one usually hears of a young child who starts talking obsessively about his or her

past life. Such children often give very specific details, often reporting names of family members and describing people and houses. These details sometimes aid later in efforts to reunite the child with the family remembered from a previous life. Amal told me that this is a very difficult and stressful experience for young children. The memories (from a previous life) that preoccupy a child in effect place the child in a tug-of-war between two competing worlds.

> They don't exactly understand what's happening. It's very hard for them to reconcile the past and the present. Nejwa [the young girl who experienced the memories of Amal's mother] became so obsessed and disturbed that she couldn't handle being in kindergarten. They had to take her out of school and that was when they started looking for, and finally found, us.

I asked Amal what exactly it was that had so preoccupied five-year-old Nejwa that people saw it as necessary to pull her out of kindergarten. Nejwa herself was refusing to go to kindergarten "because she was obsessed with concerns about her children, she wasn't able to concentrate at school. She didn't think about her studies, or her father, or her mother, or her grandfather, or her siblings." Reconciling the past and the present can be disruptive and confusing for children like Nejwa whose memories of a previous life stubbornly persist.

When her mother tried to get her to eat she refused food, insisting that she wanted to take care of her children. She would often say that she had another family. The first thing she said along these lines was, "I have a girl; her name is Amal."

"That's the first thing she said!?" I asked.

> It was the first thing because she died between my hands . . . The last time someone came to her it was me. But we are educated people and so, you know, we were not [a pause] we did not go to the village right away in order to see this girl. But my grandmother went.

Detailing the specifics of these persistent memories is another common element in reincarnation stories. A large orange tree in a courtyard, the color and texture of a child's hair that needs combing, whether someone was sick or unfed at the moment of death—these are the kinds of bold descriptive details that arise in and animate reincarnation stories. They also function as proof of the identity of the "previous personality," as some psychologists have come to call it.

Certain elements tend to recur in reincarnation stories. It is the specific nature of what people like Nejwa actually say, their "testimony," and sometimes their mannerisms that help the family who is approached decide whether or not the child in front of them is a reincarnated member of their family. The family member will have died at about the time the child in front of them was conceived or born. When I was told these stories, key passages of reported speech (quotes) were repeated to me. These were central to the story because they were critical in supporting any case for reincarnation.

The reunion is also a key element of reincarnation stories. How people actually come to be reunited, who is or who is not convinced, to what degree relationships are maintained after a reunion are further elements of the reincarnation genre. Among the stories I encountered, recorded, and analyzed, these elements regularly recur. Another element that is common across stories, apart from literary or structural concerns, is the fact that the entire process is fraught with mixed feelings and bittersweet emotions. There are also partial stories—stories of children who grew up and never had a reunion with the family they had memories of from a previous life. Some adults recalled for me a period when they had clear memories of a previous life, but which gradually dissipated and never developed into an obsession. Some parents similarly can remember when a child of theirs spoke about another family they belonged to, but this would pass like other stages of childhood.

RECONCILING COMPETING AND OVERLAPPING WORLDS

Those children whose memories do not pass like other stages of childhood can suffer mild to severe psychological distress. Two worlds are competing in their consciousness and are competing for their loyalty. As a way of easing this emotional difficulty, when Amal's family met Nejwa, they would not address the young girl as "mother," nor would they treat her as though she were in fact their mother. Amal's family accepted her, treated her with kindness, and were often amazed with little things Nejwa would say and do that reminded them so much of their mother. They understood that a part of their mother existed in Nejwa. But they held back and tried to treat her like just another little girl.

> We don't love her like we loved our mother. We don't have those kinds of feelings, those emotions. We love her, because she is a child. You know what I mean? I don't say to her "mama" because she needs to live her life like a child, naturally, without anxiety.

Amal's family held back from getting too attached because of the bald fact that Nejwa could never substitute for their mother. They were sincere about their fondness for Nejwa, but they deliberately interacted with her as though she were a child and not the shadow of their mother. To have encouraged a full transference of "mother" onto Nejwa, despite being convinced of their mother's presence within her, would only make things more emotionally difficult all around.

Holding back from total identification with Nejwa as mother was also, Amal said, in Nejwa's interest. They wanted to protect Nejwa from becoming too confused by the competition between the worlds of her past and her present. Once Nejwa met with Amal's family, she began to relax and behave in a less troubled and distressed fashion. She returned to school. It seems that this meeting, and the ongoing relationship she maintains with Amal's family, resolved something for Nejwa and put her world in order.

For many years previous to that, however, Nejwa's father had prevented a meeting between the two families. In retrospect he regrets this, once he saw how it improved his daughter's state of mind. He had hoped that Nejwa was simply going through a stage, which happens sometimes with other children. Also, he would say to his daughter that if they went to find this other family, perhaps they would not accept Nejwa or want to meet her. His aim was to spare Nejwa any disappointment, while also hoping her obsession would pass. Her father's strategy was ineffective; Nejwa's concerns only increased as she got older. Eventually, Nejwa's paternal uncle, a relative holding a place of influence and authority in the family, insisted that Nejwa's other family be found. With the details of Nejwa's stories to go on, her father finally set about looking for Amal's family. It was only after the families met that Nejwa started to "reintegrate" into her current life. Amal described Nejwa as having been psychologically ill until she had the chance, after reuniting with Amal's family, to somehow reintegrate these competing worlds and selves in her five-year-old consciousness.

The guarded behavior of Nejwa's father, upon hearing claims to reincarnation by his child, is not unusual. In another story, some members of a family were approached on the street by a young man who claimed to have been their brother/son who had died suddenly in a farming accident about a decade ago. The family, taking a cue at the time from the father, gave a cool response to this person. But several years later, after the family returned from working abroad, one of the brothers in this family decided to see what this individual had to say for himself. Despite outward differences, the major elements in this and Nejwa's story are shared.

THE COMFORT OF POETRY

In spite of the difficulties associated with reincarnation for the people involved, it still can be a kind of emotional comfort during the period of mourning. Certain phrases that index reincarnation during mourning, as well as elegaic poetry chanted by old women specializing in the genre, together worked to lend a sense of calm and catharsis to Amal's family after their mother died.

During the mourning period, a steady stream of people visited the family home to pay respects to Amal's deceased mother. During the first seven days of this period, in addition to paying their respects, visitors brought all kinds of cooked meals for Amal's family. The family of the deceased, it is assumed, will be unable to take care of everyday things in such a difficult period. For seven days Amal's family was fed by the community. Amal said, "People bring you food because at that time you have no strength and you're very upset. They help you through this by feeding you. It's really a beautiful idea, you know. The entire community brings you through a rough time."

On the seventh day of mourning Amal's family made a huge feast for the visitors who were still streaming through their house. The guests ate sparingly of it—to do otherwise would be very impolite. When the family feeds visitors on the seventh day, they signal a transition from emotional paralysis toward recovery.

What helps in this transition? How, in one week, does a family go from being unable to feed itself to being able to provide a feast for many guests? The answer lies in the words of the poets. During those first seven days, among the visitors are groups of older women dressed in the long black dresses and diaphanous white headscarves characteristic of senior Druze women. These women chant their poetry at both weddings and funerals, reciting (and improvising upon) poems passed down orally through the generations. In Amal's words,

> These women would recite certain sentences that made me remember my mother. It was like this: at first someone would say just one sentence that made me remember her and I'd start crying uncontrollably. And then these old women would continue singing their poetry. It made me cry, but at the same time it helped the pain rise out of me. Gradually the crying that their poetry caused also started to make me feel a calm, a peace, in my heart. This happened on the first day, on the second day, and for the whole week. The old women were there the whole week doing this. The recitations from the Qur'an started only after the women sang their poetry. So first it was the social cure, and then the religious.

WHAT CAN WE DO NOW, HIS MOTHER IS NOW PREGNANT?

In addition to poetry, there were certain phrases that could help lift one's spirit during mourning, expressions that referred to reincarnation. As examples, Amal mentioned these: "God-willing, she will live another life, one that is even nicer," *"Shu bidna na'amal, immu haamel fi?"* (What can we do now, his mother is now pregnant?), and "God-willing, she will be born to nice people."

Such expressions, said Amal, "give the family who has any sadness, they give them a hope. After all, what can you do? There's nothing to do. 'His mother is already pregnant with him now.' This gives people some hope." In Druze reincarnation, the idea of immediate rebirth is very important, which is why referring to a mother "being pregnant already" with the to-be-reborn soul makes sense. This belief gives hope that any unfinished business with the deceased might be taken care of within this lifetime. This contrasts with other systems of reincarnation, such as the Hindu and Buddhist, in which a soul is not necessarily reborn right away, but can linger indefinitely before going on to their next rebirth.

Amal wanted me to know that she thought these expressions were not so different in essence from those of Christians and Sunni Muslims when they are mourning, expressions that essentially convey that someone "has gone to eternal paradise [heaven]." Many people get comfort from the thought that somehow the deceased continue to exist, and under favorable circumstances.

Like Christians and Sunni Muslims, the Druze also believe in heaven as an ultimate destination. However, the Druze believe that a soul must go through seven generations or stages before the process of reincarnation reaches its culmination and the person or soul can enter heaven. The belief in seven rebirths signifies that there is justice in the world and that everyone has the chance to live every kind of existence. For example, Amal's sister, Semah, has been married for 14 years but has never been able to have children. This is a source of sadness for her, but she says that perhaps in a previous life she had so many children that she never stopped working and that this life is her time to have a rest.

COMIC RELIEF

Amal loved a good joke. She often joked about how much better her next life simply had to be compared to her current one. This would afford her some much-needed comic relief when times were hard, as they often were. Because of the death of her parents, Amal had become since age 18 the primary caretaker of her younger siblings. She made a meager salary at the University of Damascus. Her commutes across the city were long and tiresome. Her extended family was always giving her trouble, and never seemed to help out enough. Most of her income came on the side, outside of her full-time university job, through tutoring foreigners in Arabic.

Amal enjoyed her foreign students and would often get into long discussions with them. Sometimes the issue of death would come up. Amal found this strange—sitting around having a conversation about death. But she tolerated her international students' quirks and when the topic arose, her students invariably said, "I'm afraid of dying, I don't want to die." Amal's reply tended toward the following: "This is natural, you know. Of course! It's more or less the same thing with me, to be afraid of dying, but I'll joke with them. I'll tell them 'yeee I won't die because I'll live many lives and, besides, I want a better life than this one!'"

Once Amal was asked whether she had gone to visit her least-favorite cousin, to which she replied, "oh, maybe in my next life I'll go visit her."

References to or conversations about reincarnation are not an everyday thing. Amal emphasized that from day to day, "it [reincarnation] does not occupy the mind. Mostly just during the mourning period, not all the time. I have to live now. I can't just sit around imagining another life. I have to work to improve my life now."

LIVES GO ON

These days, Amal's family sees Nejwa about once or twice a year during major holidays or school vacations. Typically Nejwa, who is in high school, makes the trip from Suwayda to Damascus, a 90-minute bus ride, and visits for a day or two.

Although the Druze have a belief in reincarnation, not everyone necessarily understands and relates to it in the same way. Many Druze who spoke with me on the topic point out that there is the problem of proving reincarnation scientifically, and many people are quite skeptical about it. Nonetheless, reincarnation stories abound and offer recurring literary, structural, and emotional patterns.

Amal often pointed out to me that although it seemed unusual to many people, reincarnation is just one example of people trying to find meaning and hope in death. For my Druze friends the way that people express themselves during mourning, whether or not they believe in reincarnation, gives people hope that something about the deceased person continues on. It is important to assert in some way a sense of immortality of the person who has died. Certain kinds of formulaic expressions help people deal with death, whether they are Druze, Christian, or Sunni Muslim. These expressions differ from group to group, but all of them ultimately work to give mourners a sense of hope and continuity.

SUGGESTED READINGS

Betts, Robert Brenton. (1988). *The Druze*. New Haven: Yale University Press.

Stevenson, Ian. (1980). *Cases of the Reincarnation Type, Volume II: Twelve Cases in Lebanon and Turkey*. Charlottesville: University Press of Virginia.

PART IX

Material Culture, Art, and Identity

Photo by April Sievert.

Material culture refers to stuff—from the simplest stone tools to commercial airplanes, from old manuscripts to digital video disks. People everywhere produce and acquire the things needed to obtain food, shelter, and any of the other things they may need or want. Most anthropologists would agree that technology is a major component of human culture, as it represents the tangible aspects of culture.

There is no single way to study material culture. **Archaeologists** look at artifacts—things made or modified by humans—in their attempts to establish cultural histories through the past, to date objects in time, to establish prehistoric trade relations, or to figure out how people lived from day to day. **Cultural anthropologists** look at the social implications of material culture decision making.

Some anthropologists focus their studies of the material culture on the consumption of those objects that represent the modern world, such as fast food, Barbie™ dolls, and beer cans. As increased corporatization makes such objects available to more and more people worldwide, and as marketing increases, the people acquire things based on not only what is needed, but what is desired. How people change their attitudes about what they need or want can be indicative of larger global social and economic changes.

Art is a visible expression of cultural ideas extended through the mechanism of personal creativity and individual skill, and includes song, dance, and visual creations. Therefore, although artistic styles can be standardized, there is always variation in the ways in which individual artists translate ideas into compositions, creations, or performances. Sometimes, anthropologists look at **aesthetics**—what people find to be beautiful. Both material culture and art become expressions of individual and group identity.

People's attitudes toward their material goods can belie other values they may hold. For example, skyscrapers certainly serve a functional need for office space, but they also represent progress and strength, which are generally thought in industrialized countries to be positive values. On the other hand, not all members of any society are going to value the same things, like the same things, or find the same things to be lovely. Some people like old buildings, finding them to be quaint or charming, while others see only "eyesores." Anthropologists take note of these differences, and try to understand the bases for differences in attitudes about things.

Material culture can be viewed as a cultural system in its own right and, as such, contributes to how other systems—gender, politics, economics, religion—appear in the first place. Material culture and art are everywhere evident. Material culture, as culture we can *see*, creates the images and appearances that humans react to and remember. People relate to the world around them through material culture, and they express their abstract ideas through art. While material goods and art reflect individual expression, they also reflect economics, politics, and religion. Many of people's ideas may be contained within material culture, and objects serve to communicate, codify, and perpetuate their ideas. Much material culture has a symbolic component as well as an everyday functional one.

People often use art and material symbols to make political statements. Singing, writing, and painting provide ways to criticize governments, to communicate feelings, to express resistance, and to offer solutions to problems. Ideas about supernatural agents also come across in material culture and art. Inspiration derived from religious beliefs has promoted the construction of temples for collective religious worship, altars and shrines for personal devotion, equipment used in rituals, or icons worn or displayed in many different contexts.

Material culture is intrinsically economic because production, exchange, and consumption depend on objects that flow throughout the system. Material culture dictates how people look, how others perceive them, and how they interact. Clothing, accessories, ornaments, or decorations reflect the way people see themselves, or how they wish to be seen. Designer labels on the outside of garments testify that the wearer has the resources to acquire and display such goods. Uniforms convey information regarding occupation and also establish social hierarchies. And clothing still proclaims ethnic identification in many societies. For example, in the central Andes mountains in South America, indigenous women traditionally wear hats of different styles that testify to where the woman is from.

Finally, one advantage to the ever-quickening pace of technological change, and the information revolution engendered by the Internet, is that artistic styles from all over the world can now be explored and appreciated. World music and international arts are now commonplace in markets and venues across the industrialized states.

"Smoking Sage" refers to a young student, a Dakota pipe-maker, that April Sievert encountered in an introductory anthropology class. Barry Lyons takes us to the world of song, expression, tradition, and political comment in Ecuador. Alan Sandstrom and Pamela Effrein Sandstrom have worked with Nahua shaman Cirilo for many years and have learned about the representation of spirits as cut paper figures.

Other articles with reference to material culture or art:

Rosa, Weaving Women into Life by Robin O'Brian

Sunday Dinner at Hanka's by Julianna Acheson

Behind the Microphone by Debra Spitulnik

25

Smoking Sage

April K. Sievert
Indiana University

Indiana, a U.S. state without reservations, still has a small population of Native Americans from a large number of ethnic groups, from the local Miami to more distant Diné (Navajo) or Choctaw. Governmental relocation efforts, along with the promise of factory jobs, brought Native Americans into industrial cities of the Midwest during the 20th century, to join throngs of other migrants from both Europe and rural areas in the southern United States. The factory jobs have largely evaporated, but the families remain. Some of these people practice North American cultural traditions and retain ties to family members living on reservations elsewhere. Many more have not followed traditional ways, do not speak native languages, and belong to families with multiethnic backgrounds.

An awakening of interest in Native American life and the realization that whole cultures are being lost prompted many people with native ancestry to try to learn something of their heritage and to affiliate with native cultures or tribal groups. Sometimes this means seeking lost relatives and learning a "new" original language. As with any ethnic group, cultural identity often resides longest with material culture—that sum of tangible products that people recognize, use, and remember. One type of material culture that retains considerable meaning is the pipe. Used for social and symbolic functions, pipes have been used by many cultures of eastern and central North America for more than two thousand years. This is the story of a young man who was actively working to regain his Dakota identity through the medium of pipe-making. His people, once referred to as Sioux, originally comprised four large groups that occupied portions of the western Great Lakes and northern Plains regions. The easternmost group, the Santee, is made up of several distinct bands that are often collectively referred to as Dakota.

As you read, consider the following:

1. Why did Doug focus on pipes as a means to relearn Dakota ways?
2. Why did Doug not want the anthropologist to study his stone tools?
3. Does your family have objects or skills that help to reinforce ethnic identity? If so, what are they and how might they be used? How do you or your family treat these objects?
4. In today's world of mass-produced consumer items, what do you predict would be the future of handmade, traditional objects like pipes or other items?

I plopped my armful of books and syllabi down on the desk and sat on it, swung my feet and watched the students trickle in. Some looked rather weary and I suspected they had already worked a full day. A couple of men and several women wore business clothes. Others arrived in the odd array of jeans, sweaters, and sweatshirts. Most carried cans of soda. I noticed one chap, tall and lean, sporting a long, light-brown ponytail and, oddly enough for a typical Midwestern college student, excellent posture. He was talking to a voluptuous woman with curly hair, easily, as if they were old friends. They sat next to each other.

Even though the day had been chillingly cold and we were already a bit tired, the first night of the spring semester in Indianapolis always promises unforeseen treats. Human Origins is a course about human variation, so I usually begin by explaining how all humans are similar, but each is still unique. We then introduce ourselves by telling the class something about each of us that makes us unique within the class. "I have a hole in my head." "I have ugly feet." "I have a pin in my knee." Sometimes students relay cultural or historical details about themselves. "I presume I am the only student here on academic probation for grades she got in 1968," that sort of thing. The lanky student with the ponytail calmly informed us, "My grandfather was Dakota, a pipe-maker, and I am learning the craft."

At this point most of the women in the class peered in Doug Harris's direction, while the dark-haired woman next to him, Janelle, appeared enraptured. Not only was he tall and good-looking, to the students he embodied the romanticized image of Native Americans. Several men in the class also perked up. I suspected they envisioned themselves sporting the manly leather leggings popularized in *The Last of the Mohicans*, or heading out across the prairies to hunt bison, resplendent in feathers and paint. Maybe the women were the ones envisioning the leggings and breechcloth. Such is the stilted picture that Hollywood has drawn of Native American history and life.

Doug said he was one-quarter Dakota and had lived in Indianapolis basically his entire life. He was older than many of the other students in the class—maybe age 30 or so. He had, a few years before, gone out to a Dakota reservation to find his grandfather and get to know him better. He had always known that his ancestors were pipe-makers, and he had always seen and known something of the pipes that his grandfather had created. At that point he knew few Dakota words, and virtually nothing about actually making pipes. He now had rights to quarry the sacred raw materials, he was proficient at making simple pipes, and he knew how to conduct some pipe ceremonies.

I was excited because, as an archaeologist, I am always interested in learning more about how traditional manufacturing was done. Here was someone who knew about perhaps the most symbolic and sacred of all manufacturing in native North America, pipe-making, and he was in my very own classroom for an entire semester. I had recently studied some fascinating stone pipes, over 500 hundred years old, from a site in Oklahoma. I selfishly hoped I could become the student and have an opportunity to learn from Doug.

Dakota pipes are made from stone—very special stone called pipestone or catlinite. It comes from one locality only, a quarry near the town of Pipestone, Minnesota. Catlinite, the geological name given the stone, derives from the name of George Catlin, a photographer and chronicler who brought images of the Plains Indians to the eastern United States. It is a soft, red stone, nearly the color of dried blood. It takes a high polish and has been used for hundreds of years to make stone pipes. The quarries are off-limits to everyone except Native American pipe-makers. It is a limited resource, and a very important one. The stone pipes are equipped with a hollowed out bowl and a stem drilled with a narrow bore. A hollow piece of reed or sumac is inserted as a pipestem, and this guides the aromatic smoke to the user's lungs.

One evening after class I was chatting with some lingering students. Doug was among them and I asked him what sort of tools he used to make the pipes.

"They are made from quartz," he replied.

"You mean crystal quartz, or another form of quartz, like chert or jasper?" I queried. Precontact people of the Americas most often used an opaque form of quartz called chert, flint, or jasper to make tools. These stones have very small crystals and flake nicely. Quartz crystal is translucent, a semiprecious gem, and is more difficult to work.

"Oh, crystal. It is the best stone to use," Doug answered.

"Why is that?" I continued.

"It is very hard, carves the pipestone easily, and well—it's what we are supposed to use. It has, hmm, some other aspects that I really shouldn't talk about."

"Cool," I thought to myself. There are secrets to the making of pipes. That fits, considering what limited things I knew about how pipes function. They are very special, not just objects for smoking a tobacco mixture; they are objects for ritual purification and for ritual communion. Pipes are used in pipe ceremonies, conducted to usher in important occasions and cement relations between groups or lineages.

"Do all pipe-makers use quartz? Do any use metal tools?" I asked.

"Some use metal, but not the more traditional pipe-makers. For me it is important to use stone," Doug said.

I wondered at the importance of finding, in the hew and rub of hard stone on soft, a way of being and belonging. It seemed that in Doug's pipe crafting, there was more than simply an artifact being made; it was the making of one's own history.

"Do you make your own tools?" I pressed on.

"Yes, except that the quartz is hard to knap, and I sometimes get help from an elder."

I asked these questions because I study stone tools. Stone tools are almost never used today; so much of the lore about making and using them is lost. In North America, prior to contact with Europeans, most Native American tools used for cutting, sawing, drilling, carving, or scraping were made from stone. Smooth-textured stone can be made into scrapers, knives, and projectile points by removing flakes with a stone or bone hammer or punch. This process is called flint-knapping, or knapping, for short. It takes practice and skill to knap stone, and quartz is especially intractable and hard to control. I was impressed—as I thought of my own experiments in making stone tools. My attempts usually resulted in hideous chunky slabs crude even in comparison to tools made by *Homo erectus* over a million years ago.

"Do you make the handles and haft the stone bits?" I asked.

"Sure, I make and maintain all the other parts of the tools," Doug said.

As the semester wore on, I gradually learned more bits and pieces about Doug. The art of pipe-making required an apprenticeship of sorts. The skill is passed down from generation to generation, from father to son. He told me that learning to make pipes gave him a place among the Dakota, and that he was finding it easier and easier to spend time on the reservation with relatives and friends. He said that whenever there were crises or problems, he drove to the reservation. He indicated that before regaining some of his Dakota heritage, he felt out-of-place. He had little to identify with and no direction, no clear idea as to what he wanted to do with his life. When he took up pipe-making, he said he found his niche. He could learn a skill that meant something to him and to his grandfather, who was delighted to have a trainee. He said it wasn't always easy and he had so much still to learn; in particular the language was giving him trouble. He needed to learn the ceremonies involving pipes, and these required chanting in Dakota.

For a couple of weeks in midsemester, as the muck of early March descended on Indiana like a slime-mold, he disappeared. So did Janelle. I suspected that perhaps they had been forming an "attachment." They always sat next to one another, and usually arrived and left together. I hoped that Doug and Janelle had not done the sort of vanishing act that commuter students at large urban universities often do. They both had seemed so interested in the course.

About three weeks later, they were both in class again. During the break that rescued all of us halfway through the 2½-hour class, Doug and Janelle strolled up to the front to speak to me. Doug apologized for missing class.

"I took her to the reservation," he told me, gesturing toward Janelle. "She is going to have a baby."

Janelle smiled strangely, and seemed a bit uncomfortable.

"Is this a good thing?" I stammered. "If so, then congratulations." I really did not know what to say.

"Oh, it's not my baby," Doug said, almost shyly, but as if he needed to explain. "We are just friends. I have a wife, same one for some years now. Janelle needed some help so I took her to talk to some of my people, so she could get some guidance, some perspective. I think she is doing better now."

"It's really great out there," was all Janelle could muster. I wished I could have put her more at ease.

Later, as I drove the dreary 52 miles back to my home in Bloomington, I mused about these students. Never again would I assume that students led simple lives that revolved only around going to school and taking tests. I was amazed that Doug had taken time away from his job, his family, and his education to take a friend in need to the Dakota reservation to talk to elder folk. This seemed a rare dedication to a friend. It also showed how highly he valued his culture and suggested that he understood his Dakota community to have much to offer a young woman—help that she perhaps could not find elsewhere.

Although Janelle and Doug still hung around together and sat together, Janelle's attendance became more irregular. It was clear that she had concerns other than an anthropology class, taken perhaps to fulfill a science requirement. I hoped her health was okay, but did not feel like it was my place to inquire.

On another slow evening, I spoke to Doug again after class. I am interested in how stone tools are used and what sorts of wear or damage they might incur as a result of use. I thought that if I could examine Doug's quartz tools, I might be able to learn something that would help me interpret older stone tools found in archaeological sites. I asked him if I could look at the tools he uses to carve the catlinite into pipes. He said he did not really know if that would be okay; he would have to ask someone.

"I'm going out next weekend, and I can find out for sure," he offered.

A couple of weeks later, he sought me out. "I talked to the elders," he said, "you know, about looking at my tools."

"Yes?" I awaited his answer eagerly.

"They don't think that it would be a good idea." He explained that making the pipes was also a ritual activity, too. In order for the pipes to be pure and for them to "work," they had to be treated and kept by strict standards. These standards extended to include the entire manufacturing process, from the quarrying of the catlinite to the pipe ceremony itself. Having someone who was not a pipe-maker, not Dakota, not even Native American look at his tools would be a bad idea. If I put Doug's quartz carving tools under a microscope and subjected them to scrutiny, they would be ruined.

"But they see no reason why you couldn't make tools yourself and use them on pipestone to see what happens." He flopped his backpack onto the nearest desk and rummaged about for a few seconds. He brought out two fist-sized chunks of deep rose-colored stone and set them carefully on the desk. "My friends suggested I give you some fresh catlinite for your own experiments."

Although I was initially disappointed that I wouldn't be able to study Doug's stone tools directly, I was thrilled to receive the pipestone. This was indeed a precious gift. I fumbled for how to respond. "Doug, this is fantastic, but please don't feel obligated to give me the stones."

"No, I want to. I told my teachers about you and they think it's okay that you have some stone to work with." He smiled.

"Thank you so much." I caressed the soft silky surface of the catlinite. I also realized that Doug had told me much about stone tools that day. I had often wondered if the craft-working processes used to make ceremonial objects were themselves sacred. His attitude about his tools confirmed the ritual importance of the craft itself. How different from most manufacturing carried out in the United States today.

As the semester wore on, the group of students co-alesced as they came to know one another. Doug was possibly the "coolest" guy in the class in the eyes of the other students. One week a woman asked, "Could you bring us one of your pipes to show us?"

"I'll see what I can do," was his rather noncommittal reply.

At the end of the course, all the students were to give presentations, either on genetics or style change projects that they had done as final projects. Naturally, Doug did his project on pipes. He said he wished to conduct a pipe ceremony during our last night of class, if it would be all right with me.

That night Doug arrived loaded down with the accoutrements of a pipe ceremony. We rearranged the desks into a circle, so everyone could see. Doug started by pulling out bags of vegetable materials. He explained each one in turn.

"We don't smoke just tobacco in the pipes," he started out. "We use a mixture of many different plants. Wild cherry, willow, tobacco, and others. The most important plant we use is probably this sage, here." He handed the bag to one student to examine and pass around. "Sage is used by lots of Indian people around the country. It purifies." He is referring to sage from the sagebrush plant (*Artemisia* sp.), not the kitchen herb that goes into holiday turkey stuffing.

He showed us the pipe, reddish stone fit with a wooden stem and decorated with feathers and bead-work. After he explained the items used and told about the smoking mixture and the pipe, he began the cere-mony. He laid a blanket down in the center of the room and knelt at one end. Then he selected participants. He asked for volunteers, and two intrepid students, Kevin and Deanna, acquiesced. He asked me if I wanted to participate, and being an anthropologist, I said, "Sure."

I sat to Doug's right, with Deanna across from me, and Kevin to my right. Doug produced a ceramic dish and put some sage in it. "This is for purifying our ma-terials, our ceremony, and all of us as participants." Doug lit the sagebrush with a match. He waved the en-suing smoke over himself and toward each of us. It cre-ated a sweet-smelling fog that rose and twirled above our heads and spread out toward the rest of the room. I was delighted but then panic struck as I saw the smoke rise higher and higher.

"I think this is going to set off the smoke detectors," I interrupted. Doug looked up and nodded resignedly. I could just imagine the scene, sirens and fire trucks streaming down University Boulevard. Men in full turn-out gear stomping into the classroom to find some foolhardy middle-aged professor sitting cross-legged on the floor with a full Dakota ceremony under way.

At that moment, Frank, a somewhat older student, jumped up and said, "I'll handle it." He moved toward the doorway and explained, "I work for the Physical Plant, I can turn off the smoke detector for this end of the building. Just remind me to reengage it later."

"Hallelujah," I thought to myself.

As the ceremony commenced, Doug chanted the separate parts in Dakota. He filled the pipe four times, and each time, extended the end toward a different direction, then passed the pipe around to the four smokers. I took my turn and inhaled, not too deeply. The smoke tasted of the prairies and burned into my throat. The chanting, the smoke, and the company of students combined for an unforgettable effect. Doug's pipe had brought the class together as none of my lec-tures ever could. I had never seen a group so fasci-nated, so engaged. Indeed later, when I perused the student evaluations for the class, I found that a number of the students said that the pipe ceremony was what they liked best about the class—something I had noth-ing to do with.

As the students scurried off to their separate lives that evening, Doug carefully stowed his pipe and other ceremonial objects. He drew a small piece of catlinite from a leather bag and presented it to me. "A friend makes these little pendants." It was a stylized turtle, in-cised and polished, hanging on a deerskin thong along with one blue bead. "I enjoyed the class, and I'd like you to have this." Doug handed in his paper and told me that this was going to be a very special summer for him. He was going to participate in the Sun Dance, a ceremony that would cement forever his beliefs and his ties to his Dakota ancestors.

Doug even suggested that if I came out to the reservation, I would be welcomed. My regret is that I did not go. Other commitments including fieldwork in Peru prevented me from taking him up on the offer.

That night as I drove home, the little turtle hung around my neck and I mused about the semester just finished. This piece of material culture, a small red turtle, engraved on the back with the initials of the maker, now connected me, however peripherally, with a Native American people whom I would never actu-ally know. I thought about how objects can be so much more than just objects. I wondered if Doug, in gen-erously sharing his catlinite and his wisdom about the pipes, hadn't taught me much more than I had taught him.

SUGGESTED READING

Spector, Janet. (1994). *What This Awl Means: Feminist Archae-ology in a Wahpeton Dakota Village*. Minneapolis: Minnesota Historical Society.

26

Aurelio's Song

Barry Lyons
Wayne State University

Ecuador, in northwestern South America, is home to 12 million people, half of whom live in the Andes mountains, which run north to south through the country. Barry Lyons did his fieldwork in the highland village of Caparina, in Chimborazo province, in the 1990s. Caparina occupies a span of land extending from the bottom of a narrow river basin up to high mountain pastures over 4,000 meters (13,120 ft.) above sea level. Some two dozen huts and cinder-block houses dot the land, a few near the village meeting house and the primary school by the river, most perched a half-hour's steep walk or more up winding mountain paths. On pleasant days, the sun shines and the air is still, but much of the time villagers must wear heavy ponchos or shawls against the wind and the cold.

Ecuador was part of the Inca Empire when the Spanish *conquistadores* arrived in 1532, bringing their language and the Catholic religion. Over the following centuries, Spaniards and their descendants used their political power to gain control over the land, resulting in the hacienda system described in this article. At the same time, Quichua, a version of the Inca language, continued to spread among indigenous Andeans under Spanish colonial rule. About half or more of the people in the highlands today are Quichua-speaking Indians or *Runa*. Most of them are peasant farmers in villages like Caparina. They and their forebears have long been ruled over and despised by "whites" or *mestizos*—Ecuadorians who speak Spanish and identify with a European heritage. In recent decades, however, a growing Indian political movement has been demanding respect and equality.

One way Indians have given voice to their hopes is through song. Barry Lyons's chapter tells about his host during fieldwork in Caparina, Aurelio Condo, and a prizewinning Quichua song Taita Aurelio wrote. (*Taita*, literally "father," is a term of respect.) Anthropologists approach art as an aspect of culture and society, often using a song's lyrics or a musical performance as a sort of window onto broader cultural themes. Here, Lyons describes Taita Aurelio, his song, and his feelings about music in the context of the changing relationship between Indians and mestizos. Taita Aurelio considered some mestizo music such as the *pasillo* genre to be particularly refined. In his vision of equality, he imagined Indian musicians learning to compose and play *pasillos* in Quichua. In his prizewinning song, Taita Aurelio drew on local Runa mythology to comment upon mestizo landlords' mistreatment of Indian laborers and to call on mestizos to change their attitudes toward Indians.

As you read, consider the following questions:

1. What challenges do you think an anthropologist faces in translating art from one culture to another?

2. In what ways did the name of Taita Aurelio's music group, their costume, and the song express attitudes toward ethnic identity and toward changes going on in society? Compare the ways musical performances in your own society express group identities and attitudes toward social change.

3. How have changes in society affected music among Indians in Chimborazo? In what ways have Chimborazo Runa's ideas about composing and performing music been shaped by their position in Ecuadorian society and their political struggles?

4. Taita Aurelio believes in respecting Runa traditions, yet he grants more authority to the Bible. Why? What do you think the Bible means to him? What does the story of Taita Aurelio's music group and song reveal about the relationship between Caparina villagers and the Catholic Church?

5. Taita Aurelio's song proclaimed some traditional Indian beliefs, even though Taita Aurelio himself didn't literally believe in some of those traditions. Why did he nonetheless incorporate these traditions into his song?

6. Anthropological descriptions sometimes give the impression that everyone "in" a particular culture holds the same set of cultural beliefs. As you read the accounts in this reader focused on individuals such as Taita Aurelio, what sense do they give you of the relationship between individuals and culture?

When I think about my years in Caparina, a Quichua-speaking Runa or Indian village in central Ecuador, Aurelio Condo inevitably comes to mind. I usually picture him with a twinkle in his eye, his mouth and moustache formed into a wry smile. Like most of his neighbors, he has an angular face with high cheekbones and bronze skin, though his complexion is a little less brown, a little pinker, than most. He is of medium stature and a light build.

Taita Aurelio was in his early 40s when I first met him, in 1989. I wanted to do field research in one of the villages belonging to his parish. The nun who lived in the parish center had invited me to attend a two-day workshop for catechists, villagers trained to lead Bible study and prepare individuals for the Catholic sacraments. Taita Aurelio stood out as a leader among the catechists. I was struck by his intelligence as well as his friendly, gentle demeanor. A few weeks later I was pleased to learn that he had persuaded his village to accept me and that he himself would host me in his house.

Aurelio recalled as a child watching his father sponsor costly fiestas in honor of local patron saints. In those days, priests and village elders taught that God and the saints would bless the family in return. In spite of the fiesta and its promised blessings, Aurelio's mother died when he was a boy. His father then migrated to another region, leaving Aurelio, the oldest son, to be raised by his grandparents. These experiences seem to have left him with a lifelong inclination to question common beliefs and to seek a deeper religious understanding. As a young man, Aurelio studied for a time with an evangelical Protestant missionary and at another time with an Indian healer, a shaman. Later, as a catechist, he helped instruct fellow villagers in Catholic doctrine. He struggled to reconcile his faith in a loving and just God with his own experiences of the sufferings and injustices of this world. I think he welcomed me in his home because he could discuss such issues with me.

Taita Aurelio's people have historically been ruled by Ecuadorians termed "*mestizo*" or "white," whose first language is Spanish and who think of themselves as descended from Spaniards. He was deeply committed to Indian struggles for a place of respect and equality within the Catholic Church and in Ecuadorian society. Yet racism has an insidious way of shaping the values and ambitions even of its victims. Proud of his eldest daughter's light complexion, Taita Aurelio was dismayed when she decided to marry a darker-skinned young man from a neighboring village. He eventually accepted the marriage, but villagers gossiped that he did not think any local Indian boys were good enough for his light-skinned daughter.

Social inequalities also shaped his feelings about music. He was skillful at composing Quichua verses that fit local Indian rhythms. But occasionally he also closed his eyes and sang a few indistinct, nonsense syllables in a slow, melodic, romantic tone, in imitation of a *pasillo*. Pasillos are one of several mestizo musical forms that Ecuadorians often refer to as "national music." Taita Aurelio rhapsodized that someday Quichua words might be set to pasillo melodies, describing these as "refined" music. For pasillos to be sung in Quichua—that would be a sign of equality.

MUSIC AND HISTORY

The first night that I stayed in his house, Aurelio pulled out his guitar and began to teach me some of the Quichua songs he knew. He had a gently ironic, laughing way of explaining a difficult lyric and showed an almost paternal pride when I eventually learned enough to sing together with him. In the evenings, from time to time, he would call me to come with my guitar into the family bedroom where we would play and sing together, to the delight of his two little girls.

One time, as we were playing, Taita Aurelio paused and remarked that music was a new thing for his people. In the old days, the time of the hacienda, he said, Runa played no music. When Aurelio was growing up and until he was a young man, most of the land in Chimborazo province belonged to large estates or haciendas owned by wealthy mestizos. In an arrangement somewhat similar to serfdom in medieval Europe, Indian peasant farmers were allowed to live, grow their crops, and keep animals on hacienda land, in return for working four or five days a week for the landowner. Overseers enforced the landowners' demands with whips in hand, and even children occasionally had to serve the hacienda. Aurelio himself remembered that as a child growing up on a hacienda bordering Caparina, he sometimes had to spend cold nights outside watching over pigs. (The pigs were set loose to forage and fertilize plots that were to be planted with crops for the landowner.) This, he was saying, was a time without music.

Aurelio married a woman from Caparina and came to live with her on the estate. Caparina was then part of a hacienda owned by the Catholic diocese. Local Catholic bishops traditionally came from aristocratic, landowning families, and they saw nothing odd in the Church's position as a wealthy landowner with control over Indian peons. For many years, the diocese had rented out the hacienda to individual members of the local elite. The renter paid for the right to make use of the land, together with the livestock and people living on the estate. By the time Aurelio married in, however, a new bishop named Leonidas Proaño had ceased renting out the hacienda.

Taita Aurelio said that Runa obtained music when they began to be free from bondage on the haciendas, a transformation he felt owed much to Proaño. A man of humble origins himself, Leonidas Proaño was inspired by Pope John XXIII's call for Catholics to involve themselves in addressing the problems of modern society. In the aftermath of the Cuban revolution, and with Ecuadorian socialists and communists beginning to form alliances with Indian peasants, land reform was a burning political issue. In the 1960s and 1970s, Proaño distributed most of the diocese's hacienda lands, including Caparina, among peasants. He supported Runa around the province in their struggles with private landowners for agrarian reform. Aristocratic white landowners, used to a much more comfortable relationship with the Church, viewed Proaño's stance as a betrayal and scornfully gave Proaño the title, "Bishop of the Indians."

Taita Aurelio's claim that Runa on Chimborazo haciendas did not make music is not literally true. Laborers harvesting barley, for example, would sing in a call-and-response format known as *Jahuay* as they advanced with their sickles across the field. During Carnival, small groups of villagers would enter the yard of a friend's or kinsman's home and sing verses in honor of the head of the household, who would then be obligated to invite them inside for food and drink. There is a local Quichua musical tradition that certainly predates the land-reform period.

Did Taita Aurelio mean his comment poetically? Was he trying to tell me that the people were too beaten down to sing? It is true that the province has seen a flowering of Quichua musical creativity in recent years, linked to a new sense of Runa pride. A few groups such as Runapac Shungu (Runa Heart) and Cacha Duchicela (named after a family that claims descent from the last Inca king) have become well known among Quichua-speaking people around the province through cassette tapes, radio play, and public performances. In many villages similar groups have sprung up. They usually consist of four to eight young men who sing, play guitar, beat on a large drum, and perhaps play one or two other instruments. Sometimes they are joined by two or three young women vocalists. These village music groups perform for religious meetings and other local celebrations, and also compete for prizes in parish- or provincewide music festivals. Their music, their lyrics, the names they give themselves, and even their way of dressing for festival performances display and celebrate Runa culture and identity. The lyrics often proclaim political messages. It is hard to imagine anything similar in hacienda times:

transistor radios and cassette players did not exist. Quichua musicians did not have easy access to the airwaves or to other forms of institutional support. People working on haciendas had little personal freedom or leisure. Certainly Indians could not openly assert themselves politically without risking a beating or jailing.

A VILLAGE MUSIC GROUP

Taita Aurelio himself had begun to organize a music group, and he invited me to join. Three or four other young men from the village were regulars at our rehearsals and performances. Taita Aurelio was the natural leader of the group: in his 40s, he was 10 to 20 years older than the rest of us; he also made up or arranged most of the songs. As a catechist and political leader in the village and the parish, he had broader authority as well. With the aid of the nun who lived in the parish, he obtained some money for instruments from the diocese. The group settled on a name with local meaning: *"Los ovejeros de Caparina"* (the shepherds of Caparina). In hacienda times, looking after the hacienda's sheep in the high pasture lands was a full-time occupation; it was a burdensome duty, especially because of the hacienda practice of charging the shepherd for any lost sheep. The group's name thus reminded listeners that Caparina villagers used to work on the hacienda. Some Caparina villagers felt that that history gave them a moral claim to the flat valley land bordering the village, land that still remained in the hands of the diocese.

Dressing as shepherds for a festival performance, we wore undyed white wool ponchos—a costume with a complex meaning. Sheep and sheep's wool have come to be emblems of Runa identity and traditional rural customs. When Aurelio was a child, villagers wove their ponchos, skirts, and shawls out of the wool from their own sheep, minimizing their need for cash. In recent decades, they have incorporated colorful synthetic fabrics bought in town into their dress styles. They increasingly purchase other things too, from chemical fertilizers to roofing materials to noodles and rice. While prices of such goods have risen, however, their own agricultural production and cash income have not kept pace. So villagers sometimes look back to their old self-sufficiency with a tinge of nostalgia and talk wistfully about the loss of Runa traditions. Our shepherds' white wool ponchos, contrasting with the brightly colored clothing of many of the Indians in our audience, evoked that nostalgic view of traditional lifeways.

TAITA AURELIO'S SONG

When he was in the mood, and especially when a performance was approaching, Taita Aurelio would pick up his guitar (or mine) and compose verses. I acted as his scribe, reading or singing his words back to him when he asked. Sometimes when I had to ask him to clarify a word, his response would turn into a lesson on local culture and history. The group's greatest success came through a song Taita Aurelio composed in 1991 for a festival commemorating the late Bishop Proaño, who had passed away three years before. The Catholic radio station in Riobamba, the provincial capital, sponsored and broadcast the festival. Taita Aurelio himself did not make it to Riobamba for the performance (leaving me as the sole lead singer!), but Taita Aurelio's song won us second prize. The radio station has continued to play the song from time to time in the years since.

The song text reveals a lot about its author—maybe even a little more than he sometimes wished. Some months after the festival, the current bishop, Proaño's successor, attended a religious meeting in the village and asked to hear the song performed. Taita Aurelio encouraged me to sing it, while he stood to the side, as though not wanting to be too closely associated with it. The lyrics are irreverent in tone and threaten powerful, abusive whites with a fate that does not exactly fit with orthodox Catholic doctrine. Taita Aurelio was, after all, a catechist within the Church, under the bishop's authority. But Taita Aurelio grinned as I sang, proud, I think, to have taught me to sing in Quichua. He seemed delighted to see me giving voice to his own rebellious affirmation of Runa culture and rights vis-à-vis mestizos.

Taita Aurelio's song follows a pattern common in Quichua music in Chimborazo. Each verse comprises two couplets (pairs of lines), with each couplet sung twice. The second line of each couplet often parallels the first, with some changes in wording that make for a special poetic effect. The verses are sung to a fairly standard melody in minor key, with a driving rhythm. While the rhythm and much of the poetry of Taita Aurelio's Quichua verses are lost in translation, the surface meanings of the words are easily rendered into English.

The song is called "Taita Chimborazo, Mama Tungurahua," after two mountains in the region, the one that gave Chimborazo province its name and another, Tungurahua, a nearby active volcano. Aurelio began with a verse recounting an old tradition about the mountains:

Taita Chimborazo, Mama Tungurahua	Father Chimborazo, Mother Tungurahua
Cusandic huarmindic causacun ninmari	are living as husband and wife, it's said
Ñaupa yayacuna chashnami parlashca	Thus have our elders told us
Ñaupa yayacuna chashnami huillashca.	Thus have our forefathers informed us.

Peoples of the Andes have long viewed the mountains as powerful living beings with their own personalities and with the ability to appear in human form. Runa healers sometimes invoke the mountains' aid in curing illnesses, and elders tell stories about the mountains. The rocky marriage of Chimborazo and Tungurahua is a theme of some of these stories.

But why sing about the mountains to honor a Catholic bishop? Along with encouraging Runa to demand land and social equality, Leonidas Proaño also spoke of valuing Indian culture. Taita Aurelio's parish priest, a close associate of Proaño, learned to speak Quichua and researched Runa traditions. Where the Catholic Church for centuries viewed belief in the mountains as idolatrous or superstitious, Taita Aurelio's priest accepted these beliefs, interpreting the mountains as analogous to the official Catholic saints. So Taita Aurelio could sing about the mountains as a way of celebrating the Church's newfound respect for the Runa and their traditions.

Taita Aurelio's own relationship to those beliefs, however, was ambivalent. Several times when he shared bits of Runa tradition concerning the natural world with me, he would smile proudly and tell me that this was "Runa science." Yet his own experience and the authority he granted the Bible sometimes undermined his belief in "Runa science." During his work with a shaman healer, he was disillusioned to find the healer using what he saw as fraudulent tricks. He has worked hard to gain access to the knowledge and power that "white" people seem to derive from literacy and the Bible, first learning to read with the aid of a Protestant missionary and later becoming a Catholic catechist. Having searched the Bible in vain for references to mountains as living beings, he said he does not believe in the mountains.

His next verse alluded to the idea that after people die, they are sent to be punished for their sins inside volcanic Mount Tungurahua—a local adaptation of the Catholic notion of purgatory or hell. Inside the mountain, according to the song, was Amo Badillo, the former owner of a hacienda neighboring Caparina called Palapud. *Amo* is a Spanish word meaning "master" or "boss." Runa use the word in their language to refer to white people in general and especially to the landowners.

Amo Badillopish chaipimi puricun	Amo Badillo is roaming there too
Amo Badillopish chaipimi causacun	Amo Badillo is living there too
runacunallata fiñac cashcamanta	for so much harshness to the Runa
runacunallata macac cashcamanta.	for so many blows to the Runa.

Amo Badillo, who died sometime around the middle of the 20th century, was reputedly a cruel man. After Taita Aurelio's first wife died, he married a woman from Palapud whose own mother had been raped by the landowner. A story continues to circulate about Amo Badillo. Sometime after Badillo's death, a hacienda peon is said to have wandered into Mt. Tungurahua and encountered Badillo there, suffering and covered with sores. Badillo sent the peon back to the estate with a message for Badillo's widow to treat the Indians generously and with consideration. This story was the inspiration for Taita Aurelio's song.

The song went on:

Shuctic amocuna chaillamantic ringa	Other *amos* will go right there, too
mana pagashpalla, trabajachishpaca	for making people work, and not paying.
Mama abuelapac cocinero ringa	They'll go and be Grandma's cook
siquiman shimiman nina jicharinga.	Towards their asses and their mouths the fire will jump up.

In this life, the *amos* often have Runa maids cooking for them. Aurelio depicted them cooking for "Grandma," that is, Mama Tungurahua. (Some elders say the smoke issuing from the volcano comes from Grandma's cooking fires.) This is not the only reversal in the verse. Taita Aurelio recalled that when he was a boy, Runa had to recite elaborate greetings from afar as they approached the landlord and then kiss his hand. The reference to fire singeing the lords' posteriors—a line that never failed to evoke audiences' laughter—thus profanes what used to be virtually sacred.

Again, Taita Aurelio's verse should not be taken as a literal expression of his religious beliefs. As a child, Aurelio sometimes accompanied priests of the Redemptorist order in their travels from hacienda to hacienda, learning orthodox Catholic doctrine as he listened to them preach. Their sermons brimmed with stern warnings about sin and divine punishment. But Bishop Proaño promoted a different interpretation of Catholic doctrine, known as Liberation Theology. Liberation Theology criticizes the sort of Catholicism exemplified by the Redemptorists as an oppressive religion of fear. It emphasizes instead God's love and His call for people to work together to build a more just society. Liberation Theology has tended to undermine Taita Aurelio's belief in the fires of purgatory or hell, let alone a purgatory or hell located inside Tungurahua.

In the same vein, though, Taita Aurelio concluded his song with an appeal and an admonition addressed directly to the white elite:

Cai shuc amocuna, ama millai cangui	You other *amos*, don't be hateful
Runacunataca cuyangui-chicyari	You better treat the Runa with love
Ñatic cancunapish chashna canguichicman	You might end up the same way
Ñatic cancunapish chaipi rupanguiman.	You might go burn there too.

"Love Runa" was a call for a general change of heart and alluded to contemporary political issues as well as to the way bosses treated their workers. In June 1990, hundreds of thousands of Runa had joined in massive, largely peaceful protests around the country, demanding land, favorable economic policies, an end to racist treatment in government offices, and cultural recognition and respect. The *Levantamiento Indígena*, or "Indigenous Uprising," as it was known, marked the entry of Indians onto the national political stage as a force that had to be taken seriously. During the *Levantamiento*, Taita Aurelio remarked to me that Bishop Proaño's vision was coming to fruition. Yet a year later, when he wrote the song, large landowners were increasingly hiring private paramilitary guards to defend their land and intimidate neighboring villages. Meanwhile, Indian leaders' negotiations with the government dragged on. Taita Aurelio's sense of pride and hope, aroused by the *Levantamiento*, was mixed with growing concern and frustration.

In the years since then, Indian representatives have managed to gain a tenuous foothold within the official political system, reinforced periodically by massive protests similar to those of 1990. Yet they remain far from achieving their goals. The Runa are still economically and socially at the bottom of Ecuadorian society. The ongoing economic crisis in Ecuador, together with the policies of a succession of governments beholden both to international creditors and the Ecuadorian elite, has forced the poorest Ecuadorians to tighten their belts more and more.

I think of Aurelio often. The most recent news from Ecuador makes me think about his political activism. Today Runa villagers around the country are blocking roads and withholding their produce from urban markets, while thousands of people have evaded police blockades to congregate in the capital, Quito. This is all in protest against government economic policies designed in concert with the International Monetary Fund. The national Indigenous Confederation says that these policies place an unjust burden on the poor. The government has acted forcefully to contain and suppress the protests, resulting in a number of deaths and injuries. I wonder if Aurelio is out on the roads or in Quito with other activists, braving tear gas and hunger. I wonder also if Taita Aurelio's appeal in his song for wealthy whites to learn to love Runa has a chance. Or will the recent violent clashes intensify the sort of anger he expressed in his song and lead to worse violence in the future? Wherever he is, I imagine him continuing to strive for a better understanding of this confusing world, wondering whether his children will find respect as Runa in Ecuadorian society, and fashioning some of his thoughts into song.

SUGGESTED READINGS

Lyons, Barry. (1999). "Taita Chimborazo and Mama Tungurahua: A Quichua Song, A Fieldwork Story," *Anthropology and Humanism*, 24:1–14.

Mannheim, Bruce (1991). *The Language of the Inka since the European Invasion.* Austin: University of Texas Press.

Weismantel, Mary. (1988). *Food, Gender, and Poverty in the Ecuadorian Andes.* Philadelphia: University of Pennsylvania Press.

27

The Shaman's Art

Alan R. Sandstrom and Pamela Effrein Sandstrom

Indiana University—Purdue University Fort Wayne

Mexico is the largest Spanish-speaking country in the world, with more than 91 million citizens, and the United States' closest Latin American neighbor. Yet many people may not realize that 6.8 percent of the population (over 5.5 million people) are speakers of Native American languages. The Nahua (pronounced nä' wä) are people who speak the Nahuatl language. There are nearly one and a half million Nahua, most of whom live in Mexico, making Nahuatl the most widely spoken Amerindian language in Mesoamerica. The most famous of the Nahua peoples were the Aztecs, who were overthrown in 1521 by an uprising of the populations they had subjugated or intimidated, led by the Spanish invader Hernán Cortés. In the years following the Conquest, the Spaniards systematically destroyed the urban centers so that most contemporary Nahua now live in rural villages and towns. Members of the Nahua community we have come to know practice slash-and-burn horticulture and grow corn, beans, squash, chile peppers, and a variety of other crops. Despite the best efforts of Hispanic authorities and Christian missionaries, a great deal of Nahua culture survives in addition to language, and a rural form of the remarkable traditional religion continues to be practiced.

"The Shaman's Art " introduces Encarnación Telléz Hernández, a Nahua curer and shaman whose native language is Nahuatl. His family and clients know him as Cirilo, and he enjoys a reputation as a powerful religious specialist in the region where his village is located in the *municipio* (county) of Ixhuatlán de Madero, in the tropical forests of northern Veracruz. Through a description of daily life and ritual activities, we learn about what it is like to do fieldwork among people who consider direct questions rude and who regard indirectness and respect as ideal personality traits. The essay also portrays, quite literally, some of the concepts that underlie the pre-Hispanic practice of shamanic paper cutting. Through the medium of paper, which we take so much for granted in today's far-from-paperless society, the charismatic Nahua shaman depicts profound philosophical and religious principles in tangible form. Cirilo cuts from paper many thousands of small, anthropomorphic images for his elaborate ritual offerings. These figures symbolize the Nahua "dance of life" or animating principle.

As you read, consider the following questions:

1. What are some major challenges faced by people like Cirilo who are called to become shamans?
2. What difficulties do ethnographers face in obtaining reliable information on people's beliefs and worldview?
3. Show how anthropologists are able to discover philosophical principles and understand ritual by studying such expressions of material culture as the art of shamanic paper cutting.
4. Reflect on the different kinds of "art" that you are familiar with. Where do the paper figures that Cirilo makes fit into your ideas about art? How are creativity and individuality reflected by the paper figures?
5. Why is it important for the Nahua that the spirits and ideas found in their religion and mythology be given a tangible form?

A WARRIOR AND PERSON OF KNOWLEDGE

Encarnación Téllez Hernández lives the life of a warrior, waging a valiant fight against dangerous, disease-causing spirits or forces of disorder and disharmony—the negative consequence of disrespectful behavior.

Known widely by his nickname, Cirilo is a Nahua Indian shaman who lives in a small village of 600 people in the remote tropical forests of northern Veracruz, Mexico. Although nearly 70 years old, he carries himself with the energy of a much younger man and has a handsome face, a ready wit and willingness to smile, and a charismatic personality that compels people to listen whenever he speaks. The Nahua call a shaman *tlamatiquetl*, meaning "person of knowledge," and true to his calling, Cirilo has devoted his whole energy and knowledge—literally his life—to battling disease, drought, sorcery, and countless misfortunes that afflict his community. He has faced death on a number of occasions, once at the hands of local militia for organizing Indian resistance to local ranchers and political elites. And it is not uncommon for shamans to become targets for assassination for suspected acts of sorcery because they often deal with dark and powerful forces in the cosmos. Being a shaman is the most dangerous occupation in the Nahua world, and we have known several people who were murdered for their efforts in and around Cirilo's village, where we have conducted ethnographic field research since the early 1970s.

We first met Cirilo when he was a young man working hard to be recognized as a person of knowledge—a difficult and frustrating apprenticeship. He had to prove his worth many times over before skeptical members of his own village by engaging in the never-ending battle to create harmony between the spirit and human realms. Shamans are indeed warriors, and, remarkably, the two principal weapons in the struggle against disorder and despair among these Nahua are paper and scissors. It was Cirilo's mastery of the art of paper cutting that revealed his destiny to become a shaman.

The very use of the word "shaman" is controversial in anthropology. Some researchers believe that the term should be used only for ritual specialists among peoples of Siberia, where the concept originated. Describing people like Cirilo as shamans, however, acknowledges the connection between the activities of ritual specialists in Mesoamerica and their Arctic and Subarctic counterparts. The role of shaman among the Nahua is open to both men and women, although only a very few undergo the rigorous apprenticeship and years of work required to qualify. Fewer still are accepted by the other villagers once they have completed their training. There were never more than four or five shamans active at any one time in Cirilo's village. Each one confirmed that a person must be called by the spirits in order to enter into training for the vocation.

Cirilo received his call from dreams. To this day, he relies on his dreams as a tool for seeing into the hidden causes and consequences of events. Often, when we visit him in his house or the small shrine he has built nearby, he tells us about his dreams and interprets their meaning for us. From them, he can learn what caused a disease in one of his clients or what specific ritual attention the spirits require. In Nahua society, dreams are not considered true in the sense of being an image or reflection of actual events. Rather, they are used more like meditation devices to help people comprehend the events in their lives or the lives of others. Once, in 1986, Cirilo came to tell us that he dreamed we were dead. He told us that the cause of our demise was unclear, but he thought that it might have been an accident on the road. In fact, he knew that we would be driving back to the United States in a few weeks, and the dream was a way for him to help us focus on the potential dangers of such a long trip. He held a day-long ritual offering to help protect us in our travels. He gave us beeswax candles to burn on our home altar and instructed us how to make offerings to protector spirits.

Cirilo was a hard person to get to know. When we first arrived in his community, he had already finished his apprenticeship and he lived deep in the forest, apart from other people. Nahua shamans often have personalities that distance them from other people and Cirilo is no exception. Although he is friendly and has a good sense of humor, there is an intensity about him that others sometimes find intimidating. People are not exactly afraid of shamans, but they avoid them when possible without appearing to be rude. Before he came to know us better, Cirilo kept his distance and treated us politely but very formally.

NAHUA DAILY LIFE AND RITUAL

In the Nahua village, far removed from electricity, running water, and clocks, we saw many rituals staged, among them offerings to water and earth spirits, calendrical observances to commemorate the Day of the Dead and the winter solstice, and cures. We recorded myths and stories that helped us understand some of the key ideas underlying Nahua religion. But we had trouble getting people, shamans included, to give us detailed explanations of their beliefs and practices.

One reason for this reluctance is rooted in history. Nahua religion has survived 500 years of persecution by political authorities and missionaries in part by remaining obscure, out of the scrutiny of officials and strangers. Thus, people wisely avoid topics that might draw attention to themselves. After working many years in the village and no longer being considered strangers, we realized that many aspects of culture, especially religion, are rarely discussed in an open and systematic way. Outsiders are expected to learn about the religion in the same way that the Nahua learn about it—by attending rituals, listening to the shamans' chanting, and picking up explanations along the way. While people who seek a deeper knowledge may become shamans themselves or helpers at rituals, most are satisfied, as are many churchgoers here in the United States, to participate in rituals but leave the deeper metaphysics and theology to the specialists. Finally, shamans attract and maintain a clientele based on their secret knowledge and their ability to intervene with spirits on a client's behalf. To give away hard-won knowledge would undermine a shaman's viability.

Cirilo had gotten to know us fairly well and he welcomed us into his house on many occasions, yet he was always reluctant to talk about his deep knowledge of religious matters. He often shrugged off our inquiries, giving such evasive responses as "Who knows?" or "That's the way we do things." All the while he continued to invite us to attend curing and other rituals, showing us the proper way to make offerings to the earth and making it clear that he appreciated our interest. He treated us the way he would curious children.

Cirilo led us to understand that there is a great diversity of Nahua spirit entities that play a part in the rituals, but still we had a hard time sorting them all out. There seemed to be hundreds of earth, water, and wind spirits. Were these separate spirits or perhaps aspects of the same spirit in different guises? The many myths and stories about these entities confused as much as clarified, and failed to explain why, for example, the water spirit sometimes appears as a mermaidlike creature with the tail of a fish or, alternately, as a young girl, an old woman, a kind of earth mother, or a wild man chained to the bottom of the ocean. In addition to having no tradition of explaining the abstract aspects of their culture, the Nahua generally do not respond well to direct questions, which they consider to be aggressive and rude. We were amazed when we discovered a medium through which Cirilo could speak about religion.

THE ELOQUENT LANGUAGE OF THE SHAMAN'S ART

Nahua rituals are complex affairs that may last for days and nights on end. They always involve the construction of elaborate altars designed as beautiful places for an exchange between spirit and human realms. Ritual offerings feature food, drink, and other items such as aromatic copal incense, tobacco, corn meal, and beeswax candles. Always present are ritual chanting and dancing, and on larger occasions, sacred guitar and violin music. Cirilo and other Nahua shamans use many symbolic elements in their rituals, but probably the most fantastic are the cut-paper figures representing the spirits. These images, which Cirilo prepares specially for each ritual, may number in the tens of thousands for villagewide rituals. In most cases, the shaman destroys the figures after an offering or they are left to disintegrate on altars. In the most elaborate rituals, usually to petition life-giving rain and crop or human fertility, the shaman arranges the paper figures with great care on the altar table and sprinkles them with the blood of sacrificial chickens and turkeys. Closely identified with forces of nature and important spirits in the pantheon, and a focus of all major ritual activity, the cut-paper figures as material culture provide a key to understanding Nahua religion.

Among the Nahua, only qualified shamans cut the paper figures. Throughout the area where Cirilo lives, shamans purchase paper made in factories and cut out the images with scissors. They prefer a kind of beige or off-white paper for most images, but they also use colored tissue paper, particularly to portray disease-causing wind spirits. Some groups such as the Otomí from the Sierra Norte de Puebla and the Nahua living to the west of Cirilo's village continue to make their own paper by hand in the ancient manner. At first we were curious about the paper images, but we did not dare to ask Cirilo or other shamans for samples to study for fear of giving offense. They methodically stack the images before laying them out on the altar and treat them with a degree of reverence. Following the preparations for a ritual, they carefully collect all the scraps of paper left over from cutting and dispose of them in places where people are unlikely to come across them by accident. The scraps retain some of the power of the spirits portrayed in the images. During rituals, once offerings have been made to the sacralized images, we noted that people who are not shamans avoid touching or going near them.

Why do Nahua ritual specialists spend so much of their time making and manipulating paper cutouts? Cirilo gave us the unsatisfactory explanation that the first shamans learned how to cut paper so that they could make offerings to spirits, and he did not elaborate further. The myths explain in a general way why people make altars and dedicate offerings to various spirits, but the storytellers never specifically mention paper figures. After consulting with experts and doing some detective work in libraries, we found that paper was a highly valued substance among the great civilizations of pre-Hispanic Mesoamerica, thus linking those ancient cultures with contemporary Native Americans. Virtually all peoples of Mesoamerica made extensive use of paper, created out of fibers from the inner bark of fig trees or from leaves of the maguey plant. The Aztecs, about whom we have the best information, were practically obsessed with paper. The great wealth and strength of the Aztec empire were based on tribute extracted from conquered peoples. At its height, the imperial capital received millions of sheets of handmade paper each year as tribute payment from the provinces.

Pre-Hispanic peoples put the paper to many uses, most of which were religious. Each temple employed paper cutters to supply the priests with adornments for statues, clothing for ceremonial occasions, banners and flags, headdresses, and items for sacrifice. Practically every religious event described in the ethnohistorical documents makes some use of paper. There are records of priests cutting out shapes, probably with blades of razor-sharp obsidian, and sprinkling the paper cuttings with the blood of fowl, just as modern shamans like Cirilo do. Paper also was used to make books called codices. Aztec libraries were filled with these volumes containing pictographic paintings that priests used as mnemonic devices for their histories, almanacs, and astrological calculations. One of the first official acts of the Spaniards following their takeover was to outlaw the manufacture of paper. The link between paper and the native religion was clear to them, and they went so far as to forbid Indians to possess paper on penalty of being brought before the Inquisition. Under such pressure it is no wonder that papermaking virtually ceased throughout Mesoamerica. This fact alone makes the paper-cutting art of Cirilo and his shaman colleagues of special interest and importance.

DISCOVERING THE MEANING OF THE PAPER IMAGES

The break came unexpectedly. Cirilo was listening to us explain that we would like to examine and perhaps photograph some of his paper cuttings so that we could show them to people back in the United States. He asked, "Why do people want to see them?"

We replied, "Many want to learn more about the spirits and about religion, but they have never seen anything like the images of spirits cut from paper."

Cirilo persisted, "But why would they be interested in us?"

We said, "North Americans do not know much about the people of Mexico, and they would understand more if they could see how beautiful the *costumbres* are." The Spanish word *costumbre*, or "custom," is the term that the Nahua use for their religion, in contrast to orthodox Catholic practices.

The next day, Cirilo asked us to visit him in his small shrine. Uncharacteristically, he got right to the point and said, "I want to cut you a set of paper figures so that you can take them with you and show people about our *costumbres*."

We were astounded and very pleased. In fact, he had already spent his morning cutting out the images for us and he handed them to us one at a time. Patiently telling us the name of the spirit portrayed, he pointed out the major symbolic features of each one. Finally, to protect us from possible harm from the spirits, he sprinkled each with *aguardiente* (literally, "fire water," a high-proof alcohol made from sugarcane). That was 15 years ago and Cirilo has continued to give us gifts of his cuttings to teach others about Nahua spirits and rituals (Figure 11). Not only Cirilo but other shamans as well began to cut images for us. What started as a limited effort to identify Nahua spirits has become a major research project with sev-

FIGURE 11.   Pamela (left) and Alan Sandstrom (second from left) accepting paper figures from Cirilo (seated on the right) and recording his explanations of their meaning. *Photo by Michael A. Sandstrom.*

eral thousand cut-paper figures now in museums and archives.

Cirilo and his colleagues were able to express some of their core beliefs through the sacred paper figures. While they were reluctant to speak in generalities, they were positively loquacious in describing the symbolic features of the tangible images. The figures themselves exist in a number of forms, but by far the most common is that of a small human being with its hands held up alongside the head, not unlike paper dolls in the Euro-American tradition. Shamans cut identifying head-dresses and make small cuts in the body or silhouetted along the figure's sides. Each shaman has a distinctive style of representing the spirits but certain icono-graphic conventions prevail regardless of who is cut-ting, even among ritual specialists from different cul-tures. Some shamans are more skilled than others at the art of paper cutting, but Cirilo is by far the most tal-ented producer of paper images in the community. His reputation has grown over the years, and his clients come from great distances to benefit from the knowl-edge and skill he commands as a paper cutter.

Cirilo supplied most of the examples of the sacred cut-paper figures included here, and our brief descrip-tions of their meanings come from many conversations with him and other Nahua shamans. We also have in-cluded one remarkable example from another shaman as our final specimen.

Figure 12 shows three paper images that Cirilo cuts as part of a bundle used in curing. Cirilo said about the trio, "They go around together, making people sick." They represent *ejecatl* or "wind" spirits, signifying the disease-causing winds that infect a patient's body and surroundings. The left-hand figure is called *carus eje-catl*, "wind of the cross," and it is easy to see the design of the cross in the headdress. In the middle is *apan eje-catl*, "water wind," which Cirilo calls "bad water," and on the right is *tlali ejecatl*, "earth wind." The headdress

of the bad water image features animal horns because it is associated with the untamed natural world as op-posed to the cultured world of the Nahua. The earth wind has a rakelike headdress that probably represents the open jaws of the earth, although the precise mean-ing of this feature varies among shamans.

Cirilo used the images as a vehicle for conveying his knowledge to us. He pointed out how he cut each figure with rib holes, and it was this feature that led him to share with us his insights into the nature of dis-ease and death. He revealed that these spirits of the dead are associated with wild or untamed places such as tangled underbrush or the interior of rock. They are linked to concepts of pollution and many *ejecatl* spirits actually have in their names the word *tlasoli*, meaning "refuse" or "filth." Thus we have *tlasoli ejecatl*, "filth wind"; *apantlasoli ejecatl*, "filth wind from water"; and *mictlan tlasoli ejecatl*, "filth wind from the place of the dead." Cirilo explained that the winds represent the spirits of people who suffered bad or unpleas-ant deaths. Many represent the spirits of children or people who died young. Their angry spirits return to the village to attack the living and spread disease, mis-fortune, and death. They are attracted to antisocial be-havior such as lying, stealing, gossiping, or saying bad things.

For the Nahua, in an interesting reversal of the Judeo-Christian view of the relationship between sin and punishment, it is rare for the person who commits the malicious act to suffer directly. Disruptive behav-ior threatens the entire group because once the wind spirits are loosed in the village, they attack the weak-est members of the community regardless of guilt, and so the old and very young are highly susceptible. In contrast, engaging in moral behavior protects the community as a whole rather than just the individual. The Nahua system of morality is oriented more to pro-tecting the social group than to achieving individual

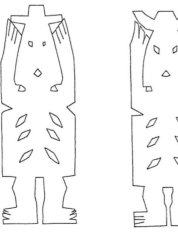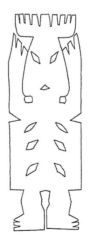

FIGURE 12.   Winds.

salvation. Shamans design the curing ritual, called a *limpia* or "cleansing" in Spanish and *ochpantli* or "sweeping" in Nahuatl, to purify patients and their surroundings by removing polluting wind spirits, and thus restore health.

The cuttings that make up a shaman's curing bundle, taken together, are symbolic of danger associated with all four regions of the Nahua cosmos: sky, earth, water, and underworld. The cross represents the sun in Nahua thought and by extension, the spirit of the cross symbolizes the celestial realm. Because the cut images of the wind spirits are associated with dead villagers, they also represent a threat from *mictlan*, the place of the dead.

Cirilo said the cuttings shown in Figure 13 represent *miquilistli*, "death" (on the left), and his wife. Death has small winglike appendages because he often flies around at night, sometimes in the form of an owl. The rib holes link both spirits to the underworld where they preside over souls of the dead. Nahua consider these spirits to be very dangerous and extremely aggressive. An important aspect of Nahua ideology is revealed in these figures. In their conception of the world, all entities exist in male and female form or sometimes as combined androgynous figures. Thus, maleness and femaleness are believed to permeate the cosmos and this idea is reflected in Nahua myths and ritual behavior. They are used in curing rituals when the patient is feared to be dying.

The two images reproduced in Figure 14 represent the spirit or life force of corn (left) and beans (right), two staple crops of the Nahua of northern Veracruz. Cirilo portrays these figures wearing poncholike *jorongos* along with headdresses and boots. The headdress of corn represents the ripening tassel or, alternately, a flower that is probably the marigold, a plant closely as-

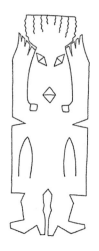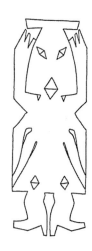

FIGURE 14. Seeds.

sociated with corn in the fields. He cuts corncob shapes from the body of this figure, while he cuts bean pods from that of the spirit of the bean plant, along with two triangular pockets. These spirits also exist in male and female pairs and Cirilo cuts them for ritual offerings held to increase crop production.

In Figure 15, the two figures on the left represent the walking stick, the most sacred symbol and treasured ritual object for the Nahua. Small dwarflike thunder spirits hold walking sticks as they carry water from the Gulf of Mexico to a cave at the top of a sacred mountain, where the water spirit releases it to the fields. By striking their sticks as they walk along in the clouds, the little men cause thunder and lightning. The image on the far left represents the stick carried by the leader of the rain dwarfs, and Cirilo calls it *el presidente*. Cirilo identified the companion image as *el juez*, meaning "the judge," to indicate that it is smaller and less important than the other one. In many ways, Nahua religion is primarily oriented to crop fertility and regulation of rainfall through symbolic means. Thus, the walking stick and its association with thunder, lightning, and rainfall become a key symbol in the culture. Cirilo makes cuts into the body of *el presidente* to depict the head of a walking stick trailing decorative ribbons, which stand for the rays of the early morning sun. The lesser *el juez* figure has the head of an undecorated walking stick cut from its body.

The third image from the left portrays the cloud spirit, called *mixtli* in Nahuatl. Its headdress is a crownlike flower, a symbol among the Nahua for fertility and abundant crops. Cirilo said that the small protuberances under the arms and above the knees represent the muscles of the clouds. He added, "The figure has muscles to demonstrate the power of the clouds. Because of their strength, it is not possible to vanquish clouds."

FIGURE 13. Death.

FIGURE 15.   Walking sticks, cloud, and thunder.

Cirilo's last figure in this set portrays the thunder spirit, *tlatomoni*, shown with a decorative cap. He cuts triangular pockets and the mushroomlike form of a copper ax from the body. After a rainstorm, villagers sometimes find small pre-Hispanic copper artifacts in their fields that they call axes, and they often form part of a shaman's sacred paraphernalia.

In Figure 16, on the left is Cirilo's image of *apanchanej*, literally "water dweller," the female water spirit who distributes water from her cave home atop the sacred mountain. She wears a crown and has cuts representing four pockets surrounding cloud symbols. In the center is her husband, or male aspect, who also has four pockets surrounding clouds. Cirilo said that he portrays these figures with empty pockets because they bring people good things, including money, from the sacred mountain. The third figure represents the spirit of the hill of the water spirit. Its headdress de-

picts the peak of the hill and the small triangular cuts in the body are empty pockets. The ornate cuttings on the sides of the body are keys that will open the door to the sacred mountain when a person asks pardon for bad behavior.

Shown in Figure 17, the final paper cutout is perhaps the most remarkable of all and best illustrates how the images relate to the underlying principles of Nahua religion. In Teposteco, Veracruz, not far from Cirilo's village, an anonymous Nahua shaman cut it from handmade bark paper. Arturo Gómez Martínez, a Nahuatl-speaking Mexican anthropologist, collected the figure in 1998. Called *tonana tlalticpac, totata tlalticpac*, literally "our mother earth, our father earth," it is also known by the name *totiotsij*, "our sacred deity." It represents the sacred cosmos in both male and female aspect.

FIGURE 16.   *Apanchanej*, her husband, and key.

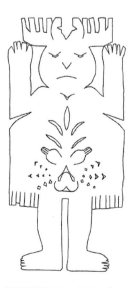

FIGURE 17.   *Totiotsij*.

THE POWER OF THE SHAMAN'S ART

At the heart of all the complex ritual practices and esoteric beliefs, and visible in the thousands of Nahua spirits depicted in paper, there is one simple truth: the cosmos itself is the deity. One day, as our collection of paper figures was growing, we asked Cirilo why there were so many spirits. He paused, and replied cryptically, "They are all the same." After much pondering we now think that the statement is literally true and that Cirilo had given us a powerful key to understand Nahua religion and perhaps the Mesoamerican religions of the past. The Nahua practice a form of religion called pantheism in which a fundamental unity underlies the apparent diversity of the world as we see it. For the Nahua, the universe is literally alive, infused with an animating principle linking humans to each other and to the world of animals, plants, and objects. The symbol they use to represent this conception is the human body. Each paper figure, even though it may represent something that in our view is inanimate, has at its center the human form that links it to the other images and to the great living unity that lies at the center of existence. Thus, all of the paper images with their elaborate iconography are really variants of a single spiritual presence.

The image of *totiotsij* in Figure 17 encapsulates this wisdom and insight. It is cut with a headdress representing the open jaws of the earth. In contemporary Nahua thought, just as in pre-Hispanic days, the earth is conceived as both provider and devourer. The shaman depicts it wearing a fringed *jorongo*, an androgynous costume. On the chest is a small V-cut symbolizing the heart. Below the heart are complex cuttings that represent vegetation—the plants that sustain human existence. Lower down is a phallic-vaginal emblem communicating that the figure transcends exclusive male–female gender identity.

We once asked Cirilo to tell us why the paper images are used in rituals. He thought for a while and then laughed. As always, he answered in ambiguous fashion, "They are *señales*." He used the Spanish word *señal* to describe them—a sign, mark, signal, reminder, or indication. It was obvious to him and to members of his community that the paper images are signs of the magnificently diverse, complex world we inhabit. The small human figure at the core of each image highlights the animating principle of life that permeates and unifies the cosmos. The art of the Nahua shaman is to understand and express the mystery of existence, using skills and powers in a heartfelt effort to better the human condition.

SUGGESTED READINGS

Sandstrom, Alan R. (1991). *Corn Is Our Blood: Culture and Ethnic Identity in a Contemporary Aztec Indian Village*. Civilization of the American Indian Series, Vol. 206. Norman: University of Oklahoma Press.

Sandstrom, Alan R., and Pamela Effrein Sandstrom. (1986). *Traditional Papermaking and Paper Cult Figures of Mexico*. Norman: University of Oklahoma Press.

PART X

Globalization

Photo by John Walbridge.

Signs advertising the latest Hollywood blockbuster in Lahore, Pakistan; large, bright-red Coca-Cola machines in Budapest, Hungary; the opening of a McDonald's in Semarang, Java, Indonesia: all are indications of the process of globalization. Globalization can be defined as the international movement of capital, goods, services, labor, ideas, and other cultural forms. In the last decades of the 20th century, the process of globalization has radically changed the world. As we enter the 21st century, we see countries, cities, and people being drawn into both closer interdependent relationships and growing competitiveness that increase international tensions.

Technological advances, especially in information technology, have been among the leading factors facilitating globalization. No longer do people have to wait to learn about events occurring thousands of miles away. Through the Internet and satellite transmission, breaking news from just about anywhere can be brought into our homes almost instantly. In earlier times, when people migrated to a new country, contact with their homelands was difficult if not impossible. With migration, **transnationalism,** the transplanting of national identities from place to place, is on the rise, and today, many people maintain homes on two continents.

The post–Cold War era also has been a factor in the globalization process. With the sudden collapse of communism, market economies, free trade, and open competition have penetrated parts of the world previously resistant to these practices and ideas. Multinational companies—both a hallmark and a generating force in globalization—are present in ever-increasing numbers in Africa, Latin America, and Asia. Their impact on these societies has been enormous as people move from their villages and towns to cities to find employment. All too often circumstances force them to live in slums where they see, first hand, extremes of wealth and poverty. This type of exposure often breeds discontent. One option that many turn to is migration to the wealthier nations in the northern part of the world. These migrations introduce peoples to new values, styles, and cultural practices. They also add to the complexity of international relations.

Globalization has had a major impact on family life and on gender relations. While an increasing number of women are migrating, men still are more likely to leave their villages for the cities or for another country in search of employment. As a result, women are left with the burdens of agricultural work or have to find new forms of work to help support their families. Thus, the traditional division of labor between the sexes has been severely disrupted in parts of the world. As with so many aspects of globalization, these changes are a double-edged sword. For some women it has meant an opportunity to move into the public sphere, to gain some control over their lives. Unfortunately, many other women and children have faced abandonment, which, in turn, can lead to prostitution and international sex trafficking. At a minimum, globalization often leads to strained relations between men and women as they sort out their changing roles in society.

Although the most forceful thrusts of globalization have flowed from West to East, it is not a process that flows one way. We need only look at changing menus in our local restaurants to see the influence of globalization on our culinary tastes. One of the strongest indications of an East to West flow of ideas has been in the areas of religion and health. Aspects of Eastern mysticism and health practices such as acupuncture have gained wide acceptance in many parts of the Western world. And we now see young girls in the United States wearing T-shirts bearing images of Hindu gods or of the Buddha. Because influences from the United States and Europe on other parts of the world have been so visible, observers assumed that the process of globalization would lead inevitably to Westernization and homogeneity. Yet it is clear that the threat of Western domination of world cultures and economies also can generate resistance, sending members of traditional societies "wherever they are found" into a conservative mode. Sometimes these reactions result in attempts to exclude new ideas and practices from a population, as in the case of the French government's effort to regulate the creeping influx of English words into the French language, or the Taliban's efforts to shut out what they consider to be non-Islamic influences in Afghanistan. We also find contradictions in people's responses to globalization. Throughout Latin America, for example, people skillfully use the tools of globalization to pitch their causes on an international stage. Ironically, though, they often protest the other side of globalization such as World Bank projects.

But many anthropologists have found that there is most often a middle path: as new ideas, practices, and products are introduced into a society, local people find creative ways to interpret and adapt them in such a way that they become their own.

In the first article, Jason Pribilsky shows us the life of Arturo, a young man whose life straddles a village in Ecuador and New York City. Driven by poverty and hope, Arturo is only one of many men from his own and similar villages seeking the wealth that the United States offers while trying to cope with the stress to their home communities that such migration brings.

Sarah Strauss introduces us to Swamiji, a former electrical engineer, and now a holy man teaching yoga in a town along the Ganges River in India. Through Swamiji's story, we see how yoga has not only become an accepted path to spiritual peace and good health throughout much of the world, but that it is also being affected by Western economics, ideas, and technologies.

Debra Spitulnik gives us a portrait of Lawson, a Zambian deejay from a small town who fulfills his dream of bringing English and American music to the air waves of Zambia while still promoting Zambian and African music. A man of great energy and charisma, he is awarded a scholarship to study at an American university, but comes face-to-face with the AIDS epidemic that plagues his country.

Liu Hui owns her own restaurant in a city in south-western China and beckons Courtney Coffey to eat there. Through Hui we learn how Western capitalism, consumerism, and images of the American good life affect her attitudes about her work and about herself as a person.

Other articles with relevance to globalization or transnationalism:

The Evil Eye Is Bad for Business by Paul Derby

Rosa, Weaving Women into Life by Robin O'Brian

Healing the Body, Healing the Soul by M. Ligaya Hattari

Tears for the Saint, Tears for Ourselves by Linda S. Walbridge

Death of an Irishman by Kathleen G. Williamson

28

Living the *Chulla Vida*

Jason Pribilsky
Syracuse University

With a population of approximately 12 million people, Ecuador is the smallest of the Andean countries that make up much of western South America. The village of Jatundeleg is located in the province of Cañar, in Ecuador's southern Andean highlands. Together with the adjacent province of Azuay, the region is famous for its *pueblos de migrantes* (migrant-sending villages) that in the past decade have witnessed a massive exodus of young men to find temporary work in the United States. Migration between Ecuador and the United States is best described as transnational, as small villages in the Andes are linked to urban areas of the United States through traffic in letters, telephone calls, remittances, and migrants themselves. Local critics often point to big houses and other consumer items bought with remittances as signs that migration perverts Andean society and fosters the loss of tradition. For young men like Arturo, migrating to the United States represents more than engaging with American consumer society. While Arturo has been successful as a migrant, firmly planting his life in New York City while maintaining strong ties to his Andean village, things are far from perfect. The realities of poverty, racism, and kin obligations are never far behind Arturo's actions.

As you read, consider the following questions:

1. What factors keep Arturo living between New York and the Andes? Why can't he settle in either one?
2. After reading this selection, how would you characterize the process of globalization? Is it creating a world of sameness or promoting difference?
3. How does the migration of today differ from the great migrations of the 20th century that moved great masses of people around the globe?
4. Has your family been influenced by migration, and, if so, how does it differ from Arturo's experience?
5. How do ethnicity and class impact Arturo's life? How, if at all, has his success as a migrant helped his status in Ecuador?

"Enjoy your youth."
—Ecclesiastes 2:2

I first met Arturo on a cold and cloudy day at the most solemn of cultural events, a funeral, in a place that was only slowly beginning to feel like home. Three months earlier I had come to this small rural village I now call Jatundeleg[1] in the highlands of Ecuador intent on learning how peasant communities were becoming inextricably linked to urban centers in the United States through the migration of young men and the back-and-forth flows of money, consumer items, and ideas. Arturo approached me with legitimate curiosity and asked me why I was snapping photos as a procession of black-clad mourners bearing flowers and in-

cense winded their way up to the church. When I described that I was here to carry out a study of the effects of migration on highland communities of the southern Ecuadorian Andes, my actions seemed to make more sense. The deceased was himself a migrant and had contracted HIV and died of AIDS complications while laboring in the United States. His death was again bringing the tensions of migration to the surface of community gossip and disdain. While if pushed, people could give a number of positive benefits of migration—more access to money, the ability to build new homes and purchase more farm lands—it took almost nothing to get them to recite the negative. New wealth was causing a divide between rich and poor families, causing the breakdown of community work projects, driving up the cost of land, and raising a sense of distrust between neighbors. During the week before the funeral, gossip circulating through the community

---

[1] Jatundeleg and Arturo, along with all other names of people, are pseudonyms.

174

told how making money in the United States had led to the deceased migrant's greed and had made him *cerrado* (closed off) from others. AIDS, villagers said, was the price he had paid for the good fortune he had made migrating.

Arturo would later help me sort out some of the complexities and ambivalence the migration of young men to the United States was causing in the village, and I quickly came to see him as a key informant. Arturo was himself a return migrant, although he could not be counted among its permanent residents. Only 23 years old, he had already made three trips back to his home village. During our early conversations though, I was convinced that Arturo was no different than the many teenage boys with whom I would occasionally hang out at night in front of the village church exchanging cigarettes for their stories. For young guys in Jatundeleg that lack education, land to work, the right color skin, and the money needed to garner a better future in their own county, migrating to the United States is an obsession, creeping its way into even the most banal of conversations. For young men who leave (women leave too, though less frequently), going to the United States means being able to shed Ecuadorian culture for that of the *iony* style, a word derived from the expression, "I [heart] N.Y." People use the term to describe return migrants who adopt American styles of speech, dress, and attitude. More than just concocted style, *iony* style became a buzzword for the hopeful path seen by some as the way to become "modern." For others, *iony* is used critically to talk about the encroachment of new values on old ones that are not seen to be in need of change. In general, for young people, mention of *iony* styles and talking about the United States initiates criticism of everything Ecuadorian and local and, as follows, a celebration of everything American, foreign, and "global." Many conversations were struck up with someone saying *"Feo* (ugly) here, no? Your country is beautiful, right? Lots of things to do there."

Arturo often chided the kids who hung out in front of the church for their idealistic and sometimes downright utopian ideas about what they perceived the United States to be like. What bothered Arturo most was not how inaccurate the young men's views about the United States really were, but rather the way heading north was framed as a fun-filled adventure to escape the boredom of village life. For his and many other poor families in the rural province of Cañar, the yearning to leave Jatundeleg reflects not just a desire to be modern. It also stems from real social pressures that young men feel to take a wife, and begin their own household, and to provide for their families. It is not about escaping boredom, but escaping poverty. As Arturo told me, "Every guy wants to get out of here if he ever wants to get married and have a family of his own.

No girl wants to marry a guy who hasn't been to the States. There is no making it without traveling north for awhile and making some dollars. It's *la chulla vida.*" *Chulla,* in the Quichua language, means to have only one of a pair (as in one sock) where the other is lost. When coupled with *vida* (life), it connotes ideas of predestination, of having a life with only one path to follow, where obligations rule out choices.

COMING NORTH

For Arturo and his family, the *chulla vida* began extremely early. In village circles they are considered *pioneros* (pioneers) as they were among the first to venture to the United States. Though, for them to have left the village at all is not unusual—the family hails from a long migration tradition. Their last name—AucaQuispe Cuzco—is not common to the indigenous groups of southern Ecuador. It is likely that Arturo's family, and most of the families in the region, descend from people forcibly moved under the rule of the Inca Empire (1438–1525) who were victims of policies to quell rebellions and transfer labor reserves from one place to the next. In more recent history—under Spanish colonial rule and directly after—Arturo's grandfather and great-grandfather traveled north each year to work as day laborers on the large haciendas in Ecuador's central Andes. In the 1960s and early 1970s, both his father and eldest brother spent full seasons away from the village, working on the Ecuadorian coast as *macheteros* (sugar cane harvesters).

Arturo was born the youngest of five children (two boys and three girls) in the house that his mother still occupies. It is a small home typical of the region, comprising three unconnected structures made of concrete brick, adobe, and rust-colored tiles with small doors that all face out toward an uncovered inner courtyard. Here the family shuck corn and beans and welcome visitors. Inside one room is a small kitchen, perpetually filled with smoke and simmering pots of soup and potatoes. Small bundles of dried herbs and animal parts hang off nails in the wall; some are used for cooking while others are amulets and charms to keep forces of evil (*mal*) from entering the household and causing sickness and misfortune. Though his mother can now afford a small gas stove, she prefers to cook over a large iron grate placed atop an open flame, pointing out that adhering to the *ñaupi tiempos* (a term carrying similar positive connotations to "old-fashioned") is still the best way to achieve good flavor. In fact, Arturo's mother remains the only one in the family to persistently adhere to customs and traditions of *ñaupi tiempos,* despite the ways money and consumer goods sent back have changed the family's life. Each day, she still dresses in what is considered traditional style, wearing the traditional full wool *pollera* skirt and a fedora-like hat. Only a new pair of Nike tennis shoes and a faded New York—Big Apple! T-shirt peeking out from under a hand-knit cardigan speak to the influences of family abroad. Few furnishings adorn the dwelling. In the living room area (*sala*), high-backed dining room chairs stand neatly side-by-side one another. Framed wedding pictures and a large photograph of the Manhattan skyline hang near the ceiling on otherwise bare and drab walls. In a far corner, a large television and stereo—gifts from the United States—stand prominently like an altar to the migrating life. The luxuries that migration has afforded Arturo's family, however, obscure the realities of poverty that have driven Arturo and so many of his relatives to seek their futures north.

Arturo spent much of his youth close to this home and to his mother. Although schooling is ostensibly free in Ecuador, even the meager matriculation and uniform costs blocked his attending for years at a time. While his older brother and father labored for months on the coast, young Arturo joined with his sisters to complete the tasks of growing and harvesting corn, potatoes, and beans, only a fraction of which could be sold at market. At one point, his mother tried to further improve the family's conditions by weaving straw hats—known popularly as "Panama hats"—for export, but soon after, cheaper markets for machine-manufactured hats in Asia eclipsed the cottage industry. As the only male in the household for months at a time, Arturo grew accustomed to assuming his father's responsibilities. Even if schooling was an option, his labor at home was too indispensable to let go.

In the early 1980s, Arturo's father could no longer find seasonal work on the coast and struggled to feed his family amid Ecuador's rising inflation. So he put his land up as collateral and paid a *coyote*, or migration broker, to get him and his eldest son to the United States, the *tierra protedia* (promised land) of jobs and dollars. When his father and brother left, migration was not yet a common way to dig one's self out of poverty and was met with fear and hostility in Arturo's household. His mother fretted over the horror stories she had heard about crime in the United States and wondered how she would ever plant the annual harvests herself. For almost six months after the father and son left, there was not a word from them. Arturo's mother became convinced that they would never return. Finally a slim letter from New York containing bad news and a few hundred dollars arrived. Crossing the Rio Grande into the United States, the letter said, *la migra* [border patrol agents of Immigration and Naturalization Service (INS)] came upon Arturo's brother and father and the other men as they attempted to cross the river. Arturo's brother, Miguel, panicked in the wa-

ter, and not able to swim, succumbed to the river and drowned. Knowing he would be unable to help his son, Arturo's father continued onward with the other men, finally arriving in New York City two weeks later. In the letter, he concluded by saying he had heard that some other migrants had retrieved Miguel's body and buried it in an unmarked grave in the Sonoran Desert.

Almost eight years later, Arturo would follow in the footsteps of the male line of his family, though the time in between would be extremely difficult. "After my brother's death, I couldn't even mention the idea of going to the United States or my mother would start crying. She carried such a tremendous *pena* (sorrow and suffering) in her chest after my brother died and my dad didn't return." In the absences of his father and brother, Arturo assumed more and more responsibility for the household. He became a skilled farmer, learning to manage a dizzying amount of knowledge about crops, weather, and soils that few other kids in the village would ever possess. His mother's overwhelming dependency on young Arturo, though, could only hold out so long. Farming was a lifeway for the family and provided them with much of their food, but it was dollars, sent each month from the United States, that ultimately ensured their day-to-day being. His father was getting old and could not work long hours like he had once done. He needed Arturo to come to the United States to work and help send money back to Ecuador. He made mention of it almost every time he called. For years, this situation caused tension between Arturo's parents, but finally his father won out when he was handed the opportunity he had always hope for. After five years of living illegally in the United States, Arturo's father received amnesty under the Immigration, Reform, and Control Act (IRCA) in 1986 and became eligible to apply for citizenship. Under the law, Arturo and the rest of his family could also gain citizenship under their father's amnesty, provided they found a way to enter into the United States. As Arturo remembers it, he got a call from his father filled with happiness. "He told me, I don't care how you do it, but just get to New York as soon as you can. We'll take care of everything else later."

In 1991, Arturo left for the United States along with 18 other men from the village ranging in age from 15 to 55. Compared to the surreptitious journey migrants heading north make today, he remembers the trip as relatively easy. Instead of stowing away for weeks at a time in the cargo hold of a boat traveling up the coast of western South America to Guatemala as is common practice today, Arturo was able to fly directly to Mexico. However, just outside of Nogales, Arizona, along the border between the United States and Mexico, the group's luck changed when Mexican immigration officials apprehended Arturo and the others from

Jatundeleg as they tried to swim their way to the United States. All the men were taken to Mexico City and placed in prison. Nearly a month later, Mexican officials released the group and ordered them to return to Ecuador. Going back home, though, was in all likelihood not an option. Regardless of the fact that his trip failed, Arturo still owed a *coyote* $5,000 for the forged visa and travel services that had gotten him as far as Mexico. The money was not his, but was tied to a loan his uncle had arranged through an illegal loan shark (*chulquero*). If Arturo could not pay back the loan, the *chulquero* and his thugs could seize his uncle's land that had served as collateral. Finally, arranging with another *coyote* in Ecuador, and again assuming a new loan, Arturo made it across the border. By the time Arturo finally reached New York City at age 17, he found himself $10,000 in debt to two different *chulqueros* who funded him north.

For a young man who had never visited his birth country's two largest cities, stepping into Manhattan for the first time proved to be a daunting experience, but one made manageable through kinship and village connections. At first, Arturo lived with his father and others from the village in a cramped and dilapidated one-room apartment in the Flushing area of Queens. Between the landlord, who rented a single occupancy to six Ecuadorians, and the village networks that helped him find work, Arturo found living illegally to be easier than imagined. Still, many of his early jobs were dangerous. Once he worked for an under-the-counter construction company removing asbestos from a building where the owner couldn't afford to do things according to code. Today, now that he holds legal residency, he works as a busboy and sometimes as a waiter in an upscale restaurant where the clientele leave big tips. Only by working 12 hours a day, six days a week can he hope to make a sufficient amount of money to send back. Still, his work provides him with respect from the people he works for. With the exception of his current job, Arturo has always worked for other immigrants, who in many cases speak neither English nor Spanish. "When I first came to New York, I knew only Spanish and was scared of not being able to communicate with people. I really wanted to learn English, because I figured it was my only way to get ahead. One of my first jobs was washing dishes and cleaning at an Italian restaurant. For a long time, I think I knew more words in Italian than I did in English."

RETURN VISITS

For Arturo, return visits to Jatundeleg are filled with mixed emotions. His life has followed such a different path than that of men his age who have not migrated.

He has forgotten much about farming and is not well versed in the ways of the village rhythms dictated by a jam-packed calendar of religious festivals. In fact, though Arturo was good at explaining the gritty details of migration, he proved a poor source of information on village life. He almost never could tell me who or what a particular fiesta was honoring and often looked puzzled at many of the questions. For a young man without fields to prepare or animals to tend to, there is little to do in Jatundeleg. On Sundays, Arturo would accompany me to the regional market in the small town of Deleg, some 25 minutes by foot from my house in Jatundeleg. Arturo looked as out of place as I did meandering between the tiny stalls, helping me to haggle prices on buckets of potatoes and overripe pineapples in his native Spanish. "Wow," he would say, "I don't know nothing here."

Still, Arturo remains a potent symbol of the changing face of highland village society in southern Ecuador. His *iony* style is a sign of sophistication, and his new position as a cultural mediator between the United States and Ecuador brings new responsibilities. If there is one thing that holds Andean communities like Jatundeleg together, it is the act of reciprocity in all aspects of daily life—what one anthropologist has called the "glue" of Andean social relations. In times past, when family livelihoods stood in the balance of survival and were easily disrupted by poor harvests and unpredictable markets for their goods, reciprocity between neighbors served as a safety net protecting those in need. For instance, when Arturo's father and brother worked on the coast, Arturo's mother could count on her neighbors to help break the land for planting that she and her children could not accomplish alone. In turn, Arturo's father would bring back goods purchased cheaply from the coast, such as machetes and cookwear, to "pay back" those who had helped his wife. Community life revolves around such activities—from the large village work parties to the exchange of cigarettes and alcohol.

For Arturo, the bonds of reciprocity link his life in New York with his natal village. By U.S. standards, Arturo's work wages place him far below the poverty line. However, through meticulous saving and cost-cutting at every turn (e.g., eating his meals at the restaurant where he works and sharing one-room apartments with multiple tenants), he finds a way to send money home each month using a delivery service in Queens. Beyond helping out his mother, Arturo has purchased cattle for his aunt so she could eke out a living selling milk and has contributed to the erection of a greenhouse being built by some cousins on the edge of the village. More significantly, Arturo and his family have begun to feel subtle pressure to assume sponsorship of the community's many religious festivals, an honor that can come with a $2,000-plus price tag. Turning down such a request could damage his family's honor, placing his relatives outside of the web of reciprocity. For now, Arturo has given more than $500 to help purchase a new stained glass window for the recently renovated church. Similarly, when Arturo is back in Jatundeleg, he participates as fully as he can in village work projects (*mingas*) and in fiestas as ways to show he is still a part of the community. When I ask him why this is so important, he returns to the gossip and rumors of the migrant who died of AIDS. "Otherwise," he says, "people will become suspect of me, like they were suspect of the guy who died of AIDS. They will turn away and stop helping my family."

Arturo's thoughts about the future could be as variable as the weather in the Andes, where in an instant scorching sunshine can change to bone-chilling wind and torrential rain. At times, Arturo took on the airs of a proud lifelong New Yorker, for whom the entire universe begins and ends with New York. Then the next day he would tell me, "Maybe next time I come back, I'll buy a truck with my money and maybe build a house. I think I could like it here." Returning to Jatundeleg to settle permanently, though, would never be that easy. Indeed, in some ways Arturo's break with the traditional custom of taking a wife in the village in his early 20s indicates that he knows that such a move would not be feasible. Arturo has only to point to his cousin, Luis, who also holds residency in the United States. Luis has a wife and a child, and is expecting another child in a few months. Because he cannot find a consistent means to make money in the community, he periodically makes trips to the same restaurant job in Chicago to help provide enough money for his family all year long.

Naively I asked Arturo, "Why don't you take your money to Cuenca and start a business?" The explanations were often the same. Even with his long absences from Jatundeleg, Arturo is still considered a *comunero* (community member) despite also being a *yoni* [one who lives in the United States]. In the provincial capital of Cuenca, or in Quito, Arturo's dark skin and high jawline would no doubt mark him as an *indio* or *mitayo*, derogatory labels used to describe Indian peoples. For Arturo, like so many return migrants who can afford it, new clothing and especially those with American brand names can help mask his rural identity. But this too often backfires, as returned migrants are often rebuffed by city folk. Though he is technically more "authentic" in his American clothing and hairstyle than the *mestizos* (mixed Spanish and Indian) and *blancos* (whites) of the city whose Calvin Klein jeans and Nike shoes are more than likely counterfeit knockoffs, his indigenous name and features exclude him from enjoying certain privileges in the city. For instance, he

lacks access to jobs in the city and could never hope to obtain a bank loan.

Once I accompanied Arturo to the *Direccion de Migracion*, a bureaucratic stopover all residents and long-time visitors to Ecuador must make in order to obtain a permission slip (*salida*) to leave the country. In all my visits, trips to the migration office have customarily been in-and-out affairs. One day you drop off your passport and the 20,000 *sucre* (about 75 cents) exit fee, and the next day the proper forms and stamps are ready and you are on your way. As Arturo approached the counter with me beside him, the uniformed man behind the counter quickly placed a cardboard shield over the Plexiglas and announced that he was taking his break. He then said it was too late in the afternoon to do all the paperwork anyway and that Arturo should come back in the morning. The next morning Arturo returned, smartly dressed in jeans and a pressed shirt, his hair neatly combed straight off his face. Again, the same man was working at the desk and again he told Arturo that the papers for his *salida* could not be processed. Either Arturo had brought the wrong size personal photos or something was wrong with how his passport was printed. In either case, the issue was trivial. Noticing my concern that he might not get his exit slip, Arturo assured me of the "dance" that would have to take place first before the paper would be issued. Like much of Latin America where hierarchies of privilege and power are cross-cut by complicated divisions based on race, ethnicity, class, and gender, the likelihood of when and how Arturo would get his *salida* depended on how much *palanca* (leverage) he had in the situation. In local hierarchies of southern Ecuadorian society, Arturo's *palanca* is low given his assumed status as indigenous (*indígena*). Because of it, he could expect to get his *salida* only after paying a hefty bribe to the migration official. In some respects, though, Arturo's *palanca* was higher than the mestizo migration official who was, because of his position, clearly lower class. He likely had more money than the official and held a coveted U.S. passport. In the end, these additional marks worked against Arturo as he was forced to pay a larger bribe because the clerk singled him out as a "*mitayo* with *migradólares*" (an Indian with migrant dollars).

TRANSNATIONAL LIVES

The last time I saw Arturo was at John F. Kennedy International Airport in New York City on a hot July afternoon. I had returned to the United States to take a break from fieldwork to see my family and help them to get ready to return with me for my last stint of research. In a strange coincidence, Arturo had the same

30

Behind the Microphone

Debra Spitulnik
Emory University

Zambia is a land-locked southern African nation of approximately 10 million people, nestled between neighbors Congo (DRC), Tanzania, Malawi, Mozambique, Zimbabwe, Botswana, Namibia, and Angola. Between 1924 and 1964, Zambia was the British colony of Northern Rhodesia. It became an independent nation-state in 1964. There are 73 different nationally recognized *ethnolinguistic* groups and over 15 different languages in the country. English is the official language of government and much of the media. With its extensive copper mining industry, Zambia is one of the most industrialized and urbanized nations in Africa south of the Sahara. Between 40 and 50 percent of the population live in urban areas, and nearly every Zambian today has had some experience with urban life, other ethnic groups, and other languages besides his or her first language.

Radio broadcasting was first introduced to Zambia in 1938. In Debra Spitulnik's article, we meet Lawson Chishimba, a radio DJ at the state-owned and operated Radio Zambia. Readers are introduced to the Zambian media landscape and they get a glimpse of Lawson's voice, his love of music, and his attachments to Western forms of music and consumption. What does it actually mean to sit behind a microphone and imagine an audience?

As you read, look for how issues of technology, social status, globalization, language, and music interrelate. Think about the following questions:

1. What are some similarities and differences between Lawson's deejaying style and the style of radio DJs that you have heard in the United States?
2. How is the role of radio different in Zambia from that in the United States?
3. What do you learn from this story about the way that American media and American influences have become part of contemporary life in Zambia?
4. In what ways did Radio Zambia contribute to changing attitudes and increases in foreign influences in Zambia? How was Lawson Chishimba instrumental to this?

A ROLLER COASTER OF SOUNDS AND WORDS

I wish I could honestly say that I remember my first time hearing the wonderfully melodic voice of Lawson Chishimba on the airwaves of Radio Zambia, but I cannot. It wasn't until I was in Zambia for nearly a year that I actually met him. And then I became an instant fan.

I was conducting dissertation research on the role of state radio broadcasting and how it built a feeling of a collective national identity in the multilingual, multiethnic country of Zambia. In the late 1980s the economy was collapsing and with each passing month people saw their standards of living drop dramatically. Radio had almost nothing to say about this and people were tuning out. At the same time, I was learning that certain areas of entertainment programming, such as those featuring Lawson Chishimba, were very popular and that radios themselves were important focal points for socializing and status-building. Radio was immensely powerful as a messenger of both Western and Zambian ways of being modern. It also bolstered the nation's power elite. It gave visibility to some languages and some ethnic groups at the expense of others and it helped spread certain kinds of English language usage. English is Zambia's official language, the language of over 60 percent of all radio broadcasting, and the second language of over one-quarter of all Zambians.

I chose as my ethnographic focus both ends of the mass communication spectrum. I studied the institutional life of broadcasters as well as the everyday experiences of listeners. For the first component of this study, I lived in the capital city of Lusaka and conducted participant–observation research in the hallways, studios, and offices of the Zambia National Broadcasting Corporation (ZNBC).

There I met Lawson Chishimba in February 1989. And from that time his voice burned a permanent mark on my auditory memory. How do you describe what is distinctive about a person's voice? Lawson's riveted me. His voice had more contours, more ups and downs than those of most Zambians I met. But it was more than that. His voice was more unpredictable. It had an element of mischief in it, as if he were up to something, as if you couldn't quite pin him down. It was a gravelly voice, but not deep—more like the voice of a smoker or someone who can't clear his throat. Yet Lawson never sounded congested. It was just as if his voice were flowing over some little pebbles at the back of his throat. And he talked fast, very animated, always making exclamations like "ooh" and "aah." So in the midst of this he would sometimes let out a little bit of a squeak. As if his voice had cracked, like he had strained it across too many fluctuating contours or too much excited delivery.

Lawson's voice was not wildly unusual, however. He actually sounded like many of the people of his own ethnicity, the native speakers of the Bemba language, who use a wide range of intonation contours, volumes, and pitches to create an animated, engaging delivery. Lawson's was just several times more exaggerated. And he was having much more fun with it all. He loved speaking, but not so much to hear himself talk, I think. Lawson's love of speaking was really about a pure delight in the art of sound—a roller coaster of sounds and words. He thrived in dramatic delivery and the rascal-like persona that emanated through it.

RADIO 4: "DAWN OF A BRAND NEW ERA"

For several years Lawson had worked as a radio announcer, producer, and part-time DJ at the ZNBC regional studio in the city of Kitwe, on the industrial Copperbelt. In February 1989, Lawson was transferred to broadcasting headquarters in Lusaka. This was a major moment in Zambian broadcasting history as ZNBC was about to launch a new radio channel and it needed the combined forces of all of its best DJs.

Up to that time, ZNBC operated one television station and two national radio channels called Radio 1 and Radio 2, collectively known as Radio Zambia. Radio 1 broadcasts a variety of programs in the nation's seven official Zambian languages: Bemba, Kaonde, Lozi, Lunda, Luvale, Nyanja, and Tonga. Radio 1 is known for its indigenous language talk shows and plays; it also runs three major daily newscasts and a range of informational programs. By contrast, Radio 2 broadcasts exclusively in English. Radio 2 focuses on news, current affairs, government informational programs, and educational broadcasts. While primarily associated with government-sponsored talk shows, it also carries a sizable amount of English language entertainment, in the form of music, drama, and sports. Through the late 1980s, ZNBC operated a third radio channel—known as Radio 3—dedicated to external (i.e., nondomestic) broadcasting for Zambia's neighbors engaged in liberation movements.

Through the early 1990s, ZNBC was a broadcasting monopoly and the most important form of mass communication in the country. Nearly two-thirds of the national population listened regularly to its radio broadcasts. And in 1989, there were only the two domestic radio channels: Radio 1 and Radio 2.

In 1989, however, ZNBC introduced Radio 4 and heralded it as a total revolution on the radio listening landscape. This new radio channel featured 24-hour "round-the-clock" musical programming, "news on the hour, every hour," and dynamic DJs who promised to bring "all the latest hits." Radio 4 was nicknamed Radio Mulungushi, after the Mulungushi Rock of Authority, a natural landmark viewed as the birthplace of Zambia's independence. During the early 1960s, Zambian leaders fighting for independence from British colonial rule held numerous political meetings in this location near the Mulungushi River, roughly a hundred miles outside of Lusaka.

The most prevalent music on Radio 4 is American and British top-40, R&B from the United States, Zambia's latest recording stars, Jamaican reggae, and popular music from Africa. Radio 4's broadcast range includes all major urban areas of Zambia (nine cities and large towns), which comprise roughly 45 percent of the national population.

Radio was introduced into colonial Zambia (then, Northern Rhodesia) in 1938 and almost from the beginning, popular hits from Britain and the United States were regularly played on the air. Moreover, for years preceding Radio 4's birth in 1989, contemporary Zambian listeners had been able to hear hit music on ZNBC's Radio 2, as well as on the foreign short wave radio broadcasts emanating from the BBC, Voice of America, German radio, and the stations of nearby Zimbabwe and South Africa. But this was not enough. And what sense did it make anyway for Zambian state broadcasting to lose its audiences to other nations' radio stations when it came to hourly news and the latest in musical trends? It was time to signal Zambia's place in the modern world. It was time to really deliver to the cosmopolitan urban listeners across the nation. The dynamic DJ from the Copperbelt, Lawson Chishimba, was now in the capital city to help make this happen.

Nicknamed "The Sweet Sensation" and "Son-in-Law," Lawson joined a small army of other trendy Radio 4 broadcasters, with on-air names such as "The Groove Maker," "Saucy Sarah," "DJ Kool," and "Captain of the Air." For my research, I regularly sat in the Radio 4 broadcast studio, notebook in hand, and talked to these broadcasters during their shifts.

Tucked away in the core of the very large Zambia National Broadcasting Corporation complex, the actual Radio 4 broadcast studio is a small 8' by 8' space. It has full soundproofing, two chairs, a table for storage and extra equipment, and a large window looking out into an anteroom, where program directors or station visitors sometimes stand. At the center of the studio is the technological heart of the broadcasting operation: A large mixing console containing countless audio controls, cables, jacks, and switches; the turntables and tape decks that sit adjacent to the console; and two large microphones hanging over the center of the console. This is where the DJ sits, spins, and leans in to speak when "on air."

This small Radio 4 broadcast studio did not contain what you might imagine to be the working inventory of a popular radio station. The room was not filled with crates and crates of records or stacks of CDs. There were no shelves of recorded music, no catalog, no reference material of any kind. One wall had a bulletin board featuring photos of distinguished visitors at the station and Radio 4 DJs at special events. It also had newspaper clippings about Radio 4 and various foreign celebrity photos and articles cut out of popular media such as *People* magazine and *The National Inquirer*. Another wall had a bulletin board with the Radio 4 weekly DJ roster, some ZNBC technical information, and various corporate memos. Besides these wall items, everything else in the studio was dull gray, shiny aluminum, or techno black.

LAWSON BEHIND THE MIKE

Lawson enters the studio fully stocked for his live four-hour shift and does not plan to leave until it is over. There are only the bare necessities: his play list, his news script, the prerecorded advertisements, and a small stack of about 25 records and tapes. Before his shift Lawson types up his play list and checks the items out from the Records Library on the first floor of the ZNBC complex. He carries these up to the studio, usually along with a few other records or tapes brought from home or borrowed from friends.

Of course, we only talk while the music or a prerecorded segment is playing. While Lawson is "on mike," I quietly observe the process of deejaying, as an ethnographer. But as an interviewer, I need to wait for "off mike" moments. While he works, Lawson talks a bit to the listeners, introduces the record, fades into it, and then switches off the DJ microphones. Then our conversation begins in the studio. At times I am worried that the mike might have been accidentally left on and that my anthropological interview is being inadvertently broadcast across the nation. To have my research burst in live onto the national airwaves for all avid Radio 4 fans to hear—what a unique form of participant–observation that would have made!

The morning news announcer, located in an adjacent studio, is finished reading the seven o'clock *Main News*. Lawson is patched back into Radio 4 airspace and it's time for him to do the channel identification and time check. He pulls his swivel chair up to the mixing console and leans into the mike: "This is Radio Mulungushi. Broadcasting to you live from Lusaka on FM stereo, and the time is comin' on to seven ten." He pauses briefly and then becomes more evocative: "Feel love? This is Donna Summer." Lawson adjusts the controls to fade the music up. It is a popular disco tune by the American artist Donna Summer. As the song finishes, Lawson fades the music down and starts to speak again: "Right, Donna Summer and 'I Feel Love.' I can't blame you. It's a cloudless sky in the morning in the capital city . . ." The Sweet Sensation is in full swing. He continues with the friendly conversation, plays another song, and then comes in with some animated boasts about the Radio 4 programming: "It's a semi-paradise. It's 24 hours a day round the clock. Giving you nothing but the very best there is in music."

What an eclectic mix there is this morning. Jimmy Cliff's reggae plays amid a Bemba religious hymn, the latest rhumba song from neighboring Congo (DRC), a popular hit by the American singer Angela Bofil, and the disco classic by diva Donna Summer. An ad by the national pharmaceutical company for allergy medicine airs throughout the morning. An agricultural and transportation company, Mulungushi Investments, has one ad spot just before the news.

Lawson now puts on a funky disco instrumental as background music. It's time to read Radio 4's frequency list. But this is no ordinary rattling off of call letters and FM frequency numbers. Instead Lawson greets different sectors of the Radio 4 audience as he creates a road map across the nation:

> We're sending you all the great waves on FM stereo-wide. From border town to border town. For those within our stereo zone, we say "Good morning to you." From Chililabombwe down to Livingstone. And we're coming live on 92.2 megahertz for those in the hub of the Copperbelt. Of course, that links you to Mufulira town, Chililabombwe, Kalulushi, and all right, Chingola town. Good morning to you. I hope you're still the cleanest town in the country. Right. If you're not, please

do clean the mess. As for Ndola city, it's 94.5 mega-hertz. Kabwe town, 92.2. As for the greater city of Lusaka, it's 92.6. As a matter of fact, the weather's fine in the capital city. It's bright and sunny . . . We're roll-ing the toughest rock this side of the world. 95.5 to Livingstone. And of course, if you happen to be getting a strong signal, we say: "Welcome to the world of Radio Mu."

THE MAGIC OF LAWSON

Lawson's magic was that he could weave an experi-ence for listeners across the nation. His fans were of many different ethnicities, age groups, and social back-grounds. Lawson's delivery was crisp and playful. His own words had a kind of packaged originality, full of fun phrases and slogans like the abbreviated "Radio Mu" for Radio Mulungushi and the echoes of song lyrics such as "Rhythm's definitely gonna catch you" and "Feel love." I asked him about what makes a good DJ. Lawson got directly to the point: "A DJ must flow and make people feel like you're with them. You must be emotional." He elaborated, "You must be natural; you must be yourself. When you come in, you have someone in mind. There are different inspirations you can create, the way you bring the music up, the way you talk."

Not everyone was drawn in by—or even exposed to—the broadcasts of Lawson Chishimba, however. The broadcast range of Radio 4 only covers the urban areas of the country, so Lawson's fan base was lim-ited to those urbanites. And given that only 25 percent of Zambians speak English as their second language, not everyone could understand his lively on-air talk. Nevertheless, radio listeners in multilingual Zambia do listen to radio, especially music programming, even when they don't fully understand the broadcast language.

Lawson's ultimate skill was in creating a seamless link between the mood of the music, his own mood as DJ, and a projected mood for everyone listening. One of his former supervisors told me that Lawson had achieved a level of expertise and professionalism that few radio DJs do these days. "There was something about the voice that made him Lawson," he explained. "But mainly it was that he was so comfortable with his job, as if it were his second nature. His broadcasts were very smooth. The flow of his programming was impec-cable. He faded in and out at just the right time. This created a richness to the color of his broadcasting."

Lawson was a favorite among radio listeners. Many stated that they liked him because of his clear enunciation and his musical selections. One radio lis-tener in Lusaka was convinced that Lawson was a large person, because of his resonant voice. He told me about

being surprised one day to actually see the DJ in pub-lic and realize that he was a fairly thin man of average height.

Lawson's popularity was clear especially when he hosted phone-in request programs. The phone lines jammed. Lawson cracked jokes and made lively con-versation with anyone who phoned in, from school children to seniors. But surprisingly, he never won any DJ awards. Every year ZNBC asks listeners to write in with votes for their favorite DJ. Winners are announced at the annual ZNBC awards ceremony. Lawson was very popular—he fared quite well in the top five, but he never won "DJ of the Year."

I don't think that this ever bothered Lawson be-cause fundamentally, Lawson was complete within himself. The fans were there, but he didn't need vali-dation from them. He was not behind the mike because he had a big ego. He simply loved the magic of broad-casting, and that was his magic. Once, I asked him why he decided to go into broadcasting in the first place. He explained with a story about one of his first experi-ences with radio:

> When I was a little boy I listened to programs in my own languages, and in Bemba they used to say "kuno kuŋanda kwa shikapepele" [here at the house of endless activity]. As a kid I would imagine that you had to crawl under all these wires and whatever you said there would be picked up. The broadcaster sat there hunched up under the wires and spoke. They also said "ŋanda ya nsalensale" [a house of wires upon wires]. As a kid I thought TV was the same. Immediately you enter this special room, that thing can be seen on the screen.

The magic and the attraction were clear. Special things happened when you entered the great place of wires.

THE SHAPE OF A CAREER

In many ways, Lawson was a loner, making him some-what of a paradox. Behind the mike he was sponta-neous, knowledgeable, charismatic, and a bit of an ex-hibitionist. In one single moment, whatever he did behind this mike all alone in that tiny studio at the core of ZNBC was transmitted simultaneously across the nation to millions of people. He was as public as it gets. Yet there was also a quiet, almost shy side to him. He lived alone for much of his adult life. He had just a handful of friends. And he married fairly late by Zam-bian standards, in the early 1990s when he was in his 30s.

Lawson was born in 1957 in the very small town of Mporokoso in Zambia's Northern Province. When he was old enough for elementary school, his parents sent him to stay a few hundred miles away with one of his older brothers who worked in the mines in Chingola, a small city on the Zambian Copperbelt. Then Lawson moved again for high school, this time to Lusaka, joining a different brother who had a government job there. After he graduated high school in 1975, Lawson joined the National Service for a two-year period of military training and service, which was required of all young Zambian men and women.

Exhibiting a pattern typical for many Zambians, by the time Lawson had reached his mid-30s, he had lived in five different Zambian cities, towns, or villages. Some moves come with changing job assignments. Other moves come about as individuals spend time with their extended families and rely on key family members who earn a regular income through formal employment. This migration pattern has been evident since the 1930s, during the early years of the British development of industrial mining on the Zambian Copperbelt. Major industries and white-collar jobs have become increasingly Zambian since independence in 1964, and employers in areas of government, education, health care, finance, law enforcement, factory work, and utilities all foster migration across the nation. Zambians, men and women, are also required to join National Service for military training and service, and this also fosters movement. Lawson entered for two years and was stationed in Chipata, the capital of the Eastern Province.

After National Service, Lawson returned to Lusaka and enrolled in Evelyn Hone College for a two-year diploma in journalism. Going to college is rare in Zambia; less than 3 percent of all Zambians have college degrees. A very low percentage of the population even graduate from high school. So at this point, Lawson was already a member of a privileged class of Zambians. Nearing college graduation, he wasted no time in applying for a job at Radio Zambia. He was quickly called for an interview and was hired. He started as an English language announcer for Radio 2. A fast-rising star, just one year on the job and Lawson was sent for a short course at the Radio and TV Institute in Cairo, Egypt. Two years later, in 1982, he was promoted from announcer to producer and was sent to the Kitwe studios on the Copperbelt. In 1988, he became senior producer, all the time keeping up his passion as radio DJ and announcer. Then in 1989 Lawson returned to Lusaka to work for ZNBC's new Radio 4.

At the ZNBC workplace, Lawson was friendly with his colleagues, but also kept to himself. His best buddy was Kenneth Maduma, a fellow English language broadcaster and the Radio 4 program manager at the time. Lawson always joked with Maduma—about his looks, about whether he had a girlfriend or not, and about why he was so reserved. Both at work

and outside of work Lawson jokingly called him "Chief," alluding to Maduma's more senior management position.

Lawson was a dedicated and polished professional who had already logged more than 10 years in the profession by his early 30s. He knew he was going places. He was interested in things American and was being considered by the Lusaka branch of the United States Information Service (USIS) for a study-abroad scholarship. At the time, USIS was a wing of the United States State Department—the cultural, informational, and educational exchange branch of our foreign embassies.

I ran into Lawson one day at the USIS library and found him checking out videos: *Born to the West*, a classic shoot-em-up Western starring John Wayne, and *All the President's Men*, a dramatic portrayal of the *Washington Post* reporters who first exposed the Watergate scandal. We talked about the second video a bit and I mentioned that as a media person he would probably be interested in the investigative journalism part of the story. I missed the mark. He answered with little interest: "Oh yeah, but I don't know much about that scandal." And then with more enthusiasm: "I really want to see it because Robert Redford stars in it."

ON U.S. GROUND

Lawson's dream to get closer to things American did come true. In 1992 he was awarded the scholarship to attend Elizabethtown College in Pennsylvania and study for a B.A. in Mass Communications. Lawson's acceptance in the B.A. program was part of an initiative in which the Elizabethtown Department of Communications received USIS funds to help train a small number of media people from Africa. USIS had a long history of cultivating relations with media professionals around the world, and it had important initiatives in developing nations where media freedom was very limited.

Being a professional who already had 2 years of college and 13 years' experience on the job, Lawson initially had concerns about what he could learn from the program. Courses for the degree at Elizabethtown covered topics such as communications theory, media law and ethics, news writing, media management, and public relations. But he was thrilled about the opportunity to live in the United States, even if it meant leaving his new wife behind. Having the degree, and particularly the stamp of the United States, would provide a major avenue to career advancement. It was a chance to earn more status in Zambia and to qualify for the upper ranks of ZNBC management. It was a chance to acquire money and valuable commodities in the United States that could be brought home, if stipend funds were used wisely. Plus, there were chances to tour U.S. radio stations, newspaper publishers, and TV stations to see how they work.

When Lawson came to the United States, I was at the University of Chicago completing my Ph.D. We often talked on the phone and I was happy at the chance to stay in close contact. In 1993, I had the opportunity to run a conference at Northwestern University on the role of radio in Africa and I invited Lawson to present a paper. He would talk about the role of Radio Zambia during the 1991 multiparty elections, the first truly democratic presidential election that the nation had had since independence in 1964. The state-run ZNBC still had a broadcasting monopoly and there had been tension over how much coverage radio and TV should give to the various political parties—and particularly on presidential candidates other than the sitting president. In the end, coverage of opposition politics was limited on ZNBC, but the opposition's presidential candidate still prevailed. Lawson knew these controversies first hand, and we had talked on the phone about them several times. It was going to be a great presentation—but it never happened. Just one day before the conference was to begin, Lawson called and said that he was canceling. He had consulted with the Zambian Embassy in Washington and they advised him not to do the paper. I was very upset, but I completely understood.

I never did figure out if this was a case of self-censorship on Lawson's part or a case of direct censorship on the part of the Zambian state. Apparently some Washington-based representative of the Zambian government felt that Lawson's intended conference paper would put the Zambian government in a bad light. Indeed, if the truth were told about state-run Radio Zambia's role during the 1991 elections, it would be a story of elaborate propaganda for the sitting president's bid for re-election and a story of suppressed coverage of the contending candidates. Someone did not want the world—or even just a small gathering of specialists at Northwestern University—to hear this story. Maybe Lawson himself decided that it would be too risky to make a public presentation that reflected badly on his employer.

A Chicago visit was not meant to be, but the next year Lawson traveled to Atlanta where I had recently moved. I brought Lawson to my department, introduced him to my colleagues, and had one take our picture. My department hallway is lined with large photos from faculty research projects. My contribution just happens to be a big glossy of Lawson's buddy Kenneth Maduma behind the mike. So taking a photo in front of it represented a new phase in ethnographer–informant relationships.

I gave my small apartment over to Lawson for four days while I stayed with a neighbor. One morning I arrived at the apartment to pick up Lawson for breakfast, only to find that my entire living room had been completely rearranged. An antique wooden bookcase, handcrafted by my great-grandfather, had been positioned as the focal point of the room. The couch was against the south wall instead of the west wall, and the floor lamp, chairs, and plants were moved accordingly. All the audio tapes on the bottom shelf of the bookcase had been restacked and neatly arranged. All the books were in order. The room looked fantastic. And I was

FIGURE 18 Debra Spitulnik and Lawson Chishimba with photograph of ZNBC broadcaster Kenneth Maduma. *Photo by Bruce Knauft. Photo taken at Emory University Anthropology Department.*

shocked. What kind of person takes such license with the contents of someone's home? I calmed my nerves somehow and said, "Wow, this looks great!"

Lawson exclaimed with a bit of mischief in his voice, "Debra, I don't know why you had this beautiful bookcase jammed into the corner over there. It needs to be the centerpiece of the room!"

While Zambian friends and relatives often take a certain liberty in handling and borrowing one's possessions, no ordinary Zambian would ever think of moving someone's furniture around, with or without permission. I remained puzzled for several years, until another Zambian friend shared a similar story. One day at work Lawson had said to him, "Boss, I'm coming to your office this weekend to fix up a few things. Can you give me two workers to help out?" Returning to the office on Monday, the boss found that all of the clutter in the office had been removed and some furniture had been rearranged. To his great surprise, the useable space had nearly doubled in size and the office looked wonderful.

My friend and I decided that if Lawson hadn't become a radio DJ, he would have made an excellent interior designer. From the seamless rhythms of his DJ style to the harmonious ambiance of a well-designed room, Lawson had a special way of making beautiful environments for people to live in.

BACK TO ZAMBIA

In 1998, two years after he returned to Zambia, bachelor's degree in hand, Lawson was promoted to public relations manager at ZNBC. Lawson began to see things differently after his U.S. training. He wanted more ZNBC resources to be spent on the basics of broadcasting rather than on big salaries and job perks for senior management. There was a need for more records, for more blank tapes to do interviews and prerecorded shows, and for more funds to support the collection of innovative news and human interest material outside the ZNBC studios and outside the capital city.

The executive who recommended him for the public relations position explained to me that "Lawson was a public figure and would find it very easy to relate to the public. And the public would take him seriously." The job didn't go so smoothly, however, possibly because people still saw him as a radio DJ. To avoid confusion of roles, Lawson was taken off the airwaves. When I spoke to him in early 1999 about it, he seemed saddened not to be on air anymore. But he wouldn't say that directly. There were also other problems. He

had recently lost his young wife and their small child to HIV/AIDS. His own health was beginning to fail.

As many as 20 percent of all Zambians have HIV/AIDS. The epidemic has spread dramatically over the past 20 years through all sectors of the population, being transmitted mainly through heterosexual intercourse, inadequately sterilized medical instruments, and an inadequately screened blood supply. The effects have been staggering, not just on individual lives and families, but on the nation's economy, as it becomes progressively robbed of its most productive citizens.

The last time I heard Lawson's signature voice, I was thousands of miles away in Atlanta. It was near the end of 1999. I had been trying to track him down by telephone and had finally reached him on his cell. He had taken a leave of absence and was at home. He insisted that there was nothing to worry about, that he just had the flu or something. He sounded a little weak and tired, but there was still the wonderful playful crackling in his voice. I feared the worst, but found it hard to talk directly about it. Lawson died less than two months later. Colleagues later told me that his deterioration had been dramatic, but that he always came back to work to show that he was strong. His death was a great loss to ZNBC and to all of those who had loved listening to "The Sweet Sensation."

It is difficult to pin down Lawson's legacy. His work may not have been particularly path-breaking or of dramatically high impact, but it was creative and compelling. And it had lasting consequences when viewed in terms of the bigger story of radio in the nation. Like many other Zambian DJs, Lawson brought foreign music and popularized English language phrases through his work. He also added a very distinctive Zambian accent to radio broadcasting, by greeting different Zambian cities, playing regional African music, and promoting local Zambian music. He contributed on a daily basis to the very concept that radio listening is an enjoyable pursuit, a modern and fun thing to do with one's time.

Lawson Chishimba was one of a long line of broadcasters who have made radio a meaningful part of everyday life in Zambia. Since the late 1930s, numerous Zambian radio personalities like him paved the way for radio's popularity and eventual place in nation-building. And since Lawson's death in early 2000, several other young DJs have stepped in behind the microphone to spin the latest numbers, talk up the audiences, and take requests from callers.

Was Lawson an agent of globalization and a contributor to the erosion of Zambian culture? Some might say that he brought too much of the Western world to Zambia and that he himself was more Western than

Zambian. I would say that Lawson was just being himself. He was a worldly and meticulous professional. He was a product of the countless social, cultural, and economic changes that have happened in Africa since the early 1900s. He loved Western music, he loved Zambian music, and he loved South African music. But most of all he loved something that perhaps is neither here nor there when one thinks only in terms of globalization: he loved the art of sound. He loved creating an experience, a playful connection between two people separated by space yet linked through the magic of radio.

SUGGESTED READINGS

Abu-Lughod, Lila, Faye Ginsburg, and Brian Larkin, eds. (In press). *Media Worlds: Anthropology on New Terrain*. Berkeley: University of California Press.

Appadurai, Arjun. (1991). Global ethnoscapes: Notes and queries for a transnational anthropology. In *Recapturing Anthropology: Working in the Present*, ed. Richard G. Fox. Santa Fe, N.Mex.: School of American Research Press, pp. 191–210.

Tacchi, Jo. (1998). Radio Texture: Between Self and Other. In *Material Cultures: Why Some Things Matter*, ed. Daniel Miller. Chicago: University of Chicago Press, pp. 25–45.

31

The Model Worker Talks Back

Courtney Coffey
University of Arizona

The People's Republic of China is a country about the same size as the United States but with over four times the population. China initiated economic reforms in 1978, and these have spawned dramatic changes in recent years. China continues to shed its communist economy for one directed more toward market capitalism, and people laid off from government jobs are finding new ways of making a living. The Chinese state promotes "model worker" stories, commending former factory workers who have become successful entrepreneurs. Incomes have generally risen several hundred times over since the reforms began. The effect on women is enormous: they can set up businesses, earn their own living, and be independent of male control. These gains in status and power come with a price, including increased competition among women and family members.

Over the last two decades, the gap between the haves and the have-nots in China has increased. The reality is that unemployment is now as high as 25 percent in the cities undergoing economic restructuring. Starting a business can be difficult and frustrating, especially for women, who are still influenced by traditional gender roles.

Courtney Coffey introduces us to Liu Hui, a restaurateur whose story shows that becoming a businesswoman in China requires determination, extremely hard work, and sacrifice. It also demonstrates the impact of globalization on Chinese society. Market capitalism and consumerism are accompanied by a fascination with American and European lifestyles and values. Images of the West arouse envy and longing for what appears "better." Liu Hui's story reveals the conflicting messages that Chinese receive, especially about gender behavior, from their own traditions, from the Chinese state, and from the Western media.

As you read Liu Hui's story, consider the following questions:

1. How do entrepreneurs like Liu Hui view the West, and how does this view influence their attitudes? Is this view realistic?
2. How has the changing economy in China affected social relations among women, and between women and men? How is this affecting social relations among family members?
3. How does globalization affect women's behavior and the way they see themselves? Are Chinese women simply imitating Western women or is the situation more complex than this? Explain.
4. What challenges face Chinese people who want to start their own businesses? Are these challenges the same for both women and men? What differences are there?

Come, have some food . . . what would you like to eat? Come, have some food . . ." The woman accosting me on the street wore her hair long and fringed with bangs. Annoyed at first by her aggressiveness, I was won over by her friendly smile. She told me her name was Liu Hui. I liked Hui, so I kept going back to her humble restaurant, even though the food was mediocre.

Hui's restaurant was one of many on the street by my apartment complex in Kunming. Kunming, a city of four million, is the capital of Yunnan province in southwestern China. "Yunnan" means land of the southern clouds, and indeed the province is blessed with many beautiful mountains and landscapes. Yunnan also has a reputation as one of the friendliest provinces in China. The people I met, mainly middle-class city-dwellers, were incredibly generous and open toward me and my research project.

Like most of the restaurants near my apartment, Hui's place was small, with an open kitchen visible from the street. Her cook stood all day before his giant wok, steam and sweat beading his face as he tossed mixtures of meat, vegetables, garlic, and chilies into fast-and-spicy dishes for impatient customers. Diners sat at plastic tables (invariably covered with brightly colored velvet tablecloths) that extended out onto the sidewalk. During the lulls between customers, Hui sat and talked with me, always on the lookout for more people to pull in for a meal.

I was impressed with Liu Hui's confidence and energy. Whenever I stopped by, she seemed to be in constant motion: chatting with customers, supervising the chef, smiling broadly at passers-by as she tried to generate more customers. Hui was probably the most independent woman I met in Yunnan. In a society that tended to criticize women who were perceived as too independent, I was particularly eager to find out more about this woman who appeared so strong and self-assured. But as I found out more about her, I realized that beneath her self-assurance lay much bitterness.

As an unmarried working woman, Liu Hui was bitter about the harsh precariousness of her life. She was not alone in these feelings. Married women were often bitter because they had to carry the burdens of housework and child care in addition to working full-time jobs away from home. Men were bitter also because they perceived women to be "taking over" both jobs and domestic life.

Hui worked in the restaurant nearly all of her waking hours. Hui's customers and associates would describe her as a working-class *laoban*, or boss. She was one of the few working-class individuals that I came to know well. Her sun-weathered face set off by sparkling eyes accented by fine lines at the corners, Liu Hui wore the same practical outfit every day and had rough, callused hands and a brusque manner, all qualities that set her apart from the middle-class women I met. Most middle-class women were decidedly "feminine" in their communication styles, body language, and choice of clothing.

In Yunnan, middle-class women are also relatively independent and often chafe at the male dominance that has been traditional in China. Yet maintaining a reputation as a "good woman" requires such women to present themselves as "feminine." Hui was actually less critical of male dominance than she was of the poverty that she had known in her childhood and that still threatened her if her business did not succeed. I admired Hui's independence, yet she seemed to feel no pride in it. Indeed, she felt ashamed. She was ashamed that she could not afford the fine clothes and habits that "modern women" enjoyed, and she was ashamed that she had to work so hard just to survive.

THE MODEL WORKER TALKS BACK

In some ways Hui is a model Chinese worker, the kind of worker that the Chinese government with its state-run media use to promote self-reliance. A former factory worker, she quit her job and opened her own business. Yet Hui was deeply unhappy and complained about the difficulties she faced. State rhetoric sends the message that anyone can (and should) open and run his or her own business if laid off from a government job. Hui's experience, however, challenges this rosy image. The life of a small entrepreneur is fraught with difficulties that the state does not wish to see. And these difficulties multiply when the entrepreneur is a woman.

From Hui's perspective, China itself is partly to blame for her economic struggles. She resents the fact that she was "born Chinese," which for her meant a childhood of poverty and only the prospect of years of hard work. As images of American and European life flash across TV and movie screens, many urban Chinese talk about the West as inherently "better" than China, in every way imaginable. In the Chinese imagination, China and its people have become associated with "lack" and "inferior" and the West with "plenty" and "quality." It seemed important for Hui and others I met to imagine a place where life was easier. I felt it was useless to attempt to convince my friends that, while working people back home might have more money, they were probably equally harried and overworked.

Late one evening, after closing her restaurant, Hui came to my apartment. The sprawling complex of white concrete buildings had been built in the mid-1980s and was considered relatively old. Multistory apartment buildings like these popped up like mushrooms across the Kunming landscape in the 1990s, part of a construction boom fueled by a rapidly growing economy. To reach my apartment, we had to pass by the guard posted at the entrance to my section of the complex. The guard, a woman who was a retiree from another line of work, sat in a small room from morning to midnight, watching who came and went with an attentive eye. Members of the neighborhood committee organization, apartment guards are part of the old system of community surveillance. Once in the building, Hui and I walked up the six flights of stairs to my apartment, took off our shoes at the doorway, and went inside for a cozy cup of tea.

With her rough hands cupped around the tea for warmth, Hui responded to my questions with an enthusiasm and speed that kept my pen flying. I wanted to hear how Hui viewed the image of the "modern woman." After all, she was a successful businesswoman. Hui began by saying that the modern woman is one who is economically independent, specifically, not dependent on men. She added that in addition to being economically independent, the modern woman talks candidly and is smart. Yet to my surprise, Hui said that she's not a modern woman. Hui explained, "I can't be modern. *Zuo bu dao xiandai*. I don't have the money to play and dress in fashionable clothes like a modern woman. I'm conservative . . ."

Hui continued, in direct contradiction to her previous comments, to describe the modern woman as a lazy woman who depends on men. Young, attractive women who rely on wealthy men for support, or whose attractiveness and availability were used to get a job, were widely criticized. One young woman noted that "such women's lives are empty." Hui wanted to make a contrast between herself, as *baoshou* (conservative), and a morally suspect woman who uses her looks (and implied sexuality) to support herself. No doubt Hui's unmarried status contributed to her wish to be viewed as conservative. As a single woman who runs a business, Hui risked appearing antifeminine and in some way unnatural. She emphasized how *baoshou* she was as a defense against possible accusations that she was unfeminine and immoral. In this regard, Hui was similar to other middle-class Yunnanese women I knew.

ECONOMIC DISPARITY BETWEEN SIBLINGS

Hui's emphasis on not having the money to "play and dress in fashionable clothes" reflects bitter feelings related to her inability to afford many of the new goods and services available. Indeed, commercialization was the most striking characteristic of urban Yunnan in the late 1990s. From rhinestone-studded clothes to bowling alleys, urbanites with money to spare had choices as to where to spend this money. These goods also offered symbolic sustenance. Many people have commented on the spiritual and moral vacuum that engulfs contemporary China. People are searching for something—something different and new, something to believe in, something to enrich their lives. Consumerism promises to fulfill many intangible needs, including the need for emotional security, reassurance of self-worth, a sense of power, a creative outlet. Not everyone, of course, can afford to indulge in the new luxuries, leading some to feel dissatisfied and frustrated. For Hui, this frustration may have been amplified by the relative success of her younger brother.

Hui's brother Liu Zhusheng was also an entrepreneur. He had recently opened up a small laundry and dry cleaning business not far from his sister's restaurant. Operating the laundry seemed much less demanding than the restaurant. His work was not so physically challenging and he had more free time. Yet Zhusheng was making more money and enjoying himself more than his sister. Zhusheng struck me as a "wheeler dealer." He told me that he was interested in getting to know me better because he thought I could help him generate business ties with other North Americans. I was skeptical. Yet I was curious how Zhusheng, with his cell phone and minivan, enjoyed so much more prosperity than his hard-working sister. So one night I agreed to join him, his girlfriend, and another couple for a night on the town. We went out for pizza (the few Western-oriented restaurants in Kunming were very popular with the newly rich and upcoming younger set) and then to a blaring disco. Hui was not invited. I wanted to ask why but sensed that this was a sensitive topic. Nor was I ever able to ask Hui or her brother directly about their financial affairs. I was dying to ask them why China's economic reforms seemed to be helping Hui's brother so much more than they were helping her.

THE IRON RICE BOWL SPLIT IN TWO

Liu Hui had just opened the restaurant a few months before we met. She had accomplished this mostly on her own. Her parents had never supported her, so her success in operating this suburban restaurant came through her own hard work. Before she opened the restaurant, she had been working in a factory. Her factory job was rolling cigarettes for 600 yuan a month, or about 75 U.S. dollars. Six hundred yuan was a fairly good wage in 1997, but Hui said the conditions were bad and that she had to work long, monotonous hours in a dirty environment. Other factory workers she knew were "let go" (*xia gang*) from their jobs. *Xia gang* is becoming well known in cities throughout China, where unemployment sometimes reaches as high as 25 percent. A popular saying pokes fun at the situation:

> *Mao Yeye qing women xia xiang,*
> *Deng Yeye qing women xia hai,*
> *Jiang Yeye qing women xia gang.*

> Grandpa Mao asks us to go to the countryside,
> Grandpa Deng asks us to go into business,
> Grandpa Jiang asks us to go home.

The references to Mao (Mao Zedong, autocratic leader of China from 1949–76) and the "countryside" reflect the policy of sending urban and "intellectual" people (i.e., those with a high school education) to work with (and ostensibly learn from) rural farmers during the Cultural Revolution (1966–76). Deng and "business" refer to the economic reforms begun by Deng Xiaoping in 1978. Jiang refers to Jiang Zemin, the current president of China, who has continued and deepened Deng's economic reforms, including closing down inefficient state factories and sending workers "home." In the past, the Chinese economy was called the "iron rice bowl," so called because state workers were assured a minimum standard of living and were notoriously impossible to fire.

According to Hui, nowadays a person has to have a good relationship with the factory leader in order to keep a job. Hui claimed that "some people would resort to flattery, and if you were not polite to your boss, you might be fired." "Most bosses think they are like gods," Hui said. She seemed bitter about these political games in the work place. Whether a person was fired or not depended more on flattery than on performance. Flattery, apparently, wasn't all that was used to keep a job. Perhaps she was exaggerating but she told me that "nowadays women with no self-esteem might even sleep with the boss to ensure their jobs."

As her own boss she liked the fact that "no one else controls you." Hui's street-side restaurant was open seven days a week, 12 hours a day. She was always there, hawking the restaurant to passers-by, overseeing orders, buying fresh vegetables and meat, supervising her staff. Hui was not alone in her resentment of women who appear to survive—or succeed—through good looks and sexual favors.

Since the reforms, it is common to hear people say that pretty women who use their looks for profit "eat Spring food." In other words, youth and beauty fade fast. The saying *"ta chi qing chun fan"* (she gets by on her youth) expresses disapproval of a woman who is "very pretty but knows nothing." It also implies that she is immoral. As a group, older women tend to view younger women, especially working-class young women, as immoral. In a climate of economic uncertainty, resentments fester toward groups that appear to have some advantages, whether based on youth or good looks.

But do young, pretty women really have so many advantages? If being a young and attractive woman is an advantage, this "advantage" works only to the extent that society supports the exploitation of particular kinds of female beauty, beauty that does not last and is easily expendable. And, like older women, these pretty young women are also likely to lose their jobs when there are mass layoffs. Women of all ages and types are the first to go when a factory decides it needs to cut back. Furthermore, some companies actually require women to score twice as high as men on an entrance exam in order even to be considered for employment. Considering all of this, the fact that a pretty young woman might be preferred for certain kinds of jobs

(such as restaurant hostess or office receptionist) seems like a slim reward for being young, attractive, and female.

Women like Hui aren't the only ones feeling threatened by female competitors. Many men feel nervous and insecure in this era of economic "restructuring," as state-run factories lay off thousands of workers. Even though women are laid off in much higher numbers than men, fear and anxiety lead men to target women as the scapegoats. When I would pick up a popular magazine, I could often find articles portraying women as domineering. The magazines commonly had commentaries ridiculing strong women. Such articles told me clearly that men fear that women are "taking over" the job market and dominating domestic relationships. In an era of uncertainty and change, the cooperative ethos of Mao's era seems far away.

IMAGINING THE "WEST"

How does the hard-working Hui envision her future? What hopes does she have? On one occasion she talked of the kind of man she would most like to marry (assuming that she might meet someone besides her idle, lackadaisical boyfriend). He had to have a good temperament and a "good heart" and earn a good salary. Looks were not important. On another occasion, she envisioned a different future for herself:

> I would like to leave, go somewhere, go somewhere and be anonymous. Like Australia or America, to go and live like a cowboy. I can just imagine myself on my ranch, with my dogs and a big kettle on the stove . . . I hope I can make some money and travel, explore, go travel to America.

Over and over again, I heard urban Yunnanese tell me how much they wanted to travel to "America" or Australia, or possibly to Europe. Young people in particular are deeply interested in Western cultures and lifestyles. For Hui it is the West within the West that is her dream destination—the Western United States or the Australian outback, where she has a nostalgic view of herself living an adventurous yet homey lifestyle.

Hui has lived under community surveillance in the city all her life. Whether it is members of the Communist Party–controlled neighborhood committee or just busybody neighbors, someone is always watching. Many Chinese friends complained to me about the lack of privacy and the constant gossip that follows one everywhere. Living abroad would mean an escape from that type of prying and control. Living the life of a cowboy would be the ultimate escape for her. Hui's ideal future also reveals the different ways that America is imagined in China. While Chinese propaganda

FIGURE 19 Liu Hui and the author talk and drink tea at Hui's restaurant. *Photo by Kurt Thomson.*

paints the West as decadent and materialistic, Hui imagines something completely different: the cowboy, the ultimate individualist.

One afternoon, as we sat sipping tea at a sunny table set on the sidewalk for her customers, Hui suddenly seemed very taken by my eyes. "Your eyes, what color are they?" she asked, leaning toward me. Overcome by their apparent strangeness, Hui opened my eyelids wider with her fingers and peered intently at my eyes. Hui seemed possessed by a hungry fascination with my eye color (green). I think from her point of view my facial features were a physical manifesta-

tion of how Westerners/Americans were born into a life of wealth and plenty. "Americans," she told me, "grow well. Being born American means you are automatically lucky."

China likes to send the message that its economic reforms bring nothing but happiness and opportunity to its people. The Chinese media portray people such as Liu Hui as examples of the success of the "new China." She is an entrepreneur. Thus, she has the good life. They don't talk about the bone-wearying hard work that is involved. And all of her hard work did not land Hui the lifestyle that the economic reforms and the Chinese media seemed to promise in its propaganda. She has neither fashionable clothes nor leisure time. Hui might scorn younger women who use their looks to get these things, but she is also envious of them. On the other hand, some men might envy her. After all, isn't she a woman taking away their opportunity for a good job?

For me, Liu Hui's story indicates how disruptive rapid economic change can be on the social fabric of a society. This disruption is intensified by the availability of information from the outside world—information often distorted by Hollywood. While I respected Hui for her courage and independence, she found nothing to admire in herself. She neither conformed to any traditional standard of Chinese beauty and behavior, nor did she live up to the images that she could watch on a movie screen. How could state rhetoric about her being a "model worker" sound anything but hollow?

SUGGESTED READINGS

Lull, James. (1991). *China Turned On: Television, Reform and Resistance*. London: Routledge.

Watson, James L., ed. (1997). *Golden Arches East: McDonald's in East Asia*. Stanford: Stanford University Press.

Index